VAN BUREN DISTRICT LIBRARY
DECATUR, MICH

W9-CDV-573

DISCARDED

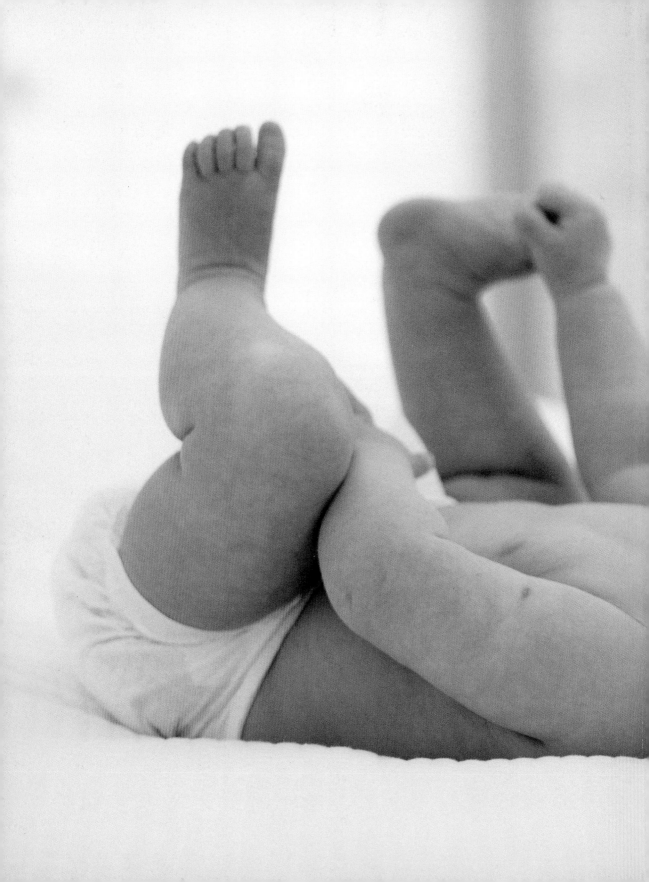

complete baby & childcare

Dr. Miriam Stoppard

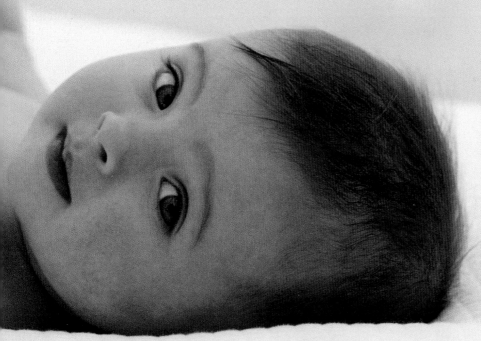

649.1
sto

LONDON, NEW YORK, MELBOURNE, DELHI

For Esmé

Revised edition
Publishing Director Corinne Roberts
Managing Editors Jemima Dunne, Penny Warren
Managing Art Editors Lynne Brown, Marianne Markham
Editors Jinny Johnson, Elise See Tai
US Editors Jennifer Williams, Christine Heilman
US Pediatric Consultant Aviva Schein, MD
Senior Art Editor Helen Spencer
Senior Designer Ian Spick
Project Art Editor Sara Kimmins
Designer Iona Hoyle
Picture Researcher Liz Moore
DTP Designer Traci Salter
Production Elizabeth Cherry
Special Photography Ruth Jenkinson

First published by Dorling Kindersley in 1995
Reprinted 1995, 1996, 1997, 2001

This revised edition published in the United States in 2006
by DK Publishing, Inc., 375 Hudson Street,
New York, New York 10014

Copyright © 1995, 2001, 2006 Dorling Kindersley Limited
Text copyright © 1995, 2001, 2006 Miriam Stoppard

All rights reserved under International and Pan-American Copyright Conventions.
No part of this publication may be reproduced, stored in a retrieval system, or transmitted in
any form or by any means, electronic, mechanical, photocopying, recording or otherwise,
without the prior written permission of the copyright owner. Published in Great Britain
by Dorling Kindersley Limited.

DK books are available at special discounts for bulk purchases for sales promotions,
premiums, fund-raising, or educational use. For details, contact: DK Publishing Special Markets,
375 Hudson Street, New York, NY 10014 or SpecialSales@dk.com

A Cataloging-in-Publication record for this book is available from the Library of Congress.

ISBN: 0-7566-1707-3

Reproduced by Colourscan, Singapore
Printed and bound in Singapore by Star Standard

Discover more at
www.dk.com

Preface

There would hardly seem to be room for another baby book. Having worked on this subject for over 25 years, however, I've always felt that even the best baby books have gaps. Very few, for instance, deal with three- to five-year-olds. I also feel sure that women who have children with special needs or children with chronic ailments and disabilities feel short-changed by most baby books, including mine, because their babies aren't given enough space or emphasis. Fathers continue to be a neglected group, and there's a tendency to overlook the impact of a new addition on the family as a whole. With more and more families having two working parents, choosing childcare is a more universal problem than it once was.

In my previous books there was never enough space to deal with important subjects like caring for twins, to illustrate the treatment of illnesses, from glue ear to hydrocephalus, and to go fully into complicated subjects like baby first aid. Most of all, I never felt that I had the freedom to explain how a baby's physical, mental, and social development relates to the acquisition of skills. This is a subject that's crucially important to parents. For instance, without the knowledge that a baby can't hold a bladder full of urine until her nerves and muscles have matured, parents will continue to enforce "potty training"—a completely outdated and cruel idea.

The scope of this book has given me the chance to plug some of those gaps and to enlarge on those two very important preschool years. Three-year-olds make huge strides in all areas of development when they're introduced to preschool classes and need a great deal of patience, understanding, and support from parents if they're going to realize their full potential—which is every child's birthright, after all.

So as well as dealing with the everyday aspects of baby and childcare, this book encompasses the acquisition of skills, your role as teacher, and—something I've longed to write about—the differences between boy and girl babies, to offer parents guidance on how to treasure and nurture the best parts of being a girl and being a boy.

In 25 years of writing about childcare, my aim has always been to help parents feel independent, confident, and free to follow their instincts—which are nearly always right. In this new edition of my book my goal remains the same and I have taken the opportunity to bring the information right up to date and include all the latest advice and research on many aspects of childcare. While this book is not definitive, it's as near complete as I've ever hoped for.

Contents

Introduction

Whether you're a mother expecting your first baby, have just given birth, or are an expectant or new father, you may be feeling apprehensive about your new role. Don't worry: while parenting may be one of the most responsible and challenging jobs around, it's also one of the most rewarding.

YOUR NEW BABY

You have just experienced the creation of newborn life. Your baby is probably smaller than you imagined, and she may seem very vulnerable. You may be overwhelmed by feelings of joy, but you will also be anxious to know whether your baby is healthy, and whether the sounds and movements she makes are normal. Your healthcare provider will be able to reassure you, and you will probably be surprised at just how much your baby can do.

EVERYDAY CARE

In the first months of life, your child depends on you for everything: you will have to feed, dress, and change him, and carry him around. If he is your first child, you are bound to be nervous. You may wonder whether he is getting enough milk and putting on weight fast enough, whether he is waking too often in the night, or why he seems to cry so much. You'll be surprised at how quickly caring for your baby becomes second nature; in fact, you will hardly believe there was once a time when you didn't know how to change a diaper! You'll be surprised, too, at how quickly the time comes when your child is able to do things for himself: to spoonfeed himself, to walk, to dress himself, to use a potty…. In a few short years he will be able to look after his own basic needs and be ready to go to school.

PLAY AND DEVELOPMENT

Sharing your child's pleasure in new skills and knowledge is one of the great joys of parenthood. It's also the most important thing you can do to promote your child's development: physically, by allowing her to explore her own capabilities in a challenging and safe environment; mentally, by taking time to talk to and play with her; and socially, by providing her with the love and security that will make her a well-adjusted and happy child. In these early years, play is your child's main tool for learning. By understanding how she learns and develops, you can help her to get the most from play and from her toys.

FAMILY LIFE

However much getting married or deciding to live with your partner may have changed your life, the birth of your child will change it far more. You need to balance your partner's needs and the needs of your baby with your own. If you've had twins, you will be very much in need of practical help and support. Your extended family may suddenly start to figure more largely in your life. Whether you see this as a good thing will depend on all sorts of personal factors, but your child will undoubtedly benefit from the loving interest of his relations, and this continues to be true even—or rather, especially—if the relationship between you and your partner is under strain.

SPECIAL NEEDS

All parents want their children to grow up into happy, well-adjusted adults, and to live rich and fulfilling lives. If your child has special needs—and this applies to a wide variety of children, from those who are very gifted to those born with a chronic physical condition such as cerebral palsy—then achieving this is going to require a lot of extra effort from you. If your child is ill, then at the same time you will have to cope with your own feelings of confusion, anxiety, and perhaps guilt. Over the months that follow the diagnosis of your child's condition, however, you will learn a lot about what you can do to help your child, and you will almost certainly cope better than you had thought possible. There are many support networks available that offer help to parents of children with special needs; be sure to make use of them.

MEDICINE AND HEALTHCARE

You are responsible for promoting your child's good health, recognizing when he is ill, and acting accordingly. Your child can't always tell you what's wrong with him, but you will become sensitive to the signs that tell you something is amiss, and you will learn when you can take care of him yourself and when you need to call the doctor. It is your duty as a parent to learn basic first-aid procedures, and you should attend a training course to do this rather than try to learn from a book. (To find a course, look up your local Red Cross chapter in the telephone book and call for information.) Be sure to learn emergency first-aid procedures by heart, and refresh your memory often.

CHAPTER I

Your new baby

Your feelings about the birth of your new baby are likely to be pride, wonder, and exhilaration mixed with exhaustion. You may feel fiercely attached to your baby right away, or bonding may take a little longer. You will almost certainly be surprised at his appearance: his oddly shaped head, wrinkled face, and tiny hands and feet.

From the moment of birth, your baby will exhibit reflexes and behavior that help him survive. In such things as his sleeping patterns and crying bouts, you will see the beginnings of a personality.

The first question in every new parent's mind is, "Is he alright?", and medical staff will carry out tests immediately after the birth and in the first few days to reassure you on this point. Your baby will be given all the special attention he needs. If he is premature or small for his dates, he may need to be kept in a special neonatal unit, but you'll still be able to bond with him and take part in his care.

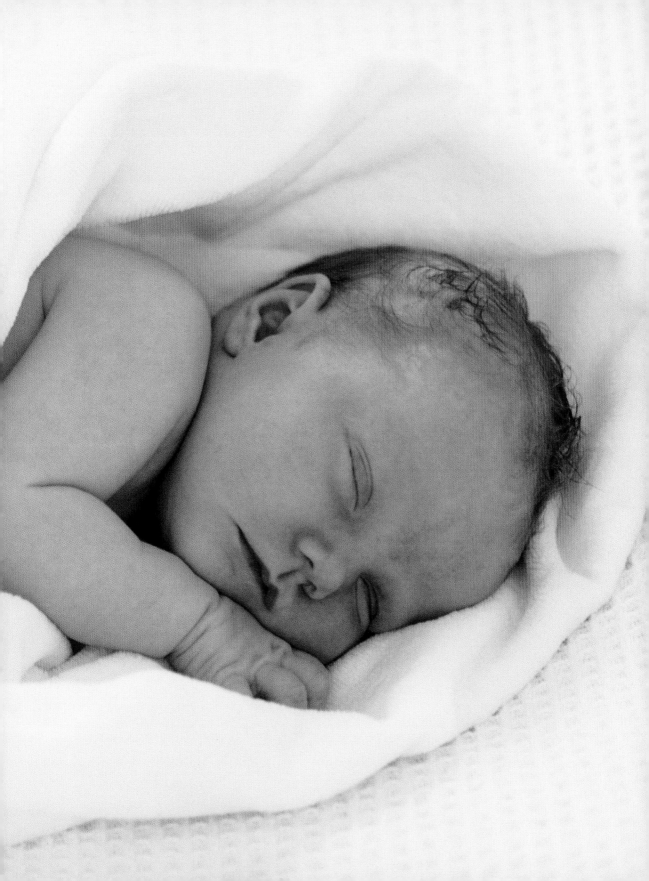

LOVING YOUR BABY

Most mothers find that they establish a genuine bond with their newborn babies within the first 72 hours, but a "bond" doesn't necessarily mean instantaneous and ecstatic love at first sight.

Attending to the physical needs of your newborn baby is so exhausting that it's easy to forget your baby also has an active emotional life. In the long term, the most serious damage to a baby's health may stem from inadequate love and attention—so in the next few weeks and months, heap as much upon your baby as you can.

Maternal love is partially hormonal, so if you don't feel it immediately, it's not your fault. Motherly love usually comes in with the milk, 72 hours after the birth of your child, though it may come in later and it may grow quite gradually. One of the hormones that stimulates lactation is also, in part, responsible for motherly love.

Some mothers are shocked to find that they lack maternal feelings when they first hold their babies. This may be due to a variety of factors, such as complications with the delivery, unrealistic expectations of childbirth, sheer exhaustion, fluctuating hormone levels, and even the mother's own experience in early childhood. Maternal "indifference" can last from an hour to a week, but rarely much longer.

Your newborn

Whatever you had expected—bigger, smaller, quieter, less slippery—your baby will surprise and delight you. Experienced parents discern a personality at birth, but first-time parents may think their newborns are oblivious to the world about them. Babies, however, rapidly build up a vocabulary of sensory experiences from birth. When awake, a baby will be alert and listening. She can respond when spoken to, recognizes you by smell, and has an intent gaze. At birth, she can recognize a human face, and she will move her head in response to noise. She is born wanting to talk and will "converse" with you if you talk animatedly about 8–10 inches (20–25 centimeters) from her face where she can see you clearly. She will react to your smile by moving her mouth, nodding, sticking out her tongue, or jerking her whole body.

HANDLING YOUR BABY

The need for physical contact throughout childhood is well documented, and this is especially true of the first weeks of life. The majority of newborn babies spend much of their time asleep, so it is important that you're there to hold and mother your baby when she's awake. If your baby is in an incubator, ask to be allowed to stroke her and change her diaper. One young mother I met, whose ten-day-old baby had been in an incubator for the first 48 hours, was too terrified to pick him up because she thought he might "break." Babies are stronger than you think so don't worry—the important thing is to give her plenty of cuddles.

Bonding
Your baby will be happiest next to your skin, where she can feel your warmth and hear your heartbeat.

BREATHING

Apart from crying, you may not hear anything more from your baby because it can be difficult to hear a newborn's light breathing. In some cases, a baby may even stop breathing entirely for a few seconds, but this isn't abnormal. All babies make strange noises when they breathe— usually a noisy snuffling sound—and their breathing is often irregular.

Your baby's lungs are still weak, which means that her breathing is naturally much shallower than yours or mine. This is nothing to worry about; her lungs will gradually get stronger each day.

SUCKLING

For the first three days after your baby's birth, your breasts produce not milk, but colostrum, a thin, yellow fluid that contains water, protein, sugar, vitamins, minerals, and antibodies for protection against infectious diseases. During her first 72 hours of life, colostrum helps protect your baby against infections. To stimulate your breasts to produce milk, you need to feed her frequently; the sucking action of the baby stimulates hormones that, in turn, stimulate milk production. Even if you don't intend to breastfeed, it's a good idea to suckle your baby as soon as she's born, because the colostrum will be beneficial to her, and the act of suckling will help you bond with your baby.

As soon as your baby is born you can put her to your breast. She will have a natural sucking reflex, and the sucking action will encourage the production of the hormone oxytocin. Oxytocin makes the uterus contract and expel the placenta. Touch your baby's cheek on the side closest to your nipple to stimulate her rooting reflex. Rather than just sucking on the nipple, her lips should be on the breast tissue with the whole nipple in her mouth.

INVOLVING YOUR PARTNER

Because the experience of childbirth is so focused on the mother, it is common for the father to feel neglected or excluded. It is important for father and baby to bond, too, and touch, smell, and sound are good ways to do this. Soon after his baby is born, her father should hold her against his skin; this way his baby will come in contact with his specific smell, and over a period of weeks she will learn to associate this with comfort and reassurance. The father should also speak to his child, since she will quickly become familiar with his voice. In fact, if he talks to the baby while she is in the uterus, she will recognize her father's voice when she is born.

It's common for the mother to take prime responsibility for a newborn's care, but the father should be encouraged to take an equal role and should build up a tactile relationship with her. Make sure he becomes involved with day-to-day routines such as bathing and diaper-changing. Even if the baby is breastfed, he can learn to bottle-feed her using expressed breast milk from the mother. Both parents should cuddle her when you and she are naked so that she can feel and smell your skin and hear both of your hearts beating.

YOUR BABY'S FIRST BREATH

In the uterus, your baby's lungs are redundant—she gets all the oxygen she needs from the placenta, so the lungs are collapsed.

The very first time your baby takes a breath, her lungs expand, and the increased pressure in them shuts a valve just beyond the heart, so that the blood that used to pass to the placenta for oxygenation now goes directly to the lungs. These two crucial steps make her an independent being, able to survive without you, and they happen in an instant.

Nothing should interfere with your baby's ability to take her first breath. That's why doctors and midwives clear air passages immediately, and if the first breath is delayed, they resuscitate the baby.

Newborn babies cannot make vitamin K, so your baby is given a vitamin K injection soon after birth.

SPOTS AND RASHES

Most newborns have harmless skin irritations such as spots and rashes in the first few days. They generally clear up when the skin begins to stabilize at about three weeks old.

Milia These small white spots, found mainly on the bridge of the nose, but also elsewhere on the face, are the result of a temporary blockage of the sebaceous glands, which secrete sebum to lubricate the skin. Never squeeze them—they will disappear of their own accord within a few days.

Heat rash If your baby is too warm, he may get small red spots, especially on his face. Make sure that he isn't over-wrapped in clothing and blankets, and that the room temperature is well regulated (see p.123).

Erythema toxicum This is a type of rash where the spots have a white center and a red halo (see p.292). It is quite common in the first week, and it may recur for a month or so. There is no need to treat it; it will disappear quite quickly.

YOUR BABY'S APPEARANCE

When you are given your baby to hold for the first time, you will probably be surprised by his appearance. Although your baby is undoubtedly a bundle of joy, many mothers mistakenly expect a clean and placid bundle, similar to the babies who appear in advertisements for baby products. As you now suddenly discover, however, real life is a little bit different.

Skin Your baby's skin may be covered in a whitish, greasy substance called vernix, which is a natural barrier cream that prevents the skin from becoming waterlogged. In some hospitals the vernix will be removed immediately, but in others it may be left on to give your baby some natural protection against minor skin irritations, such as flaking and peeling.

Your baby's skin may be rather blotchy in color; this is because the tiny blood vessels are unstable. Black children are often light-skinned at birth, but the skin begins to get darker as it begins to produce melanin, its natural pigment; it will reach its permanent color by about six months.

Head Your baby's skull is made up of four large plates that don't fuse, so they can move across each other, especially during labor, when your baby's head is compressed by pressure from your vaginal walls. The sliding skull bones enable him to pass through the birth canal without hazard, though his head may become slightly elongated or misshapen in the process. This is entirely normal, and does not affect the brain. There may also be some bruising or swelling, but it will disappear during the first few days or weeks.

The soft spots on the top of your baby's skull where the bones are still not joined are called the fontanelles. The skull bones won't fuse completely until your baby is about two. Be careful, especially with a very young baby, not to press the fontanelles.

Eyes Your baby may not be able to open his eyes straight away due to puffiness caused by pressure on his head during birth. This pressure may also have broken some tiny blood vessels in your baby's eyes, causing small, red, triangular marks in the whites of the eyes. Entirely harmless, they require no treatment and will disappear within a couple of weeks. Conjunctivitis, which results in a yellow discharge around the eyelids, is quite common. Although this is not serious, it may need treatment by a doctor if it persists for more than a day or so, since it can lead to other problems, such as ear infections.

Your baby can see clearly up to a distance of 8–10 inches (20–25 centimeters), but beyond that cannot focus both his eyes at the same time, and this may cause him to squint, or look cross-eyed. Both of these conditions will clear up as his eye muscles grow stronger (usually within a month). If your baby is still squinting (see p.287) at two months, you should consult your doctor. You may find it difficult to get your baby to open his eyes at first, but never try to force them open. One of the easiest ways I have found to get a baby to open his eyes is to hold him above my head.

Most newborn babies' eyes are blue regardless of race, and your baby's eye color is likely to change after birth because it is only then that babies acquire melanin, the body's natural pigment.

Hair Some babies are born with a full head of hair, while others are completely bald. The color of your baby's hair at birth is not necessarily the permanent color he will acquire later on. The fine, downy hair that many babies have on their bodies at birth is called lanugo, and this will often fall off soon after birth.

Genitals Many babies, both male and female, appear to have enlarged genitals shortly after birth, and babies of both genders may have "breasts." This is due to the massive increase in hormone levels that you've experienced just before giving birth; some of the hormones have passed into your baby's bloodstream.

With a baby boy, this can lead to an enlarged scrotum and enlarged breasts; he may even produce a little milk. This is not abnormal, and the swelling will gradually subside. A baby girl may have a swollen vulva or clitoris and a small "period" shortly after birth.

Umbilicus The umbilical cord, which is moist and bluish-white at birth, is clamped with forceps and then cut with scissors. Only a short length of cord remains; this dries and becomes almost black within 24 hours. The stump will shrivel up and fall off about seven days after, but your baby will feel no pain.

UMBILICAL HERNIA

Some babies develop a small swelling near the navel, called an umbilical hernia. This is caused by weak abdominal muscles, which allow the intestines to push through a little.

Umbilical hernias are most obvious when the abdominal muscles are used for crying. They are very common, and virtually always clear up within a year. If your baby has one and it enlarges or persists, consult your doctor.

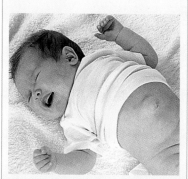

Site of swelling
The hernia forms where the umbilical cord entered the baby's abdomen, because there is a gap in the abdominal muscles at that point.

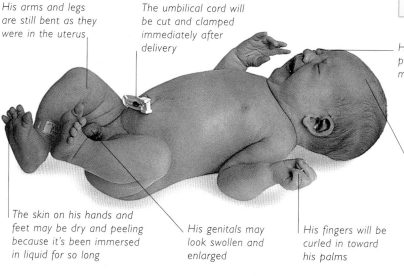

His arms and legs are still bent as they were in the uterus

The umbilical cord will be cut and clamped immediately after delivery

His eyes may look puffy and be closed most of the time

The skin on his hands and feet may be dry and peeling because it's been immersed in liquid for so long

His genitals may look swollen and enlarged

His fingers will be curled in toward his palms

The soft spots at the top of your baby's skull are known as the fontanelles. You may be able to see a pulse beating beneath the scalp

ABOUT BIRTHMARKS

If you haven't found a blemish anywhere on your baby's body, it's probably because you haven't looked long enough.

Virtually every child is born with some type of birthmark, no matter how tiny. Most marks will fade and disappear on their own by the time your child is three years old, although some of them may remain and increase in size.

Both my sons had stork-bite birthmarks at the back of the neck just under the hairline (which is a very common place to find them). They disappeared, however, by the time they were six months old.

Other likely places are the eyelids, the forehead, and the neck, although one might be found on any part of your baby's skin.

Superficial birthmarks are nothing to worry about. They do no harm and need no treatment.

MEASUREMENTS

Your baby's weight, head circumference, and length will be measured to give an indication of her maturity and development. These measurements can be used as a baseline for her future development. Although routine measurements are inevitably compared to "the average," don't worry about this too much. An average is just an arithmetical calculation, so the "average child" is only theoretical and doesn't exist.

Weight Newborns differ greatly in weight. Nutritional, placental, and racial factors all have a bearing. The weight range for babies born around their expected time is 5½ pounds to 10 pounds (2.5–4.5 kilograms). If you are tall or heavy or if you are diabetic, your baby is likely to be on the heavy side.

Women who suffer from chronic hypertension, kidney disease, or preeclampsia, and women who smoke during pregnancy, are likely to have lighter babies. A woman whose pregnancy is shorter than 40 weeks is also likely to have a lighter baby. Girls generally weigh slightly less than boys, and babies born as twins are each likely to weigh less than a single baby.

It is normal for your baby to lose weight in the first few days after birth as her body adjusts to new feeding requirements. She must now process her own food, and it will take a while for her to feed consistently. In general, weight loss at this time can be as high as ten percent of your baby's birth weight. After a few days, you can expect your baby's weight to begin increasing.

The significance of a baby's weight gain is what it tells us of her overall physical health. Steady weight gain indicates that her food intake is sufficient and is being absorbed, while poor or erratic weight gain or weight loss signals that food intake is insufficient or that it isn't being absorbed.

Head circumference Your baby's head is disproportionately large in comparison to her body size, taking up one quarter of her entire length. The younger a baby is, the larger her head is in proportion to the rest of her body. The average circumference of a newborn's head is about 14 inches (35 centimeters). Measuring head circumference is regarded as an essential part of the

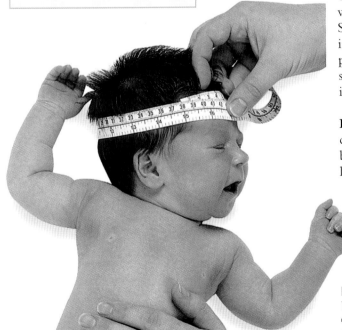

Measurements
Your baby's length and head circumference will be measured, and he will also be weighed.

examination of a baby because the growth of the head reflects the growth of the brain. An unusually large or small head circumference may be an indication of an abnormality of the brain.

Chest and abdomen The circumference of your baby's chest will be smaller than that of her head. Her stomach might appear to be very large, and even distended, but given the weakness in her abdominal muscles, this is to be expected.

THE FIRST DIAPERS

Your baby's stools and urine may not look as you expect them to, and if you have a baby girl there may be some vaginal discharge. None of these necessarily means that anything is wrong.

Stools Your baby's first bowel movement will consist of meconium, which is mainly digested mucus and looks blackish-green. Some of this is accumulated from swallowing amniotic fluid while inside your uterus. The first meconium stool should be passed within the first 24 hours, and it is not unusual for her next bowel movement to be two days later; this is especially true if you are breastfeeding (check, however, that your baby is wetting her diaper regularly). After the fourth day she may have four or five bowel movements daily.

You will notice that the color and composition of her stools change from dark, greenish-black sticky meconium to greenish-brown, and then to a yellow semi-solid type. If you are bottle-feeding your baby, the stools might resemble scrambled eggs.

Most babies fill their diapers as soon as they have eaten, due to a perfectly healthy gastrocolic reflex, which makes the bowel empty itself as soon as food enters the stomach. Some babies have bowel movements much more infrequently, but as long as your baby does not have to strain too much and her stools are soft and a normal color, there is no need for concern. If her stools are infrequent or hard, it is a good idea to give her a small amount of water (one tablespoon or 15 milliliters) two or three times a day.

Urine A newborn baby passes urine almost continuously because her bladder muscles are underdeveloped. She's unable to hold urine for any length of time—usually no longer than a few minutes—so it's quite normal to find that she wets her diaper up to 20 times in 24 hours. When she does, her urine will contain substances called urates that may stain her diaper dark pink or red. This, too, is normal for a newborn.

Vaginal discharge Newborn girls sometimes produce a clear or white vaginal discharge. In some cases, you may notice a small amount of vaginal bleeding, but this is perfectly normal and will clear up naturally after a couple of days. If you are really worried, contact your doctor for reassurance.

TYPES OF BIRTHMARKS

Most birthmarks are just abnormal collections of small blood vessels under the skin. They are harmless and don't cause your baby any pain. These are some common types:

Salmon patches Harmless but very common, these reddish marks may be present at birth on the eyelids, nose, upper lip, and nape of the neck. No treatment is needed and most fade during infancy.

Strawberry hemangiomas These pink discolorations of the skin usually fade with time, sometimes within a few months. They usually first appear as small red dots that are not always obvious at birth. They may grow during the first months of life into red raised lumps, but these start to shrivel and disappear without leaving a scar—30 percent by three years, 50 percent by five years, and 70 percent by seven. Very few need treatment with lasers and steroids.

Spider birthmarks (naevi) These small marks appear shortly after birth as a network or a cobweb of dilated vessels. They generally disappear after the first year.

Pigmented naevi These brownish patches can occur anywhere on the body. They are usually pale and nearly always enlarge as the child grows, but they seldom become darker.

Port wine stains Found anywhere on the body, these bright red or purple marks are caused by dilated capillaries in the skin. They can be removed with laser treatment, or camouflaged with special make-up.

Mongolian spots It is common for dark-skinned babies to have harmless, dark bluish-black discolorations of the skin, usually on the back or buttocks; these will fade naturally.

New parents

Case study

Parents' names Katharine and Adam Winterton
Age 34 years and 30 years
Katharine's past medical history High blood pressure (140/90)
Family history Several cases of high blood pressure on paternal side
Obstetric history First pregnancy. Mild preeclampsia (a condition that causes swelling of the legs, fingers, and face) diagnosed in sixth month.

During pregnancy, Katharine's whole view of giving birth changed drastically. She had wanted to do everything naturally, she didn't want any drugs, and the thought of a cesarean horrified her. When she was told she had high blood pressure, she began to panic. Symptoms that virtually all pregnant women

experience at some point, like faintness, headaches, or indigestion, seemed terrifying to her. Because he had had three years of medical training, Adam thought he would take the birth in stride. But he found things more difficult than he expected.

Katharine was very concerned that she might develop eclampsia during labor, which can lead to seizures. In fact, as I explained to her, this is a rare condition that is unlikely to occur even when preeclampsia has been diagnosed. Due to her high blood pressure and the weight of the baby (estimated at about 9 pounds/4 kilograms), Katharine agreed to being induced when she was two weeks overdue.

THE LABOR

In the end, although it was long (17 hours), labor went relatively smoothly for Katharine. She was induced at 9 a.m. on Monday, and at 1 p.m. felt relaxed enough to send her husband Adam to her mother's for lunch… on the condition that he bring her back some of her favorite homemade cake.

Katharine used a TENS machine, which stimulates the body's natural painkillers through the transmission of electrical impulses. She was put on it

late, however, so she's not sure whether it helped or not. At midnight, 15 hours later, she asked for an epidural—something she had sworn not to do—and after that everything was fine. Adam felt better, too, because Kath was no longer in excessive pain. He says, "That was when I felt the most useful, because she needed someone to take her mind off what was going on. We even started planning what we were going to do once we got Daniel home." At 1:45 a.m. on Tuesday, Katharine had an episiotomy (which she didn't feel at all), and about ten minutes later the doctor used forceps to pull Daniel out.

FIRST REACTIONS

"I got a bit of a shock when I saw him," recalls Katharine, "because his face was very red and scrunched up, his head looked slightly lopsided because of the forceps, and he seemed to be gasping for air, but not making any sound. I kept asking the nurse, 'Is he alright?! Is he alright?!' The nurse turned away for a second and I was absolutely convinced Daniel was dead. That was actually the worst moment during the whole labor, and I started to cry uncontrollably.

"In fact, the nurse was only doing the Apgar scores and, as it turned out, Daniel scored highly. About 30 seconds later, we were handed a perfect little baby boy breathing normally.

"I was quite surprised that he had his eyes wide open and seemed to be looking at me and Adam in a very alert, quizzical manner. He just stared for about five minutes without crying at all. Daniel is my first child, and so I wasn't prepared for the combination of sheer joy, love, and relief that flooded over me when he was placed in my arms for the first time.

"The placenta came out after only ten minutes, which I'm told is a bit unusual without the use of Syntocinon, and then the doctor clamped the umbilical cord in two places, and Adam cut it."

LOOKING BACK AT THE BIRTH

The one thing Katharine regrets about the whole pregnancy is having had an episiotomy. She is sure she would have stretched enough had she been given another half hour. Although she felt no pain at the time, due to the epidural, she says the episiotomy was the only physical problem associated with the birth that didn't clear up in the first two weeks.

Three months later the episiotomy scar was still sensitive, and she said that the feeling she may tear during intercourse had put her off sex completely. I explained to her that, although this fear is genuine, it is almost certain she would have lost her sexual appetite for a time after giving birth, with or without an episiotomy. Although the latest research indicates that tears heal better than episiotomies should the mother not stretch enough naturally, a forceps delivery always necessitates an episiotomy.

THE FIRST DAYS

Katharine found that despite her elation after the birth of Daniel, she soon got what are commonly known as the "baby blues," a feeling of deep depression that stayed with her for three days. She found it very difficult to relate to all the people around her, including Adam. She also felt guilty because she had not expected these feelings to accompany the birth of a normal, healthy baby.

"Baby blues" are caused by the huge increase in hormones in a woman's body during childbirth. It takes quite a while, sometimes weeks or months, for the body to readjust, and in the meantime a new mother may have to deal with difficult bouts of depression.

In Katharine's case, things improved when she arrived home from the hospital. Although she was physically exhausted, psychologically she felt much more in control.

"It was only when we walked through our own door with Daniel that I felt the three of us were a real family."

Katharine's tips

• Try to be flexible and positive. The only thing to be sure of is that it probably won't turn out as you planned—but that isn't necessarily a bad thing.

• Although I only had my husband with me during labor, a lot of women I spoke to in the maternity ward also had a friend or a relative. I will definitely consider this next time if the hospital allows.

• If you reach the stage where the pain becomes overwhelming, don't be afraid to ask for an epidural—it really did make a difference for me, and after that I enjoyed the birth much more.

• Ask your doctor to let you have the time to stretch naturally if at all possible, rather than attempt an episiotomy too early.

Newborn behavior

EYE REFLEXES

Your baby will close his eyes, blink, or move them from one side to the other, depending on what is happening around him.

• If light shines in his face, he will blink—usually whether he has his eyes open or not (you should never shine bright light directly in your baby's eyes).

• He will also blink if you tap the bridge of his nose or blow gently across his eyes, or if he is startled by a sudden noise.

• If you lift your newborn up and turn him to the left or right, his eyes will not normally move with his head, but will stay fixed in the same position momentarily. This is known as the "doll's-eye response," and will usually disappear after about ten days.

Once your baby is born, it may take you a while to get used to his behavior. It is worth studying his reactions to various stimuli, and becoming familiar with some of the traits that will mark his personality. Young babies have far more individuality than they're usually given credit for, and this is a useful fact to bear in mind as you get to know your child.

REFLEXES

One thing common to all healthy babies is a number of reflexes that can be stimulated from the very first moments after birth. These reflexes are unconscious movements that eventually, at about three months, start to be replaced by conscious movements.

Grasp reflex
If you put something in the palm of your baby's hand, he will clench it surprisingly tightly. The grasp of a baby is often tight enough to support his entire body weight (although you should never try this).

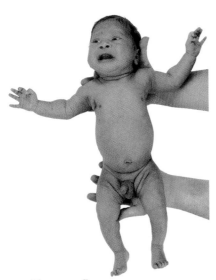

Moro reflex
Should your baby's head drop back, you might notice he throws his limbs up with fingers outstretched, then lets them fall back slowly toward his body.

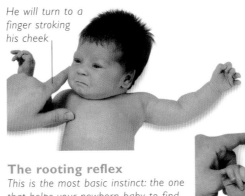

He will turn to a finger stroking his cheek

The rooting reflex
This is the most basic instinct: the one that helps your newborn baby to find your breast and suck it. If you gently stroke your baby's cheek, he will turn his head in the direction of your finger and open his mouth. If you touch the center of his upper lip, you will also see that his mouth opens.

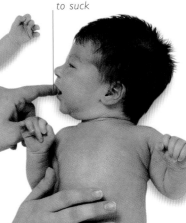

He instinctively opens his mouth to suck

You might notice that your newborn baby responds in a positive way to your presence by momentarily contracting his whole face and body. As he learns to control his movements, you will see that his reactions become more directed and less random. For instance, at six weeks, instead of scrunching up his whole face, he may show you a distinct smile.

TESTING REFLEXES

Until your baby's physical and mental capabilities develop, it will be his instinctive reflexes that provide an indication of his maturity. Doctors can test these reflexes to check your baby's general health and see that his central nervous system is functioning well. Premature babies will not react in the same way as full-term babies.

Although there are more than 70 primitive reflexes that have been identified in newborn babies, your doctor is only likely to test a selected few. The two most commonly recognized reflexes that you can easily test yourself are the rooting and the grasp reflex. Don't try to test the Moro reflex at home, as this could distress your baby and make him cry.

GETTING TO KNOW YOUR BABY

Spend as much time as you can playing with your new baby—it's vital for his development.

• Watch his expressions and you'll soon start to recognize his needs. When he's content, he'll look tranquil and quiet. When he's feeling miserable or uncomfortable, he'll look red and flustered.

• Play with your baby. Don't worry about looking silly—make funny faces and use a high-pitched voice as you tell him how much you love him. He'll answer by nodding and moving his mouth. He may stick out his tongue, too, and jerk his body.

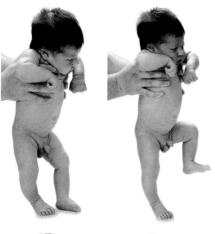

Walking reflex
If you hold your baby under the shoulders so that he is in an upright position and his feet are allowed to touch a firm surface, he'll move his legs in a walking action. This reflex disappears in three to six weeks, and is not what helps your child learn to walk.

Your baby takes up a crawling position when he's placed on his stomach

Placing reflex
This is quite similar to the walking reflex. If you hold your baby in an upright position and bring the front of his leg into contact with the edge of a table, he will lift his foot as if to step on to the table. The same reflex is present in the arm; if the back of your baby's forearm touches the table edge, he will raise his arm.

"Crawling"
When you place your baby on his stomach, he will automatically assume what appears to be a crawling position, with his pelvis high and his knees pulled up under his abdomen. When he kicks his legs, he may be able to shuffle in a vague crawling manner. It is not real crawling, however, and this behavior will disappear as soon as his legs uncurl and he lies flat.

YOUR NEWBORN GIRL

Many behavioral traits that are typical of girls can be observed in your baby as soon as she is born.

- Hearing in girls is very acute, and they can be calmed down with soothing words much more readily than boys.

- A baby girl cries longer than a boy if she hears another baby crying.

- Baby girls use their own voice to get their mother's attention earlier and more often than boys.

- Baby girls can locate the source of a sound without difficulty.

- Girls respond enthusiastically to visual stimulation from birth.

- Baby girls are interested in the unusual.

- Girls prefer the human face to almost anything else. Later in life, this trait shows as intuitive reading of facial expression regardless of cultural differences.

CRYING

Assume that your baby will cry a lot and you might be pleasantly surprised if she doesn't. If you think she won't cry and then she does, you may find yourself overwhelmed and disoriented.

Remember that there are really only three states your newborn baby can be in: asleep, awake and quiet, or awake and crying. If she is crying, there are a variety of possible reasons. The most likely causes are tiredness, hunger, loneliness, and discomfort—she is too hot or too cold, is in an uncomfortable position, or needs changing. You must accept, though, that sometimes a baby will cry for no discernible reason. This type of crying can be the most stressful for a parent.

Responding to crying Leaving a child to cry on her own is never a good idea. If a baby is denied attention and friendship in her early weeks and months, she may grow up to be introverted, shy, and withdrawn. Research on newborns shows that if parents are slow to respond to their baby's crying, the result may be a baby that cries more rather than less. A recent study found that babies whose crying was ignored in their first few weeks tended to cry more frequently and persistently as they grew older.

Often people confuse spoiling a child with loving a child. In my opinion, a baby cannot be "spoiled" enough. A six-month-old baby who is picked up, nursed, cuddled, and talked to soothingly and lovingly is not learning about seeking attention; she is learning about love and forming human relationships—and that is one of the most important lessons a child will ever learn in terms of her future emotional and psychological development. What we tend to call spoiling is both a natural response of a mother to a distressed child, and the natural need of the baby.

SLEEP PATTERNS

Once you bring your newborn home, you'll have some sleepless nights unless you are very lucky. Although most newborns usually sleep when they are not feeding—typically spending at least 60 percent of their time asleep—some will remain active and alert for surprisingly long periods during the day and night.

One young mother was shocked to find that her new baby never dozed for longer than one or two hours at a time until she was four months old. This is a very long time for any parent to survive without a full night's sleep, especially when your body may be in need of rest after an exhausting pregnancy and birth. If you have a very wakeful baby, be consoled by the fact that as long as she isn't left bored on her own, every minute that she's awake she's learning something new— and in the long run you will be rewarded with an eager, bright child.

All babies are different, and their sleep requirements depend on individual physiology. For this reason it's nonsensical to lay down rigid sleeping times that correspond to the average baby. As I've said before, the average baby doesn't exist.

Most newborns fall asleep soon after feeding. At first, a baby's wakefulness is likely to depend on how much feeding she needs, which in turn depends on her weight (see below).

SOUNDS YOUR BABY MAKES

Babies make a variety of strange noises, whether asleep or awake, and this is quite normal. Most of these are due to the immaturity of her respiratory system and will soon disappear.

Snoring Your baby may make some grunting noises when she's asleep. This is not a true snore, and is probably caused by vibrations on the soft palate at the back of her mouth as she breathes.

Sniffling Your baby may sniffle so loudly with each breath that you think she has a cold or that she has mucous at the back of her throat. In most babies these sniffling noises are harmless and are caused because the bridge of the nose is low, and air is trying to get through very short, narrow nasal passages. As your baby grows older, the bridge of her nose will get higher and the sniffling sound will gradually disappear.

Sneezing You may also think your baby has a cold because she sneezes a lot, but sneezing is common in newborn babies, particularly if they open their eyes and are exposed to bright light. This sneezing can be beneficial—it helps clear out your baby's nasal passages.

Hiccups Newborn babies hiccup a lot, particularly after a feeding. This leads some mothers to fear that their baby has indigestion, but this is rarely the case. Hiccups are due to imperfect control of the diaphragm—the sheet of muscle that separates the chest from the abdomen—and they will disappear as your baby's nervous control of the diaphragm matures.

YOUR NEWBORN BOY

From the moment of birth, baby boys show characteristic male behavior, some of which will persist throughout life.

- Hearing in boys is less acute than in girls, so boys are more difficult to calm down.

- If a newborn boy hears another baby cry, he'll join in, but will stop crying quite quickly.

- Baby boys don't make sounds in answer to their mother's voice early on. This hearing response lasts throughout life.

- Newborn boys have difficulty in locating the source of sounds.

- Baby boys require more visual stimulation than girls. They quickly lose interest in a design or picture, and lag behind girls in visual maturity up to the age of seven months.

- Baby boys are interested in the differences between things.

- Boys are more active, and are interested in things just as much as in people.

- Boys want to taste everything, touch everything, and move things around more than girls do.

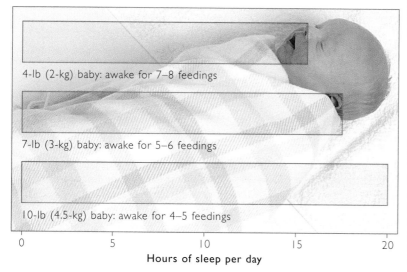

4-lb (2-kg) baby: awake for 7–8 feedings

7-lb (3-kg) baby: awake for 5–6 feedings

10-lb (4.5-kg) baby: awake for 4–5 feedings

0   5   10   15   20

Hours of sleep per day

Newborn sleep requirements
A newborn's sleep pattern is determined by her weight and feeding requirements. This means that in the first weeks of life, the less your baby weighs, the more often she will need to be fed and the less time she will spend sleeping, and vice versa. The chart is a very rough guide to sleep requirements according to varying birth weights, but all babies have their own sleep/wake pattern.

Newborn health

Immediately after birth, your baby will undergo five short tests to assess his health.

Your baby is given a score of 0, 1, or 2 for each category. If he scores over 7 in total, he is in good condition. If he scores under 4, he needs help and will receive resuscitation. Most low-scoring babies score highly when tested again a few minutes later. The five checks are:

Activity This shows the health and tone of your baby's muscles.

Pulse This indicates the rate and strength of the heartbeats.

Grimace/crying Facial expressions and responses show how alert he is to stimuli.

Appearance A pink skin color shows his lungs are working well.

Respiration Breathing shows the health of his lungs.

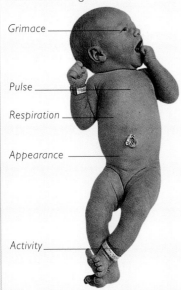

Grimace

Pulse

Respiration

Appearance

Activity

Assessing a newborn
The baby is checked to be sure her lungs and heart are working and her responses are healthy.

When your baby is born, your doctor or midwife will see to it that he is given uninterrupted expert attention until breathing is well established. Any major problems should be identified within a matter of minutes, so that if special care is required, it will begin at the earliest possible moment.

Immediately after delivery, the doctor or midwife will test your baby against the Apgar scale (see left), a series of short tests to determine his general physical well-being. Devised by the late Dr. Virginia Apgar, a renowned anesthesiologist, they are designed to detect whether your baby is in need of immediate special attention. The doctor or midwife will then examine your baby to assess his general condition. The sort of checks your doctor will do involve:

• Making sure that your baby's facial features and body proportions are normal.
• Turning your baby over to see that his back is normal and there is no spina bifida (see p.28).
• Examining his anus, legs, fingers, and toes.
• Recording the number of blood vessels in the umbilical cord—normally there are two arteries and one vein.
• Weighing your baby.
• Measuring your baby's head and body length.
• Checking your baby's temperature and warming him if he needs it.

This preliminary examination takes less than a minute when performed by an experienced doctor or midwife. You can then rest easy in the knowledge that your baby is healthy and normal.

THE NEXT DAY

Once the initial tests have been carried out and you've held and suckled him for as long as you and your partner want, your baby will be wrapped up snugly and put in his crib in order to keep warm. He'll be given a thorough examination about 24 hours later to ensure that all is well. This takes place when your baby is warm and relaxed. At this time you will have an opportunity to discuss your baby's exam, and any worries you might have, with the doctor. Maternity staff can be very helpful in this regard as well, so don't hesitate to ask questions.

Your baby is placed on a flat surface in a good light and at a convenient height for the doctor, who may be seated. You can have the examination at your bedside if you are immobile, but should you be absent, never fail to get the results of the examination. Generally, your doctor will start examining your baby at the top of the head and work down to the toes.

Head and neck The doctor will look at the skull bones and the fontanelles, and check for any misshaping that occurred when the head passed through the birth canal during delivery. He will look at the eyes, ears, and nose, and check the mouth for any abnormality, such as cleft palate, and for any teeth. Although rare, some newborn babies do have teeth. If they are loose or growing at an unusual angle they will be removed so that there is no risk that they will fall out and be swallowed. The doctor will also check your baby's neck for any cysts or swellings.

Chest and heart The heart and lungs are checked with a stethoscope. The lungs should be expanded and working normally. After birth, the workload of a baby's heart increases substantially when he becomes responsible for his own circulation. This may cause heart murmur (a sound that the doctor hears with a stethoscope), but most murmurs soon disappear. Your child will be examined during the postpartum checkup to see if a heart murmur persists.

Arms and hands The doctor will check each arm for a pulse, and for normal movement and strength. He will also check your baby's fingers and palm creases. Nearly all babies have two major creases across each palm; if there is only a single crease, your doctor will look for other physical abnormalities.

Abdomen and genitals The doctor will press his hands gently into your baby's abdomen to check the size and shape of the liver and spleen. Both may be slightly enlarged in a newborn baby. He will check the testes to ensure that they are properly descended if your baby is a boy, and check that the labia are not joined and that the clitoris is a normal size for a girl. The doctor will also check the lower spine and anus for congenital abnormalities (see pp. 28–29).

Hips, legs, and feet Your doctor will hold both thighs firmly and move each leg to see whether the head of the thigh bone is unstable or lies outside the hip joint, suggesting developmental dysplasia of the hip. Testing the hips is not painful, but your baby may cry at the movement. The doctor will examine the legs and feet to make sure they are of equal size and length. If the ankle is still turned inward as it was in the uterus, your baby may have a club foot. This can be treated with manipulation and perhaps a cast.

Nerves and muscles Your doctor will put your baby's arms and legs through a range of movements to make sure that they are not too stiff or floppy. This will tell him about the health of your baby's nerves and muscles. He will make sure that the normal newborn reflexes, such as the grasp, walking, and Moro reflexes (see p.20) are present, and check your baby's head control.

JAUNDICE

Jaundice is not a disease and, in the majority of newborn babies, is not dangerous.

Jaundice is likely to occur when a baby is about three days old. It is caused by the breakdown of red blood cells shortly after birth. This breakdown creates an excess in the blood of a pigment called bilirubin, causing a yellowish tinge to the baby's skin.

A newborn is unable to excrete the bilirubin sufficiently rapidly to prevent jaundice until his liver is more mature, at about one week. In most babies, jaundice doesn't require treatment and clears up by itself within a week. The level of bilirubin can be checked with a blood test. Some babies do need treatment, usually with phototherapy.

Rhesus compatibility (incompatibility between the blood types of mother and baby, usually a Rhesus-negative mother with a Rhesus-positive baby) is now a rare cause of severe jaundice in newborn babies, since it is usually diagnosed and treated prenatally. Other less common causes are hepatitis and biliary atresia, a rare condition in which the bile duct fails to develop properly.

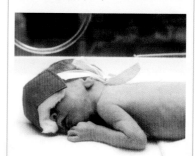

Phototherapy
Jaundice in a newborn may be treated by exposure to ultraviolet light for about 12 hours.

BONDING

You should make every effort to establish bonds with your premature baby as soon as possible through your smell, your voice, and your touch.

Much research has been done to illustrate the positive effects of physical human contact on young babies, and this applies equally to those that are premature.

If you are a new mother expecting to have your baby in your arms right after birth, it is obviously distressing to find that she will be kept behind a glass screen, and be surrounded by many machines.

Mothers who don't have early contact with their babies may start to feel cheated of motherhood. They are likely to blame themselves for having "failed" their babies, and these feelings of guilt are intensified because they are unable to comfort their babies, who are obviously in need of help.

It is important to realize, though, that effective bonding can take place with your baby in an incubator—indeed, it is essential that it does. No baby is so ill that you can't place your hand inside the incubator and stroke her gently. Try not to be intimidated by all the machinery; ask the hospital staff to show you what to do.

PREMATURE BABIES

About one in 20 babies is premature. A premature baby is one that is born at less than 36 weeks. All premature babies need special treatment, but not necessarily in a neonatal intensive care unit.

When we say a baby is premature, we mean that she hasn't yet matured to the point where she can cope easily outside the security of her mother's uterus. Although the chances today of a premature baby surviving and thriving are vastly improved in comparison to our mothers' generation, it's still a troubling experience to see your baby being taken away to an intensive care unit immediately after the delivery.

Understanding why a baby needs special treatment for a few days or weeks will help lessen your anxiety. Premature babies have very weak muscle tone and don't move much. They often have calcium and iron deficiencies, as well as low blood-sugar levels. If they are very premature, their eyes may still be sealed. They have very red and wrinkled skin. Their heads are disproportionately large in comparison to the rest of the body, and the bones in their skull are soft. They are more than usually prone to jaundice (see p.25).

SPECIAL NEEDS OF A PREMATURE BABY

A premature baby needs to be fed more frequently than a full-term baby because she burns calories more quickly. You can understand why she needs to be fed so often if you think of a tiny hummingbird; it never stops feeding, since its weight is so low compared to its volume that it needs constant food to stoke up the metabolic burners and keep the temperature normal. The smaller the baby, therefore, the more often she needs to feed and the less time she spends asleep (see p.22). For premature babies, the challenge of living outside the uterus is

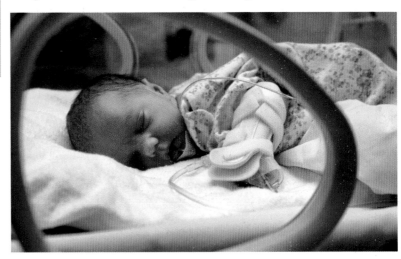

Incubators
A premature baby will be placed in a closed, thermostatically controlled cabinet to maintain her body temperature, and will be given oxygen if necessary. Her temperature and breathing will be constantly monitored.

clearly an exhausting one. The lack of stimulation from being in an incubator and the inability to move very much means that, apart from frequent feeding, premature babies spend most of their time sleeping.

BREATHING PROBLEMS

A premature baby may stop breathing for short periods. This is called apnea, and although it sounds frightening, it is not uncommon. Most babies start breathing again after gentle stimulation, such as a tap or stroke. Other respiratory problems can arise from fluid inhaled into the lungs, or a lack of surfactant—a substance produced in the lungs that stops the lungs from collapsing inward. If a baby's lungs don't have enough surfactant coating them, they don't expand as well as they should. This can cause the smaller air sacs to collapse inward, leading to a condition common in babies born before 28 weeks, known as hyaline membrane disease, or respiratory distress syndrome (RDS).

Babies suffering from any of these complications can be given oxygen either by way of a face mask or by a small tube inserted directly into the windpipe. Sometimes a ventilator is needed to do the breathing for the baby.

TUBE-FEEDING

Most premature babies don't have the strength to suck milk from a nipple or bottle, and their intestines may be too weak to absorb food. There are three alternative ways of feeding:

• Intravenous feeding is used for babies who are very sick or so premature that they can't swallow or digest food for themselves. It may continue for weeks and subsequent feeding will be through a nasogastric tube.
• With nasogastric feeding, a tube is passed through the baby's nose and into the stomach or intestine. The tube is very fine and soft so your baby hardly knows it's there, and it's a very comfortable way to feed.
• When your baby is older, a combination of breast- or bottle- and tube-feeding will suffice; the baby feeds as much as she can from breast or bottle, and then tube feeding supplies the rest. Combination feeding can be used once the rooting and sucking reflexes (see p.20) are established and will continue until your baby is strong enough to feed from breast or bottle only.

PROGRESS

The development of a premature baby can be slow and erratic. It is often a great shock to see just how tiny your premature baby is, but she will have a strong will to live. For a premature baby, every day can be an uphill battle. Periods of improvement may be followed by setbacks, and this constant uncertainty can make you and your partner feel anxious, moody, and restless. It is encouraging to know, however, that most babies born after 32 weeks develop normally. Of those babies born at 28 weeks, six out of seven will survive.

HEALTH RISKS

Premature babies are ill-prepared for life outside the uterus, and can have the problems listed below.

Breathing Due to the immaturity of their lungs, many premature babies experience difficulty in breathing, known as respiratory distress syndrome (RDS).

Immune system An under-developed immune system and a body that is too weak to defend itself properly means there is a greater risk of infection than with a full-term baby.

Temperature regulation A premature baby's temperature control is inefficient and she is likely to be too cold or too hot. She has less heat insulation than a full-term baby, since she lacks sufficient body fat underneath the skin.

Reflexes Inadequate development of her reflexes, particularly her sucking reflex, creates difficulties in feeding. Premature babies often need tube-feeding.

Digestion A premature baby's stomach is small and sensitive, which means she is less able to hold food down, and so is more likely to vomit. The immaturity of her digestive system can make it difficult for her to digest essential proteins, so they may have to be given in a pre-digested form.

SPINA BIFIDA

If the neural tube (the developing spine) doesn't fuse properly in early pregnancy, the meninges (the coverings of the brain and spinal cord) may be left exposed.

The affected part of the spine may be covered by skin and marked only by a dimple or a tuft of hair (spina bifida occulta); the meninges may protrude and the bulge may be covered with skin (meningocele); or, in the most serious form, the spinal cord itself, covered only by a thin layer of meninges, may protrude as a raw swelling over the spine (myelocele). A high percentage of all spina bifida babies have some degree of hydrocephalus (see opposite). Women with a family history of neural tube defects are at a particularly high risk of successive infants being affected.

In babies with severe defects, problems may include complete paralysis of the legs, double incontinence, and mental retardation. Urinary incontinence can be helped by the use of a catheter (a sterile tube that is inserted into the bladder), and physiotherapy is important to encourage mobility.

Spina bifida can be detected in pregnancy by ultrasound. According to the March of Dimes, spina bifida affects 1,500–2,000 babies (one in every 2,000 live births) each year in the US. The introduction of folic acid before conception and during pregnancy has reduced the incidence of spina bifida lesions.

CONGENITAL CONDITIONS

Congenital handicaps are rare. Some are genetic, while others are due to the effects on the fetus of drugs, radiation, infections, or metabolic disturbances. The fetal tissues that are most actively growing at the time when the adverse factor operates are the ones most likely to be affected. An increasing number of defects can be detected before birth and successfully treated just after birth.

Talipes (club foot) Some infants—twice as many boys as girls—are born with the sole of one or both feet facing down and inward, or up and outward. The cause of club foot is not fully understood, but it can be inherited. The foot will be manipulated over several months, and braced or splinted in position between manipulations. If surgery is necessary, it can be carried out up to the age of nine months. Talipes can be a feature of spina bifida.

Dislocated hip In about 0.4 percent of infants, the ball at the head of the thigh bone doesn't fit snugly into its socket in the hip bone. In a newborn, this is a potential rather than an actual problem. It is much more common in girls than in boys and following breech births and in pregnancies where there is an abnormally small amount of amniotic fluid in the uterus.

Your doctor or midwife will check your baby's hips for excessive mobility as part of routine tests after birth (see p.24). Treatment, such as manipulation and splinting, can prevent trouble in later infancy. In severe cases, an operation may be needed.

Hypospadias In a very small number of male babies—about 0.3 percent—the urethral opening is not situated at the end of the penis but farther back on the underside of the penis. In most cases, it lies toward the end, but in some it is on the underside of the shaft of the penis. In severe cases, the penis is curved. Rarely, the urethral opening lies between the genitals and the anus. Surgery for this condition is usually carried out before the age of two years, allowing the normal passage of urine and, in later life, normal sexual intercourse. The condition, even in its most severe form, doesn't cause infertility.

Congenital heart disease The most common form of heart disease in newborns is a hole in the ventricular septum—the thin dividing wall between the right and left ventricles (the two main chambers of the heart). Symptoms include breathlessness, particularly during feeding, crying, and poor weight gain, but there may be no symptoms and the doctor may simply notice a murmur and pick up the condition during a routine examination. Small holes usually close spontaneously, but if they don't, surgical treatment may be necessary.

Cleft lip and cleft palate A cleft is a split or separation of parts. In the early part of pregnancy, separate areas of the baby's face and head develop individually, then join together. When joining doesn't take place or is incomplete, the baby can be born with a cleft lip on one or both sides, with or without a cleft palate. Breastfeeding is sometimes possible, perhaps using a nipple shield; or special bottles and nipples are available.

A cleft lip will be surgically closed soon after birth or some weeks after. The palate will be closed from about six to nine months. Further operations may be necessary for some children.

Some affected children will be treated at a cleft palate center, by a multi-disciplinary team of doctors, dentists, and speech therapists. Others may be treated by an ear, nose, and throat (ENT or otolaryngologist) doctor, or by a plastic surgeon.

Down syndrome This is by far the most common of a range of conditions called trisomies, in which one pair of chromosomes has an extra chromosome, making three. In Down syndrome, there are three number 21 chromosomes. Affected infants characteristically have a round face, a tongue that tends to protrude, and slanting eyes with folds of skin at their inner corners. The back of the head is usually flat. They tend to be rather floppy infants and have short, wide hands with a single transverse crease across the palm. Other problems may include congenital heart disease.

Down syndrome babies are usually mentally handicapped, though the degree of handicap varies widely; many are near normal. They are usually affectionate and happy children. With early education and careful attention, they often do very well, and some manage to live independently as adults.

Pyloric stenosis In this condition, the pylorus, the passage that leads from the stomach into the small intestine, is narrow because of a thickening of the muscle. The cause is unknown, and it is more common in boys than in girls. Symptoms usually first appear at two to four weeks, though they can appear earlier. The stomach contracts powerfully in an attempt to force a buildup of food through the narrow pylorus. This is impossible however, and the contents of the stomach are vomited up so violently that they may be propelled up to 3 feet (1 meter)—projectile vomiting. The baby may also suffer constipation, and dehydration is also a risk, so seek medical advice quickly. Ultrasound may be carried out to confirm the diagnosis. An operation to widen the pylorus can cure the condition.

Imperforate anus Very rarely, a baby's anus is sealed at birth, either because there is a thin membrane of skin over the opening or because the anal canal, which links the rectum with the anus, hasn't developed. The baby must be referred for surgical treatment at once. This condition is routinely checked for at every birth (see p.24), and is treated immediately if present.

HYDROCEPHALUS

Also called water on the brain, hydrocephalus often occurs with other neurological defects, such as spina bifida.

A rare condition, most common in preterm babies, it is caused by a blockage in the flow of cerebrospinal fluid or a buildup of the fluid in the brain cavities. Cerebrospinal fluid bathes the brain and spinal cord, protecting them from injury. The head swells because the skull bones are still soft, and the soft tissues between the skull bones and the fontanelles become wide and bulging.

If hydrocephalus is suspected, frequent ultrasound checks will be performed and your baby's head circumference measured every two to three days. If a child is born with hydrocephalus, a shunt may be inserted to drain off the fluid. Mental development is usually adversely affected, but some children with advanced hydrocephalus are of normal intelligence.

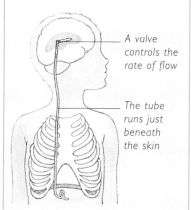

A valve controls the rate of flow

The tube runs just beneath the skin

Shunt
A system of tubes with a valve drains off excess cerebrospinal fluid to where it can pass into the bloodstream, usually the abdominal cavity. The entire device is enclosed in the body.

CHAPTER 2

Everyday care

Confronted with a new baby, many parents worry
that they won't know what to do. Will he start to
breastfeed automatically? How much sleep should
he have? How much food does he need? What
if he refuses food?

Fortunately, caring for a baby doesn't require
special skills—just some basic knowledge,
common sense, and a willingness to ask for advice.
In the space of a few weeks, your confidence and
experience will increase dramatically, and you
will know the best way to change, hold, comfort,
and feed your baby. You will learn that if he
needs something, he will usually find a way
of communicating with you.

As your child gets older, he will become more
independent. By the age of four, he will be able
to feed, wash, and dress himself, and he may be
quite opinionated about the clothes and foods he
does and doesn't like. His physical needs will no
longer take up so much of your time. Your role
in his everyday care is to keep him strong and
healthy by meeting his dietary needs and
looking after his health and hygiene.

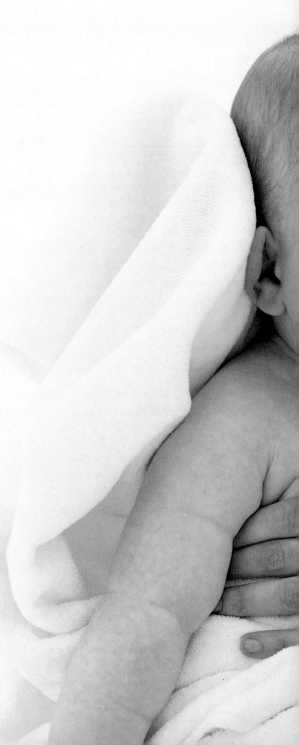

Equipping your baby's room

SAFETY

When planning a baby's room, bear in mind that your child will be mobile before long.

• Make sure there are no sharp edges or corners on the furniture.

• Choose a nonslip floor covering and consider adding bars and locks to the windows.

• The furniture should be stable so your child can't pull it over.

• Toys should be stored at floor level so your child doesn't have to stretch to reach them.

• Choose wall-mounted lamps to avoid trailing cords.

• Don't overheat the room; overheating is a risk factor in crib deaths (see p.122).

Your baby may have a room of her own or share yours; once she is sleeping through the night, however, she should have her own space. You'll need little special equipment, and you can improvise with household items—a sink will do as well as a baby bath, for example, and a folded towel as a changing mat—but many parents do delight in equipping their baby's room.

If this is your first child, ask friends with children which items they found most useful, and weigh up their advice against your own lifestyle. If there's anything you're unsure about, shop around and take a look through a variety of baby catalogs before making your final decisions. There will often be many things that you can manage without. The only essentials are somewhere for your baby to sleep, her clothes and diapers (see pp.82–83 and 106–107), and her feeding equipment.

You don't have to buy everything brand-new; look for secondhand items advertised in local papers or on notice boards at the clinic or grocery store. A carrier will last only a couple of months, since babies grow so quickly, so it makes sense to borrow one from friends if you can. If you buy secondhand items, check for general wear and tear, and make sure that all surfaces are smooth and free of rust for your baby's safety. Check, too, that they still comply with the latest safety regulations. Beware of painted items; old-fashioned paints may contain lead, which is poisonous. Never buy secondhand car seats or harnesses.

Basic equipment

Sleeping
Baby carrier, crib
Mattress with waterproof cover
Fitted crib sheets
Cellular blankets
Swaddling shawls (optional)
Baby alarm

Transportation
Convertible carriage/carrier (suitable from birth), carriage, or stroller
Baby sling
Infant car seat

Bathing
Baby bath
Cotton balls
Large, soft towel
Washcloth or sponge
Baby brush
Baby bath lotion
Blunt-ended scissors

Other
Bouncing chair
Burp cloths

DECORATING YOUR BABY'S ROOM

Although a newborn's vision is limited, cheerful colors and decorations will provide a stimulating environment.

• Light, cheerful colors are the most suitable for your baby's room. Yellow, blue, and grassy green—the colors of nature—will be soothing to your baby, and vivid splashes of primary colors will enliven the room.

• A newborn baby has a very limited range of vision—only 8–10 inches (20–25 centimeters)—so hang mobiles above the crib and the changing area. Their colors and movement will make your baby alert to her surroundings.

• Put an unbreakable mirror on the side of the crib so your baby can see her face; the human face is fascinating to very young babies.

• Choose fabrics and wall coverings that are washable.

• A folding screen may be useful to shelter the crib from bright sunshine or from cold drafts.

• Carpet is warm and will absorb noise, but can be difficult to keep clean; a good alternative is a vinyl floor covering with a couple of nonslip rugs.

ARRANGING A BABY'S ROOM

Planning your baby's room, like buying equipment, is best done before your baby is born: once you bring her home, you'll be far too busy feeding and changing, and you're likely to be tired, too.

Try to ensure that the room is as easy as possible to keep clean, with wipe-clean surfaces. Choose furniture without hard edges or corners, and make sure that any painted surfaces are nontoxic and lead-free. You will need plenty of storage space, especially near the changing area. This could be a wide-topped chest of drawers with some shelf space above, or you may like to build your own. Be sure the top is wide enough for the changing mat and smooth as well as washable. Cork tiles and berber carpets are ideal floor coverings, as they are warm and hard-wearing.

The baby's room doesn't have to be very warm, but should be kept at a constant temperature. Around 65°F (18°C) is suitable if your baby is covered with two blankets and a sheet; if the room is warmer, she should have fewer blankets (see p.123). It is a good idea to install a dimmer switch so that you can gently bring up the lights without startling your baby. If you like, the light can be left on low as an alternative to a night light.

Safety is the most important thing when choosing equipment for your baby.

• Make sure the crib you choose is sturdy and is finished with nontoxic paint or varnish. Check it for sharp edges and screws.

• The mattress can be new or secondhand, but should be firm and in good condition.

• Choose closely woven blankets that don't trap fingers.

SLEEPING

The best choice for your newborn is a bassinet or a convertible carriage/carrier; some carriages convert to strollers for use when he's able to support himself sitting up. Your baby will outgrow baby baskets or cradles quite quickly, so don't splurge on an expensive one unless you're sure you can afford it. When your baby outgrows his bassinet or carrier, you'll need a full-sized crib. Choose one with side rails that are set closely together—a distance of 1–2½ inches (2.5–6 centimeters) is suitable—and drop sides so that you can lift your baby out easily. The mattress should fit snugly, so your baby can't get his arm or his

Sleeping equipment
Your newborn baby will spend much of his time asleep, and he'll be able to sleep just about anywhere. A basket or carrier is best at first, and easily portable, but once he outgrows these he'll need a crib.

Handles should be near the hood end to take the weight evenly

Mattress can be covered in PVC or other wipe-clean materials

The gaps between the bars should be in the range of 1–2½ inches (2.5–6 centimeters)

The drop side should have safety locks so your child can't let it down

Caster locks

Casters for maneuverability and for "rocking"

leg, or even his head, trapped down the side. The crib will last you until your baby is big enough to climb out, when you'll need to buy a bed—at about two or two-and-a-half years. The crib mattress should be a foam type. Some have air holes that allow your child to breathe if he turns over onto his front while asleep. Travel cribs are very useful for going on vacation or taking your baby out for the evening. They have fabric sides and are collapsible so that they can easily be carried. All sleeping equipment must comply with safety standards.

Because a young baby can't regulate his body temperature effectively, you should use a cotton sheet and cellular blankets for the crib so that you can easily add one or take one away. Once he is a year old, a crib comforter will be suitable. Make sure that any bedding you buy is fire-retardant and conforms to current safety standards.

Sleeping temperatures Research into crib death has shown that babies who get too hot are at a greater risk of crib death. While the temperature of the room is an important factor, the number of blankets is even more so. If the room is at 65°F (18°C), then a sheet and two layers of blankets will keep your baby at an ideal temperature. If it is warmer, you should use correspondingly fewer blankets (see p.123). Similarly, crib bumpers and pillows can make your baby too hot. Babies lose heat through their heads, so if your baby's head is buried in a pillow or bumper, heat loss will be reduced. These days, fleeces and baby nests are not advised because the baby is at risk of overheating.

BABY MONITORS

A baby monitor will allow you to keep in touch with your baby, even when he's in another room.

- Baby monitors are available in different versions: battery, AC-operated, or rechargeable.

- Lights indicating whether the batteries are low, or the baby unit is out of range, are useful.

Keeping in touch
Monitors come in two parts— the baby's transmitter, and the parent's receiver (see left).

Sleeping accessories

The first requirement is a mattress that is thin and fits closely into the crib with no gaps between the edges of the mattress and the frame. You will also need sheets and covers as suggested here.

- Crib comforter (not for babies under 12 months)

- Cotton sheets

- Cotton cellular blankets

- Fleecy blanket

- Tie-on waterproof sheet to protect mattress

Bright colors
Nowadays, there's a wide range of fun bed covers that look attractive and are stimulating for your baby.

CHOOSING A STROLLER

A stroller or carriage will probably be the most expensive thing you buy for your baby, so choose carefully.

• Think about how and where you will use it most? Do you need something that is easy to get in the car? Or are you more likely to travel on public transportation and need something that folds easily?

• Before making your purchase, ask the salesperson to demonstrate the stroller or carriage so you are sure it is easy to deal with.

• Check on what guarantee the product carries and how easy it is to get repairs should you need them.

WALKING AND CARRYING

Your baby will spend most of her time being carried, wheeled, or secured in some way, and there is a wide variety of carriages and carriers available. When choosing equipment of this kind, safety and portability will be your main considerations.

Slings are the most popular way of transporting a newborn; they're light and comfortable, and allow you to carry your baby close while keeping both hands free. Try one on with your baby in before you buy it, and make sure it has a head support for your baby. Backpacks, which have supportive frames that make it easier to bear a larger baby's weight, are suitable once your baby can sit up by herself.

For longer trips, you will need a carriage or stroller in which your baby can sit or lie down. One in which your baby can lie flat should be used for the first three months, until she has head control. The carriage you choose will depend on your budget and lifestyle. Consider where you will keep it and whether you will need to take it on buses and trains or up stairs. Whatever carriage you choose, it should have a safety harness, or rings to fasten one in place.

CARRIAGE OR STROLLER?
For the first three months, your baby must be able to lie flat. Reclining strollers are available, but a combination carrier/carriage is more versatile. Some models can be converted into strollers.

A hood shield will protect your baby from rain

The top lifts off and can be used as a carrier

Make sure the brakes are easy to use

BOUNCING CHAIR

Your baby can be propped up so that she can look around her in a special made chair. When she's on solids, you can sit her in the chair and feed her, but make sure she is safely strapped in to prevent her from slipping.

Put the chair on the floor, never on a table or counter

SAFETY HARNESSES

Your young baby has no fear of falling, so wherever she sits, she will have to be strapped in for her own safety.

• A five-point harness, which has straps for the shoulders as well as the waist and crotch, is safest.

• Your baby's carriage should have a built-in harness, or anchor points so that you can attach one.

• High chairs often have a built-in crotch strap, and should also have rings to take a safety harness, which you can buy separately.

• Many harnesses come with reins that can be attached when your baby is old enough to walk.

CARRYING YOUR BABY

Using a sling
Your baby will feel safe and secure inside a sling, and it leaves your arms free.

The sling should support your baby's head

Using a backpack
You can carry your baby in a backpack once he becomes too heavy for a sling. Make sure that he is comfortable and is not restricted by the leg openings.

MILK: THE IDEAL FOOD

In the first few months of life, your baby will get all the nutrients he requires from breast or formula milk.

Calories The energy content of food is measured in calories. Infants require about two-and-a-half to three times more calories than adults for their body weight.

Protein Vital for building body cells and tissues, a baby's protein needs are three times as great as an adult's on a body-weight basis.

Fats Minute traces of fatty acids are needed for growth and repair.

Carbohydrates These are the major source of calories.

Breastfeeding
Suckling helps to form a very strong bond between you and your new baby.

Feeding and nutrition

Your baby depends on you for the provision of adequate nutrition, and for a newborn, breast milk or formula will provide all he needs. Breast milk is the ideal food for a baby (see below), but if you choose to bottle-feed, rest assured that your baby will still thrive. Feeding takes a great deal of a parent's time, so it's important to choose a method that is suitable for both parent and baby. Well before delivery, you should decide whether you are going to breastfeed or bottle-feed and prepare for whichever you choose.

It's quite normal for all babies, breastfed or bottle-fed, not to take much colostrum (see p.40) at first, since they take a while to get the hang of feeding. Your baby will cry when he is hungry, and you should take your lead from him in setting the pattern of feedings.

Babies grow most rapidly during the first six months of life—most babies double their birth weight in around four to five months. Your baby's nutritional needs reflect this tremendous growth. A healthy baby's food has to contain adequate amounts of calories, protein, fats, carbohydrates, vitamins, and minerals (see left and opposite), and until he's at least six months old, your baby will receive all these nutrients from breast or formula milk.

WHY BREAST IS BEST
Human breast milk is the perfect food for babies. Because it doesn't look as rich and creamy as cow's milk, you may think that it isn't good enough, but don't be put off. It contains all the nutrients your baby needs, and in just the right amounts.

Breast milk has many benefits for your baby. Breastfed babies tend to suffer less than bottle-fed babies from such illnesses as gastroenteritis and chest infections. This is because antibodies from the colostrum and the mother's milk are absorbed into the bloodstream, where they act to protect the baby against infections. In the first few days of life, they also protect the intestines, reducing the chances of intestinal upsets.

Breast milk has other advantages for a baby's digestion. Breastfed babies don't get constipated, since breast milk is more easily digestible than cow's milk, although they pass few stools because the milk is so completely digested that there is little waste. They are less prone to ammoniacal diaper rash (see p.110), too. From a mother's point of view, breastfeeding is far more convenient than bottle-feeding: there is no need for the milk to be warmed up, there are no bottles to sterilize, no formula to make up, and no equipment to buy. Breastfed babies usually sleep longer, suffer less from gas, and spit up—that is, regurgitate food—less, and the spit-up smells less unpleasant. It is difficult to overfeed a breastfed baby, so don't worry if your baby seems fatter than other babies of his age. Each baby has his own appetite and metabolic rate, and yours will be the right weight for his own body.

You may feel that one of the few drawbacks of breastfeeding is that until your milk supply is well established enough for you to express and store milk for later feeding by bottle, you are the only person who can your feed your baby. However, this stage doesn't last long.

Some women worry that breastfeeding will make their breasts sag. This is not the case: breasts may change in size or sag after a baby is born, but these changes are due to being pregnant, not to breastfeeding itself. In fact, breastfeeding is good for your figure, since it promotes the loss of any weight gained during pregnancy. While you are breastfeeding, the hormone oxytocin (see p.40), which stimulates milk flow, also encourages the uterus to return to its pre-pregnant state. Your pelvis and waistline will also get back to normal more quickly.

Studies have shown that breast cancer is rarer in those parts of the world where breastfeeding is the norm, and it is possible that breastfeeding may provide some protection against the disease.

BOTTLE-FEEDING

Every woman is capable of breastfeeding her baby, and you should try to do so. Many women feel that they must breastfeed to be a good mother, and feel guilty if they decide not to. On the other hand, some women find it emotionally or psychologically difficult to breastfeed; others find that, however much they try, they can't master breastfeeding. If this is the case, then you should forget about it and concentrate on giving your baby a good bottle-fed diet: he will still thrive.

You may consider bottle-feeding because you feel that breastfeeding will tie you down, particularly if you intend to return to work very soon after the birth. This may be the best solution for you, but remember that it is also possible to express enough milk so that your partner or a caregiver can feed your baby in your absence. That way, your baby can have the benefits of your milk, and you can still have the flexibility of bottle-feeding and the freedom that this gives you.

One of the benefits of bottle-feeding is that your partner can be involved with feeding the new baby. He should try to do this as soon as possible after the birth, so that he can learn to handle the baby confidently, and if possible he should share the feeding equally with you. Encourage him to hold the baby close and talk to him while feeding, so that the baby gets used to the feel of his skin, his smell, and the sound of his voice.

VITAMIN AND MINERAL NEEDS

As well as the basic nutrients (see opposite page), milk will supply your baby with necessary vitamins and minerals.

Vitamins Vitamins are essential to health. Formula milks contain all your baby's vitamin requirements, but breast milk does not contain as much vitamin D, which is manufactured by the skin when stimulated by light, as formula milk. You should ask your healthcare provider whether your baby needs vitamin supplements.

Minerals Calcium, phosphorus, and magnesium, which are necessary for the growth of bone and muscle, are contained in breast milk and formula. Babies are born with a reserve of iron that will last about six months; after this, they have to be given iron, either in solids or as supplements.

Trace elements Minerals like zinc, copper, and fluoride are essential to your baby's health. The first two are present in breast and formula milk, but fluoride, which protects against dental decay, is not. Never give fluoride supplements without checking with your healthcare provider, since excessive amounts can cause fluorosis (discoloration of the tooth enamel).

Bottle-feeding
Make feeding a time of closeness and intimacy for you and your baby.

ENSURING A GOOD MILK SUPPLY

Caring for yourself properly is the key to a good milk supply. If you stay relaxed, eat well, and drink enough fluids, you will have plenty of milk for your baby.

• Rest as much as you can, particularly during the first weeks, and try to get plenty of sleep.

• You produce most milk in the morning when you are rested. If you become tense during the day, your supply could be poor by evening. Go through your prenatal relaxation routines and lie down for a little while every day.

• Let the housework go; do only what is absolutely necessary.

• Try to give yourself a few treats; relax with a glass of wine at the end of the day.

• Eat a well-balanced diet that is fairly rich in protein. Avoid highly refined carbohydrates (cake, cookies, candy, and so on).

• Ask your doctor about iron and possibly vitamin supplements.

• Drink about 3 quarts (liters) of fluid a day; some women even find that they need to keep a drink on hand while they are feeding.

• Express any milk your baby doesn't take in the early feedings of the day to encourage your breasts to keep producing milk.

• The combined contraceptive pill can decrease your milk supply, so avoid it while breastfeeding. The progesterone-only pill may be prescribed instead, but discuss methods of contraception with your doctor.

ALL ABOUT BREASTFEEDING

Breastfeeding has to be learned, and it's a good idea to seek support and advice from your family, from friends with babies, and from your healthcare provider. Above all, you'll learn from your baby, by understanding her signals and discovering how to respond to them. No special action is required to prepare the breasts for feeding unless you have an inverted nipple. If you do, use a breast shell to make your nipple protrude so that your baby will be able to latch on to it. While you are in the hospital, make sure the nursing staff know that you intend to breastfeed, and don't be afraid to ask for help. Suckle your baby as soon as she is born—in the delivery room, if possible—to form a bond with her as early as possible and let her get used to the action of suckling.

COLOSTRUM AND BREAST MILK
During the 72 hours after delivery, the breasts produce a thin, yellow fluid called colostrum, made up of water, protein, and minerals. Colostrum contains antibodies that protect the baby against a range of intestinal and respiratory infections. In the first few days, your baby should be put regularly to the breast, both to feed on the colostrum and to get used to latching on to the breast (see p.42).

Once your breasts start to produce milk, you may be surprised by its watery appearance. When your baby sucks, the first milk that she gets—the foremilk—is thin, watery, and thirst-quenching. Then comes the hindmilk, which is richer in fat and protein.

THE LET-DOWN REFLEX

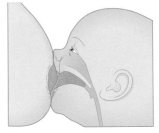

Hormone messages
Your baby's sucking sends messages to the hypothalamus, which stimulates your pituitary gland to release two hormones: prolactin, responsible for making milk in the milk glands, and oxytocin, which causes milk to pass from the glands to the milk reservoirs behind the areola.

BREASTFEEDING POSITIONS

Lying down is ideal for night feedings; when your baby is very small you may need to lay her on a pillow so that she can reach your nipple. You may find a lying position the most suitable if you have had an episiotomy and sitting is uncomfortable. If you've had a cesarean section and your stomach is still tender, try lying with your baby's feet tucked under your arm.

Lying position
Breastfeeding positions that allow you to lie down are a restful alternative and can keep a wriggling baby off a tender cesarean incision.

Sitting position
Make sure that your arms and back are supported and you are relaxed.

Nursing bras

You should always wear a supportive nursing bra when you are breastfeeding.

Try it on in the store before you buy, and look for one with front fastenings and wide straps that won't cut into your shoulders. Drop-front or zip-fastening bras are easy to undo with one hand while you hold your baby. A good bra will minimize discomfort if your breasts become sore.

SUPPLY AND DEMAND

Milk is produced in glands that are deeply buried in the breast, not in the fatty tissue, so breast size is no indication of how much milk you can produce; even small breasts are perfectly adequate milk producers.

Milk is produced according to demand—you supply what your baby needs, so don't worry that you'll run out of milk if your baby feeds very often. Your breasts are stimulated to produce milk by your baby's sucking, so the more eagerly she feeds, the more milk they will produce, and vice versa. During the time that you breastfeed, the amount of milk available will fluctuate according to your baby's needs, and once she becomes established on solids, the breasts will produce less milk. I'm against babies being fed by the clock so I'm reluctant to show any kind of chart, but the following will give you an idea of what to expect.

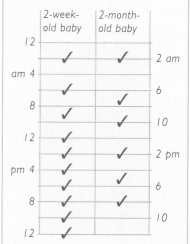

Frequency of feedings
This is an example of what may happen. At first your baby will feed little and often. By two months she will feed about every four hours and take more at each feeding than before.

HOW LONG ON EACH BREAST?

You should keep your baby on the breast for as long as he shows interest in sucking.

• If your baby continues to suck after your breasts have emptied, it may be that he is just enjoying the sensation; this is fine if it's not making your breasts sore.

• When your baby has finished feeding from one breast, gently take him off your nipple (see below right) and put him onto the other breast. He may not suck for as long on the second breast.

• Alternate the first breast you offer at each feeding. To remind you which breast was last suckled, put a safety pin on your bra.

BREASTFEEDING YOUR BABY

Breastfeeding creates a strong bond between mother and baby if feeding time is relaxed and pleasurable for both. Make sure your baby can see you, and smile and talk to him while he is suckling. He will come to associate the pleasure of feeding with the sight of your face, the sound of your voice, and the smell of your skin. Make sure you are both comfortable before you start (see p.41). If your baby still seems hungry after feeding for as long as he wants from one breast, offer the other breast, burping him before changing over (see p.55).

GIVING A BREASTFEED

The rooting reflex
Prompt your baby to look for the breast by gently stroking the cheek closest to it. Your baby will immediately turn toward your breast, openmouthed.

Latching on
Your baby should take the nipple and a good proportion of the areola into his mouth. The milk is drawn out by a combination of sucking and squeezing the tongue onto the hard palate.

Releasing the nipple
To break the suction, slip your little finger into the corner of the baby's mouth. Your breast will slip out easily instead of being dragged out.

POSSIBLE PROBLEMS

It is perfectly normal for breastfeeding not to go smoothly at first, so don't worry about minor setbacks, such as your baby refusing a feeding. Remember that he, too, is learning and that it will take time for you to get used to each other, so persevere, and ask your healthcare provider for advice and suggestions.

Refusing the breast It is quite usual for a newborn not to suck very vigorously or for very long during his first 24–36 hours. If this occurs later, however, there may be a problem that needs to be addressed. Breathing difficulties are the most likely cause of a baby's having problems taking the breast. It may be that your breast is covering his nostrils; if so, gently pull the breast back from the baby's face, just above the areola. If he seems to have a sniffly or stuffed-up nose, consult your doctor; he may prescribe nose drops to clear the nostrils.

If there's no obvious cause for your baby's refusal to feed, he may simply be fretful. A baby who has been crying with hunger, or has been changed or fussed over when he's hungry, can become too distressed to feed. You'll need to soothe him by holding him firmly and talking or singing; there's no point in trying to feed him until he's calmed down.

If there has been some delay in starting to breastfeed, your baby may find it more difficult to take the breast, and you will have to be patient and persevere. Your healthcare provider will advise you if you need to give expressed milk from a special cup until your baby can take all he needs from the breast. Supplementary bottles are rarely necessary, and they may cause mothers to give up breastfeeding. Giving expressed milk is a better alternative.

Comfort sucking Most babies enjoy sucking on their mothers' breasts for its own sake just as much as feeding. You will learn to tell the difference between actual feeding and comfort sucking. During a feeding you may notice that your baby is sucking strongly without actually swallowing. There is no reason why your baby shouldn't suck as long as he wants, provided your nipples are not sore, though he takes most of his feeding in the first few minutes.

Sleeping through feedings If your baby doesn't seem very interested in food during the first few days, make sure that he takes as much as he wants from one breast. If he sleeps at the breast, it means he is contented and doing well, though premature babies should be woken and fed regularly, since they tend to sleep a lot. If your baby does fall asleep at the breast, wake him gently half an hour later and offer a feeding; if he's hungry, he will perk up.

Fretful feeding If your baby doesn't settle down to feed, or appears not to be satisfied, he is probably sucking on the nipple alone and not getting enough milk. This may also lead to sore nipples. Make sure your baby is positioned correctly on the breast.

UNDERFEEDING

You may feel anxious that you can't see how much your baby has taken, but it is rare for a breastfed baby not to get enough milk. Remember, though, that it does take time for both mothers and babies to get the hang of breastfeeding.

• If your baby wants to continue sucking even though he's finished feeding from both breasts, it doesn't always signify hunger; he may just enjoy sucking.

• Thirst may cause your baby to go on on sucking after he's emptied your breasts. Try giving about 1 fluid ounce (30 milliliters) of cooled boiled water from a special cup.

• If he seems fretful and hungry, have him weighed at your clinic to check if he is gaining weight as quickly as expected. If you are at all worried about your baby's feeding, contact your healthcare provider.

EXPRESSING TIPS

Make expressing milk as easy on yourself as possible, and be careful to store your milk correctly.

• If you have to lean over a low surface, expressing may give you a backache. Make sure the container is at a convenient height.

• Expressing milk should be painless. If it hurts, stop immediately. Ask your healthcare provider if you are expressing correctly.

• The more relaxed you are, the easier it will be to express. If the milk won't start to flow, place a warm washcloth over your breasts to open the ducts, or try expressing while you take a bath.

• If you're concerned that your baby might not go back to breastfeeding after getting used to the bottle, try feeding her milk from a specially designed cup, or spooning the expressed milk from a cup. Make sure that both spoon and cup are sterilized before use.

• Your hands must be clean, and every piece of equipment and all containers should be sterile.

• Milk will spoil unless it is stored correctly, and could make your baby sick. Refrigerate or freeze your milk as soon as you've expressed it. Refrigerated milk will keep for 24 hours; frozen milk for up to three months in the freezer.

• Expressed milk should be put into sterile, sealable containers. Don't use glass containers in the freezer—they might crack. Sterile plastic bottle liners are ideal.

EXPRESSING MILK

Expressed milk can be easily stored either in the refrigerator or in the freezer. This will free you from feeling tied down by breastfeeding, and allow your baby to be fed with your milk if you are away. It also allows your partner to share in feeding your baby.

Milk can be expressed from your breasts using either your hands or a breast pump, which may be manual or electric. Although small battery pumps are very easy to use, many women find hand-expressing to be easier and more convenient. Before you start, you will need a bowl, a funnel, and a container that can be sealed. All equipment must be sterilized, either in a sterilizing solution, with boiling water, or in a special steam unit.

In the first six weeks, hand-expressing is nearly always a bit difficult, since the breasts have not reached full production, but don't give up. Because breasts produce milk in response to demand, you may need to express milk in order to keep your supply going—if your baby is premature and can't yet breastfeed, for example. Even if you use a pump, it is worth learning the technique of hand-expressing in case you need it. The best time to express milk is in the morning, when you'll have the most milk, although when your baby drops the night feeding, you may find the evening the best time.

EXPRESSING BY PUMP

All pumps work on suction and comprise a funnel or shield, pump mechanism, and container. The assembly and operation of the different brands of pump will vary a little, so follow the manufacturer's instructions.

Funnel

Pump
mechanism

Pump
mechanism

Container
doubles as
feeding bottle

Funnel

Container
doubles as
feeding bottle

Manual pump
Fit the funnel of the pump over your areola to form an airtight seal, then operate the lever or plunger to express the milk.

Electric pump
Electric pumps are more expensive but easier to use. They imitate a baby's natural sucking cycle more closely and are best if you need to express often.

EXPRESSING BY HAND

Massaging the outer breast

Make sure that your hands are clean. Cup your breast in both hands with the fingers underneath and the thumbs above. Squeeze the outer part of your breast gently and firmly between your fingers and thumbs. Repeat this ten times, moving around the breast as you do so.

Massaging the inner breast

Move your hands closer to the areola and repeat the squeezing procedure as above.

Massaging the breast stimulates milk flow

SUPPLEMENTARY BOTTLES

There may be times, such as when you have a blocked duct or a very sore nipple, when it is painful to breastfeed.

Hard as it is, it's best to avoid offering formula if you possibly can. There are so many benefits to your baby being exclusively breastfed for the first six months if possible. When feeding is painful, many mothers prefer to express milk from the affected breast and use this in a bottle. Giving supplementary formula feeds can undermine the production of breastmilk.

A baby who has become used to the nipple may dislike plastic nipples. Unfortunately, it can be difficult to tell whether your baby just dislikes the nipple, or is not hungry. She'll eventually get used to the bottle if you persist, but you may then find that she doesn't want to go back to the breast. If this happens, try giving the milk from a sterilized spoon or cup.

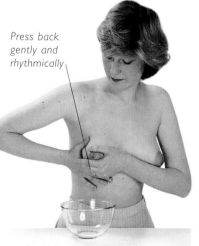

Press back gently and rhythmically

Make sure the container you use is at a convenient height for you

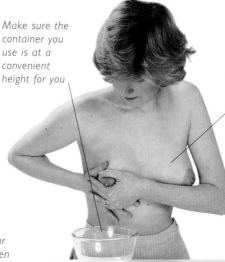

Express from each breast alternately

Emptying the breast

Continue for about five minutes, working around the areola, then move on to the second breast. Repeat the whole procedure for both breasts.

Starting the flow

Place the thumb and fingers of one hand near the areola, press them back into your ribs, then squeeze gently and rhythmically. If the milk doesn't begin to flow immediately, keep on trying.

ACCESSORIES

Although they are not essential, you will find that breast pads and shields will help keep your nipples clean and dry.

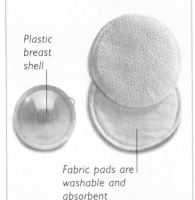

Plastic breast shell

Fabric pads are washable and absorbent

Breast shells and pads
When you are feeding from one breast, milk may drip or even flow from the other. A plastic shell can be used to collect this excess milk, which can then be stored in the refrigerator for up to 24 hours or frozen. Disposable and washable fabric pads are also available; these fit inside your bra and protect your clothes from leaks of milk.

MANAGING BREASTFEEDING

Many mothers find that breastfeeding goes smoothly right from the start, but it's also normal to be a bit clumsy at first, for the baby not to suck for very long, or for your breasts to be a bit sore. It takes time to learn, so if problems arise, persevere until things get easier.

CARE OF THE BREASTS
The daily hygiene of your breasts and nipples is very important. You should cleanse them every day with water (not soap, which strips oils from the skin and can aggravate a sore or cracked nipple), and gently pat them dry. Dry them gently after feeding. Wear your bra all the time, since you'll need lots of support. Apply a cream containing pure lanolin to the sore nipple after a feeding, or use breastmilk itself.

Once your milk flow is established, the milk may leak out quite a lot. You can use breast pads or clean handkerchiefs inside your bra to soak it up. Change them frequently, for cleanliness. A plastic breast shell with a reservoir will help to keep your nipples dry and catch the leaks of milk. Milk can be frozen or refrigerated in a sterile bottle. Wash and sterilize the shell before reusing.

IF YOU ARE ILL
You can express milk so that your partner can feed the baby if you're not feeling up to it. If you are too ill to express your milk, your baby can be given formula milk by bottle or by spoon and, although he may not like this at first, he will take the milk as he becomes hungrier.

If you have to go into the hospital you can still breastfeed. Inform the nursing staff as soon as possible that this is what you intend to do, so that they can make the necessary arrangements—for example, someone will have to be available to lift and change your baby if you are too tired or ill to do so. If you have an operation, though, you will not be able to breastfeed afterward because of the anesthetic—you'll be too groggy and, more importantly, the drugs you have been given will have passed into your milk. If you know you'll be having an operation, try to express and freeze your milk so that your baby can be bottle-fed until you've recovered. It will take up to ten days for your milk to return; your baby should suck as often as he wishes meanwhile.

DRUGS AND BREASTFEEDING
If you can, avoid all drugs when breastfeeding. Many medications pass into the breast milk and can affect your baby. Always tell your doctor that you are breastfeeding if you are already taking medications, or if you consult her for any new problems; she may prescribe something more appropriate. If you want to use oral contraceptives, it's probably

best to take the progestogen-only "mini-pill," since the estrogen in the combined pill is thought to reduce your milk supply. Your doctor or family planning clinic can help you choose the best method of contraception for you.

PROBLEMS

Your breasts will be working hard for the next few months, and problems may arise if, for instance, your baby is not latching on properly or drags on the nipple as he comes off. The best way to prevent this is to keep your breasts clean and dry and make sure your baby always empties them when he feeds. You should also wear a proper nursing bra. If your nipples do become sore or cracked, take action immediately or they will get worse.

Cracked nipple If sore nipples (see right) are not dealt with properly, they may become cracked. If this happens, you will feel a shooting pain as your baby suckles. You should keep the nipples dry with breast pads or clean tissues, and keep feeding if at all possible. See advice (see right) and if necessary express the milk by hand; it can be fed to your baby by bottle or from a special cup.

Engorgement Toward the end of the first week, before breastfeeding is fully established, your breasts may become too full and be painful and quite hard to the touch. If this happens, your baby won't be able to latch on successfully. Make sure you wear a good bra to minimize discomfort, and gently express some milk before feeding to relieve the fullness. Taking a warm bath will also help to relieve the discomfort by promoting milk flow.

Blocked duct Tight clothing or engorgement can cause a blocked milk duct, resulting in a hard red patch on the outside of the breast where the duct lies. You can prevent this by feeding often and encouraging your baby to empty your breasts, and by making sure that your bra fits properly. If you do get a blocked duct, feed often and offer the affected breast first.

Mastitis If a blocked duct is not treated, it can lead to an acute infection known as mastitis. The breast will be inflamed and a red patch will appear on the outside, as with a blocked duct. You should continue to breastfeed because you need to empty the breast. Your doctor may prescribe antibiotics to clear up the infection.

Breast abscess An untreated blocked duct or mastitis can result in a breast abscess. You may feel feverish, and you may have a shiny red patch on your breast, which is exquisitely tender. Your doctor should prescribe antibiotics; if this fails, the abscess will have to be drained surgically, but you may be able to continue breastfeeding even if you need this minor operation—ask your doctor's advice.

PREVENTING SORE NIPPLES

Suckling your baby can cause soreness around the nipples, especially if you are fair-skinned. To minimize the possibility of any problems:

• Always make sure that your baby has the nipple and areola well into his mouth.

• Always take your baby off the breast gently (see p.42).

• Keep your nipples as dry as possible between feedings.

• Make sure your nipples are dry before putting your bra back on after a feeding.

If one of your nipples does become sore, it may be due to poor positioning or your baby not latching on properly. Ask your healthcare provider's advice on correct positioning, and see pages 40–43. To prevent the nipple from becoming cracked, apply chamomile or calendula cream two or three times a day.

The shield is very soft and allows for a close fit

Nipple shield
This is made of soft silicone and fits over your nipple; the baby sucks through a small nipple on the front. Sterilize before use.

Feeding a preterm baby

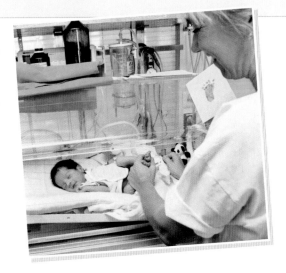

Case study

Parents' names Petrina and Mike Wehrli
Age 27 years and 34 years
Obstetric history Normal pregnancy, Benjamin born prematurely at 28 weeks
Medical history Appendectomy at 15 years
Family history Twins in previous generations

Baby's name Benjamin Wehrli
Age 39 weeks
Birth weight 2 pounds 13 ounces (1.3 kilograms)
Medical history Born prematurely at 28 weeks, and nursed in an incubator in the neonatal intensive care unit. Allowed home at 38 weeks

Petrina was enjoying a career in real estate when she gave up work to have a baby. She's a very determined woman, and prepared for her pregnancy by eating well and getting regular exercise. When she became pregnant, she read all the baby books she could, and even practiced expressing milk manually. Mike, her husband, was very involved in these preparations, attending prenatal classes with Petrina and reading baby books with her.

One night while at the movies, only 28 weeks into her pregnancy, Petrina felt sudden uterine pains, which quickly escalated to regular, strong contractions. Mike took her straight to the hospital, where Benjamin was born.

It was a shock for both Petrina and Mike to have their baby a full three months before they'd planned it; Petrina, who likes to feel in control of everything, was particularly disturbed. It was difficult for her to sit by her new baby so impersonally enclosed in an incubator, unable to cuddle and most of all to breastfeed him, something she longed to do.

MAINTAINING A SUPPLY

I explained to Petrina that although no feeding is straightforward for premature babies, breast milk is especially beneficial to them, since it provides protection against infections in the first few risky weeks of life. Benjamin had to be fed intravenously for several days and then gradually through a stomach tube because he had not had time to develop the rooting and sucking reflexes. Petrina expressed her milk from day one and stored it so that it could be used to feed Benjamin when the stomach tube was in place.

EXPRESSING MILK

She remained adamant that she wanted to breastfeed Benjamin when she could eventually take him home, and as soon as he could be released from the incubator for short periods, the nurses would encourage Petrina to put him on the breast. I reminded her that breast milk is produced in response to demand. If it's not removed by a nursing infant, then it must be expressed or production stops. This meant Petrina had to express milk to keep up production until Benjamin was able to breastfeed regularly.

Expressing milk for a premature baby is difficult because all the natural cues for milk letdown are missing: the baby's hungry cry, lifting him up, putting his mouth to the breast. In order to master the technique of expressing milk (see pp.44–45), Petrina needed persistence and support from Mike; many times she felt like giving up. Her breasts became engorged on day three and she could hardly bear to massage them. She explained her problems to the staff nurse on the unit, who arranged for a lactation consultant to help and encourage her to take off milk every two hours (as a very small baby would) and to store it hygienically (see p.44).

Petrina continued to express milk during the night, every four to six hours. By the second week, she'd become an expert, and was asked to teach other mothers how to express.

BONDING WITH A PREMATURE BABY

One of Petrina's main concerns was that Benjamin wouldn't bond with his mother and father because he couldn't hear their voices properly, and couldn't smell their skin or enjoy cuddles. The hospital staff, however, showed her how she could put her clean hand into the incubator to stroke and caress Benjamin gently. Within a week, Benjamin was showing signs of loving this contact and responded by wriggling when she touched him. Quite naturally, she would talk to him as he did this, and during the second week she saw him flick his eyes in recognition at the sound of her voice. She thought of this as their first conversation and continued to babble to him happily during their time together.

COPING WITH THE DEMANDS

The hospital staff encouraged both parents to spend as much time as possible with Benjamin, and to help feed and change him as their confidence grew. But two-and-a-half weeks after Benjamin's birth, Petrina experienced a crisis. The shock of the premature birth, the anxiety of the first few days, and the loss of sleep because of expressing at night were all having their effect, and she felt that she had no emotional resources left. When one of the nurses found her sobbing, she realized immediately that Petrina herself needed some tender loving care. She suggested that Petrina talk to Mike about her feelings. Mike had thought that Petrina was totally absorbed with Benjamin, but was only too willing for them to have some time alone together each day for cuddles and sharing. Petrina also started to take some time for herself and to spoil herself now and then with nutritious treats like strawberries out of season. She drank lots of mineral water to keep herself healthy for breastfeeding.

PREPARING TO GO HOME

Before Benjamin was ready to leave the hospital, the staff established him on breast milk from a bottle so that he learned to suck well before he was put onto the breast. In the last week before he was due to go home, he was taking five meals out of eight from Petrina's breast, so she got over the tricky stage of getting Benjamin used to the breast in the reassuring environment of the hospital. When Benjamin was 38 weeks, and 5 pounds 8 ounces (2.5 kilograms) in weight—ten weeks after he was born—Petrina and Mike took him home and felt like a real family for the first time. At home, Petrina had to continue expressing so that she always had enough milk if Benjamin showed signs of being hungry after a feeding. A week later, Benjamin weighed in at 5 pounds 12 ounces (2.6 kilograms) and was thriving. However, I explained to Petrina that she must count his age as if he were still in her womb: he wasn't two months old, but 39 weeks, and she shouldn't expect him to catch up completely with full-term babies of his age until he was two years old.

MILK FORMULAS

A variety of milk formulas are available, all carefully formulated to make them as close as possible to breast milk: in fact, formula has added vitamin D and iron, levels of which are quite low in breast milk.

Most formulas are based on cow's milk. Some formulas are available both in powder and ready-mixed forms. There are soy-based formulas available, but never give these to your baby without the advice of your healthcare provider. Ready-mixed milk comes in cartons or ready-to-feed bottles and is ultra-heat treated (UHT), which means it is sterile and will keep in a cool place until the "best before" date. Once the carton has been opened, the milk will keep for 24 hours in a refrigerator. Ready-mixed milk is more expensive than powdered formula, but it is very convenient, and you may want to use it when you are traveling.

If you use powdered formula, it is essential that you make it up precisely according to the manufacturer's instructions. Some parents are tempted to add extra powder to make the milk "more nourishing," but this will lead to your baby getting too much protein and fat, and not enough water.

If you add too little powder, your baby will not be getting the nutrients she needs for healthy growth.

BOTTLES AND MILK

The majority of babies will have a bottle at some stage—if not continuously right from the start, then often after weaning or with supplementary bottles. New infant formulas, bottles, and nipples appear on the market regularly, all with the aim of making bottle-feeding as convenient and as similar to breastfeeding as possible.

The one thing you can't give your baby if you bottle-feed from the start is colostrum (see p.40), so even if you're not intending to breastfeed your baby, you will be giving her a good start if you put her to the breast in the first few days. If you decide not to do this, the hospital staff can take care of your baby's first feedings.

One of the good things about bottle-feeding is that the new father can be involved at feeding times. Make sure that your partner feeds your baby as soon as possible after the birth. This way he can get used to the technique and won't be afraid to handle the baby. He should open his shirt so that the baby nestles up to his skin when she feeds, and bonds with his smell.

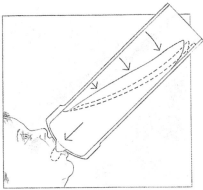

Disposable bottles
Bottles that use disposable liners are convenient when you are traveling. The liner is collapsible, so air doesn't enter the bottle as your baby draws the milk and there is less likelihood of gas.

Bottles and nipples

There is a range of different feeding bottles and nipples. You may need to try a few to find out what suits your baby best. Here are some examples:

Bottles (left to right)
• Tapered bottle
• Waisted bottle
• Easy-grip bottle
• Disposable bottle

STERILIZING THE BOTTLES

It is wise to practice with your feeding equipment before you go into the hospital, so buy it well in advance of your delivery date. Large department stores and drugstores sell bottle-feeding packs that have all the essential equipment.

I always found it most convenient to sterilize and make up a full batch of bottles (see p.52), and refrigerate them until needed. After the feeding, rinse the bottle in warm water and then put it aside. It is a good idea to continue sterilizing all milk-feeding equipment until your baby is six months old.

Most sterilizing units usually hold only four to six bottles. Your newborn baby, however, will be taking around seven feedings in 24 hours, so you may have to sterilize and prepare the bottles twice a day—morning and evening—to be sure you have enough ready for whenever she is hungry. The number of feedings will decline as your baby grows, so you'll only have to prepare one batch a day.

STERILIZING TIPS

- Put all the equipment into a large, covered, plastic container and use sterilizing tablets (or fluid) and water.
- Steam sterilizing units quickly and effectively destroy bacteria on your equipment.
- Sterilize your equipment in the microwave using a specially designed steam unit, as long as the feeding equipment is suitable for microwave use.
- Wash the equipment and boil it for at least ten minutes in a large, covered pot.

Cleaning in a dishwasher
Once your baby is over 12 months you can wash feeding equipment in a dishwasher. Clean nipples before they go in (see column, right). Run the dishwasher on the normal cycle.

Boiling
You should boil the bottles for at least ten minutes. Then remove and allow to cool down before using.

TAKE CARE

To reduce the risk that your baby will contract a gastrointestinal infection, make sure that everything that comes in contact with your baby's food is thoroughly cleaned or sterilized before use. You can use a sterilizing tank, steamer, microwave sterilizer, or immerse bottles and nipples in boiling water (see left). Make sure that you wash your hands before handling any formula or equipment. Pacifiers and teething rings should also be thoroughly cleaned each time they are used.

Always store prepared bottles of formula in the refrigerator, and never keep them longer than 24 hours. It's best to make up formula when you need it, not in advance. If your baby doesn't finish a bottle or if you warm up a bottle for her but she doesn't want it, throw it away—reheated bottles are prime sources of infection.

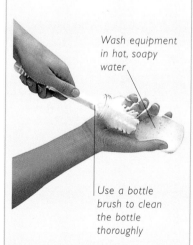

Wash equipment in hot, soapy water

Use a bottle brush to clean the bottle thoroughly

Washing bottles
All equipment should be washed in hot, soapy water. Scrub the insides of the bottles with a bottle brush and rub the nipples thoroughly to remove any traces of milk. Rinse the bottles and nipples under warm running water to remove any soap.

BOTTLE-FEEDING YOUR BABY

Using a ready-made formula is more straightforward than mixing your own, but strict rules of hygiene should still be observed.

- Before opening the carton, use a clean brush to scrub the top of the carton, paying particular attention to the cutting line.

- Cut the corner off the carton with clean scissors. Avoid touching the cut edges, as you could contaminate the milk.

- If you're not using all of the milk, leave the excess in the carton; it can be stored in the refrigerator for 24 hours.

- Don't store milk that your baby has left in the bottle; it will have been contaminated with saliva.

When you're bottle-feeding, there are a couple of essential points to bear in mind. The formula should be properly made up so that your baby gets correct amounts of both nutrients and water, and your baby should be able to draw milk at a comfortable rate. You can make up one bottle at a time, mixing it in the bottle according to the manufacturer's instructions, or you can make a batch of several.

MAKING UP A BATCH OF FORMULA

Equipment
The equipment should be rinsed with boiled water and drained before use.
- *Bottles and lids*
- *Plastic knife*
- *Measuring scoop from formula pack*
- *Nipples*
- *Caps*

Measuring
Fill the feeding bottle with the correct amount of cooled boiled water. Using the scoop provided, measure out the required amount of formula and add to the bottle. Use a knife to level off each scoopful; don't pack the formula down into the scoop.

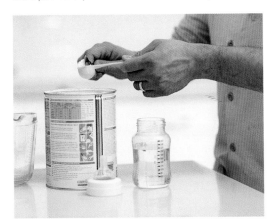

The flow of milk

The hole in the nipple should be large enough to let the milk flow in a stream of several drops per second when the bottle is inverted.

If the hole is too large, your baby will get too much too fast and splutter; if it is too small, your baby will get tired from sucking before he is satisfied. To enlarge the hole in a nipple, insert a fine, red-hot needle gently through the hole to melt the rubber (stick one end of the needle into a cork so you can hold it over a flame to heat it). Sculpted nipples, which are shaped to fit the baby's palate and allow him control over the flow, are best.

Mixing
Put the cap and nipple on the bottle. Shake the bottle until you're sure that there are no lumps or residue and the mixture is smooth. Refrigerate filled bottles immediately until required. Never add extra formula when making up bottles or the milk will be too concentrated and could be dangerous for your baby.

GIVING A BOTTLE FEEDING

Make sure you're comfortable and your arms are well supported. Hold your baby half-sitting with his head in the crook of your elbow and his back along your forearm; this will allow him to swallow safely and easily. Keep your face close to his and talk to him all the time.

If you prefer, there are other positions that are suitable for feeding. For example, you could try lying down with your baby tucked under your arm—this position is especially comfortable for night feedings. Try different positions until you decide which one suits you best (see **Breastfeeding positions**, p.41).

Before you begin, test the heat of the milk; you should already have tested the flow (see opposite). Slightly loosen the cap of the bottle so that air can get in. If your baby is having difficulty drawing the milk, gently remove the bottle from his mouth so that air can enter the bottle, then continue as before. Hold the bottle at an angle so that your baby doesn't swallow air with the milk.

BOTTLE-FEEDING

Feeding
Talk to your baby as you feed. Let him pause in mid-feeding if he likes. Switch him to the other arm at this stage to give him a new view and rest your arm.

Removing the bottle
If you want your baby to release the bottle, gently slide your little finger into the corner of his mouth. This will break the suction on the nipple.

Giving the bottle
Gently stroke your baby's nearest cheek to elicit his sucking reflex. Insert the nipple carefully into his mouth. If you push the nipple too far back, he may gag on it.

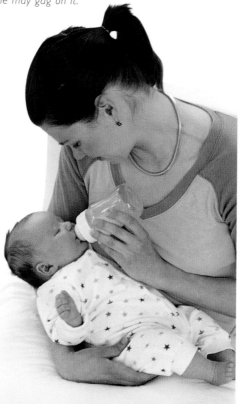

WARMING THE BOTTLE

Some parents like to warm the bottle, though it will be perfectly alright if it has simply been brought to room temperature. Don't warm the bottle in a microwave oven; it does not always heat evenly, and may create "hot spots" in the milk that could scald your baby's mouth.

Warming the milk
Place the bottle in a jug or bowl of hot water for a few minutes. You could also run it under the hot faucet, shaking it all the time.

Testing milk temperature
Try a few drops on your wrist: it should be neither hot nor cold to the touch.

BOTTLE-FEEDING TIPS

Bottle-feeding is simple and straightforward, but you will need to make sure that your baby can swallow properly, and that she is not taking in air with the milk.

• Never leave your baby with the bottle propped up on a pillow or cushion; it can be dangerous. She could become very uncomfortable if she swallows a lot of air with the feeding, and she could choke. Moreover, she will miss the cuddling and affection that she should enjoy while she feeds.

• Tilt your baby on your arm. It's very difficult for your baby to swallow when she is lying flat, so don't feed her in this position; she may gag or even be sick.

• If your baby has a stuffy nose, she can't swallow and breathe at the same time. Your doctor can give you nose drops to be used before each feeding.

• Don't change your milk formula without first consulting your healthcare provider, even if you think your baby doesn't like it. It's very unusual for a brand of milk to be responsible for a baby not feeding well; very rarely, cow's milk causes allergies in babies, but never change to a substitute formula without seeking medical advice.

• Your baby knows when she's had enough, so don't try to force her to finish the bottle after she has stopped sucking.

BOTTLE-FEEDING ROUTINES

Bottle-fed babies tend to be fed less frequently than breastfed ones. This is because formula milk takes longer to digest and contains slightly more protein, and therefore delays hunger for longer. A four-hourly regimen of six feedings a day seems to suit most bottle-fed babies after the first two or three days, whereas breastfed babies will probably take seven feedings a day. When first born, your baby will probably not take much over 2 fluid ounces (60 milliliters) at each feeding, but as she grows she will take fewer and larger feedings.

Never feed your baby according to the clock; let her determine when she is to be fed. She will let you know quite clearly with cries when she is hungry. Your baby's appetite will vary, so if she seems satisfied, allow her to leave what she doesn't want. Don't feel that your baby has to finish the bottle at each feeding. She will only get too full and spit up (see opposite); or worse, become overfed and fat. But if your baby is still hungry, give her some extra from another bottle. If this happens regularly, start to make more milk for every feed.

NIGHT FEEDINGS

Your baby will need feeding at least once during the night, and this break in your sleep on top of all the other things that you have to do may make you extremely tired and tense. The problem isn't so much the sleep that you lose, but more the way in which your sleep patterns are broken over long periods. For this reason, it's important that you get adequate rest, day and night, and share the jobs with your partner.

REDUCING NIGHT FEEDINGS

At first, your baby won't be able to sleep for more than five hours at a time without waking with hunger. Once she reaches a weight of about 11 pounds (5 kilograms), try to stretch the time between feedings until you are getting about six hours of undisturbed sleep at night. Although your baby will have her own routine, try to time her last feeding to coincide with your own bedtime, which should be as late as possible. You may find that she still wakes up for the early morning feeding, but you'll just have to be patient until she no longer needs it.

OVERFEEDING

Chubby babies can be attractive, but fat cells, once produced, can't be removed, and a fat baby may grow into a fat adult, with all the attendant dangers to health. Unfortunately, it is easy to overfeed a bottle-fed baby. The reasons for this are twofold; first, it is tempting to put extra formula into the bottle, but you should always follow the instructions precisely (see p.52), otherwise you'll be giving your baby unwanted calories. Second, in your anxiety to feed her "properly" you will want to see your baby finish the last drop of her feeding, but you should always let her decide when she's finished. Introducing solids too early and giving sweet, syrupy drinks also cause overfeeding.

UNDERFEEDING

This is rare in bottle-fed babies. Your baby should be fed on demand and not at set times; demands may vary from day to day. If you insist on feeding to a schedule, never give extra milk in a bottle, and don't allow any interim feedings even though your baby is crying for them, then she won't get all the milk that she needs.

If your child consistently seems fretful after she drains each bottle, she may well be hungry. Offer her an extra 2 fluid ounces (60 milliliters) of formula. If she takes it, then she needs it.

If your baby demands frequent feedings but doesn't take much, the nipple hole may be too small (see p.52), meaning that she is having difficulty sucking the milk and is tired before she gets enough.

BURPING

Burping releases any air that has been swallowed during feeding. It's unlikely that gas causes your baby discomfort, and many babies are not noticeably happier or more contented for having been burped. Swallowing air is more common in bottle-fed babies, but you can prevent it to some extent by tilting the bottle more as your baby empties it so that the nipple is full of milk and not air, or by using disposable bottles. Whether you breast- or bottle-feed, burping your baby makes you pause, relax, slow down, hold her gently, and stroke or pat her, and this is good for both of you.

SPITTING UP

If your baby tends to bring food straight back up (some babies never do), you may wonder if she's keeping enough down. My youngest son had a tendency to spit up, and I worried that he wasn't getting enough to eat. I simply followed my own instinct, which was to offer him more food. If he didn't take it, I assumed that he had rejected an excess that he didn't require. The most common cause of spitting up in very young babies is overfeeding, and this is another reason why you should never insist that your bottle-fed baby finishes her feeding.

Forceful vomiting, especially if it occurs after several feedings, should be reported immediately to your doctor; vomiting is always very serious in a small baby because it can quickly lead to dehydration.

Burping your baby
Hold your baby close to you and stroke or pat her gently to help her bring up air bubbles.

HYGIENE AND PREPARATION

To protect your baby from bacteria, make sure all feeding equipment is scrupulously clean, and take care with the storage and preparation of formula.

- Follow all sterilizing instructions very carefully.

- Wash your hands before sterilizing, preparing, or giving feedings.

- Never add any extra formula; follow the instructions very closely.

- Give the milk to your baby as soon as it has been warmed up.

- When making batches, cool the formula as soon as it is made up. Don't store warm milk in a thermos; germs will easily breed there.

- Keep all prepared bottles refrigerated until they are needed.

- Keep any opened packages of ready-mixed formula in the refrigerator.

- After a feeding, throw away any leftover milk.

GIRLS' WEIGHT

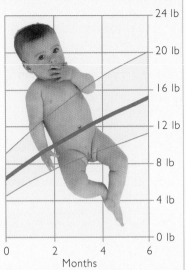

— 24 lb
— 20 lb
— 16 lb
— 12 lb
— 8 lb
— 4 lb
— 0 lb

0   2   4   6
Months

Your baby's weight
In the first six months, your baby girl will be growing fast and will more than double her birth weight. Any weight within the colored band is normal.

INTRODUCING SOLIDS

During your baby's first year, there will be a time when you will have to start to wean him onto solid foods, although not before he's six months. Before this, your baby's digestive tract is incapable of digesting and absorbing complex foods. If solids are introduced too early, they'll pass through largely undigested, and will put an increased strain on your baby's immature kidneys.

Breast milk (or its formula equivalent) is the only food that your baby needs in the early months, and if a baby is introduced to solids too young, it can lessen his desire to suck. Breastfed babies will take less milk from your breasts, and you will respond by producing less milk. Either way, your baby will end up having an unsatisfactory diet for his needs.

WHEN TO WEAN
As your baby grows, he'll need to drink more and more milk to maintain this growth. But your baby's stomach can only hold a certain amount of milk at each feeding; eventually, he will reach a point when he's drinking to full capacity at each feeding, but still doesn't have enough calories for his needs. Your baby will let you know that he needs more to eat by a change in his feeding habits. He may start to demand more milk and appear very unsatisfied after each feeding, or he may start demanding a sixth feeding, having previously been quite content on five. A classic case is a baby who has been sleeping through the night starting to wake for a nighttime feeding. This is the time to

Growth charts

The charts shown here and on pp.62–63, 66–67, and 318–25 show the wide ranges of weight or height within which a "normal" child may fall. The middle line represents the 50th centile: 50 percent of babies will fall below this line and 50 percent above it. The lines at the top and bottom represent extremes outside which only a tiny proportion of children will fall; if your child does, you should talk to your healthcare provider.

Examples of weaning stages

Feeding	1st week	3rd week
1st feeding	Breast- or bottle-feeding	Breast- or bottle-feeding
2nd feeding	Half breast- or bottle-feeding Try one or two teaspoons of purée or cereal, then give remainder of feeding	Half breast- or bottle-feeding Two teaspoons of cereal Remainder of feeding
3rd feeding	Breast- or bottle-feeding	Half breast- or bottle-feeding Two teaspoons of vegetable or fruit purée Remainder of feeding
4th feeding	Breast- or bottle-feeding	Breast- or bottle-feeding
5th feeding	Breast- or bottle-feeding	Breast- or bottle-feeding

introduce solids. Many babies do this at around six months, when their intense desire to suck lessens, though it can be later. You should be aware of the signs that your baby gives you, and follow his lead for the introduction of solids. Some people think the first tooth indicates the need for solids. Talk to your healthcare provider if you are unsure.

GIVING THE FIRST SOLIDS

Have a small amount of prepared food ready and then settle in your normal position to feed your baby. Although your baby is ready for the calories that solids provide, he will still prefer what he knows is satisfying—milk. Start by feeding him from one breast or giving half the usual bottle. Then give him one or two teaspoons of food. The midday meal is ideal because your baby will not be ravenous, but will be wide awake and more cooperative.

Never force your baby to take more food than he wants. When he's eaten the solid food, give him the rest of the milk. Once he becomes used to solids, he may prefer to eat them first. As soon as your baby is having any quantity of solid food, he will need water as well as milk to drink. Start him off with 1 tbsp (15 milliliters) of water between and after feedings, and whenever he's thirsty during the day. Avoid all sweetened drinks, since these will damage your baby's teeth. Give no more than 4 fluid ounces (120 milliliters) of water a day; milk is still your baby's main source of nutrition. Dentists recommend that you avoid fruit juice for a few months yet.

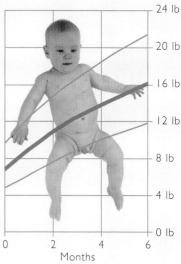

BOYS' WEIGHT

Your baby's weight
Your baby will put on weight faster during this period than at any other time in his life, and is likely to more than double his weight in the first six months. Any weight within the colored band is normal.

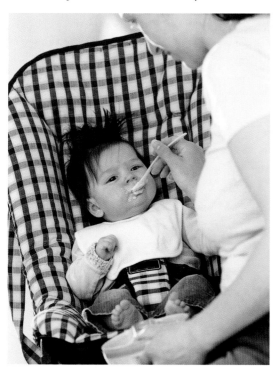

Giving the food
Halfway through her normal breast- or bottle-feeding, scoop up some food on a small spoon and insert it gently between her lips. Don't push the spoon in too far or your baby may gag. She may take a month or so to get used to using a spoon. Your baby may push more food out than she takes in. Gently scrape the excess onto her lips; she will turn away once she's had enough.

Weaning tips

Your baby may be reluctant to try new foods, so give him time to get used to each food and don't persist if he seems to dislike something.

• Give one new food at a time. Try it once and wait for several days before giving it again to see if there's a reaction.

• Use dry baby cereals rather than ready-mixed ones; they are more nutritious.

• Don't give foods containing gluten, nuts, dairy products, or egg before six months, to avoid developing allergies later.

Vegetarian weaning

Case study

Parents' names Penny and David King
Age 30 years and 35 years
Obstetric history First baby, normal delivery, no complications

Baby's name Sam King
Age 9 months
Medical history Born at full term. Umbilical hernia cleared up by six months. Breastfed

Penny and her husband David are vegetarians and have been since they married three years ago. They know that a vegetarian diet that excludes meat, poultry, and fish but contains eggs and milk can provide all the nutrients necessary for health and vitality as long as a proper balance of the different food groups is maintained. They want Sam to be a vegetarian and became particularly concerned when he was six months old and ready to start on solids.

Penny was nervous about not giving Sam a really balanced diet with enough protein, vitamins D and B12, calcium, and iron, even though she knows many vegetarian foods are fortified with extra B12 and protein. I told her that a growing baby can get all the nourishment he needs from a carefully planned diet, although if she wished to bring up Sam as a vegan (no animal foods whatsoever, not even dairy produce or eggs) she would need to see a baby nutritionist for advice.

When Sam was six months old, Penny started gradually to wean him by replacing milk feedings with solid foods so that Sam would end up on three meals a day.

Penny and I planned a schedule in which she would introduce one food at a time, withdrawing it if it didn't suit Sam and trying it again ten days later. Sam's diet had to include foods from each of the major food groups (see p.66).

Sam would get protein, essential for growth in a young baby, from egg yolks, legumes, cheese, and milk as well as sunflower-seed spread, soy yogurt, and grains. I pointed out to Penny that she shouldn't replace cow's milk with sheep's or goat's milk before Sam was 12–18 months old and that egg whites shouldn't be given until Sam was one year old.

Foods made from cereals and grains provide carbohydrates to give Sam the energy to grow and develop, while fruit and vegetables supply essential vitamins and minerals. I told Penny that vegetarian diets tend to be bulky and lower in calories than a diet including meat. This can be hard for a baby because Sam could get full before he's eaten all that he needs, so Penny should give him a wide variety of foods that are low in fiber such as eggs, milk, and cheese. We drew up a menu plan and I gave Penny a few tips.

• Choose a time when Sam is hungry, but not very hungry, such as the middle of the day, to try the first solids.

- Sam's first foods should be smooth in texture and mild in taste. Baby rice cereal, cooked puréed fruit such as apples and pears, or vegetables such as carrots or potatoes (with no added salt) are ideal.
- Avoid adding lots of seasoning or sugar.
- Adding a spoonful of Sam's usual milk to the food would help him recognize the taste.

I also advised Penny that when preparing fruit and vegetables, she shouldn't overcook or keep foods hot for a long time; this destroys their vitamin content. Fresh fruit should always be peeled and have all seeds or pits removed. Sam sailed through his weaning. He seemed to really enjoy foods without salt and sugar, foods Penny thought he would find too bland. Penny found that Sam adored pease porridge made from lentils, a food she introduced when Sam was seven months old. He also relished the yolk of an egg finely chopped and then mashed with soy yogurt. The more solid food he ate, the more fluid Sam wanted to drink, and a little unsweetened orange juice diluted half and half with water became his standard drink. In hot weather, Penny found that Sam could easily drink more than a cup of this favorite drink every day.

Sam is now nine months old and very much one of the family, eating more and more family food, which only needs sieving or mashing to suit him. He loves gravies and sauces, and Penny has found that these help him to accept almost any new food. Ice cream has become such a favorite that Penny has to limit this treat to once or twice a week so that Sam isn't getting too much sugar and fat. He's gaining weight steadily, but he's not fat.

Penny is eager to introduce Sam to new flavors. She asked if there were any foods she shouldn't give, and I advised her to introduce strongly flavored vegetables such as broccoli, onions, or peppers gradually, and not to give whole-wheat bread or unpeeled fruit until Sam is a year old.

Vegetarian menu for nine-month-old baby

Breakfast	Breast- or bottle-feeding Baby yogurt dessert	Breast- or bottle-feeding Breakfast cereal with milk	Breast- or bottle-feeding Baby rice cereal
Lunch	Diluted unsweetened fruit juice or cooled boiled water Cooked puréed lentils with vegetables Puréed fruit	Diluted unsweetened fruit juice or cooled boiled water Hard-boiled egg and spinach with bread slices Puréed fruit	Diluted unsweetened fruit juice or cooled boiled water Cheese with vegetable purée Mashed bananas and yogurt
Snack	Breast- or bottle-feeding	Breast- or bottle-feeding	Breast- or bottle-feeding
Dinner	Mashed potatoes with grated cheese and broccoli Soaked dried fruit, mashed	Thick lentil soup Baked apple with rice or wheat germ	Puréed cabbage with tofu and pita bread

Your baby's main source of calories is still breast milk or formula, so give this at each feeding, but you should also give drinks of cooled boiled water.

INTRODUCING CUPS

You can introduce your baby to drinking from a cup when she is about four months old. Aim to give up bottles by 12 months.

• Cups with spouts are best, since your baby will have to half-suck and half-drink to get anything. Soft spouts are the easiest to use.

• As your baby progresses, she may prefer to move on to a two-handled cup that she can grasp easily. Those with specially slanted lips are excellent because the contents come out with very little tipping.

Training cup
Lunchtime and late afternoon feedings are probably the best times to use the cup; these are times when your baby is more likely to eat solids.

Feeding and nutrition

During her first year, your baby will move on from mere "tastes" of solids with her milk feedings, to three solid meals a day, with drinks of water, diluted fruit juice, or milk.

Once your baby is happy with a couple of different solids, it's important to introduce a variety of tastes and textures. Not only will she be able to deal with foods that have been puréed, mashed, or chopped, she'll also learn to enjoy chewing and sucking on larger chunks of food (see **Finger foods**, opposite), but it's important to remember that every baby has different requirements and appetites. If you are in any doubt, just feed your baby as much as she will eat happily. The amount of milk she requires will lessen as the number of solid meals she eats increases. Since she'll be getting most of her calories from solids rather than from milk, your baby will become thirsty. When she does, give her plain water or diluted fruit juice to drink, rather than milk. Never give your baby a processed drink containing sugar or colorings.

FEEDING YOUR CHILD

You will probably begin by feeding your baby in an infant chair or on your lap, but once she's used to the idea, you may like to use a high chair or feeding table. With a feeding table, you will have to bend down to feed your baby, and at first you may have to prop her up with cushions, so a high chair is probably the better option; make sure your baby is properly strapped in.

Your child should always be supervised while she's eating. Almost all children choke on some food at some stage, and it is essential that you react quickly. A new texture, taken for the first time, may make her choke out of surprise. If she does, pat her firmly on the back and encourage her to cough until the food is dislodged. Talk soothingly and gently rub her back, and she'll be more able to swallow the new food. If your baby's choking is severe, and especially if she loses consciousness, you must know how to administer first aid (see p.326).

SELF-FEEDING

Your baby will soon look forward to meal times as an opportunity to play as well as to eat, so feeding will become messier. Keep your baby's high chair away from the walls, and put newspapers on the floor in case she starts throwing food. Within a month or so of starting solids, your baby will be able to take food from the spoon. Learning to feed herself is a huge step in your baby's physical and

FINGER FOODS

Self-feeding
Allow your child to feed himself if he wants to as his manual dexterity improves.

Whole-wheat bread without whole grains is suitable

Pretty shapes will make food look appealing

Cut vegetables into shapes that are easy to grasp

If your baby has difficulty using a spoon, she will find finger foods easier to handle; even if the food is hard, she will suck it.

intellectual development and you should encourage all her attempts. Her manual dexterity and hand–eye coordination will greatly improve with self-feeding, so let her experiment if she shows an interest and be prepared to cope with the mess. Food provides your baby with the perfect motivation for speeding up muscle coordination and balance.

It may be several months before your baby becomes proficient at feeding herself. You can help by giving her nonrunny foods that will stick to the spoon, such as oatmeal, egg yolks, or thick purées. If she finds trying to use a spoon frustrating, let her try finger foods. Food will be a plaything, most of which will land on the floor rather than in your baby's stomach, but there's no cause for concern; at the time a baby starts to self-feed, the initial growth spurt is beginning to slacken off, so she needs less food.

The best way to ensure that your baby gets at least some food is for both of you to have a spoon. Use two spoons of the same color and type so that you can swap your full spoon for her empty one when she has difficulty scooping up the food.

Food for self-feeding

Fruit and vegetables	Cereals	Protein
Any fresh fruit that is easy to hold, like bananas, cut into slices with the skin or seeds removed	Small pieces of dried, sugar-free cereal	Whole-wheat bread
	Boiled rice	Pieces of soft cheese
Vegetables, particularly carrots, cut into a stick or shape that is easy to grasp. Don't cut vegetables too small	Whole-wheat bread or crackers (without the complete grains)	Toast slices with cheese
		Small pieces of white meat in easily held pieces
Mashed potatoes	Pasta shapes	Low-fat cheese
		Filleted fish in firm chunks
		Sliced hard-boiled egg yolk

GIRLS' WEIGHT

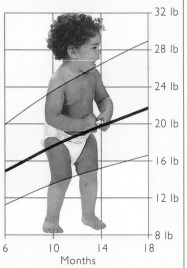

— 32 lb

— 28 lb

— 24 lb

— 20 lb

— 16 lb

— 12 lb

— 8 lb

6   10   14   18

Months

Your baby's weight

The rapid weight gain of the first few months slows down, but your baby is still putting on weight steadily. Any weight within the colored band is normal. (For a full explanation of this chart, see **Growth charts***, p.56.)*

YOUR BABY'S NEEDS

Your baby will always eat enough food to satisfy his needs. If he doesn't want to eat, then he doesn't need to. This means that there will be days when he will eat hardly anything, but these will be followed by periods of eating a lot.

To eat a balanced diet, your baby should have foods from all the different food groups in the correct proportions (see below). This doesn't have to be on a daily basis, though, so when you're considering whether he is eating well, you need to think in the long term: look at what he has eaten in the last week, not just today. Viewed like this, a binge of eating nothing but bread for two days is nothing to worry about, since your baby will probably take in enough fruit and vegetables during the week to balance this out. What is important is that he should be given a wide variety of foods to choose from: he can't eat the foods he requires if they are not made available to him.

Your baby will gradually come to eat many of the same foods as you do, prepared in a form that he can manage. It would be wrong, however, to suppose that his needs are the same as yours, or that a diet that is recommended as healthy for you will be good for him. You may aim to reduce your fat intake by using low-fat dairy products, for example, but you should give your child whole milk until he is two years old; after that you can introduce reduced-fat milk if you wish. The benefits to health of limiting sugar intake, though, apply just as

The food pyramid

This table shows the proportions in which the main food groups should be eaten in order for your baby to take in the right balance of nutrients. The two most important groups are carbohydrates, and fruit and vegetables, followed by protein-rich foods like meat, legumes, and dairy products. Sugars, fats, and oils should form the smallest part of your baby's diet—in fact, the amounts of these that occur naturally in other foods will be more than enough. By following these guidelines for your baby, you will be helping him form good habits for life.

Fats, oils, and sugars

Proteins: Meat, fish, eggs, dairy foods, and legumes

Fruit and vegetables

Carbohydrates: Bread, cereal, rice, and pasta

Suggested menus—age 8–10 months

Day 1	Day 2	Day 3
Breakfast	**Breakfast**	**Breakfast**
Rice cakes	Mashed bananas	Cottage cheese
Hard-boiled egg yolk	Whole-wheat toast	Whole-wheat toast
Milk	slices	slices
	Milk	Milk
Lunch	**Lunch**	**Lunch**
Strained vegetable and chicken	Mashed potatoes and cheese	Strained lentils and mixed vegetables
Stewed apple	Pear slices	Bananas and yogurt
Diluted fruit juice	Diluted fruit juice	Diluted fruit juice
Snack	**Snack**	**Snack**
Whole-wheat toast slices	Rice cakes	Homemade graham crackers
Orange segments	Apple pieces	Fresh fruit
Milk	Milk	Milk
Supper	**Supper**	**Supper**
Cauliflower with cheese	Pasta and tomato sauce	Tuna and mashed potatoes with steamed zucchini
Semolina and fruit purée	Yogurt with fruit purée	
Diluted fruit juice	Diluted fruit juice	Rice pudding
		Diluted fruit juice

BOYS' WEIGHT

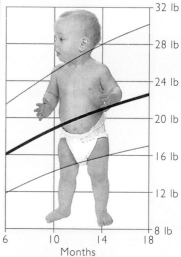

Your baby's weight
*The rapid weight gain of the first few months has past, but your little boy is still getting steadily heavier. Any weight that falls within the colored band is normal. (For a full explanation of this chart, see **Growth charts**, p.56.)*

much to babies as to adults. Never add any salt to your baby's food; his kidneys are too immature to cope.

A FLEXIBLE ATTITUDE

The sample menus shown above are intended as a guide to your baby's main meals. Remember, a baby's stomach can't hold very much, and he'll need to eat more often than an adult; so don't insist he finishes his meals, and be prepared to give snacks in between. Of course you should encourage your baby to have regular meals, but if you try to make him eat at mealtimes only, they will become battlegrounds, and he may end up not getting the food he needs when he needs it. If he shows that he's had enough, don't try to make him eat more.

Of course it's frustrating if you've spent a lot of time preparing a meal and your baby refuses it, or it ends up on the floor. The answer is to make feeding times as easy on yourself as possible: don't spend a lot of time preparing complicated dishes, and take precautions to protect the walls and the floor from thrown food.

KITCHEN HYGIENE

**Scares about food poisoning
in recent years have made
parents much more conscious
of the dangers of poor food
hygiene. The following
commonsense precautions
will protect your baby.**

• Always wash your hands with soap
before handling food, especially after
going to the bathroom or changing
a diaper, and after playing with pets.
Make sure your family does the same.

• Be scrupulous about keeping
the kitchen clean, especially work
surfaces, cutting boards, and utensils
used in food preparation.

• Always use a clean dish towel or
paper towels to dry dishes, or let
them dry in a rack after rinsing them
with hot water.

• Keep the kitchen trash can
covered. Empty it often, and rinse
it out with hot water and a little
disinfectant each time you empty it.

• Cover any food that is left
out on the counter.

• Any leftover food in your baby's
dish should be thrown away.

• Keep separate cloths for dirty
tasks and for washing your child's
high chair. Change or boil cloths
every week at least.

FOOD PREPARATION

Once your baby is on solids, it's no longer necessary to sterilize all
feeding utensils, though bottles and nipples used for milk should still
be sterilized until your baby is about a year old. Cups, bowls, and
cutlery can be washed in hot, soapy water and rinsed with hot water.
However, you need to take precautions to protect her from the effects
of harmful bacteria—salmonella and listeria poisoning, for example.

BUYING AND STORING

The most important thing to look for when buying food is freshness.
Shop often, and use food as quickly as possible. Bruised or damaged
fruit and vegetables deteriorate quickly, so don't buy them. Always
wash fruit if the skin is to be eaten, since there may be a residue of
insecticides or other chemicals. Check the "sell by," "best before,"
or "use by" dates on packaged foods and make sure that there are
no signs of damage to boxes, bags, cans, or jars.

Store food in the refrigerator in clean, covered containers. Store
cooked and raw foods on separate shelves, and put raw meat and
fish on a plate or in a drawer so that the juices can't drip on to food
on the shelf below. Check the packaging to see if food is suitable
for freezing, and never freeze foods for longer than the time
recommended by the manufacturer Always defrost frozen foods
thoroughly before using them, and never refreeze food once it has
been defrosted.

Coarse grater

Hand-held blender

Preparation methods
*At first you will need to purée or
grate foods for your baby. Steaming
is a fast method of cooking that
helps to preserve nutrients.*

Steamer

COOKING AND REHEATING

Always cook your baby's food thoroughly; this applies especially to meat, poultry, and eggs. You should never give raw or soft-cooked eggs, liver pâté, soft cheeses, or nut products to your baby. It's best not to give your baby reheated leftovers or chilled or frozen foods. If you're preparing food in bulk quantities, don't leave it to cool before putting it into the refrigerator, since this will just give the bacteria a chance to multiply; put it in a cold dish, cover it, and put it straight into the refrigerator or freezer.

PREPARATION

At first you'll have to purée all your baby's food, but this stage won't last very long, so if you don't have a blender, you can use a cheap hand-operated food mill. At first, a sieve will be perfectly adequate. As your baby gets older, you can feed her coarser foods. By the time she is seven to nine months old, she'll be able to cope with mashed or minced foods, and by nine to 12 months she'll enjoy soft pieces of food and finger foods.

You can use a variety of liquids to thin down home-prepared foods: the water you've used to steam fruit or vegetables is ideal. To thicken foods, you can use ground, whole-grain cereals, cottage cheese, yogurt, or mashed potatoes. If you feel you need to sweeten your baby's food, use naturally sweet fruit juice or dextrose rather than refined sugar.

Preparation tips

Do	Don't
• Use fruit and vegetables as soon as possible after buying	• Buy bruised or wrinkled fruit and vegetables
• Peel tough-skinned fruit and vegetables if the skin is likely to cause your baby problems	• Prepare vegetables a long time in advance or soak them in water, since this destroys the vitamins
• Cook soft-skinned fruit and vegetables in their skins; this helps to retain the vitamins and provides additional fiber	• Crush or bruise fruit and vegetables; this destroys vitamin C
• Cook fruit and vegetables in a steamer or tightly covered pan with as little water as possible. This helps to retain the vitamins normally lost in cooking	• Give red meat more than twice a week—it has a high saturated fat content
• Give your baby cooked and puréed meat or fish. The purée can be thinned with vegetable water or soup	• Overcook canned foods, since this destroys the vitamins
• Use sunflower or corn oil. Never cook with butter or saturated fats	• Add salt or sugar to your child's food; her immature kidneys can't handle a lot of salt, and giving her sweet foods will encourage a sweet tooth
	• Let prepared food cool at room temperature; refrigerate it right away

USING PACKAGED FOODS

Packaged foods are more expensive than homemade ones, but they are convenient, especially if you're in a hurry or you're traveling. Always observe the following guidelines when using them.

• Check the ingredients listed on the can or jar. They are listed in order of quantity, so anything that has water near the top of the list will not be very nutritious.

• Avoid foods with added sugar or modified starch. Also avoid foods that contain peanuts or honey, both of which have been known to cause very serious allergic reactions in some babies and small children. Avoid foods that contain added salt or monosodium glutamate (MSG).

• Make sure that the seal is intact; if it is damaged, the food could be contaminated.

• Don't heat the food in the jar—the glass might crack.

• Don't feed your baby from the jar if you intend to keep some of the food, since he leftovers will become contaminated with saliva. You can feed her from the jar if she's likely to eat the whole thing.

• Don't keep opened jars in the refrigerator for longer than two days, and never beyond the "best before" date.

• Never store food in an opened can; transfer it to a dish, cover, and refrigerate.

• Check the ingredients lists carefully if you are introducing food types gradually—many contain eggs, gluten, and dairy products. Some even contain nuts.

GIRLS' WEIGHT

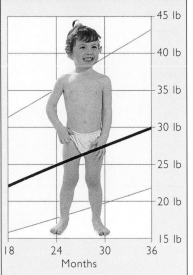

45 lb
40 lb
35 lb
30 lb
25 lb
20 lb
15 lb

18   24   30   36
Months

Your toddler's weight
*Weight gain may be irregular during spurts of growth, but any weight within the colored band is normal. (See **Growth charts**, p.56.)*

A balanced diet
Variety is the key to a good diet. Choose foods from each of the groups in the chart.

Feeding and nutrition

As your child grows, his nutritional needs increase proportionately; greater quantities are needed during growth spurts, and when he's learning to walk. Your child should have a diet containing sufficient amounts of protein, carbohydrates, fats, vitamins, and minerals, and he will get all of these as long as you provide a wide variety of foods. Because he is growing, he still needs more protein and calories for his body weight than an adult.

Although, broadly speaking, a variety of foods from three of the four food groups (see p.62)—carbohydrates, fruit and vegetables (fiber), and protein-rich foods—will fulfill your child's needs, some foods within the groups have particular nutritional value. All fruits and vegetables

Food groups	Nutrients
Breads and cereals Whole-wheat bread, noodles, pasta, rice	Protein, carbohydrates, B vitamins, iron, and calcium
Citrus fruits Oranges, grapefruits, lemons, limes	Vitamins A and C
Fats Butter, margarine, vegetable oils, fish oils	Vitamins A and D, essential fatty acids
Green and yellow vegetables Cabbage, Brussels sprouts, spinach, kale, green beans, squash, lettuce, celery, zucchini	Minerals, including calcium, chlorine, fluorine, chromium, cobalt, copper, zinc, manganese, potassium, sodium, and magnesium
High protein Chicken, fish, lamb, beef, pork, eggs, cheese, legumes	Protein, fat, iron, vitamins A and D, B vitamins, especially B12 (naturally present in animal proteins only)
Milk and dairy products Milk, cream, yogurt, ice cream, cheese	Protein, fat, calcium, vitamins A and D, B vitamins
Other vegetables and fruits Potatoes, beets, corn, carrots, cauliflower, pineapples, apricots, nectarines, strawberries, plums, apples, bananas	Carbohydrates, vitamins A, B, and C

provide carbohydrates and fiber, for instance, but leafy vegetables are particularly high in minerals, while citrus fruits are a good source of vitamins A and C (see chart opposite).

SNACKS

Until the age of four or five, your child will prefer to eat frequently throughout the day. His stomach still can't cope with three adult-sized meals a day, so he is not ready to adopt an adult eating pattern. He may want to eat between three and 14 times a day, but the typical range is five to seven times. What he eats is more important than how often he eats. As a rule, the more meals your child has, the smaller they will be.

You may be accustomed to thinking of snacks as "extras," but they are an integral part of any child's diet and should not be refused. As long as the snacks do not reduce your child's daily nutrition, and are not being used as substitutes for "meals," snacks can be wonderfully useful for introducing new foods gradually without disrupting your child's eating patterns. Avoid giving your child highly refined and processed foods like cookies, candy, cake, and ice cream, which contain a lot of calories and sugar and very few nutrients. Fresh fruits and vegetables, cubes of cheese, and cheese sandwiches made with whole-wheat bread or white bread with added vitamins, and diluted fruit juice all make good, nutritious snacks.

Planning snacks Snack foods should contribute to the whole day's nutrition, so don't leave them to chance; plan them carefully, and coordinate meals and snacks so that you serve different foods in the snacks and in the meals.

• Milk and milk-based drinks make very good snacks, and contain protein, calcium, and many of the B vitamins. You should use whole milk until your child is at least two years old; then you can use reduced-fat but not skim milk unless your child is overweight (see p.70). Raw fruit juice drinks are also very nutritious, and contain a lot of vitamin C. If you buy fruit juices, avoid those with added sugar.
• Your child may become bored with certain kinds of foods, so try to give him plenty of variety, and make snacks amusing if you can: you could use cookie cutters to cut cheese or bread into interesting shapes, or make a smiling face by arranging pieces of fruit on a slice of bread.
• A food that your child rejects in one form may be acceptable in another: yogurt can be frozen so that it becomes more like ice cream, and a child who rejects cheese sandwiches might enjoy eating pieces of cheese and tomato out of an ice cream cone.
• You can also increase your child's interest in food by involving him in planning or even preparing part of a snack. He will take great pride in eating a sandwich if he has helped you choose the filling or wash and tear the lettuce, for example, and if you allow him to assemble the bread and filling himself.

BOYS' WEIGHT

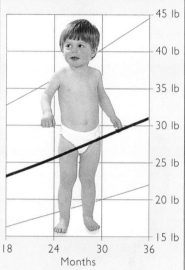

Your toddler's weight
Your child may have spurts of growth, but these will balance out with periods of slower weight gain. Any weight within the colored band is normal. (For an explanation of the chart, see **Growth charts***, p.56.)*

Little and often
Your child will need more snacks than you do, since he can't eat large meals.

Your child can eat at the table in her usual high chair, but there are other types of seats available that are more portable and will give her greater independence.

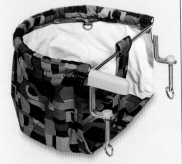

Clip-on chairs
These light, collapsible chairs are suitable for babies over six months of age. Some will grip the table when your toddler sits in the chair; others are attached to the table by clamps. These are not necessarily suitable for all tables, so be sure to read the manufacturer's recommendations carefully before buying.

Booster seat
Help your child reach table height with a booster seat, suitable for children over 18 months. It is more stable than a cushion or pillow, and can be strapped to a chair.

FEEDING YOUR TODDLER

By the age of 18 months, your baby will already be eating more or less the same foods as you, and she will probably have about one-third to one-half of an adult portion at meals. You should ensure that she has at least one protein food at each meal, and four servings of fruit and vegetables a day. Aim to give a good mixture of foods from the different food groups in the chart on p.66.

Don't give your child highly seasoned or sugary foods—fresh fruit or yogurt rather than sweet desserts should be offered. You should also avoid any small, hard pieces of food that your child could choke on, like whole nuts or popcorn, fruits with pits or seeds, or very small pieces of raw fruit or vegetables.

FAMILY EATING
Now that your toddler is feeding herself, she will enjoy sitting at the table during family mealtimes. Although she's eating the same food as everyone else, you may need to mash or chop it so that she can eat it without much help. A very messy eater can be fed beforehand, then allowed to sit at the table with some finger foods. Difficult eaters feel encouraged to eat more at family meals.

It will be some time, however, before your child is ready to sit still during mealtimes. If she wants to get down from the table, let her go, and don't try to make her come back to finish her food if she has obviously lost interest in it; she will make up for it by eating more at the next meal.

MESSY EATERS
Your child may regard mealtimes as just another game, and will see nothing wrong in getting food everywhere. Although it may seem like she's doing it on purpose, it's just a phase, and her coordination will improve eventually. Make mealtimes easier on yourself by surrounding the high chair with newspaper that can be gathered up after each

Keeping clean
Bibs and easy-to-wash plastic equipment help to keep messy mealtimes manageable.

meal. Being neat can be turned into a game: you could draw a circle on the tray of the high chair to show your toddler where her mug should go; if she keeps it there, reward her.

MENU PLANNING

The menus below assume that your toddler will eat three meals a day and several snacks. If you find in practice that she eats fewer meals and more snacks, just make sure you choose snack foods that you would have served at mealtimes.

Suggested menus—age 18 months

Day 1	Day 2	Day 3
Breakfast	**Breakfast**	**Breakfast**
½ slice whole-wheat toast	½ cup cereal plus ½ cup milk	1 cup diluted fruit juice
1 chopped hard-boiled egg	1 cup diluted fruit juice	1 tablespoon baby granola with ¼ cup of milk
1 cup diluted fruit juice	1 sliced pear, without skin	½ mashed banana
	½ slice whole-wheat toast	small carton of fruit yogurt
Lunch	**Lunch**	**Lunch**
2 oz white fish	1 beefburger in a whole-wheat roll	1 cheese sandwich made with whole-wheat bread
¼ cup brown rice (dry weight)	¼ cup steamed broccoli	pieces of raw carrot
1 tablespoon sweet corn	1 medium tomato	1 sliced apple, without skin
1 cup diluted fruit juice	1 cup diluted fruit juice	1 cup milk
Snacks	**Snacks**	**Snacks**
1 cup water	1 cup milk	1 orange in pieces
1 small yogurt	1 unsweetened whole-wheat cookie	1 small yogurt
1 banana	1 cup water	1 cup diluted fresh fruit juice
1 whole-wheat bread roll	1 rice cake	1 bag unsalted chips
Dinner	**Dinner**	**Dinner**
½ cup cauliflower with ⅓ cup grated cheese	½ whole-wheat roll	2 sardines (not in oil)
⅓ cup fava beans	⅓ cup fava beans	¼ cup baked beans
2 oz chicken pieces, without skin	2 oz chopped liver	1 medium tomato
½ banana blended with 1 cup milk	2 oz whole-wheat pasta (dry weight)	1 cup milk
1 small whole-wheat roll	1 cup water	

MAKING FOOD FUN

Making mealtimes exciting for your toddler will encourage her to try new foods. Fun foods don't have to be difficult or time-consuming; a little imagination is all it takes.

Smiley pizza face
Cheese, vegetables, and fresh fruit decoratively arranged on top of a plain pizza can be very appealing, and makes a highly nutritious child's meal.

OVERWEIGHT

Obesity is one of the most common nutritional problems among children in prosperous western societies. Most plump children, however, are not medically overweight and no special action is needed as long as they are healthy and active.

If you think your child is overweight—that is, markedly fatter than his friends—consult your doctor, who will be able to tell you if your child's weight is above the normal range for his height.

The most common causes of being overweight are a poor diet and lack of exercise. The best way to help the child is often for the whole family to adopt a healthier diet: less fat and sugar, more fresh fruit and vegetables, and more unrefined carbohydrates.

You should never aim to make your child actually lose weight, but for his weight to remain stable while he grows in height. The following guidelines may help:

• Bake, grill, and boil foods rather than roasting or frying them.

• Give water or diluted fruit juice when your child is thirsty. Never give sweetened drinks.

• Give whole-wheat bread, raw vegetables, and fruit as snacks.

• Whole-wheat bread and pasta and brown rice are more filling than their refined equivalents.

• Encourage your child to be active by playing lively games with him.

• No child needs more than a pint of milk a day. Reduced-fat or skim milk can be used for overweight children over the age of two years if vitamin supplements are also given.

FEEDING PROBLEMS

Some young children are "picky eaters," but in many cases the real difficulty is with a parent who expects their child to conform to an eating pattern that doesn't suit him. If you approach feeding problems with sympathy and a flexible attitude, they will usually just disappear. If there is a genuine problem, such as an intolerance of, or very rarely allergy to, certain foodstuffs, consult your doctor. Never try to isolate a food allergy yourself; always seek medical advice.

FOOD PREFERENCES

In the second year, your child will start to show likes and dislikes for certain foods. It is very common for children to go through phases of eating only one kind of food and refusing everything else. For example, he may go for a week eating only yogurt and fruit, then suddenly refuse yogurt and start eating nothing but cheese and mashed potatoes. Don't get annoyed with your child about this, and don't insist that he eats certain foods. No one food is essential, and there is always a nutritious substitute for any food he refuses. As long as you offer your child a wide variety of foods, he will get a balanced diet, and it is far better for him to eat something that he likes—even if it's something you disapprove of—than to eat nothing at all. The one thing you must watch out for is your toddler's refusal to eat any food from a particular group—refusing any kind of fruit or vegetables, for example. If he does, his diet will become unbalanced, so you will have to think of ways of tempting him to eat fruit and vegetables, perhaps by cooking the food in a different way or presenting it imaginatively (see p.69).

If you spend time cooking food that you know your toddler doesn't want, you'll feel annoyed and resentful when he doesn't eat it, so give yourself and him a break by cooking food that you know he'll enjoy.

Don't try to camouflage a disliked food by mixing it with something else, or bargain with your child by offering a favorite food if he eats the disliked one; he may very well end up refusing other foods as well. If you are introducing a new food, make sure your child is hungry; that way, he is more likely to take it. Never try to force him to eat something he doesn't want; if he thinks it's very important to you, he will just use it as a way of manipulating you.

REFUSAL TO EAT

Not eating is an early indication that your child may be unwell, so observe him carefully. If he looks pale, and seems fretful and more clumsy than usual, check his temperature (see p.278) and speak to your doctor if you're worried.

Occasionally your child may have eaten a lot of snacks or had milk before his meal, and he won't have his usual appetite. As long as the snacks are nutritious, this is okay. If he refuses to eat for no reason that you can see, don't let yourself worry. Your child will always eat as much food as he really needs, and if you insist on his eating, mealtimes may become a battle that you will always lose.

FOOD INTOLERANCE

The inability to fully digest certain foods has to be distinguished from a true food allergy, which is quite different and very rare. Intolerance occurs when the digestive system fails to produce essential enzymes that break down food inside the body. One of the most common forms of food intolerance in children is lactose intolerance—the inability to digest the sugars in milk. The enzyme, in this case lactase, may be absent from birth, or its production may be disrupted by an intestinal disorder, such as gastroenteritis. Pale-colored, bulky, smelly stools are characteristic of the disorder. Sometimes food intolerance occurs for reasons that are not known. If your child regularly has symptoms, such as diarrhea, nausea, or pain, after eating a particular food, intolerance may be the cause. The best remedy is to avoid the food concerned, but don't try to identify it yourself; you will need medical advice.

FOOD ALLERGY

Most cases of suspected food allergy turn out to be no more than intolerance, or the combination of a picky child and a nervous mother. A true food allergy is quite rare, and occurs when the body's immune system undergoes an exaggerated reaction to a protein or chemical it interprets as "foreign." It is a protective mechanism, and symptoms can include a headache, nausea, profuse vomiting, a rash, widespread red blotches in the skin, and swelling of the mouth, tongue, face, and eyes.

At first the allergen—the substance that causes the reaction—may produce only mild symptoms, but these may become more severe if the child is repeatedly exposed to the food concerned. Some foods that commonly cause allergic reactions are wheat, shellfish, strawberries, chocolate, eggs, and cows' milk.

In the 1980s, food allergies attracted a great deal of attention, and were blamed for behavioral disturbances in children, including hyperactivity. More recent studies have cast doubt on these claims: parents continued to report behavioral disturbance even when, unknown to them, the suspect food had been withdrawn from the child's diet. In a very small number of cases it has been proved that food was responsible for the behavior, but in very many more cases, bad behavior is a way of seeking love and attention from neglectful parents. I feel very strongly that too many parents have been willing to blame foods for behavioral problems rather than look to their own attitudes as a cause. Meanwhile, many children have been needlessly deprived of nutritious foods.

You should never attempt to isolate a food allergy on your own without medical advice, and never assume an allergy is present without a clear diagnosis from a pediatric allergist.

WHEN YOUR CHILD IS SICK

Loss of appetite is often one of the first signs of illness in a child, but this need not be a cause for concern if the illness is short.

• Your child must drink plenty of fluids, especially if he has been vomiting or had diarrhea.

• Most doctors recommend that drinks containing milk should be avoided if your child is suffering from gastroenteritis.

• There is no need for a special diet, though it is sensible to avoid rich or heavy foods if your child has an upset stomach.

• Offer some of his favorite foods to cheer him up, and give smaller portions than usual. Because your child is resting, he will probably not want much.

Giving drinks
Your child's appetite may be poor when she is sick, but make sure she drinks plenty of fluids by offering her favorite drink.

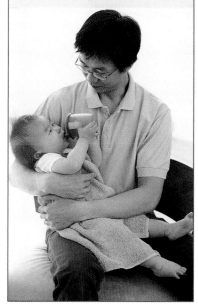

TREATS AND REWARDS

Every parent knows that there are times when it's important either to reward good behavior or to offer a bribe in return for some form of cooperation.

Candy might seem like the most suitable reward, since it's always appreciated by children. However, you may feel that to give sweets routinely as a reward undermines the consistency of your approach to eating candy in general. There is no hard and fast rule on this, and there is no reason why you shouldn't occasionally reward your child with sweets as long as you make it clear that it is a one-time gift.

It's worth making an effort, though, to devise other forms of reward: a favorite yogurt flavor, a small toy or a new box of crayons, or a specially extended bathtime or bedtime story.

I don't believe in placing a total ban on candy, because this can encourage children to be secretive and dishonest.

I do believe in rationing candy, though, and this always worked with my own children. If you let your child have one candy after lunch and one after supper, and encourage her to brush her teeth afterward, you will be encouraging self control, good eating habits, and good oral hygiene.

Feeding and nutrition

Your preschooler will eat much the same as you—taking care of her needs may even encourage you to improve your own diet. As well as making sure she is eating well, you'll probably want to start teaching her adult behavior and manners at mealtimes. This is a good time to teach her table manners that will last into adulthood.

FAMILY AND SOCIAL EATING

For many families, mealtimes are about much more than making sure everyone has enough to eat; they are social occasions when all the members of the family sit down together, exchange news, and enjoy each other's company. For a small child, these times form an important part of her learning process; she can appreciate this social aspect of mealtimes and will learn most of her behavior at the table from her early experience of family eating rather than from any number of lectures at a later age.

Every family has its own accepted standards of behavior, and I'm not going to lay down rules about what these should be. What is important, however, is that your child learns to fit in so that the family can enjoy their mealtimes together without repeated disruptions caused by bad manners and arguments about behavior.

As soon as your child first sits in her high chair at the family dining table, she will be watching and learning. She will want at least to try the foods that you are eating, and will often join in the conversation. Try to include your child in family meals as often as possible. Encourage her when she attempts to follow your (good) example. Give praise, for instance, when she asks for something to be passed to her instead of attempting to grab it from the other side of the table.

Children learn most naturally and easily by example and will rapidly pick up the norms of behavior that the rest of the family observe. If yours is a family where everyone leaves the table when it suits them, for example, rather than waiting for the others to finish eating, it will be hard to persuade your child to sit still and wait.

There will be occasions when you want your child to behave especially well at mealtimes—usually because you are having guests. Allow her to join in the excitement of a special meal by letting her help with the preparations beforehand, such as setting the table with extra care. If she understands that some occasions demand an extra effort from everyone, she will find it easier to understand why you want her to be particularly well behaved and will therefore react better to your wishes.

KEEPING MEALTIMES RELAXED

It's important to prevent meals from becoming a battleground for more generalized family conflict. The association between food and love can be very close, and arguments about food and eating can be associated with tensions over other issues. In such cases, food and eating behavior—for example, refusal to eat—can become a weapon that the child uses either to gain attention or to express anger, distress, and other emotions. It is best, therefore, to be fairly easygoing about table etiquette with your child, to make mealtimes as relaxed as possible, and not to be drawn into arguments. Insist only on the aspects of table manners that you consider essential; refinements can come later.

EATING AWAY FROM HOME

A small baby can eat only what you give her, but an older child will have pronounced preferences about what she wants to eat, and the opportunity to follow them. There are likely to be more occasions when your child is eating outside the home, and while you obviously can't account for every mouthful she eats, you should try to ensure that the good habits she has learned at home are not undermined once she starts to eat elsewhere.

   If your child goes out to daycare, preschool, or school, try to make sure she has a good breakfast before she goes. If she doesn't, she will become hungry again long before lunchtime, and both her temper and her concentration will be adversely affected. A healthy mid-morning snack like a piece of fruit or cereal bar will help tide her over until lunchtime. If food is going to be provided for her, try to find out what will be available; if you are not satisfied, or if there are no arrangements to feed your child, then provide her with a nutritious packed lunch instead. Lunch need not always be sandwiches; you could give chicken pieces and potato salad, pieces of raw vegetables with yogurt dip, or other foods that your child can eat with her fingers. Children are often encouraged to try new foods because they see their friends eat them, and you may find once your child starts at daycare or school that she starts to eat foods that she previously rejected at home.

FAST FOODS

Do try not to resort to fast food restaurants too often when you are out with your child and want to stop for something to eat. Most of the foods available in these restaurants—hamburgers, fries, and sugary drinks—are high in salt, fats, or sugar, and low in nutrients. If you can, bring a supply of healthy snack foods with you, or choose somewhere that offers more healthy foods, such as sandwiches and salads. If your child particularly asks for hamburgers and fries, however, you may like to indulge her now and again—but make it clear that such foods are to be eaten only occasionally. My family used to eat at a hamburger restaurant once a week, for Saturday lunch. This satisfied everyone and is not so frequent as to damage good health.

EATING OUT

There will be many occasions when you'll take your child out to eat. Being prepared will make the experience more enjoyable.

• Try to find out beforehand what facilities will be available at the restaurant you choose: if you are making reservations, mention that you will be bringing small children, and find out whether there will be room for your child's stroller, and whether a high chair can be provided if you need one.

• Some children's menus are very limited and offer just hamburgers, pizza, or fish sticks—all with fries. If you don't want your child to have these foods, ask whether you can order a small portion of a suitable dish from the main menu, and whether you will be charged full price for it.

• Most children will enjoy the experience of eating out, and you should involve your child fully, allowing her to choose her own meal and to give her own order to the waiter if she isn't too shy.

• Bring along your child's booster seat if she normally uses one. If you think she will have difficulty drinking from a glass, you could also bring along her training cup.

• Many restaurants positively encourage children, and will be happy to provide straws for drinks, bibs and high chairs for young babies, and even small gifts such as paper hats or pictures to color in.

PUTTING YOUR BABY DOWN

You should always lay your baby on his back.

Research has shown that babies who sleep on their fronts are at greater risk from crib death than those placed on their backs, and publicity about this finding has resulted in a significant drop in crib deaths.

Holding and handling

A newborn baby may appear very vulnerable and fragile, but he is more robust than you imagine. With this knowledge in mind, you will be able to inspire confidence in your child rather than uncertainty. For your baby's comfort, and for your own peace of mind, it's important to feel at ease when you handle him; you must be able to hold your baby confidently in order to bathe, dress, and feed him successfully.

HANDLING YOUR BABY

When you move your baby, the action must be as slow, gentle, and quiet as possible. You'll find that you instinctively hold your baby close, look into his eyes, and talk soothingly to him. Not surprisingly, it has been proven that all children benefit from intimate physical contact, particularly being in a position to hear the familiar sound of your heartbeat. Premature babies, for example, gain more weight when they are laid on fleecy sheets, which give them the sensation of being touched, than when they are laid on smooth ones. Your newborn baby will find comfort in any kind of skin-to-skin contact, but the best way to give him this is for both of you to lie naked in bed. Here he can smell and feel your skin, and hear your heart beating. In this way, too, you can make sure that he becomes familiar with the smell of his father's skin.

PICKING UP YOUR BABY

Lifting your baby
Slide one hand under your baby's neck and the other under his back and bottom to support his lower half securely. Pick him up gently and smoothly and transfer him to a carrying position.

Whenever you pick your baby up and put him down, do it in a way that supports his head; until he is about four weeks old he'll have little control over it. If his head flops back, he will think that he is going to fall, his body will jerk, and he'll stretch out both arms and legs in the Moro, or "startle," reflex (see p.20).

Put your baby down and pick him up with your whole arm supporting his spine, neck, and head. You may like to try swaddling your baby: wrap him firmly in a shawl or blanket so that his head is supported and his arms are held close against his body. Once he lies down in the crib, you can gently unwrap him. Swaddling your baby tightly makes him feel secure, so it's a useful way of comforting and calming a distressed baby.

CARRYING YOUR BABY

One way to carry your baby in your arms is to cradle his head in the crook of either arm, which is slightly inclined. The rest of his body will rest on the lower part of your arm, encircled by your wrist and hand, which support his back and bottom. Your other arm will provide additional support to his bottom and legs, and your baby can see your face as you talk to him and smile at him.

The second way to carry your baby is to hold him against the upper part of your chest with his head on your shoulder. Your forearm should be placed across his back and your hand should support his resting head, leaving your other hand free. This can be used to provide support for your baby's bottom, or to help you balance. Your sense of balance will change at first as you get used to carrying your new baby.

Supporting and cradling
Hold your baby's head and support the length of his body when carrying him. Holding him close will make your baby feel secure and relaxed, especially if he can see your face.

SLINGS

Young babies are best carried in slings worn on the chest, where they feel close to you and secure.

• Look for a sling in a washable fabric, since it will get dirty as you carry your baby around.

• Make sure your sling is easy to put on and comfortable to wear. Try it out with your baby before you buy it.

• Your sling should support your baby's head and neck, and keep him secure; he must not be able to slip out of the sides.

• The shoulder straps must be wide enough to support your growing baby's weight. Wide shoulder straps make carrying more comfortable.

• It has been said that a baby shouldn't be carried in a sling until he can support his own head. This is not true. Use a sling as soon as you and your baby are happy about it.

Slings
These lightweight fabric supports are a comfortable way of carrying a young baby.

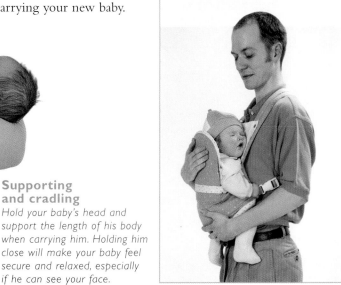

BENEFITS FOR PARENTS

Massage is a delightful and valuable activity that has advantages for you and your partner as well as your baby.

• Massaging your newborn helps to enhance the bonding process between you and your child.

• If you are anxious or have had little experience with children, massage allows you to get used to handling your new baby.

• Massage is an ideal way to soothe an unsettled baby and can also help to calm your nerves with its relaxing effects.

• You will find that massaging your baby's soft, smooth skin is a sensual experience for both of you.

BABY MASSAGE

Massage can have all the benefits for a baby that it has for an adult: it is soothing and can calm a fretful baby, and is a marvelous way of showing love. If you massage your baby every day, she will learn to recognize the routine and will show pleasure as you begin. You can continue to massage your baby as she gets older; a massage is often the ideal way to calm an excited toddler.

Provide a relaxed atmosphere before you start. Since this will be a new experience for you both, any distractions can spoil the mood and upset your baby so choose a time when there is no one else around and unplug the phone. Make sure the room is nice and warm and lay your baby on a warm towel or sheepskin, or on your lap. Work from her head down using light, even strokes, and ensure that both sides of her body are massaged symmetrically. Make eye contact with your baby throughout the massage and talk quietly, gently and lovingly to her.

GIVING A MASSAGE

Head
Start off by lightly massaging the crown of your baby's head using a circular motion, then stroke down the sides of his face. Gently massage his forehead, working from the center out and moving over the eyebrows and cheeks to finish around his ears.

Make sure you massage both sides of your baby's body symmetrically

Arms
Stroke down his arms to his fingertips. Using your fingers and thumb, gently squeeze all along his arm, starting at the top.

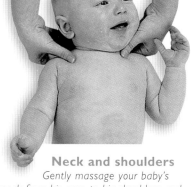

Neck and shoulders
Gently massage your baby's neck from his ears to his shoulders and from his chin to his chest. Then stroke his shoulders from his neck outward.

Chest and abdomen
*Gently stroke down your baby's chest,
following the delicate curves of his ribs.
Rub his abdomen in a circular motion,
working outward from the navel.*

BENEFITS FOR BABY

Your baby can only gain from the pleasures and sensations of a loving massage.

• Your baby loves being with you, and the intimate contact of massage enhances this. She will recognize it as a clear sign of your love.

• If she is unsettled, your baby will be calmed by the soothing strokes of your hands, which will make her feel secure and relieve anxiety.

• Massage can often ease minor digestive upsets, such as gas, that may be making your baby fretful.

• Babies need touch. Research has shown that they would rather be stroked than fed.

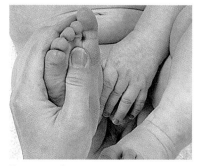

Feet and toes
*Rub your baby's ankles and feet,
stroking from heel to toe, and then
concentrate on each toe individually.
End your massage with some long, light
strokes running the whole length of the
front of your baby's body.*

Back
*Once you have massaged your baby
on the front, turn him over and work
on his back.*

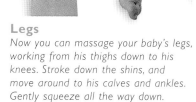

Legs
*Now you can massage your baby's legs,
working from his thighs down to his
knees. Stroke down the shins, and
move around to his calves and ankles.
Gently squeeze all the way down.*

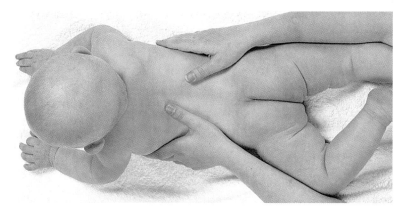

HOW WE
HANDLE GIRLS

According to research, we start preparing our girl babies from the day they are born to conform to a feminine sexual stereotype. When handling girls, we:

• Coo, whisper, and smile gently, and cradle them softly.

• Don't handle them excitingly, so they never know the sensation of flying through the air.

• Make bathtimes for girls much more sedate than for boys.

• Give them soft, cuddly toys and discourage them from rough, dirty, or dangerous play.

• Sympathize with slight injuries and make no attempts to stop them from crying, so they grow up thinking shows of helplessness and emotion are acceptable.

If you would like your daughter to grow up tough, independent, and self-assured, you should adjust your behavior and treat her more like a boy (see opposite page).

Holding and handling

By now you should be quite relaxed about carrying your baby. You will probably settle on a couple of favorite ways of carrying him, depending on whether he wants to be cuddled or to look at what is going on all around him. He is much heavier now, so make sure that you adopt a method of lifting him that won't strain your back.

PICKING UP AND CARRYING YOUR BABY

Your baby can now control his head, so there is no longer any need to support it as you did when he was newborn. Now you can pick him up simply by putting your hands under his armpits and lifting him forward toward you. This is also a very good way of putting him into a high chair: his legs will dangle and he can be slipped into the chair. Alternatively, you can lift him with one hand curled diagonally around his back, and the other supporting his bottom.

You can carry your baby in the crook of your arm, against your shoulder so that he faces you, or with your arm stretched diagonally across his back and holding his thigh as he sits astride one hip. A sling can be used, although for longer journeys a backpack will give you more support.

CARRYING POSITIONS

Facing forward
Hold your baby securely around the waist, so that she can look around her. You can use your other hand to support her, or keep it free.

On one hip
Your baby can now support herself well enough to sit astride your hip. This allows her to look all around.

Rocking
You can make this activity into a boisterous game by swinging your baby quite high, or just doing it gently to soothe her.

Bouncing
Lift your baby up and down on your knees rhythmically. You should always support her so that she doesn't slip backward.

SWINGING AND BOUNCING GAMES

All babies love to be bounced and swung, but just how much they enjoy it will depend on how they're feeling. Being swung up in the air is exciting for your baby, as he can look at his surroundings—and see your face—from a whole new perspective. Sometimes he'll prefer to be bounced on your knee or simply gently rocked. Always give your baby a chance to relax after boisterous games by cuddling him quietly for a few minutes.

Swinging
Raise your baby up high, then swoop her down between your legs. She will love looking down at your face from a height.

HOW WE HANDLE BOYS

Experiments have shown that we handle baby boys differently from baby girls, and that we persist in this stereotyping even if we are merely fooled by, say, their wearing pink or blue clothes. When handling boys, we:

• Speak, laugh, even shout out loudly, and grasp them firmly.

• Swing them around so that they get used to lots of action and physical movement.

• Encourage them to splash and kick in the bathtub.

• Give them tough, hard toys and praise adventurousness, even naughtiness, with encouraging words or phrases.

• Act efficient rather than tender when a boy grazes his knee, discouraging shows of emotion and applauding independence.

If you want your son to be more in touch with his gentler side, adjust your behavior so you treat him more like a girl (see opposite page).

LIFTING YOUR TODDLER

Make sure you know how to handle heavy weights in a way that won't strain your back.

Once you have a baby, there are many opportunities for putting a strain on your back. Your child requires constant lifting and carrying, and carriages, strollers, and other equipment must be handled. It's important that you learn to lift without injury and strain. Keep your back straight, bend your knees, and, using the powerful thigh muscles to do all the work, lift. Never lift with your legs straight and your back curved forward.

Safe lifting
Even young children can be surprisingly heavy. Always kneel down to pick up your toddler so you don't strain your back.

Holding and handling

Never refuse your toddler a hug; although she will need less holding than when she was a young baby, she will often ask to be carried like she used to when she's generally tired and cranky. She's likely to be clingy when she feels pain or discomfort, when a tooth is coming through, or if she is feeling under the weather. Always respond to her signals and don't hesitate to give her a hug for comfort and affection. Your child will make it clear when she has had enough reassurance and will get down and run off. Babies who are given love and cuddles when they need and ask for them usually grow into independent and self-confident individuals.

The desire for physical affection remains with us always. Parents should never scoff at their children's needs, and always respond. When my children were growing up, they liked a cuddle every now and then, especially when they were tired, if they had been scolded by a teacher at school, if they were fearful about my departure or absence, or if the world simply didn't feel right.

"CLINGY" CHILDREN

Older children will still occasionally want to sit on your lap. When they feel ill at ease in strange circumstances, they may even want to eat sitting on your knee, particularly if strangers are present and they feel that they are being watched. Let them do so if it's convenient; you will find that just a few moments of intimacy will give your child the confidence to handle any situation.

Bedtimes are particularly important times for showing affection. In my opinion, a child should never have to go to bed without some cuddling. A cuddle will provide a sense of security and the conviction that you really do care. The rule is that you should always be there with a comforting arm and a kind word when your child is hurt, worried, puzzled, or frightened.

THE UNRESPONSIVE CHILD

From a very early age, some children stiffen their bodies and cry when you hold them and usually grow up to be children who avoid physical contact—who turn away if you try to kiss them, for example, and make no physical advances themselves. Such children may never enjoy physical affection comfortably, and a parent may find this hard to cope with because it seems like rejection. If your child behaves in this way, don't insist on cuddles that she clearly doesn't want. Give your physical affection only when she shows you that she wants it.

SHOWING AFFECTION

By the age of three or four years, your child will be much more independent, and you may assume that she needs fewer overt displays of affection. While this may be true, it would be a mistake to think that she wants to go without any physical affection at all. You should pay special attention to boys, who are often expected to give up cuddles and kisses at a very young age because it's not considered to be "masculine" behavior.

It is all too easy to lose the habit of showing affection, so hold and touch your child as often as you can every day, whether it's letting her sit on your knee or putting an arm around her while you read the paper, or giving her a cuddle when you put her to bed. I made it a rule to tell my children every day that I loved them.

Older children often become self-conscious about being kissed or cuddled in public, so be sensitive to this. Choose private moments when they can enjoy your care, attention, and love.

DIVIDING YOUR ATTENTION

It can be difficult to divide your time and attention evenly between several young children. A friend of mine, who had twins, adopted a pragmatic approach to this problem: rather than trying to give each twin an equal share of her attention at all times, she decided to attend to whichever twin needed her at any one time, and assumed that it would even out over the years. Her example is a good one to follow; for much of the time you will give your children equal attention, so if one of them demands more, you should feel free to give it.

COMFORT AND ENCOURAGEMENT

With any luck, your child won't be averse to a cuddle even after she's reached adulthood, but cuddles do change and get more grown-up, and you have to give the kind of cuddles your child needs rather than the ones you want to give. So adapt your style of cuddling to what gives her most comfort.

Preschool children need plenty of cuddles every day, especially congratulatory ones, as when they've mastered something like getting their shoes on the right feet. Comfort cuddles are essential at the first sign of tears. A child responds much better to a cuddle than a reprimand. Therapeutic cuddles reduce the pain of a bump, a scrape, or a cut (even a big one) in seconds. Never let your child go to sleep without a huge hug and an "I love you."

As your child gets older, cuddles are transformed into other actions, but they have the same bolstering, encouraging effect. A hand on the shoulder, a small caress, or just taking your child's hand is a sign of love and her confidence will soar. Your child craves your love and approval; never leave her in any doubt that she has both in full measure.

As a parent, you have a responsibility to give your child the will and ability to form loving, open relationships with others as she grows up.

Babies are born into the world able to both give and receive love from the outset. We must both answer their demands for love and affection and respond to their need for it.

Giving comfort
Many of your child's troubles can be solved with a hug and a few sympathetic words from you.

GIRLS' CLOTHES

Unisex stretch suits and rompers are ideal for everyday wear, but you may prefer more feminine clothes for special occasions.

• Make sure all clothes are machine-washable—they won't stay clean for long.

• Avoid very fluffy or lacy sweaters. Fluffy ones will irritate your baby's skin, and tiny fingers catch in lacy ones.

• Hats can be both practical and pretty. Choose one with ties or elastic and a wide brim for sun protection or for warmth in winter.

Dressing

Everyone loves dressing a baby, and your friends and family will all want to buy clothes for your baby as soon as he is born. You are bound to take great pride in his appearance, and might like to buy some dressy clothes for special occasions, but there's no need to spend a lot of money—he will grow out of clothes very quickly. Remember that as far as your baby is concerned, anything goes as long as it's soft and comfortable to wear, and can be put on and taken off without too much disturbance.

Your baby will dribble and spit up on his clothes, and there are bound to be accidents and leaks from diapers, so buy only machine-washable, colorfast clothing, and avoid white—it quickly gets dirty, and frequent washing makes it drab. Look for soft and comfortable clothes with no hard seams or rough stitching. Terry cloth, cotton, or pure wool clothes will feel nicer on your baby's skin. If you buy clothes made of synthetic fibers, make sure they feel soft.

Always choose clothes that are flame-retardant, and avoid open-weave shawls and sweaters, because your baby's fingers could easily get caught in the holes. Check the fastenings, too: snaps in the crotch allow easy access to the diaper area, and snaps at the neck mean your

All babies will feel snug and comfy in a one-piece suit

Loose-fitting shoes with soft soles allow movement

Dressing up
For special occasions, your little girl will look very pretty in a frilly dress, sweater, and hat.

Choosing clothes
Easy-fitting clothes will give your baby the most comfort and warmth. Pay special attention to the cuffs, ankles, and neck, where fastenings could cause discomfort.

Basic layette

- 6 wide-necked cotton T-shirts or sleeveless vests

- 1 hat

- 1 shawl for swaddling

- 8 stretch suits

- 2 woolen jackets or sweaters (4 in winter)

- 2 nightgowns with drawstring ends

- 2 pairs of socks and booties

- 2 pairs of mittens (for winter)

- 1 padded or fleecy one-piece suit

baby won't grow out of something quickly just because her head is too big for the neck opening. Babies hate having their faces covered, so look for wide envelope necks or clothes that fasten down the front. Front-fastening clothes also allow you to dress your baby without having to turn him over. This will make dressing more comfortable for him and easier for you.

Make a note of your baby's measurements and bring this with you when you're shopping. Babies of the same age vary a great deal in size, so look at the height and weight given on the label rather than the age. If in doubt, buy the larger size: loose-fitting clothes are warmer and more comfortable than clothes that are too small, and your baby will soon grow into them.

Loose-fitting cuffs give your baby plenty of room to move

An envelope neck allows you to take the nightgown off more easily

A drawstring keeps your baby's feet inside and allows for easy diaper-changing

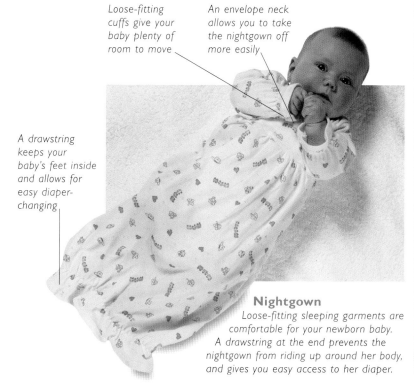

Nightgown
Loose-fitting sleeping garments are comfortable for your newborn baby. A drawstring at the end prevents the nightgown from riding up around her body, and gives you easy access to her diaper.

BOYS' CLOTHES

Look for clothes that are practical as well as attractive to dress your baby boy.

- Strong primary colors look good on both sexes.

- A jeans-and-T-shirt set is comfortable and looks good. Look for pants with snaps at the crotch so that you can get at your baby's diaper easily.

- Hats with tie-down ear flaps are cozy in winter.

- Don't think tights are just for girls; babies lose socks and booties very easily, so tights are practical as well as warm.

- Jogging suits are very comfortable and allow easy access to the diaper.

Everyday wear
Overalls with snap fastenings are ideal for your little boy. Match them with soft footwear.

KEEPING YOUR BABY WARM

You may worry that your new baby isn't warm enough, but a few commonsense precautions will keep her comfortable and safe. Remember that babies can easily become too hot; this could lead to heat rash, and is also a factor in crib death.

• A great deal of body heat is lost through a bare head; make sure your baby always wears a hat when you take her outdoors.

• Very young babies are unable to conserve body heat, and should be undressed only in a well-heated room and out of drafts.

• Your baby's room should be at a constant temperature, and the number of blankets she needs will depend on this temperature (see p.123).

• If your baby is cold, you may need to warm her up. Adding a layer of clothes is not enough in itself; you need to put her in a warmer place first so that she can regain her normal body temperature, or hold her close to share your body heat.

• Never leave your baby to sleep in the sun, or close to a source of direct heat such as a heat register.

• Wrap your baby up if you take her outdoors, but remove outdoor clothes once you bring her inside again, otherwise she won't be able to cool down efficiently.

DRESSING YOUR BABY

At first you may be nervous about dressing your baby and trying to support her while manipulating the garments. Dressing will become easier with practice, so just be gentle and patient.

You should always dress and undress a young baby on a nonslip, flat surface, as this allows you to keep both hands free—a changing mat is ideal. Your baby is very likely to cry as you take off her clothes. This is because young babies hate the feel of the air on their naked bodies; they like to feel snug and secure. It's not because you're hurting her, so don't get flustered by it.

DRESSING

Put T-shirt over head
Lay your baby on a flat, nonslip surface and make sure her diaper is clean. Roll the T-shirt up and pull the neck apart with your thumbs. Put it over your baby's head so that it doesn't touch her face, raising her head slightly as you do so.

Armholes
Widen the left sleeve or armhole and gently guide your baby's arm through it. Repeat with the other arm. Pull the shirt down.

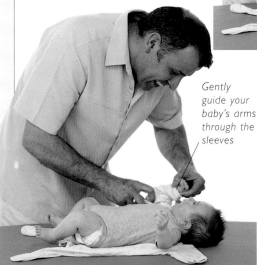

Gently guide your baby's arms through the sleeves

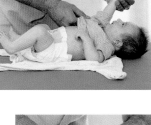

Put on stretch suit
Lay your baby on top of the open suit. Gather up each sleeve and guide her fists through. Open up each leg and guide her feet into the stretch suit. Fasten the suit.

UNDRESSING

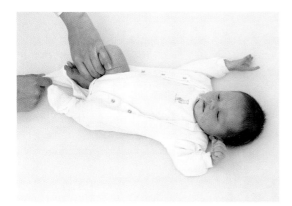

Undoing the suit
Put your baby on a flat surface and unfasten the suit. If his diaper needs changing, gently pull both legs out of the suit so that his top remains covered while you change him.

DRESSING ON YOUR LAP

When your baby is three or four months old, she will have enough muscle control to sit on your lap while you take off her clothes.

Sit with your legs crossed so that your baby will fit neatly in the hollow of your legs and cradle her with your arm, since her back will still need some support. You may find it easier to deal with the bottom half while she's lying flat.

Removing the top
Grasp each sleeve by the cuff and gently slide your baby's hand out. If he's wearing a T-shirt, roll it up toward the neck and gently pull his arms from the sleeves, holding him by each elbow as you do so.

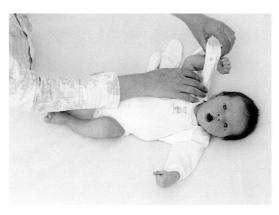

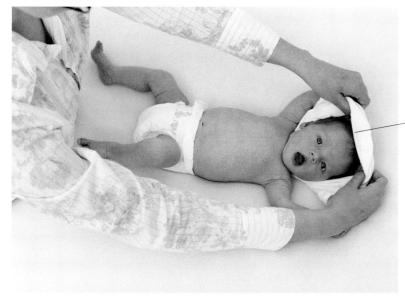

Stretch the neck of the shirt as wide as you can

Taking off his T-shirt
Pull the neck wide open and lift the shirt over your baby's head, keeping the fabric off his face.

Dressing

OUTDOOR CLOTHES FOR GIRLS

Your little girl is more active now, so she won't always be bundled up in her one-piece suit when she's outdoors. Look for outdoor clothes that are comfortable and won't restrict her movements.

• Thick tights are warm and comfortable, and can be bought in colors and patterns to match your daughter's dress.

• In very cold weather, a short cape over your little girl's coat will keep her extra-warm.

• Gloves can be clipped to sleeves or joined with a ribbon or elastic band and slipped through the sleeves.

• Sun hats are not just pretty; they are essential if your child spends any length of time in bright sunshine.

Once your baby has learned to crawl, he'll be far less willing to sit or lie still while you dress him. On the other hand, he is now better able to help you as you put on his clothes. For example, an 11-month-old baby can make a fist or stretch out an arm, if you ask him to, or hold his arm still while you pull his sleeve into place. If he's very restless, you can sing a song to him or distract him with a toy, or involve him in the whole process by naming each item of clothing as you put it on or take it off, and getting him to repeat the names after you, for example. You could also turn dressing into a peek-a-boo game: "Where's your foot? Oh, look, here it is!"

If it's difficult to get your baby to keep still here are some tips:

• Stand him between your legs so that he's immobilized while you pull up his pants.
• Sit him in his high chair so that you can put on his shoes.
• You can make a game out of his putting on his shoes by placing them at the bottom of the stairs and getting him to step down into them carefully while you steady him.

CHOOSING CLOTHES

Now that your baby is more active, you will need to look for clothes that allow easy movement. He will be awake for longer, and moving around, so his clothes are more likely to get dirty and you'll therefore need more of them. You'll also have to consider whether they are tough enough for the wear and tear that your child will give them: look for sturdy fabrics that last well, and strong fastenings that won't break or fall off. When you're buying clothes, check the label to see what kind of material they are made from. Natural fibers are both strong and comfortable, so look for pure cotton or a fabric with a high cotton content. Terry, denim, and corduroy are all strong and hard wearing. Look, too, for clothes that can be easily pulled down or up once your child is learning how to use the potty, and avoid zippers or tricky fastenings; elasticated waists are by far the easiest for him to manage.

Until he's walking, socks or woollen booties are all your baby needs, even when he's crawling. Fabric booties with elasticated ankles stay on better. Make sure there's plenty of room for movement; the bones in your baby's feet are so soft and pliable that even tightly fitting socks could deform the toes if worn regularly.

Choosing clothes
Ensure that knees are protected if your baby is crawling.

CHOOSING SHOES

Once your baby begins to walk, he'll need shoes. When you are buying your child shoes, always go to a reputable store where the staff have been trained to measure and fit children's shoes. The store clerk should measure the length and the width of your child's foot before trying any shoes. Once your child tries on a pair of shoes, the clerk should press the joints of the foot to make sure that it is not restricted in any way, and that the fastenings hold the shoe firmly in place and don't let your child's foot slip around. Make sure your child stands up and walks in the shoes to check that the toe doesn't pinch and hurt when he's walking, and to double-check that there's no slipping.

A sturdy, well-made pair of leather shoes is most suitable for general outdoor wear, especially once your child is running around and playing. You should, however, get a pair of rubber rain boots for wet or muddy conditions. Although leather shoes and sandals are solid and sensible and last well, there is nothing wrong with inexpensive canvas shoes or sneakers as long as you make sure that they fit properly. If your child suddenly becomes less steady on his feet, it may be a sign that he is outgrowing his shoes. Well-fitting shoes are essential to ensure that your child has good feet in adult life. You should never try to save money by buying secondhand shoes; they will have molded themselves to the previous owner's feet.

OUTDOOR CLOTHES FOR BOYS

Choose clothes that leave your little boy room for growth and allow him to move freely.

• Always put a hat on your little boy if he's out in the sun. Baseball caps worn backward protect the nape of the neck.

• Buy outdoor clothes on the large side. This leaves room for extra layers underneath, and allows your little boy to grow into them.

• Cut the sleeves off an outgrown jacket to make a vest.

Shoes for healthy feet
Choose a sturdy leather pair for outdoor wear. Your child's feet must be unrestricted but held firmly in place and unable to slip out. The toes shouldn't curl up or hurt when he walks. Never buy secondhand shoes.

There should be space between your child's big toe and the end of the shoe: at least ¼ inch (0.5 centimeters), but no more than ½ inch (1.25 centimeters)

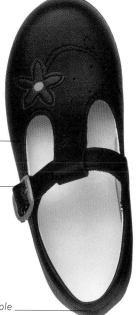

Wide toes allow your child's toes to fan out. Make sure the box on the toe is high enough so that it doesn't put pressure on the toenails

Surfaces should be easy to clean or polish

Adjustable fastenings hold the foot firmly in the shoe. Buckles and Velcro are easier for young children to manage than laces

The heel should be no higher than 1½ inches (4 centimeters) from the sole

The sole should be light and flexible, with a nonslip surface

Getting dressed

Your little girl will try to dress herself now, so choose clothes that she can manage easily. She's growing fast, too, so don't spend a lot of money on clothes that she'll quickly outgrow.

• Buy dresses with fastenings at the front; ones that fasten at the back are too difficult for your little girl to manage.

• Show her how to get her tights the right way around, and how to roll them up before she tries to put them on.

• Avoid very tailored clothes; they don't leave much room for growth.

As your child grows older, she'll develop the coordination required to dress successfully. You should encourage her in her attempts at dressing or undressing, however slow or awkward—they're a sign of growing independence and maturity. Learning to manage by herself will improve a child's coordination and increase her confidence, so be patient with her first clumsy efforts.

Lay out your child's clothes in such a way that she can put them on easily. For instance, you could drape a cardigan sweater on the back of a chair so that she just has to sit down and slide her arms into the sleeves. Let her do as much as she is capable of, and don't step in to help unless it's really necessary, though you'll have to deal with most of the fastenings yourself until your child is old enough to manage them.

At 18 months she will be trying to manage fastenings, and by two-and-a-half she will be able to close a button in a loose buttonhole, and put on her own underpants, T-shirt, and sweatshirt. By the age of four she will probably be able to dress or undress herself completely and will have enough dexterity to put her clothes away neatly. There are several things you can do to make getting dressed easier for your child.

• Teach her how to button from the bottom upward.
• Sew large buttons on to a toddler's clothes so that she can handle them easily.
• Velcro fastenings will be easy for her to manage, but don't use them where they might chafe her skin.

Room for growth
Loose-fitting clothes with adjustable fastenings are suitable now that your child is growing fast.

Dressing himself
By the age of three, your toddler may be able to dress himself completely, though it will take him quite a long time. Allow him his independence, and don't step in to help unless you're really needed.

Jumpers or overalls with ties or buckles can be adjusted to fit your child as she grows

Little hands can grasp a zipper more easily if it has a ring attached to the tab

- Buy pants with elasticated waists to avoid zippers.
- Children find it difficult to put sweaters on the right way around, so explain that the label always goes at the back.

Choosing clothes As your child becomes more involved in dressing herself, she will become more conscious of the clothes themselves. Babies are largely unaware of what they are wearing as long as it is comfortable and doesn't impede their activities, but toddlers gradually begin to notice the colors and type of clothing they put on, and your child may develop preferences. Clothes that seem similar to those worn by Mommy or Daddy might seem especially attractive. The feel of a garment will also be important to her—whether, for example, it is soft or itchy, tight or stretchy. If she takes a dislike to a garment, it may be because it doesn't fit properly and is therefore uncomfortable to wear.

Your child's concerns should be taken seriously when you are buying her clothing. Once your main requirements, which are practical ones—warmth, durability, washability, and cost—are met, there is no reason why you shouldn't indulge her; the image of a favorite cartoon character or a particular color may be the deciding factor as far as she is concerned. Allowing her to choose which clothes to wear each day is also important. You may want her to wear pants on a cold day, but let her choose which pair.

She may develop seemingly irrational likes or dislikes for certain items of clothing—insisting on wearing a particular T-shirt every day, for example, or refusing to wear the sweater that Grandma gave her for her birthday. The easiest policy is to go along with these preferences as far as possible, though occasionally bribery, or at least negotiation, may be in order: you could offer a special treat in return for wearing that pullover on the afternoon that Grandma comes over for dinner.

DRESSING A BOY

Help your little boy to dress himself by making sure his clothes don't have tricky fastenings.

- Boys are usually slower than girls at learning to use the potty, so it is particularly important to avoid awkward fastenings on your little boy's pants.

- Look for adjustable straps on overalls, or add a button so the straps can be lengthened.

- Pants with elasticated waists are easiest, but, if he has pants with zippers, show him how to pull the zipper away from him as he closes it to prevent it from catching.

- Show your little boy how to sit down to put his feet into his pant legs, then stand up to pull them up.

Choosing fastenings
Until your child has enough dexterity to manage buttons and zippers, you need to choose clothes and shoes with manageable fastenings.

Sliding buckles can be adjusted for the best fit

Hooks are easier to manage than buttons

Let him fasten his own shoes if he can

Shoes
Velcro fastenings rather than laces or buckles will allow your child to fasten his own shoes very easily.

WASHING A GIRL

There is no need to open the lips of your baby girl's vulva to clean inside, and you should never try to do so. Just wash the skin of the diaper area and dry it carefully.

When you are washing your baby girl, take care to wipe from front to back—that is, toward the anus—when you clean the diaper area. This will avoid soiling the vulva, and minimize the risk of spreading bacteria from the bowels to the bladder or vagina, which could cause infection.

Bathing and hygiene

Part of your daily routine will be to keep your baby clean. Many new parents worry about handling a very small baby in the baby bath, but you will soon get used to bathtime and look forward to it as an opportunity to have fun and play with your baby. Instead of feeling apprehensive, set aside half an hour, have everything you need around you, try to relax, and you will enjoy it.

A young baby doesn't need bathing very often because only his bottom, face and neck, and skin creases get dirty, so you only have to bathe him every two or three days, and even then you can "top and tail" him instead of putting him in the bath (see below). This allows you to wash the parts of your baby that really need washing with the minimum of disturbance and distress to him. Use clean, cool water for a newborn, but when your baby is a little older you can use warm water straight from the faucet. Do wash your baby's hair frequently to prevent cradle cap from forming (see p.93). There is no need to use soap on a newborn; from about six weeks, you can use bath lotion, soap, or other baby toiletries.

Many young babies don't like having their skin exposed to the air, so you should keep your baby undressed for as short a time as possible at bathtime. Warm a big, fluffy towel on a heat register (not too hot)

TOPPING AND TAILING

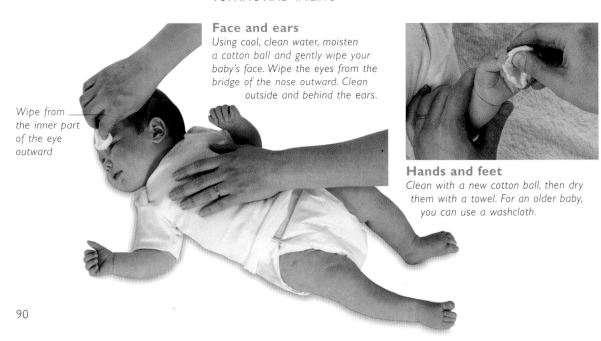

Face and ears
Using cool, clean water, moisten a cotton ball and gently wipe your baby's face. Wipe the eyes from the bridge of the nose outward. Clean outside and behind the ears.

Wipe from the inner part of the eye outward

Hands and feet
Clean with a new cotton ball, then dry them with a towel. For an older baby, you can use a washcloth.

while you are bathing him and have it ready to wrap your baby in as soon as you are finished.

BODY CARE

Once you have taken care of your baby's diaper area, and made sure that his skin is kept free from any traces of food or dirt that might cause irritation, the rest will take care of itself.

Eyes, nose, and ears Wash your baby's eyes with cotton balls and some cool, clean water. Work from the inner part of the eye to the outer, and use a different cotton ball for each eye to avoid spreading any infection that may be present.

Don't poke around inside your baby's nose and ears; they are self-cleaning, so don't use nose or ear drops, except on your doctor's advice. Just clean ears using moist cotton balls. If you see wax in your baby's ears, don't try to scrape it out; it is a natural secretion of the canal of the outer ear, is antiseptic, and protects the eardrum from dust and grit. Removing it will only cause the ear to produce more. If you are concerned, consult your doctor.

Nails Your newborn baby's nails should be kept short; otherwise, he may scratch his skin. The best time to cut them is after a bath, when they are soft; use a pair of small, blunt-ended scissors.

Navel During the few days after birth, the umbilical stump (see p.15) dries and shrivels, and then drops off. You can bathe your baby before the stump has healed, as long as you dry it thoroughly afterward. Allow the area to stay open to the air as much as possible to help speed up the shrinking and healing process.

WASHING A BOY

Never pull your baby boy's foreskin back for cleaning; it's quite tight and could get stuck. Wash the whole diaper area and dry carefully, particularly the skin creases. By the time your son is three or four years of age, the foreskin will be loose and can retract without force.

If your baby has just been circumcised, you should watch carefully for any signs of bleeding. A few drops of blood is quite normal; so is swelling and slight inflammation, but this will settle down. If bleeding persists, however, or if there is any sign of infection, consult your doctor. Make sure that you get advice about bathing your baby and special care of the penis, and what to do about the dressing if one has been applied.

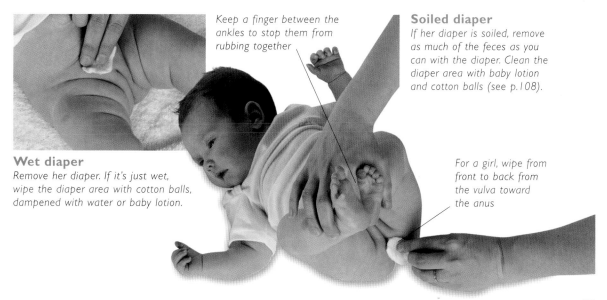

Keep a finger between the ankles to stop them from rubbing together

Soiled diaper
If her diaper is soiled, remove as much of the feces as you can with the diaper. Clean the diaper area with baby lotion and cotton balls (see p.108).

Wet diaper
Remove her diaper. If it's just wet, wipe the diaper area with cotton balls, dampened with water or baby lotion.

For a girl, wipe from front to back from the vulva toward the anus

TOILETRIES

A newborn's skin is delicate. You should not use soap or wipes until your baby is at least six weeks old, as it will remove the natural oils from her skin and leave it dry and uncomfortable. Special baby toiletries are mild and won't irritate your baby's skin— many are hypoallergenic.

• A little baby oil in your baby's bath water is a good moisturizer for very dry skin.

• For delicate skin, like the diaper area, baby lotion is an ideal cleanser and moisturizer.

• Baby powder can be drying to your baby's skin. If you use it, shake it on to your hand first, or it may be inhaled by your baby. Never use powder on the skin creases, where it can cake and cause irritation.

• Zinc and castor oil cream or petroleum jelly are waterproof and will protect your baby's skin from urine. Medicated diaper creams containing titanium salts are good if your baby has diaper rash (see p.111).

GIVING A SPONGE BATH

If your baby really hates being undressed, or if you are a bit daunted by giving her a bath, give her a sponge bath. Hold your baby securely on your lap while removing only the minimum amount of clothing at any time. If you find it difficult to maneuver your baby while she is on your lap, put her on a changing mat and follow the same sponge bath method, keeping one half covered while you wash the other half.

SPONGE BATH

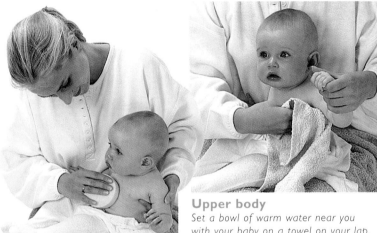

Upper body
Set a bowl of warm water near you with your baby on a towel on your lap. Undress his top half and wash his front with a sponge or cloth. Pat him dry. Lean him forward over your arm and wash his back.

Diaper area
Either wash your baby's hair at this stage, or put some clean clothes on his top half and remove his lower clothing and diaper. Clean the diaper area (see p.108).

Use cotton wool and baby lotion to clean your baby's diaper area

Lower body
Using the sponge or cloth, wash your baby's legs and feet. Gently pat his skin dry, put on barrier cream (if you use it) and a clean diaper, and dress him.

CARE OF THE HAIR

From birth, you should wash your baby's hair every day, though not necessarily with shampoo—bath lotion dissolved in water will do. After about 12 to 16 weeks, wash her hair with water daily and once or twice a week with baby shampoo. Use a no-sting variety of baby shampoo, but still take care to avoid her eyes. You can use a "football carry" (see picture, right) for a small baby, or you can sit on the edge of the tub with your baby across your legs, facing you. (She will feel secure this way.) Don't be nervous about the fontanelles (see p.14); the membrane that covers them is very tough, and there's no need to scrub the hair, so you can do no harm as long as you're gentle.

Hair washing
Tuck the legs under your armpit. Support the back and cradle the head.

Apply the shampoo or bath lotion to your baby's hair, and gradually work it in until a lather forms. Wait about 15 seconds before rinsing it off: there is no need to apply it a second time. To rinse the hair, just use a washcloth dipped in warm water to wipe the suds away. Try to remove every trace of soap. When drying your baby's hair, try not to cover her face or she may panic and start to cry.

DISLIKE OF HAIR-WASHING

Many babies hate having their hair washed, even if they enjoy taking a bath. If this is the case with your baby, it may be best to keep hair washing separate from bath time; if your child associates the two, she may start to make a fuss about taking baths, too.

The main reason for dislike of hair-washing is that babies hate water and soap in their eyes. Shields are available that fit around the hairline and prevent water and suds from running down your baby's face. She'll be less distressed if you hold her in your lap while hair-washing, and use a washcloth to wet and rinse it rather than pouring water on her head.

Never try to force the issue, and never forcibly hold your baby still while you wash her hair. If hair-washing is very distressing for her, give up for two or three weeks before trying again. You can still keep her hair reasonably clean by sponging it to remove any dirt, or brushing it out with a soft, damp brush. The hair will probably become greasy, but this won't do any harm.

CRADLE CAP

Occasionally, red, scaly patches may appear on your baby's scalp. Cradle cap is extremely common, and is not caused by a lack of hygiene, or by any shampoo you're using. It usually disappears after a few weeks.

Prevent cradle cap from forming by gently washing your newborn baby's scalp every day with a very soft bristle brush and a little baby shampoo dissolved in warm water. You should comb through the hair, even if she has very little, to stop scales from forming. If cradle cap does appear, smear a little olive oil on her scalp at night to soften and loosen the scales, making them easy to wash away the following morning. Don't be tempted to pick them off with your fingernail—that will only encourage more scales to form. If the condition persists or spreads, consult your doctor or pharmacist, who may recommend using a special shampoo.

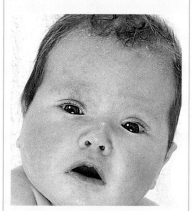

Cradle cap
Scaly patches on a baby's scalp are very common. They are harmless, and usually clear up after a few weeks without any need for special treatment.

BATHING TIPS

Make bathtimes as pleasant as possible for you and your baby.

• Before you start, make sure that you have everything that you need close at hand.

• Always put cold water in first. Test the final temperature with your elbow or the inner side of your wrist.

• Keep the bath water shallow. About 2–3 inches (5–8 centimeters) is deep enough.

• Keep the time that your baby is undressed to a minimum; small babies quickly become cold.

• Wear a waterproof apron to protect your clothing; a plastic-backed toweling one will feel nice against your baby's skin.

• Warm a towel for your baby on a register, but don't let it get too hot.

• Baby bath lotion added to the bath water is better than soap, since it strips less oil from the skin.

GIVING A BATH

You can bathe your baby in any room that is warm, has no drafts, and has enough space to lay out all that you need. If necessary, you can fill the baby's bath in the kitchen or bathroom and then carry it to the chosen room, provided it's not too heavy.

A small baby can be washed in a specially designed plastic baby bath with a nonslip surface. Place the bath on a counter or table of a convenient height, usually about hip height, so that you don't have to bend too much. This will protect your back from unnecessary strain. Some baby baths come with their own stands, or are designed to straddle the bathtub, which makes bathing your baby a far more comfortable task.

GIVING YOUR BABY A BATH

Testing the water
Use your elbow or the inner side of your wrist to test the temperature of the water. It should feel neither very hot nor very cold. Until you get the feel of the right temperature, you could use a bath thermometer, which should register 85°F (29°C).

Before the bath
Undress your baby, clean her diaper area (see p.108) and wrap her in a towel. Clean her face and ears gently with moistened cotton balls (see p.90).

Washing her head
Holding your baby in a football carry, as shown, lean over the bath and wash her head. Rinse well and pat dry. A gentle brushing is good for cradle cap.

Putting her in the bath
Support your baby's shoulders with one hand, tucking your fingers under her armpit, and support her legs or bottom with the other. Keep smiling and talking to her as you place her in the bath.

Washing
Keep one hand underneath your baby's shoulders so that her head and shoulders are kept out of the water, and use your free hand to wash her.

FEAR OF BATHING

Some babies are terrified of taking a bath. Should your baby be frightened, don't force him to remain in the water; try again after a couple of days, using only a little water in the bath. You can give sponge baths or "top and tail" him in the meantime.

If your baby continues to be frightened of water, try to introduce it in a play context. Fill a large bowl and place it in a warm room (not the bathroom). Place a towel next to it, and put some toys into the bowl. Undress your baby and encourage him to play with the toys. If he seems happy doing this, encourage him to paddle in the water, keeping a firm grip on him.

After you have done this a couple of times, exchange the bowl for a baby bath and continue to let your baby play. When he tries to get into the water with the toys, you'll know he's lost his fear of water, but be patient; let him do this a couple of times before you wash him in the bath as well as letting him play.

Lifting her out
When she is clean and well rinsed, lift her gently onto the towel, supporting her as before.

Drying
Wrap your baby in a towel and dry her thoroughly. Don't use talcum powder on the diaper area; it could gather in the skin creases and cause irritation.

Be very careful when bathing your child—there are several points to remember.

• Place a nonslip bath mat in the bottom of the bathtub.

• Always check the temperature of the water before putting your baby in the tub. Even older babies need the bathwater to be considerably cooler than most adults.

• Turn the faucets off tightly before putting your baby in the bathtub.

• Cover the faucets with a washcloth so that your baby doesn't scald or hurt herself on the metal.

• Don't let your baby stand or jump in the water unsupported. A fall, even if she isn't injured, could put her off future bathing.

• If your child likes toys in the tub, choose light plastic ones with no sharp edges.

• Don't drain the water while your baby is still in the bathtub. Many babies find the noise and the sensation of the water disappearing rather frightening.

• When you lift your baby out of the bathtub, make sure that you are standing steadily. Take the strain with your legs, not your back.

• Make sure you dry your baby well after a bath. Giving her a cuddle wrapped in a warm towel can provide a comforting end to bathtime, even for older children.

Bathing and hygiene

Between three and six months old, your baby will grow too big for a baby bath, so you will have to start using the bathtub. To make the transition easier for your baby, first place the baby bath inside the bathtub so that she becomes used to this larger bath. Once she gets used to it, she will probably spend many happy hours there enjoying her favorite toys.

BATHTIME ROUTINE

Once your baby is mobile, she will get much dirtier than before and baths will become a regular feature of your day. Washing a baby is more awkward in the bathtub than in the baby bath. Spare your back by kneeling next to the tub, and make sure that you have everything that you need at hand. Keep the water shallow: no deeper than 4–5 inches (10–13 centimeters), and use a plastic suction mat on the bottom of the bath to prevent your baby from sliding around. Keep a close watch on her; it takes only a moment for a baby to slip under the water, so you should never leave her alone, or turn away from her.

By about six months your baby will feel quite secure in the water and will no longer be scared of being undressed. Try to make bath-

times fun and as trouble-free as possible.

FEAR OF THE BATHTUB
If your child finds the bathtub frightening, you'll have to be patient and let her get used to it gradually. You could try filling the baby bath with water and putting a few toys in; then place it inside the bathtub and put a nonslip bath mat next to it. Put your baby in the bathtub where she can play with the toys and

The "big bath"
Use a nonslip mat in the bathtub to prevent your baby from slipping or sliding about.

climb into the baby bath if she likes. Once she has gotten used to this, you could also add a few inches of water to the bathtub. Your child can then climb in and out of the baby bath and get used to sitting in the shallow water in the bathtub. You can gradually increase the amount of water that you put in the bathtub; after a while, you will probably find that your child doesn't notice whether the baby bath is there or not. If you feel she still needs reassurance, get into the bathtub with her and play water games with her on your lap.

BATHTIME PLAY

Once your baby is able to sit up, you can give her some extra time in the bathtub after she's been washed, and let her enjoy splashing and playing with toys. You don't have to provide special toys; sponges, bowls, and mugs will keep her entertained. If you have two small children, you could try bathing them together. It will save time for you, and your older child will be able to share games with the baby. Suds are always a great favorite, so you could add lots of bubble bath to the water (but be careful—bubble bath can irritate the vulval area in little girls). Every now and then, get into the bathtub with your baby and have fun together.

BATH TOYS

Your baby will get a great deal of fun out of playing with everyday household objects. Make sure that any bath toys you use are clean and waterproof, without sharp edges, and reasonably light. If you give your baby plastic bottles—for example, old shampoo bottles—make sure that they have been thoroughly washed to remove all traces of their previous contents and remove the lids; your baby will put all these "toys" into her mouth.

Many toys, particularly those made of hard plastic, such as rattles and cups, are also suitable for the bathtub. If you want to buy special bath toys, there are lots to choose from. The traditional boats and ducks are always great favorites, but you can also get waterproof books for the older baby, or activity centers that work when water is poured through them.

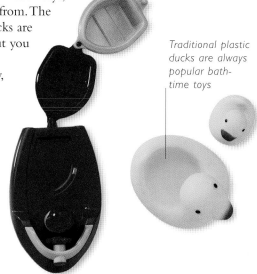

Traditional plastic ducks are always popular bath-time toys

Bathtime play
Simple floating toys will give your baby added enjoyment at bathtime.

EARLY DENTAL CARE

As early as possible, encourage your baby to form good habits with a tooth-brushing game.

Let your baby see you brush your teeth so that she can see how it should be done, then offer her a soft toothbrush to play with. She will try to imitate you by putting the brush in her mouth and moving it around. You don't need to check if she's doing it properly; at this stage, it's a game to introduce her to the idea of tooth-brushing as something she likes. When you really want to brush her teeth, wet a handkerchief and smear on a pea-sized helping of toothpaste, then gently rub it across the gums and any teeth that your baby has. You should clean the gums even if there are no teeth; it gets rid of the bacteria that cause plaque, and provides a good environment for milk teeth to grow into.

Take care

However happy and secure your baby may seem playing with her toys, no baby of this age should be left in the tub unwatched, even for the shortest period of time. Check that the water is not getting too cold; your baby may be distracted from her discomfort by play. Keep your water heater set lower than 129°F (54°C) and never add hot water while your baby's in the tub.

Bathing and hygiene

BATHROOM SAFETY

Baths should be carefully supervised, since a child of this age is still at risk from slipping and falling under the water. Although your child is now old enough to support himself in the bathtub, much of what has already been said about safety still applies (see p.96).

Toddlers are generally eager to do things for themselves—washing their own face, for example—so there is the added risk that your child may turn on the hot faucet or grab the soap or shampoo and get it in his eyes. Covering the taps with a towel is a good way to soften any falls or bumps.

A child who has previously been happy in the bathtub may take against it, especially if he has a frightening experience while bathing. Providing plenty of amusements in the bathtub, and perhaps getting him to take his bath with a sibling, can help reduce this problem. Allowing him to take a bath with you will resolve most difficulties.

Bathtime is playtime for a toddler, and you can make a game of teaching him to wash himself. Give him his own sponge and show him how to wash his face, then his arms and legs, and so on. He won't be able to make a very good job of it, so you'll probably have to go over the same areas yourself with a facecloth. Soap his hands and show him how to spread the soap over his body and arms; then have fun rinsing all the suds off.

WASHING ROUTINES
A child is often hungry when he wakes up, so it's best to leave washing until after breakfast, when your child will be more willing to stand still to have his face and hands washed, teeth brushed (see opposite), and hair combed. From the age of about 18 months, he can start learning to rinse his own hands under running water and, later on, he will learn to soap them, though he may make quite a mess with the soap and water at first.

CLEANLINESS
The younger you start teaching hygiene, the better, and the best way of teaching is by example. Wash your hands with your child: get your hands soapy together and wash each other's hands, then inspect each other's hands to see whose are the cleanest. If he finds the washcloth rough, let him use a sponge, which is softer.

Make it clear that hands should always be washed after using the toilet. You should start this at the potty stage (see p.114) and do it with your child every single time. Similarly, make sure your child washes his hands before meals or after handling pets.

Encourage your child to do this for himself. Make sure he can reach the sink and toilet easily by putting a step stool in the bathroom for him to use, and make sure that he knows which is the hot faucet and which the cold.

HAIR CARE
Your child will probably have a thick head of hair by now, and this will need regular washing to remove everyday grime. Unfortunately, there are few children who enjoy this process. You can make hair-washing as easy as possible for your child by using the following tips to help to reduce the potential for conflict.

• Keep your child's hair short; it will be easier to brush, too.
• If your child really hates hair-washing, try allowing him some control

over it: choosing whether he holds his head back for washing or forward, for example, or holding the sprayer and wetting his own hair.
• Use a "no-tears" baby shampoo and get a special halolike shield, which will keep the water and suds away from his eyes.
• You could also offer incentives to be good, such as the promise of a special game or story once hair-washing is successfully completed, or even get in the bathtub yourself and allow your child to "wash" your hair in return for your doing his.

TOOTH CARE

You will have been brushing your baby's teeth from the time that they first appeared (see p.97), and you should continue to do so at least twice a day. Always brush his teeth after the evening meal so that food particles are not left in the mouth overnight. As your baby gets older, he will probably want to hold the toothbrush and do it himself. While this should be encouraged, he will not be able to brush his own teeth effectively, and you should always follow up his efforts yourself with a thorough brushing.

Use a small, soft-bristled brush and, once your child is over three, a toothpaste containing fluoride. Nonfluorinated toothpaste is best for younger children. Use only a pea-sized amount of toothpaste, since too much fluoride while your child's teeth are growing can cause fluorosis (discoloration or mottling of the enamel). There are many "fun" flavors of toothpaste available that may give your child an incentive to brush his teeth. Never use a toothpaste containing sugar, though, so always check the ingredients before buying. Sit your child sideways on your knee, holding him securely with one arm, and gently brush the teeth up and down. If he won't keep his head still, try gently resting your free hand on his forehead.

The American Academy of Pediatric Dentistry recommends that a child has his first dental visit soon after his first tooth appears. To get your child used to the idea of going to the dentist take him with you when you go for a checkup. Most dentists are sympathetic to the need to remove any possibility of fear in young patients, and will probably be happy for your child to sit in the "magic" chair.

NAILS

Keep your child's fingernails and toenails cut short; it is more hygienic, and helps to prevent him from scratching himself or others accidentally. Long toenails may also make his shoes uncomfortable. You will probably still find it easiest to cut his nails when they are soft after a bath, and, since children's nails grow very quickly, it is a good idea to incorporate a nail-cutting session into your bathtime ritual once a week. Use blunt-ended scissors, specially designed to be safe for young children, or nail clippers. You will find it easier to restrain your wriggling child if you sit him on your lap. Follow the natural line of his fingernails and do not cut too close to the quick. Toenails should be cut straight across.

PETS AND HYGIENE

You may be concerned about the possible health risks to your toddler in having a pet. However, if you follow a few simple rules of hygiene, you should have no cause for concern, and the rewards to your child will be well worth the effort.

• Ringworm (see p.101) is a contagious skin condition, which can be caught from pets, and is commonly seen in children. If you suspect ringworm, consult your doctor right away.

• Always try to stop your child from kissing his pet, especially near its nose and mouth.

• Encourage your child to wash his hands after playing with his pet—especially before touching or eating food.

• Both fleas and worms are easily avoided by regular use of preventive treatments.

• If infestation occurs, treat it promptly and keep your child away from any pets until the treatment has been completed.

CLEANLINESS IN GIRLS

Most girls are naturally fastidious, and you can take advantage of this in teaching your child to keep herself clean.

• Encourage good habits in your little girl from an early age by showing her how to wash herself and brush her teeth.

• Let her brush her own hair; she will prefer it, and it means she can choose her own hairstyle, ribbons, barrettes, or hair band.

• Let her have her own special washcloth, soap dish, and towel; she'll be proud of her own things.

• Allow her to rub baby lotion into her skin after bathing.

• Teach her to change her underwear and socks daily.

• Provide her own laundry basket so that she can discard her own dirty clothes.

Bathing and hygiene

By the time a child has reached the age of three years, she will have developed her own views on many aspects of her day-to-day life and will want increasing control over her daily routine. This is often expressed negatively in a reluctance or even refusal to cooperate with mundane tasks, such as bathing and hair-brushing, which are often seen as unwelcome interruptions to more exciting forms of play. The best way to avoid arguments is to turn washing and brushing into a game, or incorporate a fun element into the task.

Allowing your child to take increasing responsibility for carrying out a task, supervised if necessary, or giving her some choice—choosing which comb or which shampoo to use, for example—can make it interesting and encourage cooperation. The following hints will make the daily routine easier and more enjoyable for both of you:

• Try not to rush your child to complete a task she is trying to manage by herself. It leads to tension, and may make her less willing to help next time.
• Don't leave bathtime until last thing before bedtime, or your child may be too tired to enjoy it.
• Encourage interest in tooth-brushing by using plaque-disclosing tablets once a week. The need to brush away the color is a great way to ensure that your child cleans her teeth really well.
• Make hair washing fun by letting your child see in a mirror all the silly hairstyles she can create from lathered hair.
• Offer the bribe of the use of some "special" grown-up toiletries, such as perfumed soap or bubble bath, in return for her cooperation at bath time—I believe in bribes for young children.

EXPLAINING ABOUT HYGIENE
By the age of three, your child is capable of understanding, reasoning, and comprehending why something is important. If you give her a reason why she shouldn't do something, rather than pulling rank, she's likely to desist, and you'll gain her cooperation more readily if you present arguments in favor of certain actions. Explain to your child that if her hands are dirty, they're covered in germs that could make her ill; or that if she's eaten candy it could give her toothache.

Once your child begins to understand the reasons for bathing and tooth-brushing, you must be consistent. Children are very logical, and if you have persuaded your child that it is essential to wash her hands before meals, and brush her teeth afterward, she will probably question

Hair shield
Keep soap and water off your child's face with a specially designed shield.

Soapy hair can be molded to create funny hairstyles

Make hair-washing fun
Allow your child to play games to help get over a dislike of hair washing.

CLEANLINESS IN BOYS

Boys are usually quite resistant to bathing, and you'll have to spend a lot of time reminding him to wash and brush.

• Make bath times as much fun as possible, with toys, games, and lots of suds.

• Spend some time showing him how to wash, and do this several times if necessary.

• Try not to be too picky about cleanliness; if he's in the middle of a game, let hand-washing wait until he's ready.

• Let him wash himself as soon as he can make an attempt, then clean him thoroughly yourself at the last moment.

• Encourage a daily change of underpants and socks.

• Give him his own laundry basket and encourage him to fill it.

you if you overlook it. At the same time, you should try not to be too picky about cleanliness.

CONDITIONS PASSED BETWEEN CHILDREN

As soon as your child starts to socialize with other children, she is at risk from a variety of minor disorders that are commonly passed between children. Don't be unduly upset by these; they are not necessarily a result of poor hygiene, and can all be easily treated. (For more information see **Parasites**, p.296.)

Ringworm A fungal infection affecting the scalp (tinea capitis) or the body (tinea corporis), ringworm appears as small bald areas on the scalp, or round, reddish or gray, scaly patches on the skin. These are usually oval in shape and the edges of the patch remain scaly while the center clears, leaving rings. Consult your doctor, as the condition is irritating and contagious.

Head lice The insects themselves are hard to see and most people first notice the pale, oval-shaped eggs (nits) that become firmly attached to the hair. Your pharmacist will recommend a special conditioner to treat the problem. Wash the child's hair, cover with conditioner, and comb with a nit comb. Repeat this treatment every two or three days for at least two weeks or until clear.

Pinworms and roundworms Pinworms are the most common form of intestinal worm. They live in the bowel and lay eggs around the anus, which causes nighttime anal itching. Roundworms are rare and are likely to occur only if you've been overseas. Your doctor can prescribe a drug to treat either condition.

EATING FOR DENTAL HEALTH

Making sure your child is eating the right foods is the most important contribution you can make to his dental health.

• Never give your baby a bottle of undiluted or sweetened juice to drink ad lib, since it means your baby's teeth are bathed continuously in sugar and results eventually in "bottle mouth"—a mouth full of rotten teeth as early as three years old.

• Giving sweet foods between meals increases the number of times the teeth are exposed to harmful acids, so give them at the end of a meal instead.

• If you give candy, don't choose sticky toffees, since these remain on the teeth for longer.

• Giving cheese at the end of a meal makes saliva alkaline, and helps counteract the acid that erodes teeth.

• It is better to give a piece of cake, which can be eaten in a few minutes, than a bag of candy, which will be eaten all afternoon.

• Give fruit or sugar-free yogurt as treats to avoid encouraging a sweet tooth.

DENTAL CARE

By the time your child reaches the age of three years, the basic routine of tooth care should be well established (see p.99). Morning and evening tooth-brushing sessions need to be carefully supervised by an adult, even though a child of this age will probably be eager to carry out brushing himself. Six-monthly visits to the dentist, to check that the teeth are coming through normally, are also important. These "tooth-counting" sessions are also a good way of letting your child get used to visits to the dentist.

Most people are now aware of the damage caused to teeth by sugar in the diet. Sugary foods produce acids in the mouth that damage the enamel coating of the teeth by removing calcium. Once this has occurred, the underlying tooth is open to decay and cavities will start to form. While fillings can repair cavities, the tooth is inevitably weakened and, if severely affected by decay, may need to be removed and endanger the positioning of adult teeth.

PREVENTING CAVITIES

A baby eats only those foods offered by parents and caregivers. As he gets older and gains in independence, he will begin to express his own food preferences more vigorously and will have increasing opportunities to choose foods for himself—and sweet foods are often favorites. For this reason, good eating habits can't be started too soon. Above all, try to control your child's intake of sweet treats. No child needs sugar or sweets, and you can easily find less damaging treats in the form of fruit and savory snacks. Explain to your friends and family that you would prefer that they did not give sweets to your child.

In the real world, of course, children do receive and eat a certain amount of sugary food. You can limit the damage these do to your child's teeth by incorporating them into mealtimes. Sugary snacks eaten between meals are the most damaging. If your child has eaten something particularly sweet, make sure he brushes his teeth as soon afterward as possible.

Giving undiluted fruit juice is another common cause of tooth decay even among children who eat few sweets, so you should always dilute fruit juice with water. Eating or drinking anything other than water at night after the teeth have been brushed can cause problems. The acids

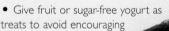

Tooth-brushing
Give your child a soft toothbrush and encourage her to use it after meals, especially once the molars are through (see p.175).

that cause tooth decay will remain in the mouth, allowing the enamel-damaging process to continue for many hours. If your child is greatly attached to having a bottle at night, give it to him before he goes to sleep, then remove it.

FIRST FILLINGS

If you are lucky, your child will need little or no dental treatment throughout childhood. Your dentist will notice any signs of decay at your regular six-monthly visits, but make an extra appointment if you notice any unusual tooth discoloration or if your child complains of pain. In cases of slight decay in baby teeth, the dentist may decide not to fill the tooth in order to avoid unnecessary upset for your child. Tooth enamel has been shown to be capable of recalcification if the cavity isn't too large.

A dentist who is used to treating children will usually have developed techniques for minimizing any fear. Great care will be taken to prevent pain with the use of local anesthetic sprays and extra-fine needles for injections as appropriate.

ACCIDENTS INVOLVING TEETH

The need for dental treatment other than for cavities in the under fives is rare. An injury to a tooth that damages the nerve can cause it to "die" even if it isn't dislodged. In this case the tooth will become discolored, but no other ill effects will follow, and it can be safely left in place until it is replaced by the adult tooth. If a tooth is chipped, you should seek the advice of your dentist. If a milk tooth is knocked out altogether, you will need immediate dental advice; take your child to the nearest emergency dental clinic, bringing the tooth with you. In some cases the tooth can be replaced in the jaw, depending on the child's age and the position of the tooth.

FLUORIDE

Fluoride is a mineral that has been shown to reduce the incidence of tooth decay by strengthening tooth enamel. It is added to many toothpastes and, in some areas, to the water supply.

• Fluoride can also be taken by mouth in the form of drops or tablets. Dentists recommend toothpastes containing fluoride for adults and children over the age of three.

• Many dentists would argue that fluoride toothpaste alone doesn't provide sufficient protection against dental decay.

• If the water in your area has less than 0.7 parts fluoride per million (you can find this out from your municipality), your child may benefit from fluoride supplement tablets.

• Always consult your dentist or doctor before giving supplements, and follow his or her advice carefully.

• It is important to avoid giving excessive fluoride. This can cause a condition known as fluorosis, in which the developing adult teeth become mottled.

Visiting the dentist
Always stay with your child during any dental treatment, or even a checkup; the reassurance of your presence is vital.

KIDNEY AND BLADDER FUNCTION

Once food has been absorbed into the bloodstream, waste has to be removed from the blood by the kidneys and eliminated as urine.

Urine production Waste chemicals in the blood are removed and dissolved in water by the kidneys. The urine then passes down the ureters and into the bladder.

Voiding Urine is temporarily stored in the bladder, which is periodically emptied through the urethra. Your baby will not even be aware of passing urine until she's about 15–18 months (see pp. 112–13). The sensation of wanting to pass urine doesn't come until several months later, because the infant bladder can only hold urine for a few minutes.

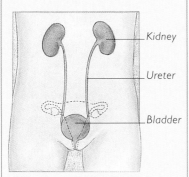

— Kidney

— Ureter

— Bladder

Kidneys and bladder
The urinary and reproductive systems are closely linked; a girl's bladder is next to the uterus.

Bowel and bladder

A newborn baby can need up to ten diaper changes a day, and, although the frequency of changes will decrease, most babies don't achieve a degree of bowel and bladder control until the second year. Although you can't speed up this process, your help and support will be very important to your child.

PASSING URINE

A young baby's bladder will empty itself automatically and frequently both day and night. As soon as it contains a little urine, the bladder wall stretches and the emptying action is stimulated. This is absolutely normal, and your baby cannot be expected to behave differently, at least until the bladder has developed sufficiently to hold urine for longer periods of time.

BOWEL MOVEMENTS

When your baby was in the womb, her intestines were filled with a sticky, black substance called meconium. Meconium is passed in the first 24 hours after delivery, and once this has happened normal bowel movements will take over.

Once your baby settles into a regular routine, her stools will become firmer and paler. You don't need to pay much attention to them, and you certainly should never become obsessive or worried about them as long as your baby is content and thriving.

The number of stools a baby passes varies greatly, and initially most bottle-fed babies pass a stool for every feeding. On the other hand, a breastfed baby may pass only one stool a day or less because there is little waste. The frequency of bowel movements gradually decreases as your baby gets older. It may be that, at the beginning, your baby passes five or six a day, but after three or four weeks she may have only two movements a day. This is quite normal and should cause you no worry. Similarly, the occasional loose, unformed stools or totally green stool are typical of a young baby's bowel movements and are no cause for concern unless looseness persists beyond 24 hours; then seek your doctor's advice.

CHANGES IN BOWEL MOVEMENTS

Don't worry if your baby's stools change in appearance from one day to the next. It is quite normal for a stool to turn green or brown when left exposed to the air. If you are worried, consult your healthcare provider, who will be able to advise and reassure you. As a rule, loose stools are not an indication of an infection. Watery stools, however, if accompanied by a sudden change in the color, smell, or frequency of passing stools, should be mentioned to your doctor, especially if your baby is "not himself" (see p.276).

Blood-streaked stools are never normal. The cause may be quite minor—a tiny crack in the skin around the anus, perhaps—but you must consult your doctor. Larger amounts of blood, or the appearance of pus or mucus, may indicate an intestinal infection, so contact your doctor immediately.

The breastfed baby By the second day, the light yellow stools typical of the breastfed baby will appear. The stools are rarely hard or smelly and may be no thicker than cream soup. Remember that the food you eat will affect your baby and that anything very spicy or acidic could upset digestion.

The bottle-fed baby A baby fed on formula has a tendency to more frequent stools, which are firmer, browner, and smellier than those of a breastfed baby. The most common tendency is for the stools to be rather hard. The easiest way to fix this is to give your baby a little cooled boiled water to drink in between feedings.

DIARRHEA

Diarrhea is a sign of irritation of the intestines, resulting in loose, frequent, and watery stools. In small babies, diarrhea is always potentially dangerous because of the risk of dehydration, which can develop very quickly. If your baby refuses food or has any of the following symptoms, contact your doctor immediately.

• Repeated watery stools and/or green and smelly stools
• A fever of 100°F (38°C) or more
• Pus or blood in her stools
• Listlessness and dark-ringed eyes

If you think your baby is dehydrated, look at her fontanelles. If they are depressed, your baby is dehydrated: contact your doctor immediately. If it is treated early, diarrhea can be cured quickly.

You can start treating your baby immediately yourself if her diarrhea is mild, and she has no other symptoms. Continue to nurse your baby if you are breastfeeding; watered down formula, however, is generally not recommended for diarrhea. Some formulas are made for diarrhea (such as Isomil DF, a soy based "diarrhea formula"), but for short term diarrhea (one to three days), the official recommendation of the American Academy of Pediatrics (AAP) is to continue regular feedings if tolerated and/or use electrolyte formulas, if there is vomiting. If mild diarrhea doesn't improve within two or three days, consult your doctor. Drinks of mineral replacement salts formulated specially for infants may help at this stage. If all goes well, you can return to feeding your baby as usual.

BOWEL FUNCTION

Food passes through the stomach into the small intestine, and from there to the large intestine. The waste products of food are stored in the rectum before finally being eliminated as feces.

Digestion The food is broken down by enzymes. Digestion starts in the mouth, then continues in the stomach and the upper part of the small intestine.

Absorption Once the food has been reduced to simple molecules, it is absorbed into the bloodstream as it continues its trip through the small intestine. It then passes through the large intestine, where any water is absorbed by the body. The waste products pass on to the rectum as feces.

Elimination Feces are stored in the rectum and expelled through the anus. A baby can't control the reflex that causes the rectum to empty— even for a second. Young babies generally have bowel movements with each feed, as a result of the gastrocolic reflex that stimulates the rectum to empty every time that food enters the stomach.

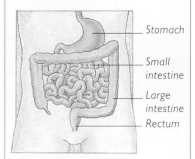

Stomach

Small intestine

Large intestine

Rectum

The bowel system
After food has been digested in the stomach and small intestine, the waste is passed as feces.

GIRLS' DIAPERS

A girl will tend to wet the diaper at the center, or toward the back if she is lying down.

• Disposable daytime and nighttime diapers are designed differently to take this into account, with the padding at its thickest where it is needed most.

• You may like to buy decorative or frilly pants to cover fabric diapers; these look pretty under a dress for a special occasion.

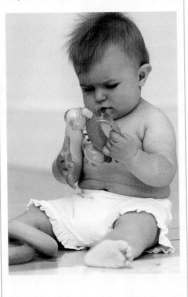

DIAPERS

Your first choice in diapers will be between fabric and disposable types. Most parents prefer to use disposables, though an increasing consciousness of environmental issues has led many parents to reconsider the virtues of fabric diapers, which create less waste. Yet the issue is not clear-cut: the detergents required to clean fabric diapers can be viewed as pollutants to the water supply, and the energy required to wash them might also be regarded as wasteful. While fabric diapers are cheaper than disposables in the long run, you need to consider the increased electricity bills for frequent washing-machine runs, and the cost in your time. What is clear is that, provided that the diaper is changed as frequently as necessary, and that the basic rules of hygiene are observed, your baby will be happy whichever type of diaper you choose.

DISPOSABLE DIAPERS

Disposable diapers make diaper-changing as simple as it can be. They are easy to put on—no folding, no pins, and no plastic pants—and can be discarded when they are wet or dirty. They are convenient when you're traveling, since you need fewer diapers and less space to change in, and you don't have to carry wet, smelly diapers home with you to be washed. You will need a constant supply, so to avoid carrying huge loads with your shopping, buy them in large batches. Some stores will deliver diapers.

Never flush disposable diapers down the toilet—they inevitably get stuck. Instead, put the soiled diaper in a strong plastic bag. The bag should be firmly secured at the neck before you put it in the garbage.

DISPOSABLE DIAPERS

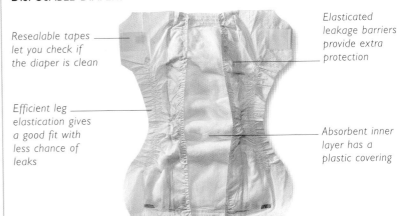

Resealable tapes let you check if the diaper is clean

Efficient leg elastication gives a good fit with less chance of leaks

Elasticated leakage barriers provide extra protection

Absorbent inner layer has a plastic covering

FABRIC DIAPERS

Though fabric diapers are more expensive than disposables at first, they work out cheaper in the long run. Fabric diapers involve much more work than disposables because they have to be rinsed, sterilized, washed, and dried after use, although laundry services are now available in many areas. You will need a minimum of 24 diapers to ensure that you always have enough clean ones, but the more diapers you can buy, the less often you'll have to do laundry. When buying fabric diapers, choose the best that you can afford. They'll last longer; they'll also be more absorbent, and therefore more comfortable for your baby.

Terry squares can be folded in various ways, depending on your baby's size and needs (see p.109). They are very absorbent—more so than most disposables—so they are good at night.

Shaped terry diapers are T-shaped, made of a softer, finer toweling than squares, and have a triple-layered central panel for added absorbency. Their shape means that they are more straightforward to put on, and fit the baby more neatly.

With fabric diapers, you will need diaper liners: choose the "one-way" variety that lets urine pass through, but remains dry next to the baby's skin, minimizing the risk of a sore bottom due to friction or moisture. Liners prevent the diaper from getting badly soiled; they can be lifted out with any feces and flushed away. You will also need at least 12 diaper pins—these have locking heads to protect your baby's skin—and six pairs of plastic pants to prevent wet or dirty diapers from soiling the baby's clothes or bedding.

There is a type of fabric diaper on the market that offers all the features of a disposable, but is machine-washable: it is shaped to fit, has Velcro closing tabs and elasticated legs, and is made of several layers of absorbent fabric with an anti-leak outer layer.

FABRIC DIAPERS

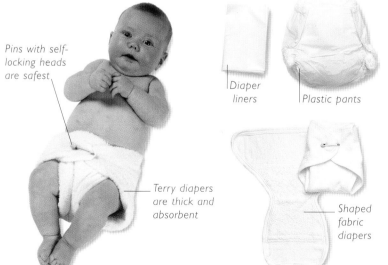

Pins with self-locking heads are safest

Diaper liners

Plastic pants

Terry diapers are thick and absorbent

Shaped fabric diapers

BOYS' DIAPERS

Boys tend to wet the front of the diaper, and boys' disposables are designed to cope with this, with extra padding toward the front.

• Fold fabric diapers in such a way that more of the fabric is at the front, particularly at night.

• Boys often urinate when they are being changed, so cover the penis with a spare, clean diaper as you take the soiled one off.

• Always tuck your baby boy's penis down when putting on a clean diaper to avoid urine escaping from the top of the diaper.

CLEANING A GIRL

Always wipe your baby girl from front to back, and never clean inside the lips of the vulva.

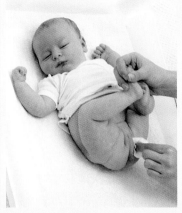

Remove urine
Use a wet cloth or cotton ball to clean the genitals and surrounding the skin.

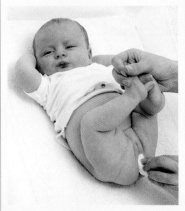

Clean bottom
Lift up her legs as shown, and wipe from front to back. Dry thoroughly.

CHANGING A DIAPER

Your baby's diaper will need to be changed whenever it is soiled or wet. The number of changes will vary from one baby to the next. As a rule, though, you'll probably change the diaper every morning when your baby wakes, before you put him to bed at night, after a bath, and after every feeding, including night feedings.

Changing disposables is straightforward, provided you choose the most appropriate diaper for your baby's size so that it fits him neatly. With fabric diapers, you can choose the type of fold that suits you (see opposite) or you can use shaped diapers. You'll need diaper liners, too.

DISPOSABLE DIAPER

Positioning your baby
Lay the diaper flat, with the tabs at the back. Slide the diaper under your baby so that the top aligns with her waist.

Fastening the front
Bring the front up between the legs and tuck it around the tummy. Peel the tabs.

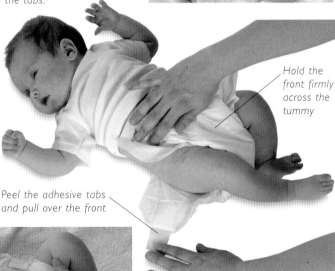

Hold the front firmly across the tummy

Peel the adhesive tabs and pull over the front

A comfortable fit
Pull the tabs firmly over the front flap and fasten the diaper. It should fit snugly.

FOLDING FABRIC DIAPERS

Triple absorbent fold

This is the most suitable fold for your newborn; its central panel provides good absorbency and it is very small and neat. It isn't suitable for larger babies, however. Start with a square diaper folded in four, with the open edges to the top and right.

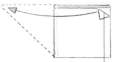

Pick up the top layer by the right-hand edge.

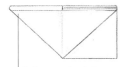

Pull it to the left to form an inverted triangle.

Turn the diaper over so the point is at the top right.

Fold in the middle layers twice to form a thick central panel.

Parallel and kite folds

These are suitable for a larger baby. You can adjust the depth of the kite to suit your baby's size. Both start with a diaper laid out in a diamond shape.

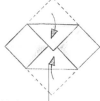

Fold the top and bottom points in to the center.

Pick up the left-hand point and align it to the top edge; do the same with the right.

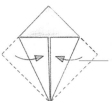

Fold the sides in to the center to form a kite shape.

Fold the top point down to the center. Fold the bottom point up toward the center, varying the depth to fit.

FABRIC DIAPER

Putting on a fabric diaper

Slide the diaper under your baby so his waist aligns with the top edge. Bring the front of the diaper up between his legs, and hold it in place while you fold the sides in to the center and fasten with a pin.

Hold in place

Fasten carefully

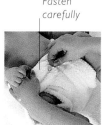

CLEANING A BOY

Boys often pass urine when released from their diaper. A tissue laid over the penis will minimize the mess.

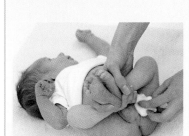

Remove urine

Wipe with a cotton ball, working from the leg creases in toward the penis. Never pull the foreskin back.

Clean bottom

Lift his legs to clean his bottom by holding both ankles as shown. Dry thoroughly.

- Use plastic tongs or gloves for lifting diapers out of the sterilizing pail; keep them nearby.

- When you change a diaper at night, keep the dirty diaper in a separate pail or a plastic bag, and add it to the new sterilizing solution the following morning.

- If you use a powder sterilant, always put the water in the powder first; otherwise, you run the risk of inhaling the powder.

- Drying diapers in a dryer, on an outside clothesline, or on a rack that can be placed over the bathtub.

- You may like to use an air freshener in the diaper pail.

Diaper pail
For sterilization, you'll need two separate pails: one for soiled diapers, one for wet ones.

DIAPER HYGIENE

It is very important to wash fabric diapers thoroughly; any traces of ammonia will irritate your baby's skin, and fecal bacteria could cause infection. Strong detergents and biological enzymes could also irritate your baby's skin, so always use pure soap flakes or powders. If you use a fabric conditioner, make sure it's completely rinsed away, whatever the manufacturer's instructions might say. If you use a sterilizing solution, then you will need to wash only soiled diapers, since wet diapers will only need thorough rinsing. There is no need to boil diapers unless they are very stained, or have become rather gray; just use hot water for both rinsing and washing. If your baby's clothing gets soiled, don't add it to the sterilizing solution, since the color will run. Just remove as much of the mess as you can, rinse the garment, and wash as normal.

WASHING ROUTINE
Establishing a routine will make life easier, especially if you aim to wash the diapers in large loads. You'll need a large supply of diapers—at least 24. You'll need two plastic sterilizing bins with lids and strong handles: one for soiled diapers, and one for wet ones. They should be large enough to hold at least six diapers, with lots of room for solution, but not so large that you can't carry them when full. There are special diaper bins, but any good-sized pail with a lid will do.

Fill the bins with sterilizing solution each morning and always rinse a diaper before adding it to the bucket. Wet diapers should be rinsed in cold water, wrung out, and added to the solution. With soiled diapers, dump as much feces as possible down the toilet and hold the diaper under the toilet spray as you flush it. Squeeze out the excess moisture and put the diaper in the "soiled" bucket. When the diapers have been soaking for the required time, wring them out. The urine-soaked ones should be rinsed thoroughly in hot water and then dried; the soiled ones will need to be washed on the hot cycle of your machine or in a tub of hot water, then rinsed and dried. Plastic pants will become hard and unusable if you wash them in water that is either too hot or too cold. Wash them in warm water with a little dishwashing liquid, then pat them dry and leave them to air-dry. If they do become hard, you can soften them in a tumble dryer with towels.

DIAPER RASH
If urine is left too long in a diaper or on the skin, it is broken down to ammonia by bacteria from your baby's stools. The ammonia then irritates and burns the skin, and this is the most common cause of diaper rash. A mild diaper rash will appear as small red dots on your baby's bottom, but if it becomes more serious, you will see an inflamed area of broken skin and possibly pus-filled pimples.

The bacteria that produce ammonia dermatitis (diaper rash) thrive in an alkaline medium. Breastfed babies are less prone to diaper rash than bottle-fed babies. If you follow the guidelines given (right), you will minimize the possibility of diaper rash.

If your baby does develop a sore bottom, check the chart below to see if she needs treatment. If not, continue your preventive measures (except for the use of barrier cream), as well as the following:

• Change your baby's diaper more often.
• Use a disposable pad inside a toweling diaper for extra absorbency at night, especially if your baby sleeps through the night.
• Once your baby has diaper rash, it is important that her skin be aired between diaper changes, for about 15–20 minutes.

Not all skin conditions occurring in the diaper area are true diaper rash (see chart below). It is important that you identify a rash correctly so that you can take appropriate action.

Appearance of rash	Cause and treatment
General redness that starts around the genitals rather than the anus. You will notice a strong smell of ammonia. In severe cases, it may spread to the bottom, groin, and thighs, and can lead to ulceration if not attended to.	Ammonia dermatitis, caused by irritation from ammonia. If the treatment outlined above doesn't work, consult your doctor.
Small blisters all over the diaper area in addition to a rash elsewhere on the body.	Heat rash. Stop using plastic pants, and leave your baby's diaper off at every opportunity. Cool your baby down by using fewer clothes and blankets.
Redness and broken skin in the leg folds.	Inadequate drying. Dry your baby meticulously and don't use talcum powder.
Brownish-red, scaly rash on the genitals and skin creases, especially the groin, and anywhere the skin is greasy—the scalp, for instance. It is very rare in babies.	Seborrheic dermatitis. Your doctor will prescribe an ointment for the rash, and perhaps a special lotion if the scalp is affected.
Spotty rash that starts around the anus and spreads to the buttocks and inner thighs. You may also notice white patches inside your baby's mouth.	Thrush, caused by a yeast infection. Consult your doctor. She will probably give you antifungal treatments.

PREVENTING DIAPER RASH

The essentials are to keep your baby's skin dry and well aired, and to make sure that diapers are always thoroughly washed and well rinsed.

• Start using a diaper rash cream at the first sign of broken skin. Ones that include zinc oxide are especially good. Stop using plastic pants, too, since they prevent the evaporation of urine.

• Don't wash your baby's bottom with soap and water, they both strip natural oils from the skin.

• Use one-way diaper liners, or disposables with a one-way lining, to keep your baby's skin dry.

• Use a fairly thick barrier cream, applied generously. Don't use this with one-way liners or disposables, however, since it will clog the one-way fabric.

• Make sure all traces of ammonia are removed from the diaper by thorough washing and rinsing.

• Never leave your baby lying in a wet diaper.

• Leave your baby's bottom exposed to the air whenever you can.

Bowel and bladder

DEVELOPMENT IN GIRLS

Bowel and bladder control usually start earlier and are complete more quickly in girls. The age ranges given are approximate.

Early stages: 1–1½ years

• The first sign that the bladder is maturing is when she gestures or makes a sound to indicate she's aware of passing urine.

• There's usually no sign of bowel control at this stage.

Middle stages: 1½ –2½ years

• One day, between 15 and 18 months, she'll bring the potty to you, and if you're quick, you may catch her in time.

• At about 18 months to two years, you may find a stool in the potty after a meal. She'll come and tell you when she needs the potty and can wait for it. Once she can wait five minutes or so, try training pants during the day.

Later stages: 2½ –3½ years

• Girls achieve bowel control very quickly. She's clean day and night with the occasional accident.

• She's dry all day. Try training pants for the afternoon nap; once she's dry for her nap, you can try training pants at night.

• She can stay dry most nights. Bowel control is virtually complete. She has very few accidents.

Once your baby starts eating solids, you will find that he soils his diaper less often. You will continue to see changes in his bowel movements as his digestive system matures, right up to the age of five or six years. After he's eaten solids for a few months, you may feel it is time he used the potty, but don't rush this (see opposite).

CHANGES IN BOWEL MOVEMENTS

In general, you can expect your baby's stools to become firmer and less frequent with age. There are some pretty standard changes at some ages; I give them only to reassure you, not so that you will obsessively examine your child's stools. All dates are approximate.

0–6 months The stools may be almost as frequent as the feedings, and are very soft. They go through color changes: first greenish black (meconium, see p.104), then yellow, then light brown.

6–12 months After your baby starts on solids, the stools become drier, darker in color, and less frequent—say, three times a day. Lots of drinks will keep the stools soft.

1–3 years As soon as your child is on the family diet, he will probably only pass two stools a day.

3–5 years The stools are identical to adult stools, except in size, and your child will rarely pass more than one a day.

MALABSORPTION AND CELIAC DISEASE

Malabsorption—impaired uptake of nutrients in the small intestine—can be caused by an enzyme deficiency, or celiac disease. This is an inflammation of the small bowel due to a sensitivity to gluten, a substance found in wheat and rye. The inflamed bowel is incapable of absorbing many foods, so your baby can become undernourished. Fortunately, this disease is quite rare.

In most cases of celiac disease, symptoms develop before the age of two, although in some children the symptoms are mild and the disease may not be picked up until adulthood. Symptoms may include poor appetite, vomiting, and diarrhea; poor weight gain and growth; and the passing of pale, greasy, foul-smelling stools. Other problems, such as anemia, can develop due to deficiencies.

It's extremely important that a baby with celiac disease is properly diagnosed, otherwise all development could be slowed down. Just as worrisome, many dietary deficiencies will develop, and his resistance to infection will be lowered. If you suspect celiac disease, ask your doctor about it immediately.

Celiac disease can be treated very simply; your baby will have to eat gluten-free foods. There are lots of products available, and foods cooked with gluten-free flour are delicious—I once attended the birthday party of a celiac child where you couldn't tell the difference from the usual party treats.

THE CASE AGAINST "TRAINING"

Babies who are allowed to achieve bowel and bladder control at their own pace learn to use the potty quickly and have few accidents. It's only when parents interfere with their child's steady progress by enforcing timetables, or expecting too much too soon, that things go awry. Babies are born wanting to be clean and dry; our job is simply to allow them to achieve this milestone happily.

An overly strict parent can do untold harm, even at an early stage, and may be responsible for problems in later life. Imagine the scenario: a domineering, insistent mother is bending over her baby telling him that he can't get off his potty until he's performed. He can't understand what she's getting at, because he is unaware of passing urine or stools— his bladder and nervous system are still too primitive. Even if he did understand, he has no "control," as you think of it. He can't figure out why something so natural to him is so important to you. And so he has no idea how to please his normally very loving mother. When he gets up to leave, you get unusually rough, he can't cope, and he's going to cry. And if you go on like this now, he is certainly going to use your obsession with training as a weapon against you later. He sees his stools as something you want and so he will withhold them when he is pitting his will against yours. The answer is to be flexible.

At no point pressure or scold. Praise every success. Let little boys see their fathers passing urine. Children who are pressured into early training tend to be bed-wetters, and more engage in pica (eating stools or other nonfood substances) and soiling than those children who develop at their own speed.

Introducing the potty

These are the ways you can help your baby to be dry and clean, but only after he indicates to you by sound or gesture that he knows he's passed urine or stools. Allow him to find his own pace, without any pressure from you.

Step 1 Give him his own "potty" chair, which is like your toilet. Let him see his mother or father use the toilet and let him see the results if he asks.

Step 2 Let him sit on the potty chair fully clothed while you read him a story.

Step 3 Gradually let him get used to sitting without a diaper.

Step 4 When he soils or wets his diaper, set him gently on the chair after you've cleaned him while you collect fresh things.

Step 5 Once he's interested, let him sit two or three times a day.

DEVELOPMENT IN BOYS

Boys are generally later than girls in developing bowel and bladder control, and bed-wetting is more frequent in boys. The age ranges given are just a rough guide.

Early stages: 1½–2½ years

• At this stage your little boy has no "control." His immature bladder can't hold on to urine for a single second.

• He still can't wait for you to get the potty after signaling that he's letting go of his urine.

Middle stages: 2½–3½ years

• Your little boy can bring the potty to you only after he can hold on to urine for a minute or two.

• He'll come and tell you he needs the potty, but will still have frequent accidents.

• When he's indicated he can wait several minutes and not before, try trainer pants during the day only.

Later stages: 3½–6 years

• He may be clean by day, with accidents, but wet at night.

• He's clean, with accidents, day and night. When he's dry all day, try training pants during his nap.

• He's dry all day but needs a diaper at night.

• He can stay dry through the night with very few accidents.

Bowel and bladder

AIDING A GIRL

Teach your little girl good habits of hygiene, like washing her hands and neatening up the bathroom after her. You'll probably find that she responds well to this.

Girls are generally neater than boys, and will enjoy turning a cleanliness routine into a game: "Now we flush the toilet... Now we wash the potty... Now we wash our hands."

Toilet hygiene
Girls are generally more receptive than boys to being taught good habits of hygiene.

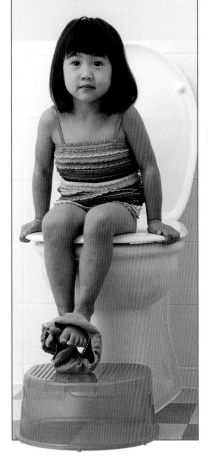

Once your child shows signs of being ready to use the potty, your aim should be to help and encourage her. If you do this, she is likely to achieve control quite quickly and without much trouble, and will remain happy and confident throughout. If you insist on her using the potty before she is ready, or try to force her, she will be unhappy at first at not being able to please you, and then guilty and resentful. Your relationship with your child will suffer and training will become a battle of nerves, which you can never win.

BOWEL CONTROL

Though a baby is aware first of her bladder emptying, she will probably achieve bowel control first as it's much easier to "hold on" with a full rectum than with a full bladder. It's a good idea to help her use the potty for bowel movements first; this is easier, in any case, because bowel movements are more predictable and take longer than passing urine. When your child indicates that she wants to pass a stool, suggest that she use the potty.

When she's finished, wipe her bottom (front-to-back for girls), then flush the toilet paper and the contents of the potty down the toilet. Clean off any trace of feces and rinse out the potty, using disinfectant. Wash your hands afterward, and encourage your child to do the same. If she doesn't want to use the potty when you suggest it, forget it for the moment and try again a few days later.

Control tips

Do	Don't
• Praise your child and encourage her to regard control as an accomplishment.	• Insist that your child sit on the potty, ever.
• Let your child set the pace. You can help your child along, but you can't speed up the process.	• Show any disgust for your child's feces. She will regard using the potty as an achievement and will be proud of them.
• Suggest that your child sit on the potty, but let her decide.	• Ask your child to wait once she has asked for the potty, even for a moment—she can only "hold on" for a very short time.
• Let her be as independent as she likes, going to the bathroom or using the potty, and praise her independence.	• Scold mistakes and accidents.
• Use training pants to give your child a sense of independence.	

BLADDER CONTROL

The first sign that your child's bladder control is developing is when she becomes aware of the passage of urine, and she may try to attract your attention and point to her diaper. As her bladder matures and is able to contain urine for longer, you may find that her diaper is dry after a nap. Once this is happening regularly, you can leave off the diaper during the nap and encourage her to empty her bladder beforehand. When she can do this and can let you know when she wants to use the potty, you can start leaving off diapers completely during the day, provided she is able to wait for a few minutes while you take down her clothes to let her use the potty. When you are out, you might find it useful to carry a portable potty; these come with disposable liners.

At this stage, your child can't hold on to a full bladder for any length of time, and accidents are inevitable, so try to take them in stride and never scold your toddler for them. Just clean up, change her clothing, and say "That's okay. We'll try again next time."

ACHIEVING NIGHTTIME CONTROL

Control of the bladder during the night is the last to come, since a child of two or three can't hold on to urine for much more than four to five hours. Once your child wakes up regularly with a dry diaper, you can leave off the nighttime diaper, but encourage her to empty her bladder before she goes to sleep. It is a good idea to keep a potty beside the bed for your child to use if necessary, but make sure that her nightclothes are easy for her to take down and that you leave a night-light on so that she can see what she's doing. Be patient if she comes and asks for your help; it's not easy for her to take responsibility for the potty herself. Try this for a week, but if your child has several wet nights, offer her diaper back for a while—otherwise she'll become very tired from disturbed sleep. If she does show signs of becoming more self-reliant, encourage her and boost her confidence. She'll still have accidents, so it's a good idea to protect the mattress with a rubber sheet, putting your usual sheet on top.

USING THE TOILET

When your child starts to use the potty regularly throughout the day, encourage her to sit on the toilet; this will save you having to take a potty with you when you leave the house. Many children are nervous about sitting on the toilet seat because they feel they'll fall off or even fall in. To make your child more secure on the large toilet seat, you can use one of the specially designed child-size seats available that fit inside the toilet rim. Suggest that she holds onto the sides so that she feels balanced. You should also stay nearby until you are sure she is comfortable on the seat. To help her to get up easily, put a small step or box in front of the toilet.

AIDING A BOY

Boys are often messier than girls in using the potty or the toilet, but there are some things that you can do to help.

Boys are more likely than girls to play with their feces. If this happens, don't show disgust; just wash your child's hands calmly, as you would if they were dirty with mud or paint.

Show your little boy how to stand in front of the toilet and teach him to aim at the bowl before he passes any urine. You could put a piece of toilet paper in the bowl for him to aim at. Let him see his father passing urine so that he can imitate him.

Potties
Specially molded potties provide support and are suitable for both boys and girls.

Bowel and bladder

TRAINING PANTS

Before your child's bladder control is fully developed, you may like to use training pants.

• Disposable training pants have easily tearable side seams so that they can be quickly removed in the event of an accident.

• Both nondisposable and disposable training pants can be left on at night. They are bulky, however, so some children find them uncomfortable.

Training pants
Your child will probably prefer training pants to diapers because they seem more grown-up.

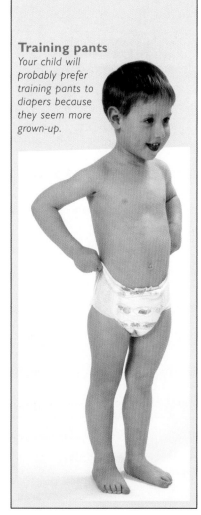

By three years of age, most children have fairly reliable bladder and bowel control, but accidents will still be common. During the day, accidents are most likely to happen when your child ignores the signals of a full bladder because he is engrossed in play or because he is reluctant to use the toilet in an unfamiliar place. You can help by reminding your child to go to the bathroom at regular intervals and by making a point of accompanying him to the bathroom when you visit new places. Encourage your child to go independently in familiar surroundings as soon as possible, but never insist on his going to a strange bathroom alone.

LATE DEVELOPERS
Some children achieve bowel and bladder control later because brain–bladder connections taken longer than average to form, so it is wrong and cruel to blame your child. Lateness in acquiring control is often hereditary; ask your parents and parents-in-law about this. If a doctor suspects there may be an underlying cause—including psychological causes—this will be investigated if appropriate. Otherwise, no action is generally taken until after the age of three or four for daytime wetting or seven for bed-wetting.

ACCIDENTS AND BED-WETTING
When your child does wet himself, remember that however badly you may feel about the inconvenience, it's likely that his embarrassment is much worse. Reassure him that you understand it was an accident and that he hasn't failed you. Being prepared for accidents will reduce anxiety for both of you; always carry spare underwear and pants on outings.

Bed-wetting at night (see p.115) can happen to a child of any age and is very common in children up to the age of six, boys being especially prone. Most children grow out of it after this age without any special help. Minimize your child's embarrassment by keeping him in diapers at night until you are confident that he has reached the point where he can stay dry all night. Once you let him go without diapers, be prepared for the occasional accident. Concern about the frequency of bed-wetting should not be communicated to your child; it only increases his anxiety. Encourage him instead by giving special praise if he has a dry night.

CONSTIPATION
Should your child's stools become infrequent—that is, less often than once every three or four days—and hard enough to cause discomfort or pain, then he is constipated. Constipation without any other signs of illness is nothing to worry about, but if it causes your child discomfort,

consult your doctor. Most doctors don't recommend using laxatives for a small child. (Constipation is rare in very small babies and can nearly always be corrected by giving your baby drinks of water.) You should never try to treat constipation yourself with laxatives, suppositories, or enemas without consulting your doctor.

Once your child is on a varied diet, he shouldn't suffer from constipation if you are giving him enough fluids, fresh fruit, vegetables, and whole-wheat breads; if he does, just give more of these. The complex carbohydrates in root and green vegetables contain cellulose, which holds water in the stools and makes them more bulky and soft, as does oatmeal. A few stewed prunes or dried figs can help, too, often producing a soft stool within 24 hours.

A child can become chronically constipated for several reasons: if you are an overly picky parent and obsessive about the frequency of his bowel movements, your child may withhold them as a means of getting attention; if he has experienced pain and discomfort when trying to pass a stool, and holds on to the stools to prevent the pain from recurring; or if he dislikes school bathrooms or other strange bathrooms and is unwilling to use them.

Chronic constipation can also cause a condition called encopresis. Hard stools become impacted in the intestine, and loose, watery movements leak out past the blockage, sometimes causing the condition to be mistaken for diarrhea.

Illness with a high temperature may be followed by a few days of constipation, partly because your child has eaten very little, so there are no waste products to pass, and partly because he has lost water through sweating with the fever. This kind of constipation will correct itself when your child goes back on to a normal diet.

Control tips

Do	Don't
• Remind your child to go to the bathroom at regular intervals.	• Scold or draw attention to any form of accident your child has.
• Take a spare set of clothes with you when you go out.	• Withhold fluids from a child in the evening.
• Accompany your child to the bathroom in unfamiliar places.	• Compare your child with others of the same age who may have better control.
• Be sympathetic and make light of any accidents.	• Make an issue out of any accident in front of friends.
• Offer praise when your child has a dry night.	• Be unsympathetic if your child needs to use the toilet at an inconvenient moment.
• If wetting or soiling occurs after a long period of reliable control, look for the cause within the family first. If it persists, consult your doctor.	

REGRESSION

Regression to night- or daytime wetting in a child who has been reliably dry for some time is usually a sign of anxiety.

The arrival of a new baby is a typical reason for your child's regressing to an earlier stage as a way of winning back your attention, but any sort of upset, such as a move to a new home or school, can cause it. Occasionally, regression can be caused by a urinary-tract infection. So when you visit the doctor for any urinary problem, take a sample of your child's urine for testing.

Bowel control, once developed, is usually much more reliable than urinary control. Bowel accidents are uncommon and, if they occur frequently, particularly after control has apparently been reliable for some time, may indicate an underlying problem such as retention of stool or some form of emotional tension. Seek advice from your doctor.

Dethronement

Case study

Parents' names Fanny and Chris Hughes
Age 32 years and 35 years
Obstetric history Son Will, age 5; normal delivery
Daughter Miranda, age 7 months; normal delivery
Past medical history Usual childhood diseases
Family history Husband Chris, aged 35, was late in
gaining bladder control, and was a bed-wetter up to
the age of six years

Name Will Hughes
Age 5 years
Obstetric history Normal birth, no complications
Medical history Minor ear infections in third year,
cleared up after treatment

Fanny had expected Will to be a bit late in mastering bowel and bladder control, since she knew boys were often later than girls in accomplishing this stage of development. She'd also read that the fathers of late developers have often been late in gaining full bladder control too, and this turned out to be the case with Chris. She therefore remained very calm and cool when Will was developing control, and never pushed him. Will, for his part, was very cooperative and eager to please, and was dry and clean by three-and-a-half years. The problem started later, when Will's baby sister was born.

When Fanny started to grow big with Miranda, Will couldn't understand what was going on. He disowned his baby sister from the start. Fanny did everything she could to reassure him, showing him pictures of babies inside their mother's tummies, letting him feel the baby kick, and involving him in all the preparations. A month before the baby was due, Will started having disturbed sleep, when he would babble about the baby, but he remembered nothing in the morning. Miranda was born at home. Will sat outside his mother's bedroom transfixed by all the activity, and refused to go in and see his new sister. That night he wet the bed, which was something he hadn't done for a full year.

FEELING REJECTED

Chris was very angry with Will for not showing more interest in Miranda, scolded him, and sent him straight to bed. That night, because of all the upheaval in the house, Will didn't get his usual bedtime story, and again, in the morning, the bed was wet. Chris, who was preoccupied with preparing breakfast for everyone and making Fanny comfortable, lost his temper with Will, who stood in the kitchen and wet himself again. "I don't know what we'll do with you," were Chris's last words to Will as he left for work.

Fanny realized that Will would never wet himself unless he was upset. When Fanny called her clinic for advice, the nurse explained to Fanny that Will was suffering from dethronement. Having been the apple of Fanny's eye for four and a half years, he felt knocked off his throne by Miranda, and Fanny would have to make him feel loved and secure again. She also told Fanny that the doctor should test Will's urine just to make sure an infection wasn't the cause of the bed-wetting (the test was negative).

SEEKING ADVICE

Fanny decided to have a heart-to-heart with her mother, who reminded her of a family rule—Dad always carried the new baby so that Mom had her arms free for the other children. She pointed out that Will wouldn't have felt left out if Chris had held the new baby so that Fanny's arms were empty for him. Then he'd have known that Fanny still had time for him and that she loved him. She reminded Fanny of a tradition in her own family that the younger children always got a present from the new baby, so that they knew they were loved by her, too. She also suggested that on the first night Will should have been allowed to sleep on the couch in Fanny's room, so that he felt special and included.

By now, Fanny felt very guilty that she had taken none of these steps to make Will feel important and secure, and she sought advice on how to give her son his self-confidence back. Her doctor explained that a child who gets upset, for whatever cause, be it a new baby or starting preschool, will regress to an earlier, more primitive phase of development, exactly as Will had done. She pointed out that Will had no control over this and that, far from punishing Will for future accidents, the whole family must be very relaxed and play them down, saying things like "It doesn't matter, Will. Let me clean you up, then we can play a game if you want." But Will was feeling far too insecure for a quick recovery, and the following morning he regressed even further and refused to feed himself: he demanded to be fed.

A PLAN OF ACTION

Fanny and Chris decided to take immediate positive action and, on the advice of their doctor, started a program to rebuild Will's confidence.

• They told Will's preschool teacher about the difficulties at home, and asked all the staff to be sympathetic and give Will lots of praise.
• Chris was to spend half an hour with Will when he came home each evening, when he would give Will his full attention and lots of cuddles.
• Fanny would also give Will half an hour of her time when he got home from school, with lots of cuddles and expressions of love, and take a deep interest in his preschool activities.
• Fanny would have regular sit-down breakfasts with Will, putting Miranda out of sight if possible in her cradle. She would never bring Miranda into the room at these special times unless Will suggested it.
• Fanny would point out to Will all the things that he had mastered that Miranda, a tiny baby, couldn't do, and suggest that perhaps Will could teach Miranda, even protect her.
• Will would have his own private bathtime, and Fanny and Chris would take turns reading him a bedtime story each night.
• Fanny and Chris would alternate taking Will out for a treat on his own each week.

Fanny and Chris put this plan into operation immediately, and within three days Will was feeding himself happily. Two weeks later, he asked to show Miranda his teddy bear, though he wouldn't let her touch him. He had no more daytime accidents after two weeks, and four weeks later he was sleeping dry through the night. Reassured by his parents' loving, caring attention, Will became more accepting of Miranda—in fact, three months later, Will said that he'd marry Miranda if he couldn't marry Fanny.

Sleep and wakefulness

A newborn baby needs a lot of sleep, and unless she is hungry, cold, or uncomfortable, it is likely that she will spend at least 60 percent of her time asleep.

Your baby may fall asleep immediately after—and sometimes during—a feeding. She will probably be indifferent to noises such as doors shutting or the radio—in fact, she may find droning noises soothing. Babies' sleeping patterns do vary, though, so if your baby is wakeful after a feeding, don't insist that she stays in her crib.

It is important that your baby learns to distinguish between day and night. When it becomes dark outside, close the curtains and turn the lights very low. Make sure that she is warm and covered and, when she wakes during the night, feed her quickly and quietly without turning the lights up, and don't play with her. In time she'll learn the difference between a daytime and a nighttime feeding.

WHERE SHOULD YOUR BABY SLEEP?

It's probably easiest to let your baby sleep in something that makes her portable, such as a bassinet. A carrier is also suitable both day and night, since it is easily movable and can be clipped on to a wheeled chassis when you go out. Later, she will need a crib.

Sleeping with you   It's lovely to cuddle and feed your baby in bed, but the safest place for her to sleep is in her own crib beside your bed. It's best not to have her sleep with you, but if you do need to for some reason, let her lie between you and your partner so that she can't fall out of bed. Never sleep with your baby if you have been drinking or have taken drugs that make you sleep heavily.

Your baby's bedroom   Pay careful attention to the temperature of your baby's room. Babies cannot regulate their body temperatures as well as adults and to maintain the right level of warmth they need a constant temperature and enough blankets to keep them warm—but not too warm (see p.123). A night light or dimmer switch will mean that you can check your baby during the night without waking her.

Sleeping outdoors   Except when it's chilly, your baby will sleep quite happily outside, but make sure she's wrapped up and visible at all times and never place her in direct sunlight; choose a shady area or protect her with a canopy. If it's windy, put the hood up on the carrier so it acts as a windbreak.

EVENINGS OUT

Because young babies are easy to carry and they sleep a lot, they're very portable, so you can still enjoy going out by taking your baby with you.

In the early weeks, it's a good thing for new parents, especially mothers, to get out of the house and relax with friends. It's easier to do this while your baby is young because she will sleep anywhere. A car seat that doubles as a freestanding chair is ideal for this; it can be safely strapped in place in the car, then carried indoors when you reach your destination while your baby sleeps.

Take advantage of this flexibility while you can; once your baby starts sleeping through the night, you will need to stick to a regular bedtime routine.

Sleeping
Make sure your baby is warm and covered, but not too warm (see p.123). A picture of a face will hold his attention if he's awake.

Clothing Your newborn will need to be changed often, and while she's sleeping she should wear something that gives you easy access to her diaper. An all-in-one stretch suit or a nightgown—one with a drawstring at the end so it doesn't ride up her back—is best.

It's important that your baby doesn't get too hot or too cold. In warm weather, a diaper and a T-shirt will be sufficient. In the winter, you can check that your baby is warm enough by touching the back of her neck with your hand. Her skin should feel about the same temperature as yours. If she feels too hot and clammy, you should take a blanket off and let her cool down.

PROBLEMS

If your baby wakes you frequently during the night or she cries when you try to go back to bed, you'll be short of sleep and you'll find it difficult to cope. It is essential that you get enough rest, and you should share the responsibility of night feedings with your partner—even if you are breastfeeding, your partner could bottle-feed your baby with expressed milk on some nights. Alternatively, you can have your partner bring you the baby to feed, and then he can change her diaper. If you're exhausted, get help from a friend or relative, relax your routine, get up late, and take daytime naps.

Encourage your baby to sleep at night by tiring her out during the day with plenty of stimulation: talk to her, pick her up, and give her lots of different things to look at. If she wakes up a lot in the night because she is wet, use double diapers or diaper liners, and if she cries when you leave her, don't immediately return and pick her up. Rocking her crib, removing a blanket, or changing her position may be sufficient to soothe her back to sleep.

Early on, swaddling or wrapping your baby in a shawl or blanket may help her sleep; the sensation of being tightly enclosed gives babies a great feeling of security. It's also a useful way of calming a distressed baby.

SWADDLING

To swaddle your baby, you need a shawl or small, light blanket. Fold the shawl in half to form a triangle and lay your baby on it, aligning her head with the longest edge. Then fold one point of the shawl across your baby and tuck it firmly behind her back. Do the same with the other point. Tuck the bottom of the shawl back underneath your baby's feet to keep them covered. Always make sure her head is uncovered. The close wrapping holds your baby's arms in a comfortable position that feels safe and secure and may also help her to sleep longer. If her limbs move while she is asleep, she is less likely to wake if swaddled.

Not all babies like swaddling, and if yours doesn't, don't worry. It's safe to swaddle your baby in cold weather, but keep a check on her temperature by touching her skin. Unwrap her right away if she feels or looks too hot.

SETTLING YOUR BABY DOWN

Here are several things you can do to ensure that your baby settles down to sleep.

- In the first month or so, wrap or swaddle your baby before you put her down.

- Give your baby a comfort suck from breast or bottle.

- Darken the room at night.

- In cold weather, put a hot-water bottle in the crib for a short time before you put your baby down—but never leave it in the crib.

- Hang a musical mobile over the crib to soothe your baby.

- If she doesn't seem to be settling down, rock her gently or stroke her back or limbs to soothe her.

- Try carrying her around in a baby sling and jogging her up and down: your closeness and heartbeat will help her to settle down.

REDUCING THE RISK

By following these guidelines, you will significantly reduce your baby's risk of crib death.

- Always place your baby on his back to sleep.

- Don't smoke, don't allow anyone in your house to smoke, and avoid smoky places.

- Don't let your baby get too hot.

- When covering your baby, allow for room temperature—the higher the temperature, the fewer blankets and bedclothes your baby needs, and vice versa (see chart opposite).

- Avoid tucking in, so your baby can throw off bedclothes if hot.

- If you think your baby is unwell, don't hesitate to contact your doctor.

- If your baby has a fever, don't bundle him up more—instead, use fewer covers so he can lose heat.

Feet to foot
Lay your baby on his back with his feet touching the foot of the crib, even if it means his head is halfway down the mattress.

REDUCING THE RISK OF CRIB DEATH

Sudden Infant Death Syndrome (SIDS), known colloquially as crib death, is the sudden and unexpected death of a baby for no obvious reason. The present rate for crib deaths in the US is 1–2 per 1,000 live births. Since the start of the Back to Sleep Campaign in 1994, the number of crib deaths has fallen by 50 percent.

The causes of crib death are unknown, and there is therefore no advice that can guarantee its prevention. There are, however, many ways in which parents can vastly reduce the risk. Recent surveys have proved that immunization reduces the risk, as does keeping your baby in your room with you at night for the first six months. Falling asleep with your baby on the sofa greatly increases the risk of crib death.

SLEEPING POSITION

One of the most crucial risk factors is the position in which you put your baby down to sleep. In most countries, babies have traditionally slept on their backs. In the UK, for example, most babies slept on their backs until the 1960s, and the number of crib deaths was low. In 1970, however, neonatal intensive care units started to lay preterm babies face down because it seemed this position improved breathing and reduced vomiting, and eventually the practice was extended to full-term babies.

The significance of sleeping position in relation to SIDS was looked at in 1965, but the evidence was not convincing, and it wasn't until SIDS rates in different communities were compared, that it became clear that SIDS was less common where babies slept on their backs. By this time, most babies were put in their cribs to sleep face downward. After the start of the Back to Sleep campaign, SIDS was most common among groups that had not been educated regarding the change.

Research in New Zealand since then has shown fewer crib deaths in babies placed on their sides, but without support, they can roll on to their tummies. The safest position for your baby, therefore, is on his back. Some people will tell you that this position may allow inhalation of spit-ups, but there is no evidence to support this.

SMOKING

A mother who smokes during pregnancy increases the risk of SIDS. (She also increases the risk of a premature or low birth-weight baby.) What's more, the risk increases with the number of cigarettes smoked. The risk of SIDS in babies born to smokers is twice that for babies born to nonsmokers, and with every ten cigarettes a day the risk increases threefold. Even more crib deaths could be avoided if mothers and fathers stopped smoking.

TEMPERATURE

There's no doubt that overheating from too many nightclothes, too many blankets, and too high a room temperature is a contributory factor, since SIDS is much more common in overheated babies.

Many parents increase the amount of bedding when a baby is unwell, but this is not what your baby needs. High temperature plus infection in babies over ten weeks old greatly increases the risk of crib death. If heat loss is prevented, the body temperature of a restless baby with an infection will rise by about 2°F (1°C) per hour. A baby loses most heat from its face, chest, and abdomen, so lying on the back allows body temperature to be better controlled.

There is no need to heat the baby's room all night unless the weather is cold; just make sure that your baby has enough blankets (see below). If you have a separate heater in the baby's room, use a thermostatically controlled one that will switch off if the room gets too warm, and switch back on again as it cools down.

CONTINUING RESEARCH

Although risk factors have been identified, the causes of SIDS are still not understood. Current research includes the development of a baby's temperature control mechanisms and respiratory system in the first six months, and the recent discovery that an inherited enzyme deficiency may cause a small number—about 1 percent—of crib deaths.

A recent study in the UK connected crib death with flame-retardant chemicals in crib mattresses, but the connection has not been definitely proven. Two-thirds of crib deaths occur in winter.

GETTING HELP

The unexpected death of an infant is a particularly painful bereavement, but support is available to help parents cope with their feelings of grief, bewilderment, and guilt (see Useful addresses, p.344).

- Many parents seek help immediately after the death—sometimes within hours—and telephone support lines are available that can provide information and a sympathetic listener.

- In the longer term, parents may seek professional help. The continued support of a healthcare provider, social worker, or religious adviser can be invaluable, so don't be afraid to ask.

- Parents may be helped by being able to talk to someone who has been through a similar experience, either in support groups or on a one-to-one basis.

- Support groups exist in some areas that continue long after professional help may have ceased, and these can be invaluable at times of particular grief, such as the anniversaries of the baby's birth and death.

- Parents who have lost one baby to crib death are likely to be extremely anxious when another baby is born. Support programs exist that involve the parents and the healthcare providers in making sure that the new baby gets the best possible care.

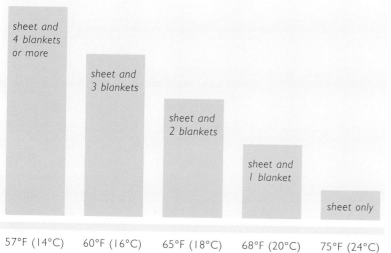

sheet and 4 blankets or more

sheet and 3 blankets

sheet and 2 blankets

sheet and 1 blanket

sheet only

57°F (14°C)   60°F (16°C)   65°F (18°C)   68°F (20°C)   75°F (24°C)

Controlling the temperature
Keep a thermometer in your baby's room so that you can see how many blankets he needs. At 65°F (18°C), a sheet and two blankets is adequate.

CAUSES OF WAKEFULNESS

Here are some of the things you can do if your baby is wakeful through the night.

• Make sure that your baby is neither too hot nor too cold (see p.123).

• Check that your baby isn't in any discomfort from a soiled diaper or diaper rash.

• Don't keep going into your baby's room to see if he's asleep.

• If your child suddenly becomes sleepless, think about the possible causes, such as a change in routine, someone new staying with you, or your going out to work. Whatever the cause, he will need lots of your attention.

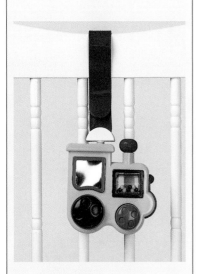

Restlessness
Put mirrors and noisy toys on the side of the crib to amuse your restless baby.

Sleep and wakefulness

Babies usually establish their sleep patterns within the first few months, and if you find that your baby sleeps a lot in her first year, she will probably do the same in her second. At some time in the first 12 months, she'll sleep through the night (though with some babies it can be much later), and once she starts to crawl, she'll be using up so much energy during the day that she may sleep for ten or 11 hours uninterruptedly.

Even though she needs sleep, however, she's able to keep herself awake so that she can stay in your company. She may whimper and cry, get crabby, and then become so tense and unhappy that sleep becomes impossible. If your baby is clingy and sleepless and appears to be insecure, the best treatment for her is you. Stay with her, hold her close to you, rock her, sing to her, soothe her, and walk up and down with her until she feels that you are not going to leave her and is reassured by your closeness. This may take half an hour, but usually she'll fall asleep in your arms after about ten or 15 minutes, and then you can put her back in her crib.

WAKEFUL BABIES
There's no question that some babies need very little sleep. Wakeful babies, as I like to call them, are usually bright, curious, intelligent, and very affectionate. They quickly catch on to the fact that you're there all through the night and that they can attract your attention with crying or calling out to you. I firmly believe that no baby's crying should be ignored. A baby that's left to cry quickly learns that adults don't respond to her cries for help and love. She will stop asking for attention and may become solitary and withdrawn. Try not to get upset because your baby is wakeful; she's demonstrating her sociability and intelligence because she's learning all the time, and you'll find as she grows up that she's a very rewarding friend. If your baby wakes before your bedtime, try carrying her around in a sling or put her in a baby bouncer so that she can tire herself out.

Solutions Wakeful babies very often need diversion, so as soon as your baby can sit up, leave some favorite soft toys or soft books in the crib. Put a mirror on the side of the crib so that she can look in it and talk to herself. A mobile above the crib that makes sounds can fascinate your baby for quite a long time, too.

I had two wakeful babies and I had to resort to extreme measures to get any sleep myself. I put up a cot alongside my baby's crib, and when he woke up in the middle of the night, I would soothe him so that he went back to sleep without really waking up. This prevented him from getting upset with a crying bout.

If your baby only whimpers, don't get up immediately because she may go back to sleep without any soothing at all. If, however, the whimper becomes true crying, then you should go and see her. The first time you go in, try soothing talk while patting her on the back. If this doesn't work, you'll have to pick her up to soothe her, then put her back in her crib, and leave the room. If she continues to cry, you may decide to go back every five minutes to calm your baby down. (If you do, try to soothe your baby without lifting her up—say, by rocking the crib or talking to her.)

BEDTIME ROUTINES

As your baby gets older, she'll require more of your attention at bedtime, and probably will have settled into some routine that she needs in order to sleep, such as a story, a song, or some kind of gentle game. Do everything you can to make your baby calm, tranquil, and happy before sleep. If necessary, forego a scolding for a minor misdemeanor; you don't want your child to face bedtime feeling tearful and upset.

Every child has the right to love her crib, and from an early age a child has to learn to calm herself down. But an older child may sometimes be happiest going to sleep in your company. As soon as she's asleep, you can take her to her crib and, instead of a lonely child upstairs becoming upset and calling out to you, you'll have a secure, calm child who in all probability will sleep through the night.

Comfort habits Your child may become attached to a comfort item of some sort: a doll, a small handkerchief, or a piece of torn blanket. You may also find that habits such as rocking, thumb-sucking, or twisting her hair will become part of her bedtime routine. There's nothing wrong with any of these bedtime rituals. By using a comforter to help her to go to sleep, your baby is using her inner resources and becoming self-reliant. She'll give up these habits in her own time.

HOW NAPS CHANGE

Some babies sleep through the night from early on, some don't. As a general rule, the more mobile your baby is and the more energy she uses, the more soundly she sleeps—sleep being divided between daytime naps and night time.

When your baby grows, night sleep usually becomes unbroken and naps are fairly regular—one in the morning and one in the afternoon for varying lengths of time.

Later, your baby's nap times will change: she may put off her morning nap until after lunch, and then need another nap at around 3:30 or 4 p.m. before going to bed for the night at around 7 p.m. Every day may be different.

Whatever time your baby is disposed to nap, take the lead from her; don't try to impose nap times on her. And try to clear your time so that you are able to take a nap with your baby; both of you will be recharged when you wake up.

Cotton vest

Fabric book

Silk handkerchief

Soft cotton blanket

Fleecy fabric rattle

Security objects
Your child may use a comforter such as a soft toy or blanket to help her sleep. This is quite normal, so don't try to take it away from her.

Sleep and wakefulness

AWAY FROM HOME

It's quite reasonable for your child to be scared or refuse to get into a strange bed—when he goes to stay with friends or grandparents, for instance, and when you go on vacation.

• Make the new bed into a playground: put lots of toys on the bed, and let your child have drinks and food on the bed, so that he associates it with pleasant experiences.

• Show your child that you're in easy reach. Get him to call out and then answer back so that he knows you're nearby.

• If he gets scared and refuses to use the bed, don't ridicule him, don't force him into bed, don't leave him alone, and don't lock the door. That will only make him worse.

• Try telling him that because he's being so grown-up in using a new bed, he can have a treat, such as a new bedtime story or ten minutes of sitting on your knee watching television.

Many two-year-olds periodically wake up during the night. If your child is one of them, this may be distressing for you and your partner, but it is both common and normal, and you should never deny your child love, comfort, and affection.

There may be some obvious problem, but often you won't be able to find out a reason for your child's waking up. It could just be that he's a bit afraid of the dark, but he can't explain to you what's wrong, nor can you reassure him with words. You have to comfort with actions, so give lots of kisses and cuddles to show your child that he's loved.

Daytime napping As your child gets older, you'll find that he doesn't necessarily want to sleep at naptime, but he does need a rest. Try to make a routine out of naptime whether your child sleeps or not by, say, playing some music or reading. You may find your child goes to sleep at naptime if you allow him to sleep in your bed as a special treat or if you give him some idea of how long the naptime will be; one way of doing this is to put on his favorite tape and say that naptime isn't over until the tape is finished.

CRIB TO BED

When your child is strong enough and well-coordinated enough to climb out of his crib and come into your room, it's time for him to start using a bed. Most children will be pleased and excited with their new bed, but if your child seems nervous, there are plenty of things you can do to help (see pp.128–29); the simplest is to let him take naps in the bed until he is ready to sleep in it at night. If you're worried that your child might fall out of the bed, you could fit a bed guard to one or both sides as appropriate.

Quiet time
During the day, watch your child for signs of bad temper or fretfulness and ensure that she rests or plays a quiet game.

Pleasant bedtimes

From the age of three onward, your child may use delaying tactics in order to put off going to bed. The way you handle this situation really depends on how much energy you have at the end of the day, and what your previous bedtime routine has been.

If you've been taking care of your child and managing the household tasks all day, you will be in need of private time and may feel you can insist that he goes to bed. On the other hand, if you have been out at work all day, you will want to see your child, so you may feel very sympathetic to his pleas for your attention.

   If you've always had quite a strict bedtime routine and your child suddenly departs from this, then it's probably best for both of you if you firmly reinstitute the bedtime with loving fairness. If, however, you've been flexible about bedtimes, then it's probably just as well for your child's happiness and your serenity to let him stay with you and make himself comfortable. He will be asleep in a few minutes if he has the reassurance of your presence in the room.

KEEPING BEDTIME PEACEFUL

I'm convinced that bedtimes should be happy times, and with my own children I was always prepared to make concessions to this guiding principle. I would do anything to avoid letting my children go to bed unhappy. I would do my utmost to prevent any crying, and whereas during the day I might punish a small misdemeanor, it would go unmarked at nighttime to make sure that my child didn't go to sleep with the sound of an angry parent's voice in his ears.

   If you have more than one child, let them enjoy their bedtimes in the same bedroom. Company is reassuring, and seeing a sister or brother in pajamas at the same time makes your child feel that bedtimes are just and fair, even if your older child is allowed to stay up slightly later. Until they get to an age where they need their privacy, it's a good idea for them to share a bedroom.

FEAR OF THE DARK

As your child gets older and his imagination becomes more fertile, it's very easy to imagine frightening things in the shadows. A fear of the dark is entirely normal—even adults retain it. Leave a night light on in the room or leave a light on outside with a dimmer switch so that your child can see his way to the bathroom if he needs it, or to your room. (If you use a night light, make sure it doesn't cast frightening shadows.) Never insist on his bedroom being completely dark, and never ridicule his fear; it's really a sign that your child is growing up and learning about the world around him. Tell him that if he wakes up and is frightened, he can always come to you for a cuddle.

PRIVACY

You can teach your child to stay within his own space as early as two years, but certainly by three, when he's open to reason. He'll learn that it's his responsibility not to disturb you thoughtlessly just because he feels like it.

Teaching him to respect your privacy is far better than shutting him out of your room, which you should never do. You can encourage mature behavior by providing him with his own private space, which is his alone, in which his belongings reside and where he can find his favorite things. Children respond very quickly to the idea of privacy, particularly if they are given a private space of their own that they can keep neat, be proud of, and go to if they want to be quiet and play on their own.

You can affirm this sense of privacy by always pointing out to your child that certain things belong to him: this is his book, his toy, his dress, and they all have a proper place. In this way, he will become familiar with his belongings and where he can find them. By about the age of four, he's mature enough to realize that if he has his things, you have yours, and that just as he doesn't like his possessions being disturbed, neither do you.

Crib to bed

Case study

Parents' names Rachel and Zac Freiman
Age 34 years and 33 years
Medical history Nothing abnormal
Obstetric history One child, Hella, age three years.
Three months pregnant with second child.

Child's name Hella Freiman
Age 3 years
Medical history Minor childhood ailments. Bowel
and bladder control now almost complete, wears
training pants at night.

There are several ways to lure a child from a crib to a bed, but the least upsetting ones always involve a bit of preparation, so it's best to plan a few months in advance. Rachel and her husband Zac decided to move three-year-old Hella into a bed when Rachel was three months pregnant with their second child, and their decision was influenced as much by the need for extra space as by Hella's age.

Rachel and Zac didn't think it was practical to have Hella in the small room with the new baby, nor did they want her to feel resentful that she was being pushed out of her own bedroom to make way for a new arrival. They decided to make the switch at the same time—a new bedroom and a new bed—before the baby arrived, so there seemed to be nothing unnatural about it. "With hindsight," says Rachel, "it may have been too much of a change all at once, because although Hella was excited about her new room, it was still an unfamiliar environment, which meant she was less settled at night."

Rachel and Zac involved Hella as much as possible, letting her choose the colors for her new room, and taking her shopping to buy her choice of comforter—a clever way of getting her excited about her new bed. If you don't really need new bedding, it's just as effective to get your child a new toy—a teddy bear or a doll—that "lives" in the bed. This will make her feel secure.

LITTLE BY LITTLE

Rachel and Zac allowed Hella a few practice runs in her bed, which is a good idea. "As a treat," says Zac, "we would hide a little toy under the covers and then let her find it. Two weeks before we planned to move her in, we started letting her take her naps there—a good tip that Rachel picked up at a toddler play group. Because Hella had the naps during the day, she got used to her bed without the complication of nighttime fears.

"I think it was a good idea to do this gradually, because children can have fears that adults never imagine. One of the new things we bought to go in Hella's room, for example, was a Mickey Mouse alarm clock. On the second night in her new bed, we heard her crying and rushed into her room. She was obviously terrified and said there was a man there. We assured her there wasn't, but she insisted

128

she could hear his footsteps quite clearly. Luckily Rachel took her seriously, and figured out that it was the loud ticking of the alarm clock that she could hear!"

Even though Rachel and Zac took the clock away, Hella refused to spend the rest of the night in her room. The night after was better, although there were several occasions during the following two weeks when she wet the bed. This seems to have been part of the adjustment process, since she hasn't done it since.

WHEN IS THE RIGHT TIME?

There are no hard and fast rules for deciding when the time is right to make the switch. In general, it is between the age of two-and-a-half to three-and-a-half years, although this largely depends on your child's temperament and your own personal circumstances; like Rachel and Zac, you may have little choice, or alternatively, your child might clearly outgrow her crib and refuse to stay in it. A child who can climb out of her crib can cause herself harm, and it's safer to put her in a low bed than run the risk of her toppling off the edge of a high crib.

Bear in mind that once your child is in a bed, she will be able to get out and investigate the nooks and crannies of her room when she wakes up in the morning. This means it is advisable to reassess safety measures to make sure that an unsupervised child won't come to any harm.

If, like Rachel and Zac, you are expecting another baby, don't move your first child out of her room or crib when the new baby arrives, since this will obviously fuel jealousy. As with everything else, it's best to give your child time to adapt to a new idea and involve her in the preparation wherever possible.

Unless you have to move your child, there is little point in trying to force the issue. While some children want to get out of their crib as soon as possible, others find the idea of a big bed frightening. They need a little more time and a bit more persuading. If all else fails, entice your child into bed by getting into it yourself—children are usually curious about what their parents are doing, and will quickly imitate you.

MAKING A SMOOTH TRANSITION

Help your child make the switch to a big bed by recreating a secure environment like the one she had in her crib. If your child is scared or unsettled, she won't sleep, and that means you won't either, so it's worth preparing your child for the move. Start off, as Rachel and Zac did, by making it a positive and exciting change.

Tell your child that now she's a big girl, she's very lucky to get to sleep in a big bed, "like Mommy and Daddy do." Put lots of her favorite toys there and consider installing a night light or just leaving the bedroom door open so that she can see the hall light. If music helps to soothe her, leave it on while she goes to sleep.

Once you have put your child to bed, don't make the mistake of disappearing suddenly—this will unsettle her, and you might find yourself back at square one. Instead, make sure she is comfortable: sing songs or read a story, leave a drink by the bed, and a potty if necessary, and then say goodbye more than once without closing the door so that she knows you are still there.

If your child is not changing rooms, put the new bed in her room for a few months before making the switch so that it's familiar. Some children are scared that they will fall out of their new bed because there is no barrier. If this is a problem, make a temporary barrier by lining a few chairs up next to the bed, or putting a row of cushions between your child and the edge of the bed.

Crying and comforting

CRYING GIRLS

The amount of crying, and reasons for crying, are different in boys and girls.

• Baby girls are less vulnerable to stress at the time of birth than male babies and less likely to cry.

• An American study has shown that girls are less irritable than boys at the age of three weeks, and therefore cry less.

• Girls are less likely than boys to cry in new situations.

• Mothers tend to give extra attention to girls who cry a lot.

Communication
Your baby can only make her needs known by crying, so always respond.

All babies cry quite a lot and so will yours, so be prepared for it. There will be times when the reason for her crying is obvious: she's hungry, too hot, too cold, bored, or uncomfortable because of a wet or a dirty diaper, or she might simply want your affection and closeness. One reason for crying that parents often fail to recognize is the desire for sleep. I well remember trying to console my newborn son in all kinds of ways before it occurred to me that he just wanted to be left alone to sleep.

Very young babies cry when they are disturbed, when they are roughly handled, such as at bathtime, or when they get a shock, perhaps from feeling that they are going to be dropped, from a loud noise, or from a bright light. A two-week-old baby always responds to the security of being firmly wrapped in a shawl or held in strong, confident arms. Once you have investigated your baby's crying, don't worry too much about it—crying is practically her only way of communicating.

Recognizing different cries Within a few weeks, you can distinguish between the different cries that mean your baby is hungry, is fussing because she's bored, wants to be put down to sleep, or wants a cuddle. Of course your baby is learning about you, too, and how to communicate with you. She cries out of need and you respond by giving her what she wants.

RESPONDING TO YOUR BABY
I believe you should respond quite quickly to your baby's cry. If you don't respond, then your baby feels as you would if you were ignored in a conversation. There's quite a lot of research to show that your baby is affected by how you respond to crying. For instance, mothers who respond quickly to crying tend to have children with more advanced communication skills, including speaking and outgoing behavior. Babies who are ignored cry more often and for longer in the first year than babies who are attended to quickly. It seems that mothers cause

their babies to settle into a pattern of crying often and persistently because they fail to respond, and a vicious circle is set up in which the baby cries, the mother fails to respond, the baby cries more, and the mother is even less inclined to act. A sensitive response from you promotes self-confidence and self-esteem in later life. Some mothers believe that always responding will spoil their babies. A young baby has a limitless capacity for soaking up love and there's no way that you can spoil a baby by giving her attention in her first year.

CRYING SPELLS

Most babies have crying spells. Often crying occurs in the late afternoon or early evening, when your baby may cry for as long as half an hour. If your baby has colic (see p.133), evening crying spells can last up to two hours. You should always try to console your baby during a crying spell.

Once your child establishes a pattern of crying spells, they may go on for several weeks. It's your baby's way of becoming adjusted to being in a very different world from that experienced inside your uterus. The more sensitively you respond and take your lead from her, the more rapidly she'll become acclimatized to her new lifestyle; the sooner you accommodate her likes and dislikes, the sooner crying spells will stop.

NIGHTTIME CRYING

There's no doubt that every parent finds crying spells difficult to cope with, especially if they occur at night. Don't get frustrated because your child doesn't respond to your attempts to soothe her. If walking up and down, singing songs, wrapping, or swaddling don't work, you could take her for a drive; the motion of the car may send her to sleep.

During the night, crying will almost certainly make you feel impatient at the least, and at the worst, that you will do anything to stop your baby from crying. These feelings are normal, so don't become frightened and tense, otherwise the crying will simply get worse. When my five-day-old baby cried persistently during the night, I actually thought that if I threw him against the wall he would be bound to stop. I didn't, of course, but it's quite normal to think such things; it would only have been abnormal if I had done it.

WHY DOES MY BABY CRY SO MUCH?

There's research that shows that your child may cry despite your efforts to console her, regardless of whether or not she feels any discomfort. For instance, babies of mothers who have a general anesthetic during labor or who have been delivered by forceps tend to cry more in the first weeks of life. Similarly, babies born after a long labor are likely to sleep in short bursts, and to cry quite a lot in between. There's no question that a mother communicates her mood to her baby, so if you are tense, irritable, and impatient, your baby will feel it, and cry. There are individual and racial differences between babies. Some cry a different amount even if they're given the same care and attention.

CRYING BOYS

Boys differ from girls in their reasons for crying, and in the way they respond to attempts to soothe them.

• Baby boys tend to benefit from a regular routine early on, and if the routine is disturbed, they quite often resort to crying.

• Boys tend to take longer to adapt to new situations, and may cry if pushed.

• More boys than girls tend to be labeled as difficult, but studies show that "difficult" baby boys are no more difficult than any other by the age of two years, especially if parents work hard to console them and make them happy.

• Boys seem to need responsiveness from their parents more than girls in order to be happy, and cry readily if parental attention and love is not forthcoming.

• Mothers of boys are less likely to give extra attention and cuddles when their baby is crying a lot, because they mistakenly want them to be tough.

Newborn crying
Many newborns cry a lot at first, but then settle down after just a few weeks.

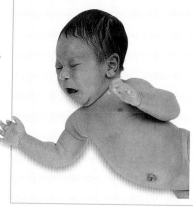

PACIFIERS

Babies are born with a sucking reflex. Without it, they wouldn't suckle and wouldn't nourish themselves. I feel it's important that babies are allowed to indulge their desire to suck.

Some babies are more "sucky" than others; I certainly had one who wanted to suck all the time, whether he was hungry or not. With all four of my sons, I used to gently put their thumbs into their mouths so that they could suck to soothe themselves. But at the same time, I see nothing wrong with using pacifiers as comforters, though very young babies will not take to one readily.

While a baby is young, pacifiers should be sterilized in exactly the same way as you sterilize feeding bottles and nipples. Once your child is being weaned, however, and starts to use his fingers for feeding himself, it is pointless to sterilize pacifiers. Careful washing and rinsing is all that's needed.

SOOTHING YOUR BABY

There are lots of remedies you can try to soothe and console your baby if he's crying. As a general rule, most babies respond to movement and sound: hence the effectiveness of taking them out in the car, where the motion of the vehicle and the steady humming sound of the engine will usually quiet them. Your baby will probably find any of the following movements or sounds soothing:

• A movement that rocks him, whether it is you, a swing, a rocking cradle, or a rocking chair.
• Walking or dancing with an emphasis on rhythm, since it reminds him of the time when he was being jogged inside your uterus.
• Bouncing him in your arms or in the crib.
• Putting him in a baby sling.
• Any form of music, as long as it isn't too loud but is rhythmic—specially recorded sleeping tapes are available.
• A noisy toy that your baby can shake or rattle.
• A steady household noise such as the washing machine.
• Your own singing voice, especially if you sing a lullaby.

UNDERSTANDING THE CAUSE

You have to learn to read your baby's signals and gain insight into his needs and desires. Once you recognize your baby's cry, you have to respond to it, otherwise he's bound to scream even louder. Always be sensitive to your baby's needs. Look, listen, and try to interpret what he is trying to say to you through his behavior. As you get to know your baby, you will learn to understand what he really wants. If you know, for example, that he's hungry, don't delay his feeding by deciding to give him a bath first, simply as a matter of sticking to your routine. Occasionally, you have to ignore routines in order to respond to your baby's crying.

There are all sorts of signs of small discomforts to which you must be alert. When your baby has a cold, for instance, his nose may become blocked, making it impossible for him to breathe and feed at the same time, so he'll become angry and frustrated and almost certainly cry.

Undressing
Many young babies cry when they are given a bath, because they hate having their skin exposed to the air.

Cause of crying	What to do
Hunger A hungry cry is nearly always the first cry that a parent recognizes, and it is the most common reason that young babies cry. They rarely cry after feeding. Babies love the sensation of a full stomach, more than being held or sucking.	Feed on demand. If you have a baby who wants to suck all the time, you don't need to feed; just give him a drink of cooled boiled water. Use a pacifier, holding it in his mouth if necessary, so that he can suck on it.
Tiredness Until they're used to their new world, babies cry when they are tired, and it takes an observant parent to realize this and to put a baby down to nap.	Lay your baby down where he is quiet and warm. Wrapping or swaddling him before you put him down to sleep helps, too.
Lack of contact Some babies will stop crying as soon as you pick them up, because they want a cuddle. Babies brought up in cultures where they are constantly in a sling or swaddled rarely cry.	Always pick up your baby as soon as he cries. Carry him around in a shawl or a sling. Lay your baby tummy-down across your lap and gently massage his back.
Startling A jerky movement, a sudden noise, or a bright light can upset your baby. If physical games are too rough, he'll cry.	Hold your baby close, rock him gently, and sing to him. Avoid sudden jerky movements, noises, and bright lights.
Undressing Most babies dislike being undressed, since it puts their bodies through movements that are neither familiar nor comforting, and they hate the feel of air on their skin. Being jerked suddenly makes them fearful.	Undress your baby as little as possible in the first few weeks, and keep him wrapped or covered with a towel as you remove layers of clothing. Keep up a running commentary of reassuring talk as you undress him.
Temperature Babies tend to cry if they become too hot or too cold. They may cry if a wet or soiled diaper gets cold or if they are suffering from diaper rash.	Keep your baby's room at 61–68°F (16–20°C) with the number of blankets suggested on p.123. Remove blankets and clothing if your baby is too hot; add another layer of clothing and a blanket if he's too cold. Change his diaper if necessary.
Pain An ear infection, colic, or some other source of pain may cause your baby to cry. If his ear hurts, he may hit it with his fist; if it's colic, his legs may be drawn up to his abdomen.	Hold your baby close, cuddle him, and talk soothingly. If you can find the source of pain, such as a diaper pin, remove it immediately. If your baby seems ill, seek medical advice.

COLIC

Colic describes recurrent bouts of unexplained crying that usually happen in the late afternoon or evening but can be at any time. The crying may be very intense and brief, or last for hours, and is not generally pacified by the usual remedies. The baby's face becomes very red, the legs are drawn up to the abdomen, and the fists clenched. Colic is not due to pain.

Colic generally stops by the age of three or four months without your doing anything at all, is rarely serious, and needs no treatment. However, parents find it distressing. It is not known why it happens, but it usually starts in the first three weeks of a baby's life. It is well recognized that colicky babies are quite healthy and continue to thrive.

All sorts of causes have been put forward, such as overfeeding, underfeeding, gas in the bowels, being picked up too much or too little, indigestion, and tension.

It has always struck me that tension is the most likely cause. You're preoccupied in the evening with bathtime and bedtime for the baby and having your evening meal. It is likely that your baby picks up on the tension, and quite normal that he would respond with a crying spell.

Since your baby is likely to cry every night for 12 weeks, I'm against using any kind of medicine to forestall the crying. Of course, you should try to soothe your baby, but don't expect him to respond readily. Try to take comfort from the fact that these spells come only at night and last for only three months, so there is light at the end of the tunnel.

COMFORT OBJECTS

When children need comfort, they may become attached to an object such as a blanket or special toy, or turn to thumb-sucking as a consolation when you're not around.

Nearly all children like to have some form of comfort that they control. Very often, comfort objects are ones that children suck or stroke in moments of anxiety or stress, to stimulate the effect of being stroked or being comforted. Let them have their comfort objects and don't interfere

Dealing with anxiety
Unfamiliar people and places make your baby anxious, so reassure her with lots of cuddles.

Crying and comforting

As your baby grows older and her world becomes more complex, the causes of crying change. In an older baby, the cause is nearly always some form of emotional disturbance: mother leaving and the deprivation of her love, or fear, anxiety, or separation.

BOREDOM

The older she gets, the longer your baby will spend being awake, and there is therefore greater scope for her getting bored. Many children cry out of sheer boredom, especially if left alone with no distractions and no one to play with. A one-year-old enjoys your company more than anything else, and is constantly interested in what you are doing.

What to do Always leave toys in the crib, especially old color magazines or cloth books. Mobiles, baby gyms, or strings of interesting objects (the strings must short so that they can't get wrapped around the baby's neck) above the crib will help amuse and distract your baby. Though it may be tiresome for you, your baby will cry far less from boredom if you keep her with you as much as you can.

FEAR OF SEPARATION

When your baby is about six to eight months, separation from a parent becomes the greatest source of distress to her and nearly always precipitates crying. Try to get your baby accustomed to separation over several months by leaving her for longer and longer periods—say, 20 minutes, then an hour, then three hours. If you go out to work, you will find your baby's fear upsetting, but this phase will pass as she gets used to seeing you go and always return. While it lasts, be very careful about the way you take leave of your baby, and make sure she's familiar with her surroundings and the people she's with. If she finds separation very unpleasant the first time, she's likely to respond with crying the second time. It's up to you to make separation as easy as possible.

What to do Be sympathetic and supportive and never make fun of your child's fears. She will respond better to reassuring actions than words, so if you make a promise to her that you are coming back, always keep it. If you say that you're only going for five minutes, just leave the room, get on with some small job, and come back in exactly that time.

INSECURITY AND ANXIETY

As your baby gets older, she becomes increasingly aware of strangers. Those situations that cause her most anxiety are being in a strange place with you, or being with strangers. As long as you're there, she can cope, but being left in a strange place with strange people completely unnerves her. Never do it. Any source of anxiety makes your child clingy. She will turn to you for comfort. She may even lose her appetite. If you become aware that your child is anxious, you should respond to her immediately.

There is an enormous amount of research showing that the child who is secure develops in almost every way more successfully than the child who is insecure. It's important to help her feel secure from the moment she is born.

What to do The best thing is extra reassurance, physical contact, cuddles, love, and soothing talk. Your child will grow out of this period of anxiety, but it helps never to force her to go to a stranger if she doesn't really want to. Explain to strangers that she's shy, and needs some time to get used to them. Your presence will help her to cope with new situations and experiences, even though she may feel fearful and uncomfortable at first. Whatever you do, always let your baby have the comforter of her choice, and always give her lots of hugs to reassure her.

This doesn't mean to say you can't gently encourage your child to be curious and adventurous. To grow up with a feeling of self-confidence and self-worth, your child needs plenty of approval, love, and praise from you, so give these every time she shows some independence.

FRUSTRATION

As your baby grows up, her desire to do things far outstrips her ability to do them, and so she becomes frustrated. This often results in crying. As she starts to crawl, then cruises along the furniture, then walks, you will almost certainly have to restrain her, which will result in added frustration and crying every time you do it. By the time she gets to 18 months, your baby's spirit of adventure is in excess of her balance, mobility, and coordination. She is likely to attempt tasks that are beyond her, and she'll become very frustrated as a result. Even though you know she is frustrated, you are going to have to stop her from doing things simply to protect her.

What to do Make your home as childproof as possible (see pp.306–11): remove precious objects from within her reach, and install safety plugs and guards around the house to make sure she can't injure herself. Distraction is a good ploy for frustration, so always have a favorite toy on hand, or be ready with a game if she becomes upset.

BEDTIME CRYING

Babies tend to cry at bedtime because they're tired, irritable, and don't wish to be separated from you. You can reassure them by establishing happy bedtime routines (see p.125).

• Make the hour before bedtime a really happy one. Sit your child on your lap, read a story or book, or play a quiet game, or sing a song to her.

• A gentle, playful bathtime will make your baby slightly sleepy, as will a warm drink before being put to bed.

• Your baby will almost certainly have a favorite game, song, or story and for a baby repetition is happiness, so do as she asks; it makes her feel secure.

Relaxed bedtimes
Spend time with your child just before bedtime in some quiet activity so he goes to bed calm and relaxed.

INJURIES

Toddlers tend to cry at even the most minor injury, such as a small scratch, an abrasion, or a tiny bruise.

In our house, I always had "the magic cream" (a mild antiseptic cream) on hand, and my children responded almost immediately to attention, reassurance, and a thin smear of the magic cream. Sometimes I had to sit down with them, hold them close, give them a big cuddle, and make very sympathetic sounds to show them that I knew how much it was hurting or how frightened they were—many young children are terrified by the sight of blood. Comfort and the magic cream nearly always had a calming effect.

Whenever your child comes to you in distress, crying over a small injury, be sympathetic. Say you know how much it's hurting and don't try to make him be brave. In a few moments he'll skip off your knee and return to his play after a kiss to make it better, a cuddle, and a favorite drink or snack.

If necessary, put some interesting idea into your child's mind to distract him from the injury, such as a special treat for supper, a special game with Dad, a picnic, or an outing to a favorite place.

Crying and comforting

As your baby's thinking becomes more sophisticated, he gains a wider appreciation of what's going on in the world around him, and his reasons for crying become more difficult to figure out. He's starting to understand what you say, not only in terms of facts but of your answers, and he's beginning to use his own reason and respond to reasoned argument. He's becoming very aware of himself and other people, and of the will of others versus his own. His fears are therefore much more related to his daytime activities and any upsets arising from them. Emotionally, he's developing very rapidly, too. He can feel guilt, shame, jealousy, and dislike, and be so upset that these emotions make him cry.

FEARS

The most common fears in this age group are of the dark and of thunder. Fear of the dark is so common as to be almost universal. It has no explanation, and reasoning with your child won't help. It's cruel to make fun of his fear, and you should never do that. Give your child an exciting night light—perhaps one with a colored bulb.

Fear of thunder and lightning is also very common, and the best way to deal with it is to distract your child while he can hear it. You can play loud music, turn on the television set, or take him into a quiet room and read him a story. You could also treat him by giving him the toy you had put aside for a rainy day.

DEALING WITH FEARS

One of the best ways to dispel fears is to talk about them, so get your child to be open and frank about what frightens him. Give him your full attention and ask questions, so that he knows that you are taking him seriously. Quite often fears are difficult to put into words, but hear your child out. Help him to explain by supplying a few examples, and confess that you have similar fears, too. Never scold or ridicule your child about his fears. Do something simple and reassuring, like demonstrating to your child that it is fun in the swimming pool and the water is nothing to dread. Your child will trust you and his fear will gradually diminish. When he's old enough, try to explain how things work: for instance, that lightning is just like a giant spark.

If your child is afraid of going to a friend's house, talk him through it step by step: "First I'll drive you to Johnny's house, and then you can play with him…" Nearly all children have some irrational fears, such as fear of monsters, ghosts, or dragons. Remember, to your child a fear is serious, so you shouldn't try to tell him that his fears are unreal.

FEAR OF SEPARATION

Even when your child is three years old, he will still have fears about losing you. When he was younger, he worried about losing sight of you; now, he is fearful that you will not come back, that you will die while you are away from him, and that he will be deprived of you forever. Again, a very good way to reassure your child is to go step by step through what is going to happen when you leave him. The more details you can give, and the more you can confirm the details, the better. What you might say is, "When Daddy comes home from work, we are both going to get ready to go out to visit Aunt Sarah. I'll take a bath, Daddy will shave, and we'll change our clothes. Then we'll put you to bed and we'll have our usual song, story, and game. Then Mommy will lie on your bed and cuddle you while we talk about your day, and what you are going to do tomorrow. Mommy won't leave you until you are fast asleep, and the next thing you will know is that it is morning and Mommy will be there."

DETHRONEMENT

Your child is bound to feel pretty distressed at the thought of a new baby brother or sister and the "dethronement" that he thinks will follow. Take all the precautions you can to make him feel good about the baby. Refer to the baby as his new sister or brother, and let him feel your tummy as the baby grows and kicks. Show him where the baby is going to sleep, and teach him all kinds of helpful things he can do to help take care of her. Well before you go into the hospital, make sure your child is at ease with the person who is going to babysit him while you're there.

When you come home, have someone else carry the baby; you should have your arms free to scoop your child up and give him a big cuddle. Don't turn to the new baby until he asks to see her. Make sure that you bring home a present from the baby for him. If you have to stay in the hospital, let him visit you as often as you like, and when he does, make sure that the baby is not in your arms, but is lying in a crib at your side so you're free to hold your child.

OVERTIREDNESS

A child of this age very often becomes overexcited and overtired toward bedtime. He'll try to put off his bedtime for as long as possible, and become more distressed. Your child might become so fragile that any small discomfort or frustration will make him start to cry inconsolably.

If you are expecting your child to have a late evening, or a special treat such as a party or a school play, make sure he takes a nap during the day so that his energy will last. If he does become overexcited and overtired, it is especially important that you remain calm and quiet. Talk to him gently, give him lots of cuddles, be infinitely patient, and take him gently to his bedroom. Sing him a song or read a story until he has become calm and quieted down.

TANTRUMS

Young children usually have tantrums out of frustration or because they are pitting their will against that of others.

Older children have tantrums because they can think of no other way of showing their determination. In the privacy of your own home, the best way to deal with a tantrum is simply to ignore it and leave the room.

It's slightly more difficult, however, in public, and you can do several things. Don't fuss, shout, or get flustered. Take your child calmly into a quiet place and attempt to calm him down. If you're in a store, take him out into the street, or into your car, or out of the restaurant into the restroom.

Fearful toddler
Always take your child's fears seriously and ask him to explain them if he can.

FEARS

Three years is a highly anxious age, but by four years your child's fears are more clearly defined.

She'll be easily frightened by sounds, for example, especially loud sounds outside, such as a fire engine. She may fear people of a different culture or appearance from herself, old people, "monsters," the dark, animals, and your leaving her—especially at night. Children of this age may enjoy being mildly frightened by an adult in play, as long as it's clearly pretend.

By five years, your child will probably have more concrete, down-to-earth fears, like bodily harm, falling, dogs, sounds, thunder, lightning, rain, storms (especially at night), and that her mother will not return home or be at home when she gets there.

Just as dislike of certain foods is suggested by chance remarks made by adults, fear of animals, cars, and thunder are suggested in a similar way. Gruesome tales and stories about ghosts, devils, and such may terrify a small child and lead to serious sleep disturbance. For this reason, you should choose bedtime stories carefully, don't let your child watch scary television programs just before bedtime, and never deliberately frighten her with stories of "bogey men" to make her behave.

Crying and comforting

The four-year-old cries a great deal and may whine if her wants are not met and there's nothing interesting to play with. By the age of five, a child cries much less, though she may cry if she's angry, tired, or can't have her own way.

Crying is now of shorter duration, and your child may be able to control it and hold her tears back. She is rarely moody and may be her usual self as soon as the crying is over. She may whine occasionally, though a lot less than she did at four years. This phase may pass, however, and give way to temper tantrums with loud, angry crying and banging around. There may be a return of moodiness, whining, and expressions of resentment, but you can often get your child to laugh when she's crying by joking with her. Your child may become astonishingly brave about real injuries, yet still cry at small hurts.

BAD DREAMS AND NIGHTMARES
Between the ages of three and five years, children quite often have bad dreams. Your child may walk or talk in her sleep, or have night terrors. This is normal because, while her understanding of the world is growing, she can't entirely make sense of it, and so she goes to sleep with unresolved questions. She's also getting more in touch with her feelings and she knows what it is to be afraid or feel that something isn't quite right. These feelings come out at night.

Often a child can't explain her dreams and has difficulty in going back to sleep. Animals may chase your child during a nightmare, or she may dream of strange, bad, or odd-looking people, fires, and deep water. Only if your child wakes up should you try to console her. If she remains asleep, don't wake her; simply stay by her. If she's sleepwalking periodically, you must put a gate across the stairs.

Night terrors Sometimes you'll find your child in bed, apparently awake, terrified, and possibly thrashing and screaming. She may be angry or desperately upset. This is a night terror rather than a nightmare, and it can be alarming. You'll feel anguished at your child's fear and pain, but all you can do is stay close and wait for the terror to pass. You can't reassure your child specifically, because she's beyond reason. Don't leave or scold her; that would simply make it worse.

PRESCHOOL NERVES
A child who goes to preschool without a backward glance, says goodbye to her mother, and gets straight into play is rather unusual.

Most children harbor fears of a strange place with strange people and separation from you. You have to give your child both the time and the opportunity to adjust to this frightening change in her life.

You can do much to allay your child's fears by familiarizing her with the trip to school, the entrance to the school, her classroom, some of the children who will be in her class, her teacher, where the games are, and what some of the routines are. Most teachers will welcome your taking your child to the school several times before she starts so that she can feel comfortable in her new surroundings. Make the first visit as casual as possible. Stay for only a few minutes, so that your child doesn't get bored or frightened, and don't make her do anything she doesn't want to do.

Making separation easy The first morning is likely to be difficult for both of you. It may be that you have to stay with your child for the whole morning, but this shouldn't happen more than once. Don't forget that it's a great transition for her to make, so be patient. Many preschools will welcome your staying to give your child confidence. Eventually, when your child realizes that you're not going to leave, she'll be happy to get on with her classroom routines as long as you sit somewhere quiet and discreet.

Maybe during the first morning, but certainly on the second, suggest that you are going out to buy a newspaper, but come back within five minutes, so that your child is reassured. Don't go if your child gets very distressed at the prospect of your leaving. Once she's happy, suggest that you leave again, this time for about half an hour, and come back in exactly the time you said you would. Over the next few days, leave for longer and longer periods according to how your child reacts. You'll find that in a short time, you won't need to stay at all. A confident child may want to be self-reliant and suggest that you leave long before you think that she's capable of being separated from you. Sometimes a teacher will advise you when it's time to go.

Starting preschool
Once your child is engrossed in an activity, she may hardly even notice when you leave.

FAMILY CONFLICTS

Your child will become very distressed if she thinks that the people dearest in the world to her, her mother and father, no longer love each other, and that there's a danger that they may separate or leave her.

Children are extremely sensitive to emotions within the home, so if you and your partner are going through a bad time, behave caringly and affectionately in front of your child and show that you have concern for each other. Witnessing a fight is one of the most harmful experiences you can inflict on your child, so that thought should act as a deterrent.

On the other hand, I don't believe in a united front between parents on every question. Your child should understand that it's alright for Mom and Dad to have different opinions, as long as they are expressed without acrimony.

Children have to get used to conflict because they're going to meet it very quickly when they leave home. The best place for them to become familiar with it is in the security of their own home.

Most children will blame themselves for any conflict between their parents and will go to great lengths to make you friends again. Reassure your child that she isn't to blame for any anger that you feel toward your partner, and that you love her regardless.

WHAT TO TAKE: YOUNG BABY

You'll need basic changing and feeding equipment, and a toy for your baby.

- Changing bag or mat
- Fabric or disposable diapers
- Baby wipes
- Diaper cream
- A sealable container or plastic bags for dirty diapers
- A bottle containing a whole feeding if you're bottle-feeding
- A change of breast pads if you're breastfeeding
- Hat
- Sweater
- A couple of favorite toys

Travel and outings

Time spent in planning your outing or travel schedule is never wasted. The younger your baby, the more you will have to plan. In the first few months, your baby's feeding schedule may not necessarily be very predictable, so you will need at least one spare bottle if you're not breastfeeding and, of course, whatever changing equipment you normally use.

When you go out, plan your route so that you know where you can stop, where you can change your baby, and where you can feed him without embarrassment or inconvenience. If you're planning to shop, it is even worth calling stores or malls to find out if they have a baby-changing room, and avoiding those that don't. Lightweight baby-changing bags containing a portable changing mat are widely available.

With a very young baby, it's simply not worth undertaking a very busy outing where you will have to walk a great deal, carry heavy loads, or use several different modes of transportation. Be easy on yourself. Try to take a friend or your partner with you if you can, so there is always an extra pair of hands and someone to help you should you have problems. Your baby can go with you anywhere as long as you're well enough prepared and have something in which to carry him—a baby sling, stroller, or car seat.

USING A STROLLER

If you don't want to carry your baby in a sling, a stroller is ideal for a small baby, who will fit comfortably and snugly into its shape. Babies are interested in their surroundings from an early age, so as soon as your baby can sit up, angle the stroller so that he can see what is going on around him.

You'll need to be adept at collapsing and opening the stroller within a few seconds without any problems, so practice it at home before your first outing. If you can't fold up the stroller efficiently, you may find people jostling to get in front of you when you are in a line, which will only add to your frustration. At the very least, you should be able to open it with only one hand, kick it shut with your feet, and know how to operate the brakes—and don't forget, you will have to do all these things while holding your baby. Here are a few safety tips:

- When you open your stroller, always make sure that it is in the fully extended position with the brakes fully locked.
- Never put your baby in the stroller without a safety harness.
- Never, ever, leave your baby in a stroller unattended.
- Should your baby fall asleep in the stroller, adjust it to the lie-back position so that he can sleep comfortably.

Baby sling
A sling can be the easiest way of taking a young baby out and about.

• Don't hang bags on the handles of the stroller; it can unbalance the stroller and your baby may be injured.

• When you stop, always put the brakes on because you could inadvertently take your hands off the stroller and it could roll away.

• Check your stroller regularly to make sure the brakes and catches work well and that the wheels are solid.

PUBLIC TRANSPORTATION

Using public transportation can really be an ordeal, since neither buses nor trains are equipped for mothers and young children. Picture yourself with a stroller, a heavy and wriggling baby, the baby bag, your handbag, a coat, and possibly a toddler in tow, and public transportation is the last thing you want to face.

Of course, you can make things easier by never traveling during rush hour or, with a young baby, carrying him around in a sling. For an older baby, a backpack makes you much more independent, and you can manage everything more easily with your hands free. Always prepare yourself well ahead of time. I simply would not leave home with my children without some distracting toys, a favorite book, and a favorite snack. All your belongings, including the stroller, should be collected together prior to leaving and in good enough time so that you can check them over to make sure that you haven't forgotten anything. The same goes for when you are getting off a bus or train; be ready to get off in plenty of time for your stop. Always ask for help from fellow passengers.

SPECIAL OUTINGS

Your baby is never too young for an outing; indeed, with a young baby, you can go just about anywhere and, provided he can look around him, he will enjoy the change of scenery even if he doesn't understand much of what's going on. When planning an outing for an older child, always try to consider what your child's personality can cope with best. If you have a quiet child who has a long concentration span, you can take him to a flower show or an antique market, and point out the things around him. If, on the other hand, he is very active, he will need more space to run around in, and a trip to the zoo, a playground, or a fair is therefore more appropriate. Wherever you go, you should be prepared to make endless stops to look at anything that catches your child's attention. Always take enough drinks and snacks to keep your child happy for the full duration of the trip. Don't take on a trip of any kind if you or your child are feeling tired or under the weather; the day is bound to be a disaster, so don't feel guilty about canceling the outing altogether.

Handling a stroller
Make sure that you can kick it shut, open it up one-handed, and operate the brakes.

WHAT TO TAKE: OLDER BABY

For an older baby, you'll need solid food, and feeding and changing equipment.

• Changing mat
• Fabric or disposable diapers
• Baby wipes
• Diaper cream
• Plastic bags or sealable container for dirty diapers
• Baby food, dish, and spoon
• Bib for feeding
• Snack, such as fruit
• Water or diluted fruit juice
• Sun hat or woolen hat
• Sweater or jacket
• Comforter
• Favorite book and toy

SHOPPING WITH YOUR YOUNG BABY

When traveling with your baby, always plan all your movements and stops in detail, so that you can use your time efficiently.

• Try to fit in a shopping trip between feedings, or, if you think that it is going to be a longer trip than the usual interval between meals, take a snack with you.

• Always bring basic changing equipment in case your child needs a clean diaper. Many stores these days have special changing areas for mothers and babies.

• If you are traveling by car, adjust your baby's seat to a reclining position so that she can sleep.

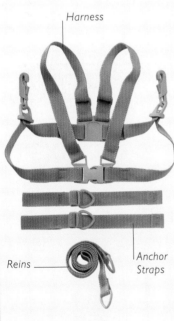

Harness

Reins — — — Anchor Straps

Harness and reins
Keep your older baby safe on busy streets with a harness and reins. The harness can also be used in a high chair with anchor straps.

SHOPPING TRIPS

Taking a baby shopping brings its own problems. Your baby can easily become bored, hungry, fretful, and difficult to manage, so it's worth planning ahead quite carefully to minimize stress. Taking a car will make a world of difference: you can feed and change your baby in it, you can put your shopping bags in the trunk and not have to carry them, and you won't have to worry about catching buses and trains. If you don't own a car yourself, it might be worth asking a friend who does to join your shopping expedition, or asking a relative if you can borrow their car. Try to shop fairly early in the day, because streets and stores may be less busy, and there are fewer distractions for your baby. Always try to give your baby a good meal before you leave; that way, you may have two or three hours to complete your purchases without her getting hungry.

Bring whatever equipment you would bring on any other trip. Toys may seem something of a burden, but they will more than pay their way, because you can attach them to the backpack, stroller, or supermarket cart for your child to play with without her being able to throw them on to the floor. Bring some kind of small snack, too, because shopping seems to make children either hungry or fretful, and a snack will deal with both.

CARRYING YOUR BABY

You need to have your hands free for shopping, and so how you carry your baby is worth some thought and attention. Once your baby is able to sit up with good head and back control, you can put her into your shopping cart. Many supermarkets now have carts with molded baby seats and harnesses, but with the older, tip-up seats, you need to strap your baby in with reins. A backpack is ideal for carrying your baby on shopping trips; her interest will always be engaged, she will feel very secure with such close physical contact, and she should be well behaved and cry very little. Best of all, your hands will be left free. Try to undertake a shopping trip accompanied by your partner, so that one of you is free to make the purchases. Reins are a very good idea for an older child, because your child will feel a sense of freedom and independence, but she will never be able to get very far away from you; a wrist link that is securely attached to her reins will prevent you from becoming separated from her.

KEEPING YOUR CHILD UNDER CONTROL

Because babies are always grasping and reaching for interesting objects, walk down the center of the aisle so that your baby isn't tempted to dislodge cans and boxes. One way to control your child is to keep her interested, and you can do this keeping up a running commentary, with observations or questions that engage your child. Your young child will love being involved in shopping decisions, and she will feel very important and needed if you act on her preferences. With items where brand is not important to you, ask your child to select products by pointing to the one she would like you to buy. As my children got older and could toddle around the shopping cart, I used to ask them to put all their choices into the shopping cart themselves, so that they were constantly engaged in looking for their favorite things, feeling a great sense of pride in finally finding them and a sense of achievement in filling up the cart.

One of the ways I used to distract and entertain my children on a shopping trip was to ask them if they were thirsty or hungry immediately on entering the supermarket, and buy them a drink or a healthy snack. That way they could munch or sip their way around the supermarket and feel quite happy and occupied the whole time. If, however, you have a wayward child who keeps on getting into mischief, the only way to handle the situation is to keep your child on reins or a wrist strap to prevent her from wandering off and bothering other shoppers or getting lost.

LEARNING

You can use your shopping trips as opportunities to teach your child all sorts of things—about colors, for example: "This can is red; that box is blue; that jar has a yellow wrapper." Your child will recognize the cornflake box that she sees at breakfast every morning and will soon understand what the words mean, so that from quite an early age, say, 18 months, you can say to her, "Can you see the cornflakes? Now, I wonder where the jelly is?" Early reading can be encouraged by teaching your child to associate the contents of a package or can with things that she actually eats at home. For example, if she drinks cocoa regularly, you only have to take the tin of the brand she sees every day from the shelf and ask "What does this word say?" for her to respond with "cocoa," because she has learned from experience that cocoa is what comes out of that tin. All my children began to read food packaging before they read anything else.

Trips to the supermarket will also teach your child about the act of shopping itself, and the choosing and decision-making that is involved. You can introduce her to the value of money, and to a certain degree, you can teach her about manners and sociability, because she will very quickly learn the politeness of allowing other people to get to the shelves when she has a great interest in doing so herself.

SHOPPING WITH YOUR TODDLER

Once your child can walk, losing her in a crowd can be a worry, so take precautions against this.

• Use reins or a wrist strap in busy places so that she can't wander.

• Dress your toddler in something brightly colored so that you can spot her from a distance.

• Have some sort of family code for your children to come back to you. I used to carry a small whistle around my neck.

• All shopping trips can be lessons, even if you only teach your child about healthy eating (e.g., fresh vegetables are better than canned).

• From as early an age as possible, make your child learn her name, address, and telephone number, so she can repeat it if she gets lost.

• Teach her never to walk off with any stranger.

• Make sure your child recognizes her surroundings when she's near home by pointing out landmarks on every journey: "There's the mailbox on the corner, and there's the blue gate, and our house is the next one down."

Wrist straps
An adjustable strap links you and your child together at the wrists to prevent her from wandering.

BABY ON BOARD

Keep the following important items of equipment in the car more or less permanently, ready for trips with your baby:

• A car seat, correctly installed and with safety harness (see p.312)

• A shade to block out bright sun

• A bag with basic changing and feeding equipment; restock it often

• Baby traveling toys

• A rug

• A couple of tapes or CDs

• Tissues

Trip checklist

As with any kind of outing with your child, the essential thing is to plan and prepare well in advance. The following tips will all help to make things go more smoothly for you:

• Try to start traveling early in the morning, or at night when the roads are quiet.

• Carry a bag of spare clothes for each child in the car, be philosophical about accidents, and change your child promptly into dry clothes.

• For safety, tape cutlery to the inside of food containers.

• Always take some soft clothing like a parka or sweater that your child can use as a pillow.

• Always have a supply of bags into which cartons, bottles, and wrappers can be placed after use.

• Take a box of baby wipes to clean dirty hands and faces.

CAR TRAVEL

Children can be very active on car trips. They're learning and taking great pride in newly acquired physical skills, like jumping, skipping, hopping, climbing, and running, and it's difficult for them to be confined in a small space. All this is intensified in hot weather because your child will become tired, touchy, and tearful more easily than when the temperature is equable. Never leave a child alone in a car, especially in hot weather, because the temperature inside the car can rise much higher than the temperature outside, causing him to become quickly overheated and even dehydrated. Always screen your child from bright sunlight by putting a special shade on the window through which the sun is shining. You might also think about attaching a canopy to your baby's seat, which serves the same purpose.

In the cramped circumstances of a long trip, your child can't be expected to behave well, and it's your job to make sure that he's cool, fed, given enough to drink, has plenty to occupy him, is taken to the bathroom without a fuss, and that accidents are accepted calmly.

SAFETY

Whatever else, your baby must be transported safely in a car. A young baby should go in a rear-facing car seat, or in an infant car seat with proper restraints in the back seat (see p.312). Never sit in the front with an unrestrained baby, because if the car stops suddenly your baby will be flung out of your arms and will certainly be injured. Once your baby is over a year old and weighs at least 20 pounds (9 kilograms) he should sit in a front-facing car seat. After any accident, you should replace your seat belts, your child's car seat, and the anchorage kit, since they will have been badly strained and may be damaged. For the same reason, you should never buy secondhand car seats, harnesses, or anchorage kits.

Misbehavior like shouting or kicking should not be tolerated; it is extremely distracting for you while you are driving and could even be dangerous. If your child does behave badly, pull over to the side of the road, stop the car, and address the difficulty. Tell your child that you are going no farther until he starts to behave himself properly.

LONGER TRIPS

Most children will become restless if they have to travel for longer than an hour and a half. Your child has no idea of time, so he'll be constantly asking you when you are going to arrive, or whether you are nearly there. Restlessness can be alleviated by stopping the car every hour for about five minutes and allowing your child to run around, explore, and generally get rid of excess energy. Warn him in advance about the stops so that he can get himself ready by putting on a coat and hat if it's cold outside.

Feeding A car trip is when breastfeeding comes into its own, because you have no preparations to make whatsoever. Never feed when the car is in motion, because your baby would be very unsafe. If you're bottle-feeding, use disposable bottles and feedings, or make up a batch of feedings, cool them in the refrigerator, and then carry them in a cooler. Alternatively, mix the formula when you need it, in a sterilized bottle with some boiled water from a thermos. Never try to keep made-up feedings warm, because you are only letting germs multiply. Once your baby is weaned, you'll need to take food, a feeding dish, a plastic spoon, a bib, a cup with a spout, a supply of drinks, and something your baby can nibble on, such as pieces of dry toast or crackers. You can feed your baby directly from the jar, but remember to throw away anything he doesn't finish, because the food will be contaminated with saliva, and germs will grow in it very quickly.

Changing Even if you normally use fabric diapers, forget the expense and take disposables with you on a car trip: they're just so convenient, quick, and easy for both you and your baby. You can always change your baby on the back seat of the car or in the trunk if he lies on a rug or towel. There is no need to do any more than top and tail your baby while traveling, but be meticulous about cleaning the diaper area. Wipes are an essential, as is a sealable container for dirty diapers.

The older child Your child will get bored and hungry, so always have some healthy snacks like raisins, unsweetened cornflakes, or pieces of cheese in plastic bags, and take more drinks than you ever think you'll need—your child often wants to drink more when he's traveling. Seedless grapes make a useful snack, because they quench your child's thirst as well as satisfying his hunger.

Take some toys to distract your child while traveling (books may be a bad idea, though, if he suffers from motion sickness), and these can be arranged in different ways for safety and convenience. Buy or make a special cover for the front headrest of your car with pockets in the back that can hold drinks, snacks, and toys, or tie toys to coat-hooks or handles so that they don't get lost under seats. Magnetized games are particularly useful in cars because the pieces cannot get lost, and you can stick Velcro on certain toys so that they will adhere to the car seat and stay in one place while your child is playing with them.

I always found it best if I allowed my child to choose some of the toys that he wanted to take on a car trip, and to be responsible for putting them into his own case or bag. Tapes or CDs of music or children's stories may give you at least half an hour of peace, so always have one ready. Word games are fun too. "I spy" is always a favorite, particularly if you join in, and will keep your children occupied for quite a long time if you make the object interesting. Keep a special treat tucked away in the glove compartment with which to relieve tension or tears.

MOTION SICKNESS

If you have suffered motion sickness, or there's any history of migraines, eczema, or allergies in the family, then your child is quite likely to suffer from motion sickness, too. There are some things that you can do to help minimize motion sickness.

- Don't give your child a rich or greasy meal before a trip.

- You can give your child a motion-sickness drug, available from doctors; always give it at least half an hour before you leave.

- Stay calm. If you're anxious, your children will become anxious, too. Carsickness is brought on by anxiety and excitement and is much more likely to happen on the outward trip, so be patient when you leave home.

- Snacks that can be sucked are a good idea, because they don't create a mess, so take along a supply of glucose candies.

- Keeping your child occupied or distracted will help prevent car-sickness, but don't let him read, since this may bring it on.

- If you notice your child becoming pale or quiet, ask him if he wants to stop. Get him to close his eyes until you reach a safe place to stop, then get him out of the car, and be very sympathetic if he actually is sick. Give him a short time to recover before you continue with your drive.

- A supply of baby wipes will help you clean up your child (and the car if necessary), should he be sick.

- Give your child a drink after he's been sick to get the taste of vomit out of his mouth.

WHAT TO PACK

Use the following checklist to make sure you have everything you need for your child.

- Passport and immunization records
- Your baby bag
- Travel crib
- Stroller or baby sling
- A bouncing chair if used
- Changing equipment or potty
- Feeding equipment
- A thermos for cool drinks
- Toys and games
- Comfort objects
- Sun hat and sunscreen
- No-iron, drip-dry clothes
- Plenty of clothes to protect your child from heatstroke or sunburn

Sun protection
Dress your child in a sun hat and T-shirt and apply sunscreen regularly when she's outside playing in the sun.

PLANNING A VACATION

Never think your baby is too young to travel. Children nearly always surprise us, and rise to the occasion in ways we never think possible. Traveling with young babies is a tradition in my family; I am told that when I was only six weeks old, my mother and father took me camping, living under canvas for two weeks by the sea! When my third son was only ten weeks old, we took him to Italy, and while we were finding our lost luggage in Rome, he was by far the best behaved of all of us. He even philosophically accepted my efforts to find the right formula for him, which took three days.

BEFORE YOU GO
A golden rule if you are going overseas on vacation is to make sure your hotel has facilities for children and really welcomes them. Things to look for in a hotel include such child facilities as a daycare, a place where you can take your child for an early supper, a children's menu, high chairs and cribs, a playroom, and an outdoor play area with trained attendants. It's worth going to some trouble to be sure these things are available, because if your children are not happy, you will not enjoy the vacation yourself. If you are going to a lake or seashore, make sure that the beaches are safe.

Vaccination Well ahead of time—six months at least—you must get advice on what vaccinations or immunizations are needed, because regulations are constantly changing all over the world. The reason for starting early is that some vaccinations need quite a long lead time, and for others, as with hepatitis, you may have to wait four to six weeks between injections, or you may not be able to follow one vaccination immediately with another. You can get information from your healthcare provider, your travel agent, or the Centers for Disease Control. Make sure your doctor gives you the correct vaccinations and vaccination certificates, plus any medication you might need, and buy water sterilizing tablets from your pharmacy or sporting good store.

Food Another golden rule for children is to introduce them to any exotic food at home so that you can determine their likes and dislikes well in advance. If your children like experimenting with food, there is no reason at all why you should not let them eat the local food, as long as it is well cooked and clean.

AIR TRAVEL
Most airlines make special facilities available to children as long as they're given warning. Try to book a flight that won't be crowded, and if you have a baby, ask for bulkhead seats, which have special folding tables for a bassinet or cradle. If these are not available, ask for any seat

that might have more leg room. Travel cribs may be available in flight. Ask the airline staff if they will heat up baby bottles for you. On some flights, children's meals might be available; if not, you'll need to take your own. Most travel agents will make all these inquiries on your behalf. Here are some things to think about before you travel:

• Aim to reach the airport early enough to avoid long check-in lines, and give yourself plenty of time to get there.
• Put all travel documents in a special bag, inside a loose, lightweight shoulder bag. If you can, fit in your baby bag, too, with spare diapers, spare clothing, and some snacks.
• Make sure that everything you take on board has an indestructible label, including your baby bag.
• Take a few of your baby's favorite toys with you, or see whether any of the games suggested for use in the car (see p.145) would work on a plane to entertain your child.
• Carry your baby in a sling so that your hands are free.
• Change your baby's diaper just before getting on the plane.
• Take a folded stroller on the plane with you; the flight crew will take it from you as you enter, and return it as you leave.
• Babies and children feel some pain during takeoff and landing, so keep aside a little treat or your baby's pacifer so she can suck on it to equalize the pressure in her ears.

SUN SAFETY

Children can get heatstroke (see p.340) in a very short time, and this is a dangerous condition. Most often it occurs when the nape of the neck is exposed to hot sun, which interferes with the temperature-regulating center in the brain.

If your baby is under six months old, never expose her skin to direct, strong sunlight for any length of time. The guidelines (below right) are for children over six months. Though the times in the sun seem short, please adhere to them and make your children wear T-shirts and sun hats the rest of the time. They should wear a sunscreen (see right) all the time that they are outdoors—even if they are swimming or if the weather is cloudy, since they could still burn.

If there have been no ill effects after the first six days, you can extend the exposure up to several hours, provided your child is perfectly happy and her skin does not become inflamed. Prevent sunburn by plastering your child with sunscreen of a SP factor of 15 or above on all parts of the exposed skin, topping it off as necessary.

A baby has to be kept as cool as possible, and this means a minimum of light cotton clothing, but something that covers almost all of her body, unless she is kept constantly under a sunshade and never exposed to direct sunlight. If you can, always make sure the carriage or stroller is placed where there is a light breeze to cool your baby's skin. Children sweat a lot more than adults do in a hot climate, so always have water with you and give your child as much as she wants.

SUNSCREENS

There are many sunscreens available. Use one that protects against both UVA and UVB rays, with a sun protection factor (SPF) of at least 15.

For a baby, you should use the strongest sunscreen that you can find—SPFs go up to 50.

What the SPF means is that you can stay in the sunshine that number of times longer without getting burned than you could have without the cream; if your child would normally burn after ten minutes, then with a sunscreen of SPF ten, she should be able to stay in the sun for 100 minutes without getting burned.

Many sunscreens say that they are waterproof, but if your child is running in and out of a lake or swimming pool, reapply sunscreen every half-hour or so.

Under other conditions, reapply sunscreen to your child's skin roughly every two hours.

Exposure times

Only let your child be exposed to hot sun for a very short time at first, and increase the time gradually. She must wear a hat.

Day 1	5 minutes
Day 2	10 minutes
Day 3	15–20 minutes
Day 4	20–30 minutes
Day 5	45 minutes
Day 6	60 minutes

CHAPTER 3

Play and development

The starting point in your baby's social development is your physical presence. As soon as your baby is born, he will become familiar with your smell and voice, and what you look like, and he will come to associate you with comfort and love. You can encourage his instinctive desire to communicate with talking, touching, eye contact, and play.

During the first year of life, your baby's brain doubles in weight, not because he acquires any more brain cells, but because more and more connections are being made between existing brain cells. "Learning to think" is a complex process of building up associations that results from observing and interacting with the world.

Your child will not only mature socially and mentally, he will also become skilled physically. He will learn to sit, then crawl, and later to walk and run, and he will develop fine manipulative skills. All of these things will open up new areas of experience for him.

DEVELOPMENT
IN GIRLS

Gender is an important factor affecting development. Boys and girls have different strengths and will develop differently, be it physically, intellectually, or socially. In general, girls:

• Do better than boys at language-based skills like talking, reading, and writing.

• Tend to be more sociable than boys and are more interested in people than things.

• Usually walk earlier than boys.

• Grow faster and are more predictable and regular in their growth patterns than boys.

• Are better than boys at jumping and hopping in the preschool years.

• Are easier to get along with than boys.

• Cope better with stress than boys.

Jumping
Contrary to expectations, young girls are better than boys at hopping and jumping.

All about development

Development is continuous, although at times your child's progress may seem very slow. The speed and ease of acquiring skills, however, is entirely individual, so don't worry if your child is slower to develop in some areas than other children of the same age.

Although you can influence the pace of your child's development by giving her the right stimulation at the right time, the stages of development occur in a strictly unchangeable sequence.

PHYSICAL DEVELOPMENT
There are a few general principles that apply to physical development in all babies. The stages or "milestones" always follow the same order, since each one depends on the previous stages. To give an obvious example, your child can't walk until she can stand.

Often, a previously learned skill may appear to be forgotten while your baby is concentrating on learning a new one, but will reappear when the new one is successfully learned. Sometimes a generalized activity makes way for a specific one: at six months your baby may make rather random leg movements that resemble walking, but they are quite different from the ones she will make when she actually starts to walk at about one year.

One important physical milestone will be when your baby's teeth start to come through. Although this might not seem like a developmental step, teeth are essential to your baby's learning to chew solid food and to speak.

LOCOMOTION
It may come as something of a surprise to learn that all locomotion—that is, walking and running—begins with the acquisition of head control. Your child can't sit up, stand up, crawl, or walk without first being able to control the position of her head. Development of any kind proceeds from head to toe, so head control is the essential first phase of locomotion.

At first your baby's movements seem random, jerky, and quite unspecific; a newborn infant may move her arms, legs, head, hands, and feet when all she wants to do is smile. Gradually, over the next three years, her movements are refined, becoming increasingly specific to match the task in hand.

Crawling, though clever, is an inefficient and clumsy way to get around, but your child has to learn balance and coordination, and acquire self-confidence, before launching herself into space.

Manipulation The primitive grasp reflex in newborns (see p.20) must fade before your baby can grasp an object purposefully. At first she uses her mouth as the main organ for touch; the fingertips take over only as she learns how to use her hands. She will refine her ability to grasp things, at first grasping them in her palm and eventually learning to use her finger and thumb. She will learn how to release as well as grasp an object.

Hearing and vision Your child's hearing is essential to her development of speech, and there are various clues you can look for very early on that indicate normal hearing: does she turn toward the direction of a sound, or respond to your voice by turning or smiling, for instance? Your baby's vision improves rapidly during the first few weeks of her life, and although she will not be able to see things at a distance, she'll be able to focus on your face at birth, provided it is only 8–10 inches (20–25 centimeters) from hers.

INTELLECTUAL DEVELOPMENT

Your baby's brain doubles in weight in the first year, due not to the growth in the number of brain cells, but to the connections between them. These connections only begin to form when your baby has to think about something. Contact with new sights, sounds, smells, tastes, and touches make your baby think, and that's why stimulation is essential from birth.

In order for your baby to understand what is going on around her, she must use her senses, her intellect, and her body to form mental connections so that she understands cause and effect. In order to pick up a favorite toy, for example, she must be able to see it, remember that she likes it, reach for it, and then pick it up.

Your baby's mental skills will advance with stimulation and teaching, so your involvement is crucial all the time, particularly when the brain goes through growth spurts in the first and third years. You are your child's first and most important teacher.

SOCIABILITY

Babies become social by imitating us and will respond to a human voice from birth, so talk to your baby from the day that she's born. Your child's personality and social skills can affect her achievement of developmental milestones. An independent and determined child will try new movements earlier than a more timid child, and a sociable child will seek social contact and communication with others and develop speech earlier than other children.

Your child's personality has three main components: sociability (the extent to which she seeks out and enjoys contact with others), activity (her prowess at, and enjoyment of, movement and energy), and emotion (her tendency to mood swings). If any of these traits is pronounced in your child, you should try to be accommodating, at the same time encouraging the development of the other two qualities.

DEVELOPMENT IN BOYS

The pace of development is affected by many things and gender is one of them; boys and girls develop according to different "timetables." In general, boys:

• Begin to talk at a later stage than girls and are more prone to language disorders.

• Tend to be less sociable than girls and more interested in objects than in people.

• Usually walk later than girls.

• Are more likely than girls to grow in sudden spurts.

• Refine jumping, running, and throwing after the preschool years.

• Are more aggressive, competitive, and rebellious than girls.

• Are more vulnerable to stress than girls and are more likely to have behavioral problems.

Active play
Toys with dials, buttons, or other moving parts encourage your child's manipulative abilities.

Promoting development

CHOOSING TOYS

Your child will grow and learn very rapidly in the first three years and toys can help stimulate development.

• Simple toys are more versatile, so they have a longer life and are better for imaginative play.

• A baby will need toys that stimulate all five senses. Introduce your baby to different colors, textures, shapes, and noises.

• Older babies enjoy games that involve building, particularly "put in, take out" toys, so bricks of different sizes are ideal.

• As your child's manipulative skills develop, he will be able to manage interlocking blocks and more advanced shape-sorters.

• Preschool children enjoy drawing, painting, and imaginative play, and simple games like Snap or picture dominoes, which improve concentration.

Painting
Give your child painting and drawing materials to allow her to develop her creativity.

The first six weeks of life are a critical learning period for your baby in which you should be actively engaged. Your role as teacher starts at your baby's birth and continues for many years; it's your job to make his world an interesting and exciting place in which he can grow and learn.

I firmly believe that the most important teacher in a baby's life is the person who most consistently looks out for his health and well-being—in other words, you. From a very early age, your baby will recognize you, first by smell and sound, and enjoy a unique bond with you which means that you are best equipped to teach him about his world, for even as adults we learn best from people with whom we feel comfortable or have a rapport. Your partner, likewise, has an important role to play. He should form a close and loving relationship with your baby as early as possible so that he becomes equally involved in teaching. Look for every opportunity to share in your baby's progress; much of his early development will be dependent on a secure and caring environment, so make sure you give him lots of attention.

PROVIDING THE RIGHT ENVIRONMENT

Your baby demands and deserves a rich, stimulating environment in order to experience as many sensations as possible while he is still dependent on his senses for learning. To ensure this, surround your baby in the first six months with a wide variety of sounds, smells, sights, and textures. In the early months, your baby can't interact with his surroundings the way he will when he learns to move and speak. His intellectual and emotional development, therefore, will only be improved through the different experiences you introduce to him.

Rather than buying your child new toys all the time, encourage him to interact with existing toys in different ways—for example, by showing him how to use a cardboard box as a car or a boat. Children don't always need store-bought toys to encourage them to play. Often, your child will get stimulation from improvised toys: a tent made out of sheets, for instance, a balancing board, a little hill made out of sod, or a tunnel made from blankets and chairs, all provide the backdrop for imaginative play.

In practical terms, the area in which your child plays should be safe, with potential hazards removed so that he can't hurt himself, or break or damage anything. Sandboxes in the back yard are ideal (but must be covered to prevent fouling by animals), or a corner of a room can be set aside specifically as a play area.

WORKING WITH YOUR CHILD

In order to allow your child to achieve his full potential, set aside time to work with him, matching your efforts to your child's stages of development. Responsible parents find the role of teacher comes effortlessly and naturally. Your child is always eager to learn new things, so make the experience fun and mutually rewarding. Take any opportunity that presents itself—intimate moments of play or telling stories, for example, to teach colors, textures, opposites, and so on.

Teaching your child is not a formal process in which specific rules and targets must be met. All teaching should be playful and be done with games. Feed your child's increasing curiosity and need for new experiences. Introduce new concepts, answer his queries, but, most importantly, praise him at every stage so that the learning process becomes unconscious and enjoyable, and one he wants to repeat over and over with you.

When you work with your child, be sure to stop the moment he shows any sign of boredom, and be careful not to put him under any pressure. If he decides early in life that learning is fun, he'll feel this way throughout his life and will thrive on knowledge.

THE IMPORTANCE OF PLAY

Your child's development will center around play, and this is the most natural way for him to learn. It is only in the last 20 years that the full value of development through play has been recognized, since playing was previously regarded as an empty activity, used to fill the time when children could not be usefully employed. We now recognize that play is an essential means of acquiring the majority of adult skills, particularly social ones. Your child will first learn to form relationships and to share with children of his own age through play, and toys will have a significant role in all your child's developmental milestones.

Choose toys for their educational value. Reading, writing, and counting proficiency requires certain basic skills that your child will acquire through building and construction toys, playing with puzzles, and matching colors, shapes, and textures. The best toys are the ones that children return to again and again because they are limitless in their appeal—usually ones that encourage inventiveness. For this reason a household item like a whisk or sieve may give more lasting pleasure than many an expensive and elaborate toy. By sharing and encouraging your child in his play, you will strengthen the bond between you as he comes to see you as a giver of knowledge and fun.

Places to play It's nice to set aside a special activity space for your child—a sand tray, for example, or an area for messy play like painting or water games—but your child can play anywhere, as long as you take the proper safety measures (see pp.306–13). The kitchen is an ideal place, provided you are there to keep an eye on your child. You could set up a dolls' corner where the dolls can be put to bed each evening and gotten up in the morning for breakfast.

TELEVISION

The average child clocks up an average of six to seven hours' television viewing a day. One hour a day is more than enough for your young child.

More than this may prevent him from acquiring communication, imaginative, and coordination skills that could be more thoroughly developed through games and storytelling. You should monitor the amount of television your child watches and be wary of using it as a convenient babysitting tool when you don't feel like amusing him. Used carefully, however, television can be a useful aid to acquiring new concepts, like telling time.

Research shows that your child could continue to live in the fantasy world of television long after he's stopped watching, causing nightmares if he's watched anything frightening or violent.

Swedish researchers have shown that bringing your child back into the real world—with a story, tooth-brushing, or laying out tomorrow's clothes—can banish this unpleasant effect of television.

HEAD CONTROL

The most important physical change in your baby's first weeks will be the development of her neck strength and head control.

A newborn's head is proportionately very large and heavy for her body, which means that before your baby can begin to control the rest of her body, she must first gain control of her head.

Once your baby can raise her head from the mattress, she will begin to increase her strength, which will encourage her to practice further locomotive skills. Holding your baby in the air in a face-down position will encourage her to raise her head, something that she will try for herself when lying on her stomach.

As she becomes stronger, your baby's head control is steadier, and her spine will gradually take more of the weight of her torso. This is the first stage in learning to sit, crawl, and walk.

Locomotion

The first few months of your baby's development are a very exciting time for you as a parent as you watch her first see the world, then move to become involved in it.

As her coordination and muscle strength increase, your baby's body control will quickly improve. The gradual refinement of her movements and her growing curiosity about her surroundings are excellent stimulation for all aspects of her development. Every child develops at her own pace, however, and the ages given below for the various stages of coordination and control are only approximations.

Newborn
Your baby will flex his limbs toward his body, which will remain curled up for several weeks as he gradually straightens out of the fetal position. His head will be very floppy at first, but you will notice that he turns it to his preferred side when lying down. Always support his head and neck when lifting him.

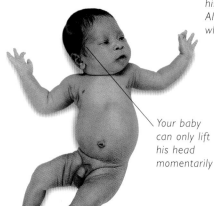

Your baby can only lift his head momentarily

If you hold your baby, he can keep his head up for a while

His neck muscles are getting stronger

1 month
Your baby will be able to lift his head slightly for a few seconds and will have lost his very newborn appearance. If you raise your baby from the mattress he may be able to keep his head up in line with his body for a second or two. His knees and hips will be growing stronger and his body will begin to straighten even more.

2 months
Your baby can hold his head up for longer now. In a prone position, he'll hold his head in line with his body and will quickly progress to raising his face from the mattress to an angle of 45°.

Your baby can hold his head up when lying prone

3 months

Your baby can now lie quite flat and take the weight of his shoulders and head on outstretched arms. There is little head lag when he is held in a sitting or standing position.

YOUR BABY'S POSTURE

Although your baby's posture will mature as her muscles strengthen naturally, you may both enjoy gentle bending and stretching exercises.

Changing time is a good opportunity to do this; your baby will come to associate the pleasure of being clean and dry with movement. Take your baby's feet gently by the ankles and bend and straighten her legs a few times. Take it slowly, and stop if your baby doesn't seem comfortable.

Your baby loves to be held in a sitting position

Your baby's head control continues to increase as he develops an interest in his surroundings

4 months

Your baby now concentrates on learning to sit up unsupported. Her head control continues to increase and she turns to the left and right when her attention is caught. She can support her chest and head weight on her forearms when lying prone, raise both legs off the mattress, and rock from side to side. She learns to roll over.

Your baby's head control and neck strength will increase with practice

5 months

Your baby has full head control even when propped in a sitting position. He may be able to take the full weight of his head, shoulders, and chest on outstretched hands. His rocking movements become stronger.

6 months

As your baby's limbs become stronger, he can take a lot of his weight on his arms. He'll sit with his hands forward for support, and hold his hands out to you when he wants to be lifted.

He may even sit unsupported for a few seconds. If you bounce your baby up and down with his feet on your lap, he can take some of his own weight with his leg muscles.

SHUFFLING

Before he can crawl, your baby may work out his own highly individual way of moving around using the coordination he has mastered.

Some babies shuffle along on their bottoms, others use crablike, sideways movements, and others devise their own unique methods. It is not important what personal maneuver your baby works out: he has managed a great achievement in moving independently, and this is all that matters.

You should never discourage your baby from his first attempts at being mobile. They are his tools for learning to control his body, and it is important that he is allowed to discover the limits of this control. Give his curiosity and spirit of adventure free rein.

ENCOURAGING MOVEMENT

Although your baby may appear to make crawling movements in his first weeks (see p.21), he'll stop this as his body straightens out from the fetal position. Before he can really begin to crawl, he must uncurl his body, control his head, lift his chest clear of the floor, and develop strength in his arms and legs.

Your encouragement and praise will make this an exciting and pleasurable time for both of you. As your baby gains head control, for instance, you can encourage him to lift his head by holding a brightly colored toy above him. As his back and shoulder muscles gain strength, help him by occasionally pulling him into a sitting position when he is lying on his back. Once he can sit up, you can play games that make him swivel in this position; call "peek-a-boo" from his side so that he has to turn to look at you. By about five months, when your baby has full head control, rocking and swinging games will give him practice in keeping his head stable.

PROPPING
From as early as six weeks, you should include your baby in daily life by propping him in an upright position with pillows. Since he can focus better by now, this will allow him to see what is going on and engage his interest in his surroundings. Once this stimulation begins, your baby will find the desire for involvement irresistible.

PREPARING TO CRAWL
Your baby has to be strong enough to hold his head and chest off the floor before he can crawl. By the time he's about six months old, he'll be able to push his chest clear of the floor and hold this position with his knees under him, but he'll be around eight months before he can pull himself forward along the floor.

It is impossible to pinpoint exactly the age at which your baby will crawl, if at all. If he's engrossed by watching what is going on around him he may hate lying on his stomach, and so leave crawling to a later stage. Some babies leave out the crawling stage altogether, but go on to learn to walk perfectly.

You can encourage your baby to crawl in a number of ways, the best being to use yourself as an enticement. Praise any efforts that your baby makes in order to divert him from feeling tired or frustrated by unsuccessful attempts. Your help and support will be far more useful to him than attempts to "teach" him to crawl by moving his arms and legs in a crawling movement.

PREPARING TO STAND
Before your baby can stand, he must have strength and balance. Although he is unlikely to have strong leg muscles or control over

them before he is ten or 11 months old, one of the most enjoyable games for a young baby is to be bounced up and down on your knee. Hold your baby facing you with his feet touching your knees and raise and lower him, making sure that his neck is supported. Your baby will really enjoy the sensation of taking his own weight, and it will strengthen his leg muscles in preparation for walking. From about six months, he'll try to bend and straighten his legs in a jumping movement whenever he is held in a standing position. These movements are your baby's earliest attempts at walking.

EXERCISES

You can encourage your baby's physical development from a very early age by playing simple exercise games, which he should enjoy. You should dress him comfortably, but in a warm room with no drafts, his diaper will be all that he needs.

Flier

Lie on your back with your knees drawn up and balance your baby on his stomach, on your shins and knees. Stretch his arms out to the side—this should make him raise his head—and then bring his arms back to the original position and begin again.

Arm stretch

Lie your baby on his back and let him grasp your thumbs. Stretch one of his arms above his head. As you then lower the extended arm, raise his other arm above his head.

Your baby will be happier if he can see you and follow your movements

Crossovers

Holding your baby's hands, stretch his arms to the side then back across his chest. Repeat.

SAFETY

From the moment your baby becomes mobile, it is vital that your home is "childproof" (see pp.306–11) to prevent accidents.

• Never leave your baby unattended. Even before he is mobile, your baby will need to be with you for reassurance and safety.

• Once your baby learns to roll, never leave him lying anywhere except on the floor in an area clear of sharp or hard objects.

• Even when he has mastered control over his head, continue to put pillows around your baby's bottom and lower spine.

• Keep all poisonous substances out of your baby's reach.

• Securely guard all fireplaces, cupboards, banisters, and stairs.

Hypotonic infant syndrome

Case study

Parents' names Catherine and Mike Dallas
Age 31 years and 30 years
Obstetric history First baby, normal delivery, no complications

Baby's name Henry Dallas
Age 16 months
Medical history Normal delivery. Nystagmus (flickering eye movements) at birth and Apgar score low for muscle tone (hypotonia). Subsequent motor development slow.

From about four months, Catherine and Mike thought that their baby Henry was a bit slow: he still didn't have control of his head, which tended to loll, and he hadn't made any attempts to sit up. If they tried to support him in a sitting position, he rolled to one side or the other. When she was dressing Henry, Catherine noticed that his arms and legs flopped back onto the bed after she'd fitted them into a sleeve or leg. Catherine and Mike have discovered from their healthcare provider that there is all kinds of help availablefor Henry (see **Useful Addresses**,

p.344). They know that one day Henry might need to have some special care, but in the meantime, they are taking Henry to regular physical therapy sessions to strengthen his muscles and improve his physical coordination. The physical therapist is very happy with the progress Henry is making, and pleased, too, to see what good teachers Catherine and Mike are becoming. They are feeling more confident in their own strength and resourcefulness now that they realize there is a great deal that they can do to help Henry.

Since Henry was their first baby, Catherine and Mike were unsure as to whether or not Henry was late in developing, but wisely decided to seek their doctor's opinion. When questioned by the doctor, Catherine could remember some other signs that all was not normal with Henry; when he was first born, she had noticed that his eyes flicked back and forth quite quickly but hadn't known that this wasn't normal in newborn babies. Henry had seemed rather weak with his sucking, and had a tendency to drool, which indicated difficulty in swallowing— but she was told many newborns have the same trouble.

After carefully examining Henry and asking Catherine and Mike some questions, the doctor said he felt that Henry should see a pediatric neurologist for a full assessment. He used the phrase "hypotonic infant syndrome," saying it had many causes and could take a bit of investigation over the next few months. Catherine was filled with fear and anxiety after hearing the doctor's opinion, and she desperately needed answers to her many questions.

POSSIBLE CAUSES

The list of possible causes of hypotonic infant syndrome is huge because the name simply describes the condition of a baby, not what's causing it. The characteristic "floppiness" can be caused by any one of hundreds of rare diseases, none of which can be diagnosed without extensive investigations. However, family history and careful clinical examination can narrow the list to one of three main categories.

Genetic This may be obvious if other family members have suffered, but may only come to light with genetic testing, performed with a DNA probe that can pick up gene abnormalities.

Muscular Muscular diseases, such as muscular dystrophy, may be tracked down with EMG (electromyography) and blood testing. The blood test measures levels of a chemical that is present in the blood when muscle tissue is being broken down. A muscle biopsy may also be carried out, so that a tiny piece of muscle can be studied under a microscope for abnormalities.

Brain The cerebellum, that part of the brain responsible for maintaining muscle tone, is situated at the back of the head and may not develop normally while your baby is in the uterus. CT (computed tomography) scans and MRI (magnetic resonance imaging) are used to give pictures of the brain that can be examined in minute detail. Very rarely the brain can be damaged at birth, but usually only in a prolonged, difficult labor.

DIAGNOSTIC CLUES

Henry's Apgar score (see p.24) had been on the low side at birth for muscle tone, an early clue to what happened later. Another clue was the nystagmus, (flicking eye movements) that Catherine had noticed at birth. Nystagmus often originates from damage to or incorrect development of the cerebellum, so already we had an indication that this should probably be the first area to examine. All the signs Catherine had noted but dismissed—weak sucking, drooling, poor swallowing, nystagmus, and low muscle tone—are early symptoms of hypotonic infant syndrome, although it's not until they're all added together that they become significant.

LEARNING TO COPE

Before any tests were started, and with the cooperation of their doctor, I encouraged Catherine and Mike to see a counselor rather than try to cope alone. It's an enormous help to chat constructively to an expert who can talk through and sympathize with conflicting emotions, and help couples to cope and plan. This turned out to be very comforting for Catherine and Mike, and they continued to see their counselor for many months.

HENRY'S DIAGNOSIS

When the tests were carried out, there was good news among the bad: the genetic tests were negative, meaning that Henry's disabilities had arisen spontaneously and future babies would most likely be perfectly normal. As far as doctors could tell, his intelligence was not impaired and the muscle biopsy showed no dystrophy. It looked as if the lesion was in Henry's brain and MRI scans confirmed this, showing a slightly small, underdeveloped cerebellum.

Henry is behind in terms of development, but this is thought to be due to his weak muscles rather than mental retardation. He is a wonderfully sociable little boy, however, and very loving; he brings Catherine and Mike much pleasure. He's slow to speak, but makes sounds, so they know he has the desire to communicate through conversation—a good sign. He has much better control over his body and is getting slowly stronger, though he will probably not walk until perhaps four or five years, and could have difficulty remaining steady. His vision and hearing are normal.

STAGES OF STANDING

As your baby learns to sit unsupported for longer periods of time, her sense of balance and her desire to walk will increase.

• From about six or seven months, your baby will begin to take her full weight on her knees and hips, but she'll need to be balanced by you. She'll test her leg strength with a sort of dancing movement—a hop from one foot to another—and as she becomes more confident, she'll practice bending and stretching her legs.

• By nine months, your baby's ability to balance will be greatly improved. She may be able to take all her own weight on her legs, but she'll still need to hold on to something. Any stable piece of furniture will support her, but she should never be left alone in this position; she'll find it difficult to sit from a standing position, and a fall may seriously affect her confidence and pleasure in standing.

• By about ten months, your baby will be able to lift one foot while she stands, provided she's supported. She'll be able to pull herself into a standing position, but will still have trouble lowering herself.

Locomotion

During her first few months, your baby achieved head control and learned to coordinate and refine her movements in stages as her muscles became stronger and her balance improved. Now she is ready to start moving around, and the next year will be an exciting one for both of you as she learns to crawl and then to walk.

It's important to remember that all babies develop at their own speed, and the ages given here are the approximate times by which most babies have achieved these skills. A few babies crawl by six months; others show no interest in crawling at all, but walk perfectly later on, so don't be too concerned if your baby's development doesn't exactly match these stages. Some babies skip the crawling stage altogether, and go straight from shuffling (see p.156) to walking. Others crawl bear-like on their hands and feet rather than on their hands and knees. Both of these are normal.

Your baby can balance on three limbs while reaching out for an object

8 months
Your baby will stretch for things that are held beyond his reach. He'll sit unsupported, briefly at first, but gradually for longer periods of time. He'll master leaning, both forward and to the sides, and will test his own balance by rocking back and forth in a sitting position or twisting around, though he'll probably fall over.

10 months
He's probably mastered crawling. He can pull himself to his feet, but you'll still have to hold him in a standing position and help him sit down again. Your baby may sit unaided for up to ten minutes.

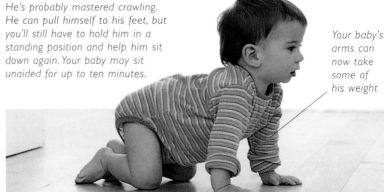

Your baby's arms can now take some of his weight

1 year

Your baby can now turn around when sitting down and can creep or crawl. When held in a standing position, she'll try stepping. She may try "cruising"—walking sideways while holding on to something.

Your baby will be able to turn and pick up an object behind her while sitting

BALANCE

Between seven months and one year, your baby will develop righting reflexes, which control her basic body movements.

These help her move from prone to standing positions and vice versa, to get to her hands and knees, and to sit up. They control the position and movement of her head and are responsible for the development of balance.

• By eight months, your baby will lean forward and backward in order to test her balance.

• At nine months, your baby can lean forward and to the side without losing her balance. She can roll over and will try to crawl.

• From ten months, she can twist her upper body while sitting. This strengthens her lateral trunk muscles and improves her ability to balance while moving.

14 months

After cruising, your baby will perfect standing alone and may even take her first independent step. Soon she'll be taking a few steps together in order to move between one stable support and another. She'll still need support to sit from standing.

16 months

Your baby's steps are high and unsteady, but her style will soon become more refined. She'll stand up and sit down without help, and can crawl up stairs. You must be vigilant about safety; now that she's mobile she'll want to investigate everything she sees around her.

18 months

Your toddler can climb stairs unaided, although she needs support to stay balanced. Her steps are lower and more steady and she rarely loses her balance. As her balance and coordination improve, she'll progress to walking backward and running.

STAGES OF WALKING

Your baby's first attempts at walking will be unsteady, and he'll hang on to objects for support, but in a couple of months, he'll be independently mobile.

• Your baby will "cruise" before he walks—that is, haul himself up on any large item, and then sidle around it. Make sure that any unsteady or lightweight furniture is secured or removed from his path.

• Next, he'll start to move one hand over the other as he cruises, rather than sliding them together and then moving both hands and feet at the same time. This is an important stage as your baby develops the confidence and balance to take all his weight, briefly, on one foot.

• His next goal is to negotiate gaps between two supports. He'll hold on to both at once, and only let go of one support when he's holding firmly on to the other.

• He'll soon progress to crossing wider gaps. Still holding on to a support with one hand, he'll move into the center of the gap and, once he's got his balance, release one support and take a step toward the next one, grabbing for it with both hands.

• Finally, your baby will begin to "toddle," staggering a couple of paces to reach the second support. He'll launch himself into the open and take several unsupported steps with confidence. He may soon lose his balance, sitting down with a thud, but he'll usually set off for his goal and waddle bow-leggedly toward it with his arms held high and wide.

ENCOURAGING SKILLS

The transition your child makes from an uncoordinated baby to an independent toddler is a major turning point in his development, and you can help by encouraging him to stand and gently urging him on during his early attempts at walking.

He needs lots of room to move in and a soft covering under his feet so that he can fully enjoy his new-found freedom. Praise him at every stage, but try not to push him to go faster than he feels he can— walking involves tricky techniques of balance and coordination and so is one of the most difficult skills your child will ever learn.

HELPING YOUR CHILD STAND

Let your baby take more and more of his own standing weight from the time he can control his head. His leg muscles, hips, and knees will gradually strengthen, and he'll relish taking his own weight on them. When you hold his hands, he'll bounce around and play standing and bouncing games. Hold him on your lap, on cushions, on a bed, or in the bath and encourage these active games.

From around nine months, your baby will take nearly his entire weight on his legs, but will still need support to do so because his muscle strength is more advanced than his balance. You can encourage him by taking him to stable pieces of furniture and getting him to grip on with his hands that he is nicely balanced. Stay close while he holds on. He'll need to develop his balance in order to stand securely, so when he is sitting, urge him to lean forward and sideways by placing toys just out of reach in front and by his sides; this will strengthen his trunk muscles. He will find it difficult to sit down from a standing position, but you can make it a little easier by gently manipulating his hips and knees. At the age of ten months, your baby is far more mobile on his hands and knees. The muscles of his trunk are getting stronger all the time as he twists and turns while sitting or crawling. Offer your fingers to encourage him to pull himself up to sit and stand. He'll be delighted at his achievement, so always praise him.

Learning to stand
Teach your baby the sensation of supporting his own weight by encouraging him to stand using the furniture around him.

HELPING YOUR CHILD WALK

Your baby will learn to walk on his own, but it's fun to help him practice if you have the time. Put your baby on his hands and knees and sit a short distance away. This will impel him to move toward you. He'll come more eagerly if you hold out your arms, call his name, or offer a brightly colored toy. To prompt your baby to twist, place a toy behind his back and support him as he turns around. When your baby reaches ten months, he'll be able to stand up if supported by furniture. While he is standing and firmly supported, bend one of his knees and lift his foot; this will help him learn to step and bear his weight momentarily on one foot.

From 11 months, help your baby to practice walking forward by holding his hands and guiding him. You can make cruising easier by positioning stable pieces of furniture close together around the room, but remove any items that could tip over easily when he pulls on them.

Improve your baby's stepping skills by calling to him while he is cruising around the room. Give him the courage to launch himself by moving the pieces of furniture slightly farther apart. Sit a little way from him and, while he is holding on to the furniture, hold out your arms and call him to you—but always be close enough to catch him if he stumbles.

From 13 months your baby can stand alone and may take his first independent step. A stable standing toy, like a push-along cart, is ideal encouragement for him to practice walking alone. At 15 months your baby can kneel, lower his body without support, and stand up unaided. A chair with arms will allow your baby to sit down without falling and will provide good bending practice for his hips and knees.

Practice more leg movements with your baby, using a large, soft ball that he can try to kick to you. This is also good for acquiring balance. Show him how to squat, and help him master hip and knee bends—which are all the more enjoyable if you do them together to music. Games that use backward or sideways steps will greatly increase your baby's walking and balancing skills. "Ring-around-the-Rosie," a game in which you hold your baby's hands while walking, sitting, and standing, is a lot of fun and allows him to imitate you, making his achievement even greater.

There's no right age for your baby to start to walk but he is most likely to take his first unsupported steps between the ages of nine and 15 months.

Toys for walking
Your toddler's mobility and independence will be enhanced by sturdy, wheeled, walking toys.

SAFETY

As your baby's independence grows, safety in his environment becomes increasingly important.

• Stay nearby when your baby is taking his first unsteady steps, and take particular care when he walks and crawls upstairs. Make sure the floor is not slippery, and don't give him shoes until he is walking outdoors.

• Give your baby plenty of clear space for his walking attempts. Trailing cords or small pieces of furniture might cause him to trip.

• Special protective edges are available for sharp-cornered furniture or door handles.

• Glass-topped items should be removed or covered with safety film.

• Fit safety gates to the top and bottom of your stairs. Gates at the top of the stairs should open onto the landing and should not have horizontal bars that your baby could climb.

• Keep all poisonous substances well out of reach, and out of sight, in a lockable cupboard. Even vitamin pills are dangerous.

• Don't leave sharp or hot objects in your baby's reach.

LOCOMOTION IN GIRLS

Girls seem to be on a faster timetable than boys all the way through their growth; they tend to grow more regularly and predictably than boys.

In the preschool years, girls are better at jumping, hopping, rhythmic movement, and balance, so they will enjoy games that involve these. Hopscotch, skipping, and dancing games will all give your little girl a chance to develop these skills.

Locomotion

Between the ages of 18 months and three years, your child will quickly progress in getting around. She will be very active on her feet, perfecting her walking and balancing skills, and you can encourage this development by involving her in your daily activities. She will begin to enjoy ball games, toys on wheels, and games that involve hopping, jumping, or climbing. Spend time with your child encouraging her in her new skills, and building up her confidence: it will be vital in her continuing physical development.

21 months
Your child can now bend to pick up objects without toppling over. Walking becomes steadier, and he can walk with his arms by his sides instead of held out high. He can run quite well, but will have difficulty turning corners and may topple over if he stops suddenly. He may be able to kick a ball, but rather awkwardly, since he can't balance well on one leg.

2 years
Your child is more fluent at ball games, both catching and kicking, and can walk backward as well as forward. He can go up and down stairs without holding on, putting both his feet on each step. He can now veer and swerve while running and can stop running without falling over.

2½ years
Your child can now jump with both feet off the ground at the same time, walk on tiptoe, and is steady on her feet—with your guidance, she can carry a breakable object or hold a baby brother or sister on her knee. She can now run quite well and can glance over her shoulder without losing balance.

HOW TO HELP

Your child's toddler years are a time of great activity for both of you. She will be interested in everything she sees and is developing the skills that will allow her to take part in a number of activities for the first time. This provides a great opportunity for you to involve her in many daily tasks, which will be both great fun for her and important to her development.

Give your child plenty of chances to practice her walking skills by going up and down stairs with her or leaving the stroller behind on short trips. Hold her hand if she needs support or when you go out shopping. Alternatively, reins are even safer and will give your child more freedom, making them particularly suitable for use in the park or other playing areas. Don't put too many demands on her walking abilities at this stage—she won't be able to walk farther than a few hundred yards. She is bound to have some lapses in her learning, so don't worry if she experiences setbacks in her walking, like a stumble or fall—she will soon regain her confidence.

Agility in walking and running may also be developed by playing games that involve jumping and walking on tiptoe. Encourage your child to dance to music with you. She'll need plenty of practice at balancing, and this can be developed with ball games and other suitable toys. Start with a large, soft ball. Let her try walking along the top of a low wall, holding her hand all the time in case she gets a bit wobbly. Your child is probably too young for a bicycle, but a toy with wheels that she can sit on and propel with her feet will develop her love of motion and strengthen her muscles. Indoors, give your child soft toys like a mattress or foam rubber on which to jump and somersault. An outdoor swing will help develop strength and coordination skills, but make sure these larger outdoor toys are safe (see p.310).

The more you involve your child in daily activities, such as cleaning and washing, and climbing the stairs, the more teaching and practice your child will receive. Take sensible precautions against falls and other household dangers, but don't worry unduly; toddlers are amazingly resilient and will be oblivious to most of the bruises they inevitably receive in these active and inquisitive years.

LOCOMOTION IN BOYS

In the preschool years, there is little difference between boys and girls in terms of strength and speed.

Young boys achieve jumping, hopping, rhythmic movement, and balancing skills less quickly than girls, so they tend to reach certain milestones later, such as picking up a toy from the floor without sitting down first. You should therefore give your little boy plenty of help with achieving these skills by allowing him freedom of movement. Games that involve kicking a ball, or dancing and jumping games, will all increase his skills.

Wheeled toys
A push-bike can be used indoors as well as out, and will improve your child's coordination and muscle strength.

Locomotion

ENCOURAGING GIRLS

Girls are often considered to be less outgoing and adventurous than boys, but it is important that they are encouraged to be curious and active, and to let off steam with physical activity.

• Don't be overly concerned about your little girl hurting herself or getting her clothes dirty; this attitude can inhibit your child from discovering her physical potential.

• Girls are more naturally sociable, so encourage them to play team or cooperative games such as hopscotch or jumping rope.

• Include more energetic movements with your child, in games such as "Simon says."

• Girls tend to be more gifted at imaginative roleplay games, so encourage your little girl to include more physical creativity, with constructional and spatial skills, in her fantasy games.

• Never hamper your daughter's adventurousness and curiosity; encourage her to climb and swing as you would a son.

During these two preschool years, your child is really developing his physical skills and taking pride in acquiring each new ability. At three years, your child has become much more nimble, walking upstairs with confidence.

Your child can jump off the bottom step and stand on one foot for a second. He can swing his arms when he walks and ride a tricycle. At four, he is very active and well coordinated. He races around hopping, jumping, and climbing, and can walk down stairs rapidly, with one foot per step. He can even carry a drink without spilling it. By five, your child's coordination is finely developed. He can walk in a straight line, go down stairs on alternating feet, jump rope with alternating feet, climb confidently, and enjoy fast-moving toys and games.

ENCOURAGING SKILLS

You can encourage your three-year-old's jumping skills by playing hopscotch, or holding hands and hopping on one foot. This will work off excess energy. You can practice arm-swinging with him by marching to music. Riding a tricycle will strengthen his calf muscles and encourage flexibility in his feet, while playground equipment, such as a swing, seesaw, or slide, will boost his physical confidence. At four, a climbing frame or jungle gym will give your child a chance to exercise his muscles. Help him to master jumping rope, and to try other physical games, too. Five-year-olds can jump rope and will enjoy playing on stilts and skateboards.

Wheeled toys
A three-year-old will have enough coordination to manage pedaling.

Dance will improve poise and balance

Sturdy pedals are easy to maneuver

Dance
Many little girls love the idea of being a dancer, and lessons can be an enjoyable social occasion as well as honing physical skills.

ADVENTUROUS PLAY

If your child is encouraged to be adventurous, he will be willing to push himself to the limit and develop his full potential. A child of three or four has a very clear sense of self and his abilities, and is discovering the limits of what is safe and feasible. If you are overprotective and don't allow your child to test his abilities, master a new skill, and move on, you will hold him back and he will lack coordination and confidence as a result. You must separate his fears from yours; his fears will make him circumspect and sensible, while your fears will cripple both his curiosity and his spirit.

By the time your child is three years old, he can walk and run confidently. He has boundless energy and is ready to tackle more demanding activities, so give him plenty of scope: running, climbing, and pedaling will improve his skills and help him burn off surplus energy. If you can afford it, set up a climbing frame, rope ladder, or swing in your yard where you can supervise him from the house. Depending on your child's skill and confidence, he may be ready to tackle roller skating, riding a bicycle with training wheels. Introducing your child to sports and other activities now could lay the foundations for a lifetime of enjoyment, so give him the opportunity to try lots of different things: swimming, dancing, soccer, or horseback riding. At the very least, try to make sure he has somewhere he can run, climb, or just kick a ball around.

You can always help your child to tackle new and difficult tasks at first, holding his hand and guiding him through them so that you are secure in your own mind that he is competent and therefore safe. Extend adventurousness and curiosity in your child across the board, not just in physical development, but with toys, music, painting, books, and games.

Balance and coordination
Encourage your child's adventurous spirit by providing equipment such as roller skates.

Adjustable roller skates are comfortable and allow for growth

ENCOURAGING BOYS

Boys are assumed and encouraged to be adventurous in their play, but it is a mistake to assume that all boys are outgoing and active. Some have an obvious preference for boisterous games while others prefer quiet, contemplative activities.

• Games on large, soft cushions and foam-filled furniture are excellent fun and good for promoting balance and coordination.

• Boys are usually considered to be better at "spatial relationships"— knowing, for example, how one object best fits onto another. Encourage this skill by introducing construction toys as soon as he can fit them together.

• Provide plenty of opportunities for your little boy to be creative; items such as toilet roll tubes, old egg boxes, and yogurt cartons can be turned into anything his imagination can conjure up.

Inflatable armbands give your child confidence

Swimming
Your child's muscular fitness and strength, particularly in the arms, will be developed by swimming.

YOUR BABY'S HANDS

At first, your baby has little interest in her hands, but as she becomes more aware of her body, they'll begin to fascinate her more and more.

When she waves her arms around, her hand will accidentally touch her face and she'll put it in her mouth to suck. At two to three months, she finds the movements of her fingers fascinating and will watch them for ages. By about four months, she'll grab hold of objects to "test" them in her mouth. At six months, she refines her manual skills and feels with her fingers as much as her mouth.

Manipulation

Your baby was born with the reflex to grasp anything that is placed in her palm—such as your finger—and not let go; her grip is so strong she can support her own weight (though you should never actually let her do so).

When she is not holding something, her hands will be tightly closed in a fist, although they'll probably open and close when she cries, and she will open them instinctively when she is startled (see p.20). The early reflex grasp must be lost if she is to learn to select an object, and reach out and pick it up with thumb and index finger—the basic skill of manual dexterity. Most babies will develop a mature "pincer" grip by one year of age.

Newborn
From birth, your baby has the ability to grasp an object and hold on. This grasping reflex is so strong it allows her to support her own weight.

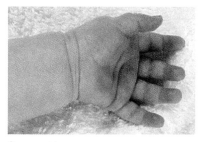

2 months
Your baby is becoming more aware of her hands and her reflex grasping action is almost gone. Her hands are much more open now, too.

Your baby will start to be fascinated by his feet

Your baby will love to play with his toes

5 months
Your baby is eager to grab things with his whole hand. He will hold his feet, or a soft toy, and transfer them to his mouth to suck.

6 months
Your baby holds his bottle or cup, and he'll be able to hold an object that is given to him between two hands.

Your baby learns to feed himself

ENCOURAGING SKILLS

Even the most simple activities can add to your baby's feelings of confidence and achievement. She needs to feel that her hard work is noticed and appreciated by you, and that you are as pleased as she is about her growing independence.

0–6 weeks Your baby must ignore her instinctive grasp reflex before she can manipulate objects. Test this reflex by letting her grasp your fingers and seeing how far you can pull her off the mattress. Encourage her to open her fingers by gently unfolding them one at a time as you play games like "this little piggy."

6 weeks Your baby's hands are opening and she is becoming aware of them. Help her to take an interest in her hands by tickling her palms and fingertips with materials of different textures: soft, furry, smooth, or ridged—corduroy, for example. A gentle hand massage or rubbing of her palms will encourage her to open her hands.

2 months Your baby's hands are more open now, so continue to provide plenty of tactile stimulation by giving her objects of different textures to hold. Lay each object across her palm, following the horizontal creases, so that she can wrap her hand around it.

3 months Your baby uses a wide open hand to grasp and reaches for things inaccurately. Encourage a mature grasp by giving her things to hold. Place a rattle in her hand and shake it a few times—she will be fascinated by the feel and the sound. Put a mobile above her crib to give her something to look at, and string toys across her carriage to swipe at—make sure they are safe (see p.310).

4 months As your baby starts to get her hand and arm movements under control, she'll reach out for things with increasing accuracy. Encourage her by presenting interesting objects while she is sitting propped up or lying down. She'll still tend to overshoot when she reaches for something, so you'll need to give her some help.

5 months Your baby will be grabbing everything within reach, and she will particularly love crumpling paper, so give her tissue paper to play with. She will love you to play with her feet where she can see them, so play "this little piggy" with her toes. Play giving and taking-away games to encourage her to open her fingers and let go. She will reach for a bottle to try and feed herself.

6 months Her finger movements are becoming more precise all the time. You can let her hold her own bottle in two hands and teach her how to pass an object from one hand to the other. As soon as this is mastered, she will joyfully start to practice her letting-go skill and throw everything on the floor.

HAND–EYE COORDINATION

From six months, your baby's coordination and manipulation skills will develop rapidly.

Once she starts on solid foods, she will be able to pick up and hold finger foods such as crackers.

Self-feeding
Your baby will like to try picking up finger foods and feeding himself, though he may not be very accurate yet at getting the food into his mouth.

RIGHT- OR
LEFT-HANDED

**Right- or left-handedness
develops in the first few
months as one or the other
side of your baby's brain
becomes dominant: if the right
side dominates, he will be left-
handed, and vice versa.**

Even as a newborn, your baby may
have shown a tendency to turn his
head more to the right than the left.
Now he may start to favor one hand.
Never try to dissuade him from
being left-handed—you could cause
psychological side effects and reading
and writing problems.

Manipulation

By six months, your baby will have learned to grasp objects at will,
and now he will gradually refine his handling skills as he learns to
use them to eat, dress, and pick things up. You'll find this time both
rewarding and frustrating—your baby is learning to do more things
for himself, but he won't be very adept at first, so you'll have to be
patient while he learns.

By 12 months, your baby will have the mature adult grasp, which is
a fine movement achieved by bringing the thumb and index finger
together (opposition). He can give something to you by releasing his
grip, and he will be able to roll a ball to you.

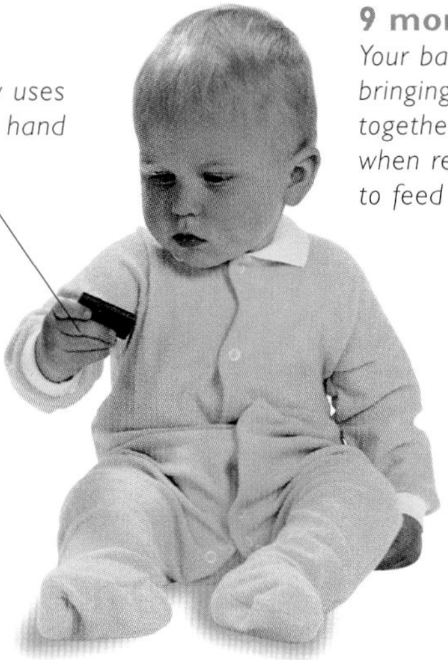

9 months
*Your baby can pick up small things by
bringing his thumb and index finger
together. He points with his index finger
when reaching for something. He's eager
to feed himself.*

*Your baby uses
his whole hand
to grip*

12 months
*Your baby still enjoys
throwing things as he
practices "ungrasping."
He can build a tower
of two blocks, and draw
lines with a pencil.
His coordination is
improving, so he
spills less food.*

*Your baby can
grip objects
between his
thumb and
fingers*

18 months
*Now your toddler can turn two or three pages of a
book at a time, and build a tower of three blocks.
She can feed herself completely with a spoon and
drink from a cup without spilling anything. She'll
put on some clothes, is fascinated by zippers, and
enjoys finger painting and scribbling.*

170

HOW YOU CAN HELP

Your baby's new skills can be encouraged as before in a variety of games that you can play together. Now that he's older, however, he'll be able to pursue some activities by himself; he'll also be able to apply himself to everyday tasks.

Everyday activities The business of getting food into his mouth will give your child a powerful motive to improve his hand–eye coordination. As soon as he is able—from about six months—let him hold his own bottle or cup while he drinks from it, and give him finger foods to encourage fine finger movements. Before long, he'll be able to feed himself with a spoon, a skill you can encourage by preparing semisolid foods that will stick to the spoon.

Dressing is another everyday activity that your baby will try increasingly to do for himself. He may be able to pull some of his clothes on and off, but won't be able to manage fastenings yet, though he will want to try.

Building blocks Once your baby is able to grasp a block, you can teach him to place one on top of another. At six or seven months, he will have mastered this, but you can continue to stack blocks—three or four high or side by side—for him to see and copy. As his grasp develops (see right), he practices the novel skill of letting go and dropping things, and will start to throw blocks. By one year old, he'll be able to build a tower of two blocks by himself, and by 15 months he'll probably manage a tower of three.

Games There are all sorts of simple games your baby can play to develop his skills. He'll love making noise with a wooden spoon and some pots and pans. Once he learns to let objects go, he will enjoy throwing them out of his stroller or high chair. You can make this into a game by showing him how to put objects into a container and take them out again.

Drawing Your baby won't be able to manage a pencil or crayon until he's about a year old, but once he starts, he will love to scribble. Give him lots of scrap paper—wallpaper remnants are good—and pin his pictures up where he can see them.

Building blocks
Help your child to develop his grasp so he can let go as well as hold on, by introducing him to toy blocks.

YOUR BABY'S GRASP

The ability to grasp small objects precisely between the thumb and finger— opposition—will be one of the great achievements of your baby's first year.

• At about five months, your baby will grasp objects in his palm on the little finger side.

• At about eight months, he will be able to grasp an object between his fingers, perhaps pushing it against the base of the thumb.

• Next he learns to "ungrasp" and practices this by dropping and throwing things.

• At about nine months he will use his index finger to point—a step toward holding small objects with the thumb and index finger.

• By the time he is one year old, he will have achieved a mature "pincer" grip, grasping objects between his thumb and index finger.

ENCOURAGING
INDEPENDENCE

Manipulation

**With so many new skills
to learn at this stage, it's
important not to expect your
child to develop at a rate that
is too fast for her.**

All children progress at their own
pace, which is decided by the speed
that their developing brain and
nerves allow. Your child will want to
please you, and may try to do things
that are more complicated than her
development will allow. Failure is
demoralizing because she feels she's
let you down. A better approach is
to give her all the help and
encouragement she needs, showing
her how pleased you are with every
task she manages, without setting
goals that are beyond her abilities.

In terms of general development, the toddler stage marks a quite
dramatic change from babyhood to childhood, and from 18 months
onward you'll really notice this transformation, especially in
manipulative skills. Over the next 18 months, your baby will be
getting more independent as she learns to dress herself and to
manage increasingly fine movements. Her creative skills also come
to the fore at this stage as her building-block houses get more
complicated and her drawings more recognizable.

Milestones
*Your child may just be able to do up a
zipper. He'll try an "unscrewing" movement
with jar tops and door knobs by the age of
two. He'll use crayons more deliberately and
may be able to build a tower of four blocks.*

*Your child has a refined
grip to clasp and
twist objects*

Fine movements
*Your child will be able to thread
large beads or spools on a string
by two-and-a-half years old.*

*Thick yarn or
shoelaces will be
easy for your child
to manage*

*Household items
like thread spools
can be threaded
on to string*

*Your child can
grip and pull
fine materials*

Getting dressed
*At two-and-a-half,
putting on and taking
off clothes will become
easier and your child
will be eager to do
these things for himself.*

ENCOURAGING SKILLS

All sorts of everyday tasks are now becoming possible for your child to manage by herself, so give her every opportunity to do things unaided. More complicated toys, especially construction or craft toys, will help her to practice and develop her skills.

Dressing By the age of two, your child will be able to cope with a number of dressing skills, though putting on her socks, shoes, and gloves will still be tricky, so let her choose her own clothes and practice getting dressed. Clothes with snaps and fairly large buttons, provided the holes are not too tight, will also encourage her to develop new finger skills. Continue to encourage her dressing ability, and she'll soon be able to put on and take off underpants, pants, and T-shirts. Once she can cope with all her buttons, including the smaller ones, she'll be able to dress and undress herself completely.

Construction toys
Interlocking building blocks are always popular toys and are ideal for developing hand movements.

Improving dexterity As soon as your child can turn a door knob with two hands and open a loose-fitting screw-top jar, give her toys that need to be fitted together. Washing and drying her hands will also be a favorite pastime, so encourage her in this. Make sure your two-year-old has plenty of colorful picture books, since she can now turn the pages of a book one at a time by herself. Your child can now build a tower of four blocks, and with encouragement she'll make more complicated structures. Building blocks that need pressing and fitting together will help develop the small movements of her hands. Intricate tasks, such as threading large beads or fitting together jigsaw puzzles made of large pieces, will boost her manipulation skills.

Arts and crafts Children enjoy drawing at this age, so give your child plenty of drawing materials, including a range of different crayons, and start her off by showing the effect of all the different colors. She will also enjoy using paints, especially if you allow her to be messy and paint with her hands. You can also help her relate her drawings to the world around her by naming the colors of the crayons and then pointing out the same colors in everyday objects. She'll soon be producing images of people and familiar objects, and by two-and-a-half years her pictures will become more recognizable.

HANDLING HER BODY

Babies usually become aware of their bodies, including genital organs, toward the end of the first year but handle them without any obvious pleasure, just curiosity.

By the time your child is a toddler, handling may bring a mildly pleasurable sensation. Later on most children of both sexes fiddle with themselves and it is perfectly normal behavior.

There is no reason to discourage it or show disapproval. If you do, the child will grow guilty and secretive. If your child masturbates in public, try to distract her rather than scolding or showing disapproval.

Choosing clothes
Encourage your child's interest in dressing himself by letting him choose the clothes he will wear.

DRAWING

Your child's improving manual dexterity is clearly demonstrated by his ability to copy a circle.

2½ years
His earliest attempts at a circle may end up as a continuous round shape, like a spiral.

3 years
His attempts become more controlled, but the circle may not quite join up or the lines may overshoot.

3½ years
Your child should be able to draw a closed figure, either a true circle or an oval shape.

Manipulation

Your three-year-old is maturing rapidly and by now can probably dress and undress himself completely, as long as the fastenings are all easy to reach. He can draw and color quite accurately and his drawings are becoming more recognizable.

By the age of four, he will have mastered the complicated action of using scissors. Building blocks are becoming too simple for him, so he is ready to move on to more sophisticated construction sets. He is already doing very simple tasks around the house, and from four years old he will get much better at jobs such as setting the table, washing his face and hands, making his bed, and putting his clothes away neatly.

Crafts
Your four- or five-year-old's ability to use scissors represents a huge step forward in manual dexterity and brain–muscle coordination. Give him simple models to make. Any scissors he uses should be blunt-ended.

Drawing
From three years on, your child becomes more skillful at drawing as she begins to master skills like copying two straight lines drawn at right angles. By four years, she begins to include more detail on her figures. Make simple puzzles for her— draw an incomplete person and ask her to finish it.

Teeth

People used to think a child's first teeth weren't very important because the adult teeth would come in later. But they are vital— they guide in the adult teeth so they grow in the correct position. And if the first teeth are lost to decay, this can spread to the bone beneath and erode the support needed by the adult teeth.

Cutting time There is no standard time for your baby to cut his first tooth. Some babies are born with one tooth, while others still have none at 12 months of age. (If a baby is born with a tooth, this is sometimes removed if it is crooked or badly positioned, for instance, or if it is loose and there is a risk of its falling out and causing the baby to choke.) As a general rule, though, teething starts at around six months to cope with solid food and a changing diet, after which many teeth appear up to the end his first year. If you are on the lookout, you will probably notice your baby's first tooth as it starts to push its way through the gum and form a small, pale bump. Your baby will be teething for most of the second year, and you should be prepared for the molars, which come through last, to be a bit upsetting.

Signs of teething You can tell when your baby is cutting a tooth because he will be irritable. The gum will be red and swollen, and you may be able to feel the tooth through the gum. Your baby's cheeks may be red, and he will probably drool. Giving your baby something to chew on can help. Symptoms such as a high temperature, vomiting, or diarrhea are never caused by teething, so you should not dismiss them—check with your doctor.

Your baby will like something firm to chew on when he is teething. This principle continues to hold good once he has all his teeth.

Chewy foods, particularly fresh fruit and raw vegetables, encourage the development of strong jaw muscles. They also strengthen the teeth and have a cleansing effect as their fibers are shredded during the chewing process. Never leave him alone with chewy foods because of the risk of choking. Your baby's diet should contain plenty of calcium and vitamin D (from dairy foods, and fatty fish such as herring) to ensure the healthy formation of the permanent teeth, already growing in the jawbones.

Safety tip
Never leave your baby alone with finger foods because of the risk of choking.

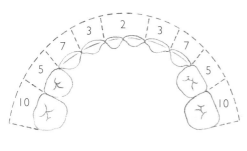
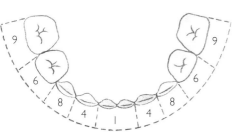

How the teeth come in
The numbers indicate the order in which the teeth arrive. The first to erupt are usually the lower front two teeth, then the upper two front teeth. Upper side teeth come next, followed by the lower side teeth. After this, the first upper molars erupt, and then come the first lower molars. The upper canines come in next, one on each side, followed by the lower canines. The second molars erupt first in the lower jaw, then appear in the upper jaw.

Vision

The development of normal vision requires two properly functioning eyes and plenty of visual stimulation. Try the following ideas to stimulate your baby's eyesight:

- From the day she's born, put a photo of a face—yours or one cut from a magazine—at the side of the crib for your baby to look at.

- A simple mobile over the crib, or brightly colored objects on elastic, will give your baby something interesting to look at.

- Your baby is never too young to go sightseeing. If she is in a stroller, she'll be able to look all around her.

Stimulating toys
Give your baby plenty of interesting toys to keep him entertained while he's awake in his crib.

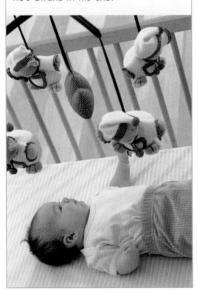

A newborn baby is not blind just because she can't change focus. She can see everything at her fixed focus of 8–10 inches (20–25 centimeters) as plainly as you or I can. Right from the moment she's born, your baby needs lots of visual stimulation in order to develop her eyesight fully.

Your newborn Although your baby's eyesight is limited, her eyes are very sensitive to the human face and anything that moves. At first, she won't be able to focus on anything more than 10 inches (25 centimeters) away, but if you bring your face to within 8 inches (20 centimeters) of hers, she'll see you, and you'll notice that her eyes move in recognition and her expression changes. A newborn baby's vision is more limited than an older child's, so you'll have to fit her visual world into a range that she can perceive. The color-sensitive cells in her eyes aren't yet fully developed, so she'll only see the world in muted shades.

Increasing recognition If you talk excitedly to your newborn, move your eyes, and open and close your mouth, your baby will respond from within a few minutes of birth by opening her mouth and sticking out her tongue. A baby of only a few hours old can train her eyes on an object and follow it if it moves. At two weeks, a baby will automatically raise a hand to protect herself from something that's moving quickly toward her. At three weeks, her whole body may react with excited jerking movements when your face comes into focus. She can fully focus by eight weeks and she'll recognize your face and respond to it with smiles and waving arms. She's also more conscious of other objects, but, because she can only focus on nearby objects, the world appears rather flat and distant details are lost to her.

Depth of vision By three to four months, your baby can take in details and is able to build up a three-dimensional picture of the world—a necessary step before she becomes mobile, since she probably won't start crawling until her vision allows her to understand depth as well as height and width. She can tell the difference between pictures with two and three items, and can recognize patterns. This eye for detail improves until, by five to six months, she can discriminate between different facial expressions, such as sadness, fear, and joy, and will respond to them with her own expression. She will show excitement when she sees her feeding being prepared.

A sense of permanence From six months, she can identify objects and can adjust her position to see those that most interest her. From now on, the biggest development in your baby's visual skill is the way her brain interprets the information her eyes see.

TESTING VISION

The first test of vision, which you can carry out at birth, is to note your baby's reaction to your face when it is held 8–10 inches (20–25 centimeters) from hers. If she sees your face, her facial expression should change; her eyes will dart to your face and she may open and shut her mouth. There are many clues that will warn parents if a child has a sight defect. If you're in any doubt about your baby's vision, or if your child's eyes water a lot and bright lights cause her discomfort, consult your doctor. The following eye conditions may show up even in a very young baby. Although you should not try to diagnose them yourself, here are some things you might observe; if you do, check with your doctor.

Lazy eye If your child suffers from weak eye muscles around one eye, she may turn her head so that the eye with better sight can more easily follow the action around her. Check that both eyelids are level when your baby is concentrating on a moving object. If she obviously favors one eye over the other, check with your doctor.

Misalignment (strabismus) If you notice that only one of your baby's eyes is focused on the object of interest and the other is pointing too far in or too far out, she may be suffering from strabismus. She may tilt her head or hold it in an unusual position to get her vision in line. Find an interesting object, such as a toy, and, keeping your child's head still (you may need another adult to help you), move the toy to spell the letter H in the air. Check that both eyes follow the toy in unison. (See also **Misalignment**, p.287.)

Color blindness The most common form is the inability to distinguish between red and green (mostly, but not exclusively, found in boys). Use colorful candies, such as jelly beans, and ask your child to pick out certain colors. If she hasn't learned her colors yet, ask her to pick out the same colors as you.

Peripheral vision To test whether your child has a normal field of vision extending wide to either side, choose a favorite toy and, with your child staring directly ahead, slowly move it from the outside to in front of her face until she sees it. Her field of vision should extend to about 45° on either side.

Visual accuracy Test the accuracy of your child's vision with the following game. Stand about 20 feet (6 meters) away and hold up some fingers. Ask her how many fingers you are holding up, or get her to hold up the same number as you. If she fails, it's probably best to check with your doctor.

THE VISUALLY IMPAIRED BABY

If your child's vision is poor, you need to be sensitive to her needs. Ensure that she receives professional attention and regular checkups.

• Far-sighted children receive six-monthly checkups to see if their prescription for glasses needs changing. A child who is far-sighted or has astigmatism may only need to wear glasses for two or three years before her eyesight develops normally.

• The earlier children start wearing glasses, the more likely they are to accept them. At first, a child may take them off and play with them, but she'll soon show a preference for seeing the world clearly.

• A visually impaired child needs stimulation by touch, noise, and smell, so choose toys that have interesting textures and make different noises. Puzzles are particularly important; those with large, colorful pieces are best.

HELPING
YOUR BABY

Hearing

By explaining sounds and playing appropriate games with your baby, you can help him to listen in a discerning way to the confusion of sounds that he hears.

• Be theatrical about explaining sounds. For example, put your finger to your lips and say, "Shhh, let's be quiet as mice" to explain the idea of quietness.

• Describe sounds and music with appropriate adjectives such as "loud" or "soft."

• Teach the concept of high and low notes with songs.

• Teach rhythm with rhymes and clapping songs—this will also help your child's speech.

• Name every new sound, such as the cat purring, and imitate it.

By the time he is four months old your baby should be able to discriminate between certain sounds. For example, when he hears your voice he will grow quiet or smile, and will turn his head and eyes toward your sound, even if he can't see where you are.

After six months, your baby should turn at once to investigate quiet noises made on each side of him, or at the sound of your voice from across the room.

Your baby needs to be able to hear the full range of sounds that are essential for speech if he is to be able to talk correctly. Only when your child proves first that he can hear, later that he can imitate sound, and eventually that he can use different sounds correctly to form speech, can you be sure that he can discriminate between different sounds across the full normal range of hearing.

Your newborn baby reacts to noises without really understanding them. If he is startled by a sudden loud noise, such as a hand-clap or a door slamming, he may throw out his arms and legs in a "startle" reflex action, as though to save himself from falling. A little later, sudden sounds will make him blink or open his eyes wide in surprise. By four weeks, he will begin to notice sudden prolonged noises, like the sound of your vacuum cleaner.

Parents with profoundly deaf children usually become aware of the problem fairly quickly. It is often more difficult to identify those with partial hearing loss, because their symptoms can be mistaken for inattentiveness, slow learning, or shyness. If you are worried about your child's hearing, you should have him examined by your doctor as soon as possible so that he can receive appropriate help.

Your baby's first hearing test may well be in the maternity ward shortly after birth. This test uses soft sounds (clapping, singing, ringing) to measure your baby's response to noise. Responses may vary from a slight movement of the head to a change in breathing rate. In some areas, though, a new and much more effective newborn hearing test is being introduced, and this should soon be available everywhere.

NEWBORN HEARING SCREENING TEST

The newborn hearing screening test is carried out only a day or two after birth and is much more reliable than the old distraction tests. One or two babies in every thousand have hearing difficulties. Screening is vitally important, since the sooner any problems are detected, the better the prospects for the child's future development. If deafness is not diagnosed until a child is two or three years old, that child has missed out on a critical stage of development in language and communication skills.

The new test is called an otoacoustic emission test. It is quick and easy to do and does not hurt your baby. You'll be asked to hold your baby while the person doing the test puts a small probe just inside his ear. Your baby doesn't even have to be awake. The probe makes a small sound, then measures the echo that is normally produced by the inner ear in response to the sound. Both ears are checked, and you'll have the results immediately. If the test does not detect an echo, this does not mean your baby is deaf, but he will need further tests.

TESTING HEARING

If your baby has not had the newborn hearing screening test (see opposite), there are simple tests you can do to check his hearing from about six months of age. For best results, the tests need to be carried out in a quiet room with no distractions.

You will need a high-pitched rattle, some hard tissue paper, and a china cup, a spoon, and a bell. Sit your baby on your lap, at least 4 feet (120 centimeters) from any wall, and ask another adult to take up a position to the side of your baby, level with his ear and outside his immediate range of vision. Your helper should stand 18 inches (45 centimeters) away for a six-month-old and 3 feet (1 meter) for a nine-month-old and make sounds at the level of the baby's ear in this order:

• Produce low-pitched and high-pitched sounds with their voice.
• Shake the rattle.
• Tap the spoon against the cup.
• Crumple the tissue paper.
• Ring the bell.

If you get no response to any of the sounds, wait two seconds before repeating it. Wait a further two seconds, and if there is still no response after three tries, go on to the next sound.

A baby of six months should turn at once to investigate quiet noises made on each side of him, or at the sound of your voice from across the room. Older babies of nine months and up should turn at once when they hear the sounds and will often smile. They should also search for quiet sounds made out of sight. A clear response to three of these sounds means your baby has enough hearing to speak. If the response is less, repeat the test within three months before seeing your doctor.

18 months to 2 years For an older baby or toddler, you might like to try judging his response to spoken instructions. Sit him opposite you at a low table, with another familiar adult (such as his father) close by. Ask your child to hand certain objects to Daddy, such as a ball, cup and spoon, doll, toy car, or building block, and see how he responds. Ask him again from different distances up to 10 feet (3 meters). For children up to three years, you could try the same test while partly covering your mouth with a piece of paper to muffle the sound and make it more difficult.

It is important that you don't carry out these hearing tests too often, because even quite a young child will come to know what to expect from them and will turn to the tester whether or not he can actually hear the sound.

THE HEARING-IMPAIRED CHILD

Children must be able to hear in order to learn to speak, read, and write by conventional methods, so it is essential to pick up any hearing impairment early and seek professional help as soon as possible.

Many children with hearing loss can function quite well with a hearing aid, and many doctors now fit them in infancy rather than at four or five years. In profoundly deaf children, however, comprehension of sound and spoken language is significantly impaired.

There are many ways to approach communication for profoundly deaf children, and they are often used in combination. Among them are cochlear implants, sign language, lip-reading, and the "oral method."

THE FEMALE BRAIN

When a baby girl is born, her brain is already sexed—that is, programmed for femaleness. Brain structure is responsible for many developmental differences between boys and girls.

• In the womb, the cortex, which determines intellect, develops sooner in girls than in boys.

• The left half of the cortex, that which controls thinking, develops earlier in girls than in boys.

• The corpus callosum, the part of the brain that connects the right lobe to the left, is better developed in girls.

• The earlier development of the left side of the brain in girls confers greater language-related skills on girls than on boys.

• The right and left sides of the brain "talk" to each other earlier and better in girls, and this gives them an advantage in reading skills, which draw on both sides.

• Girls show earlier and greater fear of separation than boys because their nervous connections mature earlier. This leads to faster message transmission than in boys, and so girls recognize earlier what's going on around them.

Mental development

Your baby is born with a finite number of brain cells, yet her brain doubles in weight between birth and 12 months. The increase in weight is due to the growth of connections between the different cells used in thinking. When your baby sees a piece of bread, points to it, reaches for it, picks it up, puts it in her mouth, chews it, tastes it, and swallows it, she's built up eight brain connections and slotted them all into her memory.

PREDICTING INTELLIGENCE

Although it's difficult to say what "normal" intelligence is, many experts in the field of development can define the sequence and rate of mental development in the average child and use this to predict intelligence. Remember that the average child doesn't exist: an average is theoretical, so you should never apply it to your own child, nor should you compare her with other children of her age.

There are major variations in the rate of development from child to child, and there is no correct age when any milestones should be reached. Most children have growth spurts and pauses. Some show a temporary developmental pause and then go on to develop normally; others appear advanced in infancy but turn out to be average in later years. Then there is the well-known "slow starter," the child who is slightly behind in infancy, yet later does very well. Very few children show a progressive slowing in the rate of development. There are children in whom it is so difficult to predict the course of development that the outlook can only be guessed at cautiously and after repeated examinations. The conclusion is that you shouldn't try to predict your baby's intelligence unless there is a very good reason to do so.

The great majority of babies turn out to be perfectly normal children. Sadly, a very small number lag seriously behind in all fields of development and, unless the lag is due to a serious physical handicap, can grow up to be educationally under par. Throughout the first three years, the mentally impaired child shows below-average concentration and interest in her surroundings. She is late in aspects of development such as head control, sitting up, and grasping her toes, and in outgrowing her primitive birth reflexes, which may persist long after the usual age.

While there are clear indicators that a child is mentally slow, it is more difficult to spot the child with above-average abilities. A particularly intelligent baby may reach developmental milestones earlier than average, but the real indicators of her superior intelligence are more subtle: she'll display a greater variety of behavior, a greater interest in her surroundings, and more interaction with her environment than the average baby.

THE PARENT'S ROLE

Very few children are developmentally disabled, and equally few are especially gifted, so the chances are that your child falls within the normal range of intelligence. Your task as a parent is to accept her abilities and to help her develop her strengths by careful teaching. Remember, too, that there are many fields of ability: we tend to think of intelligence rather narrowly as verbal and arithmetic skills, but your child may have creative and artistic abilities that are just as valuable and just as much in need of nurturing. Never push your child: accept her for who she is, give her every opportunity to develop her talents; show her and let her know that you love and respect her just as she is.

INTELLIGENCE TESTING

Modern systems of intelligence testing were developed in 1905 by two Frenchmen. Originally they were intended to predict whether children were likely to do well at school, and concentrated on judgment, comprehension, and reasoning. Modern testing views intelligence as the ability to process information, and so the tests are devised to see how well a child is acquiring thinking skills and applying them to everyday life. They are limited to skills that are important at school, and don't take account of creativity or artistic talent.

CREATIVITY

All children have some creative ability, and developing this in the preschool years is just as important as teaching letters and numbers. There are a whole range of skills and mental processes that you can encourage in your child to stimulate her creative abilities: point out the things happening around her, show her patterns, colors, flowers, animals, smells, act out empathy for other people, talk about feelings, invent stories, and imagine "What would happen if…?" Dressing up, painting and drawing, or making toys are all practical activities that can help your child developer creativity and imagination.

THE MALE BRAIN

Even while your baby is in the womb, his brain is programmed for maleness. Differences in brain structure and function between boys and girls affect the way they develop.

• A boy's brain weight and volume are greater than a girl's by about 10–15 percent.

• When the right side of the brain is ready to send connections to the left, the appropriate cells don't yet exist in boys. As a result, the fibers go back into the right side. This enriches connections within the right lobe and could explain why boys have greater spatial awareness than girls.

• Boys show less fear on separation than girls because they have slower message transmission than girls until the brain matures. From as young as nine or ten months, they bring the fear under control by activities such as playing with a toy or crawling so as to distract themselves. This mode of behavior continues into adulthood.

Making costumes
Encourage your child to make his own dress-up toys with a variety of colored paper, crayons, scissors, and tape.

YOUR BABY'S SMILE

The first time your baby smiles at you is an exciting milestone in your relationship; it's also an important sign that he is developing mentally.

When your baby begins to smile, he is demonstrating that he can recognize you and that he wants to engage with you in an exchange—he's already being sociable. He will start to respond to your talking to him with smiles, because he has learned that this pleases you and makes you talk to him more—his first attempts at "conversation" (see p.198).

Smiling is an important indicator of a baby's maturity and desire for interaction with other people, and experts consider that a baby who smiles early in a sociable way may be showing the first signs of superior intelligence.

Stimulating your baby
Encourage your child to focus on objects by rattling and shaking toys in her line of vision.

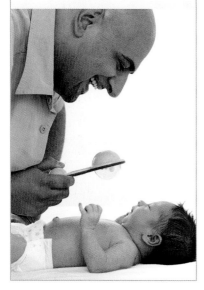

Mental development

In the early weeks, your baby is busy sorting out the most important things in his world: your face and voice will be among the first things he recognizes. He demonstrates his good memory and his hearing by quieting down if you play a recording of the human heartbeat—something that comforted him for nine months.

Getting to know you
Your baby will recognize your voice and face and will show signs of this at a very early age.

Newborn Within half an hour of birth, your baby will flicker his eyes when spoken to. After one week he knows your voice, and after two he'll show that he recognizes you. If spoken to from a distance of 8–10 inches (20–25 centimeters), where he can see your face, he will open and close his mouth in response.

1 month He will respond to the tone of your voice, becoming calm if you speak soothingly and distressed in response to rough tones. He gets very excited and his whole body jerks when he attempts to "speak." He follows a moving object with his eyes.

2 months He smiles readily in response to your face and voice. He looks around in response to sounds, and stares at objects with intense interest.

3 months Your baby is becoming more aware of his body, and will look at his hands and move them. He responds to conversation by smiling, gurgling, and moving his body

4 months Your baby is curious about all sights, sounds, and people. He likes to sit propped against cushions so he can look around him. He now recognizes familiar objects and remembers routines; he'll get excited at the sight of a breast or bottle. He plays with his feet when lying on his back.

5 months Your baby now spends longer examining things, showing that his concentration is developing. He turns toward unseen sounds, and moves his arms and legs to attract your attention.

6 months Your baby makes sounds to attract your attention, and puts out his arms to be picked up. He "speaks" and smiles to his reflection in a mirror. He may start to show shyness with strangers.

HOW YOU CAN HELP

From the earliest days, you should talk and sing to your baby. His movements and sounds are his earliest attempts at speaking, so answer them to encourage him; make sure he can see your face clearly and make eye contact with him at all times, smile a lot, and exaggerate your mouth movements.

Feed his curiosity Everything is new and interesting to your baby, so show him objects and give him a chance to hold them. By the time he is two months old, he will like to sit propped up so that he can look around him; put lots of small, soft toys within his reach where he can see and touch them. Talk to him constantly.

Encourage awareness of himself Your baby's discovery of his own body is a gradual process. When he is about eight weeks old, you can start showing him his hands, and play simple physical games. By six months he will smile at himself in the mirror.

PERCEPTION

Your baby experiences things through her senses just as you do, but he has to learn to single out what is important and what is not. Help him to connect the information given by his different senses: show him a rattle, allow him to touch it, then shake it and draw his attention to the sound. Touch is one of the main ways that your baby explores his environment, so introduce him to lots of different textures.

Using a mirror
Point at your baby's reflection and say her name, so she starts to gain a sense of herself. Use her name often to bolster her sense of identity.

TESTING PERCEPTION

From an early stage, your baby can make basic distinctions between big and small. He will also show interest in new sights and sounds, as the following test, which can be carried out from four months, demonstrates.

- Show your baby a card with a small diamond above a large diamond.

- Next, show him a card with a small circle above a large circle drawn on it. He is already starting to see the relationship between the small and large shapes.

- Now show him a card with a small triangle above a large one. Because this fits the pattern set by the first two, he will probably show no interest in it.

- If you show him a card with a large triangle above a small one, he will probably show renewed interest because the pattern of small above large has changed.

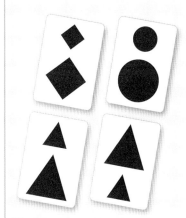

Test cards
Your baby will be able to make quite sophisticated distinctions involving pattern and shape.

183

THE RIGHT TOYS

As they develop, babies need different stimuli, and your choice of toys must reflect this.

It is very important that the toy chosen for a baby is appropriate to her age. If the toy is too advanced, she won't know how to play with it in the proper way and will gain little enjoyment. If the toy is too primitive, she will become bored.

Suitable toys for a baby under one year are those that give experience of colors, textures, materials, and interesting and varied shapes and sounds, so choose toys that give a variety of these things. Toys that make noises and react to actions, such as rattles, give a sense of control and encourage the development of manipulation skills and coordination.

Look and learn
Color, shape, and noise are all interesting to your baby, so choose toys that give a variety of these things.

LEARNING THROUGH PLAY

Babies and children learn through play, and play is a very serious business! Everything is a learning experience for your baby, and anything new is fun, so learning and playing are indistinguishable. If you are aware of the skills she's developing in her first six months, you can choose games and toys that will interest her and are best suited to encourage her abilities. At this age, toys that stimulate her senses will be most interesting to her.

Simple games Because your baby is fascinated by your face, "peek-a-boo" is one of the best games you can play with her. Hide your face in your hands or with a scarf or towel, then peek out at her, saying "peek-a-boo" as you do it. Babies develop a sense of humor quite early, and this is a game that they find endlessly amusing. When she's old enough to sit up without support, roll a large, soft ball gently toward her; she'll eventually try to push it back to you. Then you've got a real game going and she's acquiring early ball sense.

Rhymes and songs Your baby will love listening to rhymes even when she's very young, because she likes to be talked to, and rhythmic sounds are easier for her to listen to than normal speech. She will love to be sung to as well, whether it's a soothing lullaby or a more lively tune sung while you bounce her on your knee. Rhyming, rhythmic songs and games encourage early speech.

Physical activities Even a very young baby can benefit from play such as bouncing, swinging, and rocking. It will make her aware of her own body and improve her locomotive skills, such as crawling and walking, as well as balance and coordination.

Feed her senses Your baby explores the world through her senses, and she will find anything new interesting (see **Testing perception**, p.183). Allow her to spend as much time as possible propped up in a sitting position so that she can see what is going on around her, and leave small toys within her reach so she can handle them—toys that make noises or are made of different-textured materials are best. Catch her interest first by showing her the toys up close, and demonstrating how the sound can be made—even something as simple as a lidded cup filled with fairly large beans will serve as a toy. When she's older and able to grasp objects, you can give her stacking cups or rings—ones with large pieces are suitable while her grasp is still quite primitive. The kitchen is a good source of interesting toys for your child; wooden spoons, spatulas, small pans and lids, colanders and sieves, funnels, a set of measuring spoons, plastic cups, ice cube trays, or egg cartons. Let your baby create her own use for them.

A rattle is an ideal toy as your baby gradually learns to grasp objects during the first six months

By about four months, your baby explores the world through her mouth, so provide toys that are safe to chew

Toys that do different things are a good buy; this camera incorporates a mirror, makes clicking noises, and can be chewed

Your baby will love toys that make a noise, so hang an easily operated musical box over her crib or carriage

SAFETY

Safety is the most important consideration when choosing toys. With a young baby, bear in mind that she is likely to put everything in her mouth.

• Toys such as rattles should be lightweight in case your baby hits herself with them.

• Avoid toys with small holes that could trap your baby's fingers.

• Long strings could be swallowed or wrapped around your baby's neck.

• Soft toys should be made of flame-retardant material, and should also be colorfast; otherwise your baby could suck the dye off and become ill.

• Small parts that could choke your baby, such as eyes on soft toys, should be firmly attached.

CHOOSING TOYS

Many parents find it difficult to choose toys for a new baby—relatives even more so. A young baby won't be able to interact with her toys much at first, so they should be soft, simple, sturdy, and attractive to look at and touch.

Soft toys Your baby will like soft toys that she can squeeze and that are nice to touch. Make sure they are washable and colorfast, because she will keep putting them in her mouth.

Mobiles For a newborn, a mobile hung 10 inches (25 centimeters) above a crib or carriage provides visual stimulation, but make sure it's out of her reach. Change the parts around every few days to hold her interest.

Noisy toys Rattles, soft toys that squeak, and musical toys are suitable for a young baby. By six months, she loves to play with a music box that she can operate by pressing a button or pulling a string.

Books Your baby is never too young to be read to, so start as soon as she's born. Choose books with large, brightly colored pictures; point to common objects and name them while you're looking at them together. Faces always attract her, so show her pictures in magazines and point out the parts of your face, then her face, and then the same parts in the pictures.

LEARNING SPURTS

Mental development

The mental development of your baby goes in spurts, rather than moving at a constant rate.

During a learning spurt, your child will latch on to new ideas and skills very quickly, and will put them into practice immediately.

During these rapid learning phases, skills that he's already acquired may seem to slip a bit because your baby's concentration is totally taken up with learning something new. Once a new skill has been mastered, he'll regain any lost skills.

If your baby clearly enjoys certain activities, then repeat them. Don't hesitate, however, to introduce your baby to new ideas, because he can absorb information very quickly and develop new skills at an astonishing speed. Aim to entertain him over as wide and interesting a range as possible. Your baby will focus on what he wants and ignore the rest.

A learning spurt is usually followed by a period when development appears to slow down as your baby consolidates newly learned skills and prepares for the next spurt. This is a good time to help him to practice skills he has just acquired until they are absorbed into his repertoire.

Your baby is developing new mental abilities at an amazing rate, most of it through play, and you can help by giving him lots of interesting new experiences. Try to suppress any anxieties about what your child should be learning at this stage. Be guided by him and respond to his needs. He will develop much faster if you let him learn what he wants to, rather than what you think is best.

7 months Your baby is beginning to know the meaning of words and understands "no." He shows signs of determination by going for toys that are out of reach. Your baby takes a strong interest in games, and concentrates deeply on his toys. He will look around for a toy he has dropped, demonstrating a developing memory.

8 months Your baby's memory takes a leap forward at eight months when he recognizes familiar games and rhymes, and turns his head when he hears his name. He can anticipate movement and will hold out his hands to be washed, but will turn his face away from a cloth.

9 months Your baby is learning routines, such as waving bye-bye and putting out his foot so you can put on his sock. He also knows "patty-cake" all the way through. Your baby knows what a doll or teddy bear is and will pat it, and he'll look around corners for a toy, and for Daddy, if you say "Where's Daddy?" This is a very important perceptual step: he's learned that things are still there even if he can't see them.

10 months Your baby may point out things in a book by the time he is ten months old, but he won't concentrate for long. He will be constantly dropping toys out of his stroller and wanting them picked up because he's learned the "letting go" skill. He may say one word with meaning. He is also starting to understand the concepts of "here" and "there," "in" and "out," and "up" and "down."

11 months Your baby loves jokes now and will repeat anything that makes you laugh. His interest in books is growing, and he likes to have items pointed out, then he points them out if you ask him. He'll repeat his name and shake his head for "no."

1 year Once your baby is a year old, he'll kiss, and say two or three words with meaning. He'll pick up a toy and hand it to you, and may spontaneously point to an object that he recognizes in a picture. He starts to understand simple questions.

STYLES OF PERCEPTION

From about six months old, a child is developing his own "style of perception"—that is, the time and care he takes to look at a situation before making a decision. Broadly speaking, most people fall into one of two styles: reflective or impulsive. A reflective baby will look at something with fixed concentration, and remain very still, whereas an impulsive baby will become excited, and look away after only a short period of examination.

When your baby is 18 months old, you can tell which style most closely describes him by trying a simple test: show your baby a card on which there is a picture, and below, variations of this picture. Ask him to select the picture that exactly matches the picture at the top. A reflective child will look at all the options carefully before making a choice, and is usually right. An impulsive child is more likely to look at all the pictures quickly and then make a snap decision, which is often the wrong one. Reflective children often do slightly better at school, especially in learning to read. An impulsive child may therefore need more help with schooling. Reflectiveness, however, isn't always best. There are occasions when your child has to think fast, such as when playing games, and an impulsive child may be better able to make a good decision in the short time available.

HELPING YOUR CHILD'S MENTAL DEVELOPMENT

To stretch your child's memory, play hide-and-seek with a toy. Place a toy in front of your baby and let him reach for it several times, then put a piece of paper in front to hide it. Your baby will move the paper to find the toy. Give him simple tasks such as putting things in and taking them out of containers

Choose soft baby books with large colorful illustrations, and set aside time each day to read. Children love tales about mother and baby animals, and such stories will help them learn about the sounds animals make. You could also read different kinds of well-illustrated books and magazines to your baby. Try naming several items on a page, and then take your baby's hand and point to them. Name the items again.

At one year old, your baby will begin to understand cause and effect if you describe your actions while, for example, putting his coat on him and taking it off, or dressing and undressing a doll. Describe what's happening when he plays. For instance, if he knocks over his bricks, say "Fall down!" Play lots of water games with him; give him tubs, jars, and pitchers that he can use to pour, empty, and fill. Put his toys just out of reach and retrieve them when he asks. Encourage independence with self-feeding.

An older child, of around 15 months, can be given simple tasks, such as putting things away in the right place or getting something for you, to stimulate his sense of achievement and to encourage his feelings of pride. Help him to string words together to make simple sentences. Introduce the concept of possession, particularly with his own things: "That's Michael's ball, your ball."

MEMORY

Now that your baby is older, his developing memory becomes more apparent. There are many things you can do to help.

- Repeat a short rhyme to your child over and over again, until he learns how to say it himself.

- Sing a brief song to your baby, accentuating the rhythm with hand-claps, head nods, and gestures of your body.

- Reading aloud to your baby is by far the best way to develop memory. If a story is repeated several times, he will anticipate events and say them before you get there. If you hesitate dramatically in midsentence, he will supply the missing word, such as "duck," "tree," "baby," or "kitten."

- Reciting sequences of numbers will stimulate his memory, as will repeating the alphabet, especially if you give it a definite rhythm or rhyming pattern.

HOMEMADE TOYS

A baby under one year doesn't need store-bought toys. Use colorful, noisy, household items to stimulate and fascinate her.

• Anything that rolls: thread spools or the cardboard tube inside paper towels and toilet paper.

• Interesting textures: pieces of felt, a string of beads, thick strands of yarn, or bean bags.

• Interesting shapes: plastic ice cube trays, whisks, egg cartons, colanders and sieves, or plastic bottles of all shapes and sizes.

• Anything that's noisy: wooden spoons and spatulas, small saucepans and lids, cake pans, or plastic cups.

• Anything that rattles: plastic jars with seeds, beads, or paper clips inside (but make sure the lid is on tight).

Noisy
A baby will love playing with pots, pans, and saucepan lids. The more noise she can make, the more fun she'll have.

LEARNING THROUGH PLAY

Your baby learns through play, and to develop fully, she needs to engage all her senses: sight, hearing, smell, touch, and taste. To provide the necessary stimulation, her toys and games should be full of variety so that they will appeal to all these senses. While you should obviously play with your baby as much as possible, it is also important that she learns to play on her own so that her sense of exploration and imagination is given free rein.

At seven months, your baby's mouth is still an important sense organ and she'll want interesting objects that she can investigate safely. Her toys should be bright, colorful, and have an interesting shape to stimulate her perception of form and space as well as her sense of color. Primary colors are best at this age. Always name the color of an object she plays with.

Stimulate your child's hearing with toys that make ringing or rattling sounds when she shakes them. Music boxes provide endless fascination for young children, particularly ones with a string that your baby can pull. As your baby's manipulative abilities improve, she'll become absorbed by touch as well as sound. She will love toys that make a noise when she squeezes them. Activity centers, which have a series of knobs and buttons that your baby can push or turn to make noises, can be attached to a crib or a bathtub. As well as stimulating both her hearing and sense of touch, they will help her understand the link between cause and effect. Rubber balls of all sizes are always a favorite.

Any fairly small objects that are interesting to touch, with holes or handles that your baby can poke her fingers into or wrap them around, are ideal. Look for objects that are brightly colored and, if possible, make a noise, like rings with bells on them. She'll love a large, specially designed baby mirror placed in her crib for her to stare into. Never put one of your own mirrors in the crib—it could easily break.

When she is ten months to one year old, your baby will pick up small objects like pencils, crayons, and, eventually, paintbrushes. She'll be more mobile now and will enjoy being able to push or pull toys like trains, cars, or carts.

From one year to 18 months, having achieved some measure of dexterity, your baby will enjoy toys that challenge her manipulative abilities, such as puzzles. Nesting and stacking toys that can be built up or fitted together will encourage dexterity and spatial visualization. Now that she speaks and understands some words and ideas, she'll love stories and books. Those with brightly colored illustrations and different textures are best.

Toys that your baby can push or pull around help build muscles and develop coordination

Books should have large, simple illustrations, and be made of a "chew-safe" material

Building with blocks gives your baby a sense of achievement

Musical or noisy toys will attract your baby's attention

Fun with toys
Your baby will love brightly colored toys with interesting shapes and textures.

Coloring materials will satisfy your baby's need for scribbling

PLAYING TOGETHER

Your baby will enjoy playing games with you. To be sure she makes the most of new toys, show her how they can be used and encourage her to be imaginative with them.

- Roll a ball to her and encourage her to roll it back to you; her hand–eye coordination will develop.

- Show her how to build a more complicated structure with blocks, such as a bridge; she will improve her delicate manipulative skills.

- Fill a container with water or sand and show her how to fill up measuring cups and containers; she'll experience the movement of different substances.

Water play
All babies enjoy splashing in water or floating a boat in a bowl. Provide unbreakable containers to pour and fill.

TOYS AND GAMES

As your baby grows, her developing skills and mental abilities will be reflected in toys that capture her imagination. Freestanding rattles that she can swipe at while feeding, for example, will keep her amused at first. Large soft blocks are ideal for a six-month-old baby because they can be used for building and throwing, but an older baby will prefer hard blocks of wood or plastic, stable enough for more complicated structures. Puzzles and games that challenge your baby, such as simple jigsaw puzzles, are important for her development. They should have knobs to make the pieces easier to pick up, or a very few large pieces that are simple to put together.

IMAGINATION

Most children over the age of 15 months or so begin to develop a vivid imagination, and there are substantial individual differences. In general, the greater the intelligence, the greater the imagination.

Between 15 and 18 months, imagination begins to appear in doll play. At three years your child will have imaginary playmates behind the sofa, and he'll tell tall stories and play highly imaginative games with friends. His imagination may lead to the development of fears: of the dark, of noises, or of animals, for example.

Mental development

At the toddler stage, your child starts to become an independent person. His speech will progress by leaps and bounds during this phase and he'll be able to ask for what he wants, and do some of the things you want him to do—if he so chooses. He'll have an insatiable curiosity about his world and everything in it, will be able to cope with increasingly complex ideas, and will be eager to put all he learns to good use.

MILESTONES

18 months Your baby will be able to ask for food, drinks, and toys. He probably tells you when he wants to go to the potty, but can't wait and so has frequent accidents. He will carry out several simple requests and begin to understand more complex ones, such as "Please get your hairbrush from the bathroom." He may also grab your arm or use other gestures to get your attention. His vocabulary may consist of about 30 words.

2 years Your child's vocabulary of names and objects will increase rapidly. He will describe and identify familiar items. He will obey complicated orders, and find a toy that he played with before. He will talk nonstop and ask occasional questions.

Shortly after this, he will know who he is and say his own name. He'll try to build houses and castles with blocks, and repeat new words when encouraged. He'll begin to pit his will against yours and may become rather negative—saying "no" fairly often and not always fitting in with your wishes. He may know the difference between one and several, but he has little idea of the magnitude of numbers and so anything more than one may be "lots."

2½–3 years Your child will start to add detail to broad concepts, as in "A horse has a long tail," and be able to draw horizontal and vertical lines. He'll be able to say one or two nursery rhymes and find them in his book, and he'll know some colors. He will also ask "why?" and say "won't" and "can't." He may make an attempt to copy a circle that you have drawn for him (see p.174), but probably won't be able to complete it. Your child will now enjoy helping with household tasks. He will begin to grasp the concept of numbers and may be able to

Chores
Your toddler enjoys helping you with some simple household tasks, such as sweeping.

count to three. A boy will have noticed that his sex organs stick out from his body, in contrast to those of little girls he has seen.

Your child can understand prepositions, such as "in," "on," "under," "behind," and "after." At around three years old, he'll be able to form more complex sentences and his vocabulary may consist of 200–300 words. This, together with his ever-increasing curiosity, will lead him to ask incessant questions. He can distinguish between "now" and "then" and will refer to the past. He knows his own gender. He'll become more sociable and like to play with others.

REASONING

As a toddler, your child may have satisfied his curiosity, absorbing a great deal of new information in the process, but rarely related it to anything else in his life. What happens in the third year, however, is that your child starts to think about his experiences and to learn from them. Information is sifted, matched up to other experiences to see if they fit together, or if they differ greatly, and it is then put into similar or different pigeonholes. Your child is learning to reason.

Your child starts to plan ahead, and becomes much more creative and imaginative. Gradually, all the information that he has absorbed so far becomes available to apply to a given situation. This new ability to think, imagine, and create, changes his perception of the world.

Many familiar things in the house or garden no longer contain the same interest. He needs wider horizons; he needs to explore, to push the frontiers of his experience and knowledge farther and farther back. Your child becomes very interested in how things work. He's greedy for information and is constantly asking "why?".

A huge step is realizing that time is not just in the present: there is today, yesterday, and tomorrow. Planning for the future is one of the most critical aspects of our intellect, and it is during this third year that you'll hear your child say for the first time, "I will eat that later" or "We can go tomorrow."

FORMING CONCEPTS

This is an important step forward for him. One way in which it will be obvious is when, between the ages of 18 months and two years, he starts sorting objects as a form of play: he might sort his building blocks out from his other toys, for example. You'll notice, too, that he's begun to understand how things are grouped: he knows, for instance, that his ball and an apple are similar in shape and that they roll; that animals that bark and have four legs are dogs.

Some time before his third birthday, your toddler will begin to give these concepts names—round, dog. He'll use the names in all cases where they are appropriate—whether the dog in question, for instance, is a family pet, a dog he sees on television or in a book, or a toy dog. By the time he is three years old, he'll describe things in a way that shows he also understands their differences: "our dog," "toy dog."

COLORS

To help your child grasp the notion of color, always mention the color of something that you're using or wanting.

- Household items: "I'm looking for the green box"; "Where did that red can go?"

- Your child's clothes: "That's a pretty pink dress"; "What a nice red sweater."

- Flowers, animals, and especially birds: "Can you see the red cardinal?"

- Show your child how colors are made: "Look! If we mix a little bit of red with this white, we get pink; yellow mixed with blue will make green."

- Teach your child the colors of the rainbow and get him to pick them out if you see a real rainbow.

Concept of roundness
A toddler can begin to deal with sophisticated ideas. He will understand that roundness, for example, is a property of different objects.

A STIMULATING ENVIRONMENT

A STIMULATING ENVIRONMENT

One of the ways you can encourage your child's development is to foster creative play with an inviting environment.

Simply the way you display your child's toys can, to a large extent, determine whether they will be played with or not. When toys are piled randomly in a toy box, they are not inviting to a child. Well-displayed, orderly toys arranged into little scenes stimulate her to play and to make other creative arrangements. It also helps to have particular play areas, like a sand tray, a painting table, and somewhere your child can splash around in water.

Costumes
Children love dressing up, so stock a box with old shoes, shirts, skirts, dresses, hats, and scarves, and include some cheap jewelry.

LEARNING THROUGH PLAY

Play helps learning in many ways. It improves manual dexterity—building a tower of blocks or doing a jigsaw puzzle teaches a child how to make her hands work for her as tools. Playing with other children teaches her that it's important to get along with others; she will discover friendship and learn to be kind to other people.

Social play helps to make a child's language more sophisticated because the more imaginative the play, the more complex the ideas that have to be put into words. Play aids physical development; the freedom to swing, climb, skip, run, and jump helps to perfect muscular coordination and physical skills. Play also improves hearing and vision considerably.

TYPES OF PLAY

Girls and boys love dolls; dolls are children's pretend families, helping them to create a make-believe world into which they can escape. While playing with dolls, your child is understanding human emotions. She will mother the doll, give it instructions, then dress it, put it to bed, and kiss it good night. In this way your child is reenacting the things that happen to her, and learning to relate them to other people. Even action dolls for boys can bring out protective feelings. A child can also use dolls to get rid of aggressive instincts that might otherwise be directed against other children.

An important concept for a child to grasp is that of classification—whether things are the same or different. Toys of farmyard animals can help form this idea; with a variety of sheep, horses, and chickens, your child will be able to sort out the animals that look the same. You can help by showing her the differences and naming the animals as you put them into groups.

Children love playing with water, especially in the bathtub. Give your child empty plastic bottles and containers so that she can create a variety of water effects. All children love blowing bubbles; put some dishwashing liquid in a cup and shape a pipe-cleaner with a circle at one end. Wading pools, such as the small blow-up kind, are ideal in the summer and needn't be expensive. Another summer game is to lay a tarp on the ground and spray a hose over it; your child will enjoy sliding around on the slippery surface.

Painting encourages your child's creative urges. She'll love finger painting and can produce a range of interesting prints and patterns with combs, pegs, sponges, thread spools, or cardboard tubes. Try cutting star shapes and other stamps out of pieces of potato so that she can create unusual designs. Plastic egg boxes or baking sheets will make good palettes for the aspiring painter. Give your child thick brushes so that she sees bold results immediately. Provide pastry brushes, cotton balls, corks, straws, and pipe cleaners for variety.

TOYS AND GAMES

Up to two years of age, your child will spend longer on toys that she can use independently, particularly those that imitate the adult world. Dolls, toy houses, and cars, for example, will enable her to act out the scenes she sees in real life. As she gets older, she will acquire new skills and enjoy anything that tests them—building and knocking down, or constructing and taking apart. Household items, such as plastic containers and cardboard tubes, will stimulate her creativity and imagination. Drawing, painting, making shapes with clay or dough, and fitting together puzzles encourage creativity. Long before she's able to write or draw formally, your child will love scribbling and using colors, so give her crayons and lots of paper. A box of colored chalks and a blackboard and easel, set up at her height, will be useful because she'll be able to draw, then rub out her work and start again.

Children love being part of the domestic routine. A small child can be given a little bowl with some flour to mix each time you bake; she can help with carrying, and use a small dustpan and brush to help with the cleaning.

A toy will enable your child to imitate adults and feed the need for conversation and other word-play

Your toddler is able to make increasingly complex use of building toys

Your child's picture books should now introduce simple vocabulary

Fuel your child's artistic talents with painting sets or play dough

OUTDOOR SAFETY

Once a child is old enough to have large toys to play with in the yard, a whole new set of hazards can arise.

• It's impossible to provide a totally safe environment for your child, but if you take precautions, the risk of serious accidents can be greatly reduced. For example, make sure that outdoor equipment is carefully installed and regularly checked for faults.

• Young children should always be properly supervised, and never left alone to play outdoors, especially in wading pools.

• Play equipment, such as slides and swings, should be checked regularly for strength, stability, and signs of corrosion. They should be installed on a soft, flat surface, such as grass or sand—never on concrete.

• Check all play equipment to be sure that there is no risk of scissoring, shearing, or pinching injuries and that surfaces are free from snags and splinters.

• Instruct your children carefully on what they can and can't do on play equipment.

• Make sure tents, playhouses, and tunnels are made of flame-retardant material.

• Make sure that sandboxes are covered when not in use to stop animals from fouling them.

• Fence off ponds.

• Always empty a wading pool after use.

Mental development

GIFTEDNESS

It is tempting to think your child is gifted if he is farther ahead than others in one or two areas.

Truly gifted children, however, are advanced in most aspects of achievement and in the acquisition of skills. They will enjoy all kinds of brain exercises and may even find some of them very easy. A gifted child invariably learns quickly and is able to use that learning in a broad and flexible way. If this applies to your child, it will be important to provide him with plenty of stimulation, new games, new ideas for play, and plenty of creative opportunities. Otherwise he is likely to become bored and frustrated if he is not being stretched by his play (see p.252).

The development of your child as an independent and reasoning individual blossoms during the preschool years. He'll speak much more fluently and he'll start to relate speech to the written word. He'll also be much more imaginative in his play, so that he'll keep himself amused for longer periods, without expecting you to join in.

A three-year-old child will want to help with simple household tasks, such as sweeping the floor or setting the table. His steadily improving grasp of shapes and understanding of sequences will mean he can solve more complex puzzles, such as rearranging pictures into the correct order, or copying a design. His make-believe play will be more vivid, as he invents people and objects and puts them into more complex situations, which is why girls enjoy playhouses and boys make camps. And he's beginning to understand that some enjoyable things must be put off until the future, such as a visit to a favorite relative, or being able to buy an ice cream cone.

He is more independent and more self-centered at the age of four. He may be cocky, and more argumentative about getting his own way. He will have mastered the concepts of past, present, and future though he may not understand how close or far away his birthday is.

By the age of five, he'll be more sensible and controlled, and will be able to play games that have more complicated rules. He'll be able to appreciate clock time, and it will help him relate to a daily routine. His sense of humor will be more developed now and he'll be able to tell simple jokes and act out comical situations—anything for a laugh.

Puzzles
You can aid your preschool child's mental development with some simple teasers.

Ask your child which part is missing from this picture

Ask your child to put the pictures in the correct order

Make patterns with specially painted blocks for your child to copy

Make a jigsaw puzzle by cutting up a postcard or an old photograph

PERCEPTION

Perceptual style—the way in which a child takes in a situation—depends on whether he is able to shut out what's going on in the background or pays a lot of attention to it. The former is called field independency and the latter is field dependency.

Measurements of field independence or dependence show a strong difference between girls and boys. Boys are usually more field-independent, and are therefore able to pick out a shape from a complicated background more easily than girls. This could be because boys are usually far better at spatial visualization at a much earlier age than girls.

It can be quite helpful to know if your child is field-independent in his interests and personality. If he is, he will generally be able to focus on objects or tasks, while field-dependent children tend to focus more on people. This may account for the fact that baby girls, being more field-dependent, are much more sociable from the outset than boys.

TESTING PERCEPTION

You can assess your child's field-dependence or independence by seeing whether or not he is able to pick out a geometric shape from a complicated drawing. Show your child a simple shape, such as a circle, square, or triangle, and then ask him to find a figure exactly like that in a more complex drawing.

In order to find the figure, your child has to ignore the background detail (the field) and pay attention only to shapes. Generally speaking, children become increasingly field-independent as they get older. After a while, you will be able to introduce more complicated shapes—such as a hidden animal—in more and more complex backgrounds.

If your child is more field-dependent, he'll rely more on outside clues, and so will rely on your prompting and your encouragement. In contrast, however, your field-independent child, because of his greater ability to extract parts from wholes, will tend to be better at some cognitive tasks, such as those that require good spatial sense—playing chess, for example.

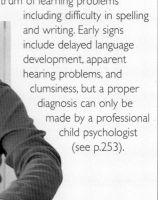

Jigsaw puzzles
Wooden jigsaw puzzles are easier to handle and don't bend like cardboard ones.

LEARNING DISABILITIES

Children learn at different rates, so apparent problems, such as a delay in learning to read, may simply be a normal variation in timing, rather than a sign of any disability. But there may be other signs that might indicate a learning disability of which you should be aware.

• Learning disabilities rarely occur alone. They are usually part of a broader picture, including, perhaps, poor coordination, poor memory, and the inability to draw and to fit differently shaped blocks into matching holes in a board.

• Common features that accompany learning difficulties include a short attention span, aimless overactivity, poor concentration, impulsiveness, aggressiveness, and clumsiness. Eyesight and hearing should be tested in a child like this in order to pick up any possible weaknesses.

• Dyslexia is a learning disability that should be spotted early on. Sometimes called word-blindness, this condition is part of a wider spectrum of learning problems including difficulty in spelling and writing. Early signs include delayed language development, apparent hearing problems, and clumsiness, but a proper diagnosis can only be made by a professional child psychologist (see p.253).

OUTINGS

Your child's insatiable curiosity needs more stimulation than your home can offer, so go to the local park regularly and plan outings to state or county parks, zoos, or nature centers.

• Let your child know in advance what to expect—say, by reading a book with her—so she'll get the most out of the experience.

• Talk about items of interest, and take crayons and paper, or a coloring book, and encourage her to draw what she sees.

• The beach is full of new sights, sounds, and smells—don't forget a pail and shovel. Sand castles are a perennial favorite.

• Provide a cheap camera to make a record of the trip and put her photos in an album.

Make-believe play
Your little girl will readily adopt a mother's role toward her doll and may create a whole imaginary world around this relationship.

LEARNING THROUGH PLAY

Play will continue to make a positive contribution to your preschool child's development. Once she has practiced her creative interests at play, she can apply them to the real world. Sometimes your child will be absorbed in a make-believe world of her own and won't need your involvement; at other times you can add to her enjoyment by suggesting new games, or new ways to play with her toys.

Make-believe play Your child will create a little world of her own as part of her imitation of adults. An instant tent or playhouse can be made from a couple of chairs or a small table draped with a blanket. Children love playing with cardboard boxes, so long as they are big enough to climb into. Small ones become boats and cars; piles of them turn into castles and houses. Boxes laid on their sides are tunnels, and laid end-to-end become trains.

Dressing up is a favorite game at this age: a few simple props can transform your child into a doctor or firefighter and, in her fantasy world, she is the adult, and a teddy bear or doll serves as the child. It often surprised me who my sons thought were family.

Messy play Any play involving water, sand, mud, or dough will stretch your child's intellect. Your child may build a wall in the sandbox, which then becomes a castle, or she may simply enjoy playing with a bucket full of water and floating objects, which will keep popping up to the surface no matter how often she pushes them down. To make your supervision easier, set aside a time when messy play is allowed and a place where the mess can be contained, and encourage your child to look forward to it.

Domestic play By now your child has mastered the coordination needed to help around the house. It's play rather than work because she's so eager to copy you. She helps in the kitchen by tearing salad leaves or arranging bread on a plate, and will enjoy setting the table, thus improving her motor and counting skills as well as her sense of independence and self-worth.

Musical play Any child with normal hearing can hear and enjoy musical sounds. She probably won't be able to play melodies, but she may be able to hum them and will enjoy banging out a rhythm. Rattles, wooden clappers, trumpets, and drums are all very good for this purpose, as are old pans or cookie sheets and wooden spoons. A xylophone will enable her to identify musical sounds and experiment with high and low notes. It's best not to buy a xylophone or other instrument until she's shown interest over the long term, and then it's worth investing in a good-quality one from a music store, which will be better for your child's developing ear.

SHARING TOYS

Your child wants to be sociable, so she has to learn the difficult skill of sharing. It's easiest if she learns to share with you first, so set a good example: "Here's some of Mommy's ice cream"; "You can have half of my apple." Then introduce the concept of "One for you, one for me." Only then say "May I have your pencil?"; "May I play with your dolly?"

SIMPLE GAMES

Your child at four or five is old enough to understand simple board games. She will enjoy uncomplicated games involving a spinning wheel, dice, or moving pieces, as well as card games which rely on pictures, such as "Old Maid" and "Snap."

• Many games will help her improve her counting skills and also her developing ability to concentrate. Games with rules that have to be followed can serve as an introduction to the concept that the real world is full of accepted standards.

• She will have to learn to take her turn and to wait patiently while others take theirs. This will help her to realize that other people have rights and needs that sometimes take priority over hers.

• The winning and losing element of games will teach her to understand and cope with disappointment and to try harder next time, as well as enjoy the success of winning. Don't concentrate too much on winning; it could make her unduly aggressive and competitive in later life.

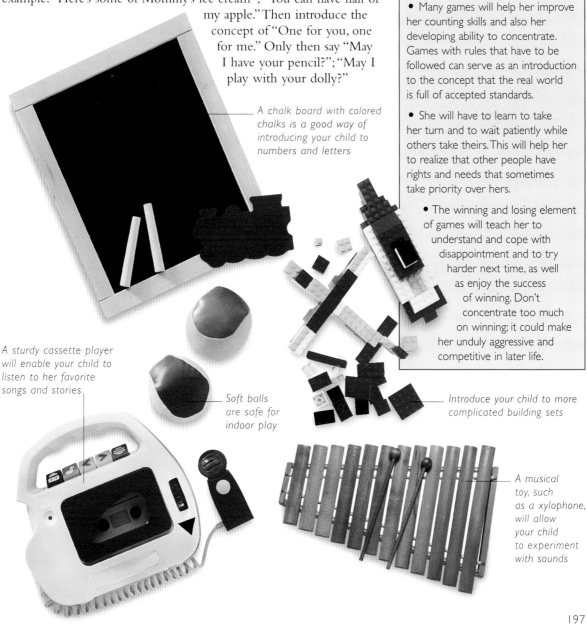

A chalk board with colored chalks is a good way of introducing your child to numbers and letters

A sturdy cassette player will enable your child to listen to her favorite songs and stories

Soft balls are safe for indoor play

Introduce your child to more complicated building sets

A musical toy, such as a xylophone, will allow your child to experiment with sounds

FIRST SOUNDS

Your baby first starts to communicate with you at birth, but without sounds.

Within half an hour of birth, your baby moves his eyes at your voice, and when you're 10 inches (25 centimeters) away from his face, he will smile and mouth in imitation and recognition of hearing speech. He is born to talk!

Crying becomes the major way of saying he's discontented; burbles of contentment don't appear for another six weeks.

Social smiling at six weeks marks his desire to converse and a few weeks later he'll start to make vowel sounds, such as "eh," "ah," "uh," "oh." By the time he's three or four months old, he'll be making a variety of sounds: vocalizations, laughing, squealing, and blowing between his lips. Around five to six months, his first consonants appear—"m," "p," and "b"—and so he may say "ma" or "pa" very early on, though he will attach no meaning to these sounds.

Talking to your baby
Your earliest conversations with your baby will involve smiles rather than sounds.

Speech and language

Babies need and want to communicate from the very earliest days, and even before they begin to vocalize, they will listen to and try to imitate sounds. The basics of languages are built into babies' brains. A deaf infant starts to babble at the same age as a child with normal hearing, so we know that auditory stimulation is not necessary for language development. Some theorists even say we have a "language acquisition device" somewhere in the brain that makes language inevitable.

Before your baby is six weeks old, he'll have learned that if he smiles or makes sounds, you will respond. What is remarkable is that even at this early stage he realizes that he can call the shots: he smiles, you are pleased and talk to him more, and he can keep a two-way "conversation" going. By smiling and talking to your baby and showing your pleasure when he responds, you are giving him his very first lesson in communication.

Newborn Your baby will respond to human voices from the moment of birth, and he will try to imitate gestures and expressions. He will sense when you are talking to him and will respond with sounds and by moving his entire body.

4–6 weeks He can already recognize your voice. He'll respond to your smiles and speech by gurgling, and wait for you to reply. Keep your face close to his when you talk to him so that he can see you, and reward his sounds with more smiles and talking.

4 months Your baby now has a range of sounds, including squeals and blowing between his lips. He communicates with you through laughter, so laugh and giggle a lot when you talk to him.

6 months There are many signs that your baby is beginning to understand what you say. He babbles and strings sounds together. Singing to him, repeating rhymes, and speaking rhythmically will all help him to understand language and encourage early speaking.

BEGINNING TO TALK

For your baby to talk, he must first understand what you say, and his understanding will increase rapidly toward the end of the first year. From six months onward, he'll understand when you say "no" firmly, and at nine months he can follow simple instructions, such as "wave bye-bye." You can help him by making meanings clear with exaggerated emphasis and gestures: read to him, show him pictures and repeat the names of the things he can see, and give him a clear, slow running commentary about everyday actions.

Children who are sung to, have nursery rhymes repeated to them, are spoken to in a rhythmical way, and are involved in singing, rhyming and clapping games, speak earlier and better than children who don't, so you should do all these things from your child's earliest days. As soon as your child says his first word, or what you think might be a word, repeat it to him. Tell him he's a smart boy and show him how pleased you are with him.

7 months By now you will be able to discern clear syllables in your baby's sounds, such as "ba" or "ka." He'll probably use a special sound to attract your attention, such as a cough or a squeal, and will have started to play games with his tongue and lips.

8–9 months Your baby's range of sounds is increasing, and he has added the consonants "t," "d," and "w" to his repertoire. He'll start to imitate real speech sounds, and may use one word with meaning. He pays close attention to adult conversations.

11 months By now your baby is almost certainly using one word with meaning, and can understand a few simple words, such as "bath," "drink," and "lunch." Praise him for every new word, and repeat it; he'll say it over and over when he sees your approval. You are your child's first model of good speech, so speak clearly and slowly when you're talking to him.

15 months Your baby is breaking gradually into jargon—that is, strings of sounds with the odd recognizable word and with the phrasing and inflections of real speech. This is a sign that he is just about to start talking. He may start to use some favorite phrase of yours, such as "oh, dear," in appropriate situations.

18 months Your baby may be able to use about ten words with meaning. His understanding is increasing all the time, and he can point out many objects in his picture books or in the world around him if you ask him to.

FIRST WORDS

Acquiring speech is a complex process, and there are a few typical ways in which children simplify pronunciation.

Your child may acquire words a little at a time, so that "dog" starts out as "d," then "do," then finally "dog." Some difficulty with consonants is normal until four or five years of age.

Double consonants are especially difficult; your child might say "pay" for "play." He'll simplify words that contain sounds made in different parts of the mouth, so that "ball" becomes "baw." You can help him by stressing the last letter of words.

Make every effort to encourage and understand your child's attempts at communication.

Teaching words
As your child learns his first words, play a game of pointing to things in books and repeating their names.

Right from the moment of birth, girls are more responsive to the human voice than boys, and they have better verbal skills throughout childhood.

Girls talk sooner than boys, and begin to string words into sentences earlier. They have better articulation, pronunciation, and grammar, and are better at verbal reasoning. They also learn to read earlier than boys.

The structure of the female brain is believed to be the reason for girls' superior verbal skills (see p.180): the speech centers are more tightly organized in the female brain than in the male brain, and have more and better connections with other functions of the brain.

Speech and language

Your baby is learning new words all the time now, and she's also starting to put them together. Her pronunciation will be indistinct, but this is no cause for worry; if she is using words with meaning and putting them together, then her language is developing.

Mild speech defects, such as lisping, are very common in children, and usually disappear without any treatment. There is great variation in the speed at which children acquire speech, so don't feel the need to compare your child with others of her age, and don't worry if her development doesn't match the timetable outlined below: I give these dates merely as average guidelines, and no child corresponds exactly to the average.

18 months–2 years Your baby's speech will become more complex during this time. She will probably have a vocabulary of about 30 words, including possessives ("mine"), and negatives, ("won't"), instead of simply "no." She is starting to combine words to make simple statements, such as "ball gone," or questions: "Where Daddy?" She understands that conversation is a two-way thing and will wait her turn to speak, and she uses language to give information, to ask for things, to tell how she feels, or to relate to other people.

Remember that she can understand a lot more words than she can use, so you can continue to help her by teaching her new words. Use adjectives whenever you can, and combine them with nouns: "good boy," "hot water," "big dog." Introduce adverbs, too: "Run quickly," "Pet the dog gently." When you use prepositions—"on," "under," "behind"—always show her what you mean.

2–3 years Your toddler probably has a vocabulary of 200–300 words by now, and she can talk at some length. She is interested in learning new words. Her attention span is longer, and she will listen to you when you explain things or give reasons. She will still mispronounce words, and may lisp, but her fluency and confidence are improving all the time. She can connect two ideas in a single sentence, "I get ball and play outside," and can use pronouns such as "I," "me," and "you" correctly.

You can help your child to increase her vocabulary by using unfamiliar words in your speech in such a way that she can guess at their meaning, and repeat them frequently so that she can learn how they are used. Read to her often, and explain new words as they arise. She will like to hear the same stories read over and over, and will be able to understand increasingly complicated narratives. Your child's use of language is becoming more social now, and she will talk more to other children than to adults, so contact with children is the best way to help her to develop her abilities.

TALKING TO YOUR CHILD

It is important that you continue to talk to your toddler, and go on introducing new words and making your meaning clear with gestures and facial expressions. It is just as important, however, that you allow her to respond so that she learns that conversation works two ways. If she initiates a conversation by showing you something or asking you a question, always give her your attention. If you are impatient, or just respond with "That's nice" without even looking at her, she'll become discouraged and give up trying to talk to you.

Talk about everything you are doing in detail. When you're dressing her, give a running commentary: "Now we'll do your buttons … one, two, three." Describe objects you are using: "Let's put the apples in the glass bowl"; "Would you like a yellow candy or a red candy?"

While you shouldn't correct your child when she makes mistakes, there's no reason why you should talk to her in her own baby language. If she makes a mistake in grammar or pronunciation— "Granny goed"—just repeat her words giving the correct form: "Yes, Granny went home."

LANGUAGE AND UNDERSTANDING

You will be able to observe the way your toddler gradually gains concepts in her use of language. She will often use the same word to describe similar things, so that apples, oranges, and peaches are all "apple," because they are all round fruits; and horses, cows, and sheep are all "horse" because they are all large animals with four legs. This doesn't necessarily mean that she can't tell the difference; only that she doesn't have words to describe all of them, so she uses the nearest one.

By the same token, the questions your child asks you may be very simple because she can't fully express what it is she really wants to know. So when she says "What's that," she may be asking "What is it? What is it called? What does it do? How does it work?" all at once. Give your child as much information as you think she can understand: "This is called laundry detergent. It's just like soap, and I put it in the washing machine to make our clothes nice and clean." Always try to answer the question she is really asking.

LANGUAGE IN BOYS

Boys are almost always slower than girls at developing their language skills, and this discrepancy lasts all through childhood.

Boys are later in talking than girls, are slower to put words together in sentences, and take longer to learn to read. Speech disorders, such as stuttering, are far more common in boys than in girls, and boys outnumber girls in remedial reading classes by four to one.

Although this difference in linguistic ability levels out somewhat during the teenage years, you can help your son's language skills in the preschool years by reading aloud to him and playing lots of word games.

Socializing
During the third year, your child's verbal skills will be improved by talking to other children.

GIRLS' TALK

GIRLS' TALK

Studies of the way children use language show marked differences in the way girls and boys speak to each other, which can be seen even in the preschool years.

The reason for these differences has to do with the way the sexes behave in groups. Girls want to be part of the group, so their talk is aimed at promoting unity and reaching compromises. Girls:

• Use language as a way of forming close, intimate friendships.

• Make suggestions when playing in groups—"Let's play house."

• Give reasons for their suggestions: "Let's play in outside because there's more room."

Girls at play
Close friendships form the basis of a girl's social world, and this will be reflected in her choice of language.

Speech and language

As your child's world becomes wider, his language will have to keep pace with new experiences and ideas. His perception of the world is becoming more complex, and so is his vocabulary; for example, he will start to realize that mauve is different from purple, and look for the words to express this difference.

Never overtly correct your child's mistakes when he's speaking. Tactfully repeat what he has just said, but correctly. If he hesitates over a word, supply it instantly to maintain his momentum and interest. When your child speaks to you, turn to him and show him that you're listening attentively.

3 years Your child will enjoy learning new words, so he listens to adult conversations carefully, and his attention span is increasing. He can understand words that describe how he feels, such as "cold," "tired," and "hungry." He is also beginning to understand words such as "on," "under," and "behind," though this will take longer. He should be able to give his first and last name. Because his mind is racing ahead of his ability to form words at this stage, he may start to stutter, but this is likely to be temporary. If he hasn't overcome his stutter by about four-and-a-half, or earlier if it is severe, it might be worth consulting a speech therapist.

4 years Children of this age talk a great deal: they boast, exaggerate, tell tall tales, and have conversations with imaginary friends. Your child will ask lots of questions, as much out of a desire to keep you talking as out of any real curiosity, because he loves conversation. He will enjoy inventing silly words, and may indulge in mildly obscene verbal play, especially to do with the toilet. He will probably start to use slang, and he may call you names and threaten you.

5 years Your five-year-old will ask innumerable questions, and now he really is seeking new information. He loves to be read to. He is aware that there is a "right" way to say things and will often ask you what it is. He can understand opposites, and it's very easy to make a game out of this, where you give a word such as "soft," "up," or "cold," and he has to give the opposite. He will also be able to define words if you ask him, and this is a very good way of getting him to use him skills of classification as well as verbal skills. In fact, all word games are excellent mental exercise, because clear speaking goes hand in hand with clear thinking.

BOOKS AND READING

Encouraging an interest in books is probably the best single thing you can do for your child, so read to him often; his attention span is increasing now, and he will be able to listen to stories with sustained interest. Words are crucial to the way our brains work; they are our main means of communicating, and they form the basis for everything your child will learn in school. Books will provide your child with new words and new ideas, and will explain to him how the world works.

Let your child know that you regard reading as a pleasure. Have plenty of books in the house and make it clear to your child that they are all available for him to look at. Store his own books on low shelves where he can easily browse through them.

Choose books for your child that are visually appealing; first reading books should be short, with only a few pages, and should have large illustrations, large print, and a simple vocabulary. Be willing to read your child's favorite books over and over again; eventually he will memorize the words, and when he is ready to start reading himself, the familiar words will be easier to recognize.

TEACHING LETTERS AND NUMBERS

Take every opportunity to help your child become familiar with letters or numbers. Show your child how his own name is spelt, and let him try to copy it. As you read to him, pick out a simple word like "cat" and point it out every time it recurs. Then show your child what it looks like, and ask him if he can find it on a certain page. When you are doing routine tasks, count out loud as you do up the buttons on your child's sweater, for instance, or lay the table. When you are out shopping, you could ask your child to fetch things for you: three packets of soup, or two oranges.

Reading to your child
From your child's earliest days, reading to her will be a very valuable time of sharing and learning.

Aids to learning
Give your child numbers and letters to play with. Magnetic ones can be attached to the refrigerator door.

BOYS' TALK

The way little boys talk to each other when at play is markedly different from the way little girls interact with one another, and this reflects attitudes that will continue all through adult life.

In any kind of group situation, boys usually want to stand out from the crowd, so the things they say are intended to enhance their status in the eyes of their playmates. Boys:

• Tell jokes and stories far more than girls, since this allows them to be the center of attention; they will often interrupt a story being told by another boy.

• Give orders and try to grab favorable positions for themselves: "OK, we're going to play doctor. I'll be the doctor, you be the patient."

• Back up their suggestions by insisting, by appealing to the rules, or even by threats: "You have to be the patient because it's your turn. I won't play with you if you don't."

Girls tend to develop social skills and enjoy the company of other people far earlier than boys do. While not all children conform to a stereotype, in general, girls:

- Are more sociable than boys, and form closer friendships from an earlier age.

- Are more compliant with adult requests than boys tend to be in early childhood.

- Show fewer competitive traits and are less socially aggressive and dominant than boys.

- Cope far more easily with physical, emotional, and intellectual stress than boys.

Social behavior

Many features of your child's personality will affect her development as well as her future prospects in life. Helpful traits include the ability to get along well with people, concentrate, and learn from mistakes; willingness to work hard; good powers of observation; thoroughness; creativity; an inquiring mind; and determination.

Less helpful traits are slowness of thought, difficulty in expressing herself, overactivity, and diminished concentration, which may occur even in a highly intelligent child.

Your newborn baby needs to interact socially, especially with you, her parents. She learns to be sociable by imitating you, first with facial expressions, then with gestures and movements, and finally with complete patterns of behavior. In this way the relationship between parent and child forms the blueprint for all subsequent relationships, so it is your responsibility to be more aware of your behavior and responses than ever before. From the moment you begin to talk to your baby, she begins to develop into a social being because she longs to converse with you.

Like all other development, social development has its own well-defined stages. Everyone has heard of the "terrible twos," when your child enters a stage of refusing to obey, and of doing what she is told not to do. This is her way of asserting her independence and, although at times you'll believe that it will go on forever, it's simply a stage in her learning to interact with other people.

PREDICTING PERSONALITY

It would be marvelous if we could predict the future personality of a child when she was still an infant. Certainly, we can do so with intelligence. Personality and character, however, derive partly from heredity and partly from environment, so there always remains the possibility that, as the result of a bad environment or the lack of secure, loving relationships, a child may not have the opportunities to grow up as a loving and lovable adult.

In view of the profound effect of environment and family on character, predictions during infancy are doomed to failure. However, observant parents with several children can detect differences in their personalities from the outset. Perhaps it's a good thing that personality prediction is so difficult. From the point of view of adoption, it would be a pity if such predictions were possible. Adoptive parents have a right to want to know the intelligence of the child whom they are thinking of adopting. They must not expect to know what her personality will be like. All parents take huge risks when having children, not even knowing if they will be mentally normal. If they're not willing to take that risk, they shouldn't consider having children.

INDIVIDUALITY

Your baby's individuality will gradually become more and more apparent as she grows and learns. You should treasure your baby's individuality and nurture her growth and strength.

The gradual insight you gain into your baby's personality is like watching a thrilling movie in slow motion. All her preferences, the things that make her laugh and cry, the foods she likes, her favorite toys, come together to create her unique personality.

Baby types There's much evidence now that within a week or so of birth, infants show a primitive form of all the traits they will show as they grow up and probably later in life. Undeniably, environment has a profound effect on character formation, but much of the child's basic character is inherited from her parents, so it's fair to say that each baby will show basic personality traits that don't change much with age.

The traits that are easily recognizable by any parent are the amount of energy your child has, how well she can control her body (as opposed to being floppy), self-reliance, social responsiveness, family attachment, communicativeness, adaptability to various situations, exploitation of the environment, sense of humor, emotional expressiveness, reaction to success, reaction to restriction, readiness of smiling, and readiness of crying. Between six weeks and three months, your baby will probably fall into one of three personality types:

She may be quite "good" or "easy"; eating and sleeping and merging comfortably with her surroundings when awake, and seldom getting overenthusiastic in her responses.

She may be what is sometimes referred to as a high-key "sparkler," becoming as demanding in her bids for entertainment and companionship as she first was for food and comfort; the zest for living keeps her growing in self-play.

She may be an "in-betweener," having "up" days and hours and "down" days and hours and asking only that you respond in kind to her moods.

While personality differences may be apparent very early on, it's in the first few months that each new baby starts to become more distinctly herself. Here are some traits you may notice:

- Easy-going, placid, daydreaming
- Cross and irritable, a leader
- Sociable, a follower
- Serious, determined
- Independent, often perverse
- Imaginative, sometimes difficult

BOYS' BEHAVIOR

Boys tend to be slower to develop social skills than girls. While not all boys will show these traits to a marked degree, in general, boys:

- Tend to be slower to develop social skills than girls.

- Are more socially aggressive.

- Have more friendships than girls, but they tend to be superficial and short-lived.

- Are more emotionally vulnerable than girls.

- Tend to have more behavioral problems, particularly when around authority figures.

Social skills
Young children play alongside each other rather than together, but will enjoy the company.

BONDING

The relationship between you and your baby begins from the moment you give birth, and every aspect of your being becomes a comfort and joy to your baby.

He'll respond to your smell, the sound of your voice, the touch of your skin, and the sight of your face. This bond is so complete, your baby will be able to single you out from others in an astoundingly short time. The same will occur with your partner if he spends time alone with the baby.

Make every effort to ensure that the contact you and your partner have with your baby is pleasant, calm, and loving, even if at times this seems impossible.

An early start
By developing a close, loving relationship with your baby from birth, you are laying the foundations of a good relationship in future years.

Social behavior

Your baby's first six months are, surprisingly, a crucial time for his social development. It is during these early weeks that your baby comes to understand the pleasure of social interaction and the importance of communication.

Your baby grows beyond the basic requirements of warmth and feeding as he begins to enjoy the social aspects of being alive. Because you embody comfort, pleasure, and security for your baby, you are naturally the best person to teach him loving relationships, the basics of which are learned through the initial skin contact that he loves so much during the first few weeks.

Newborn From the very beginning, your baby will desire close contact with you. He'll appeal to you through head nodding, mouth and tongue movements, and jerks of his body. These are his earliest conversations; he's engaging with you, and you should answer with noises, laughter, and bobbing head movements. He'll soon learn that he can make you respond.

3 months Your baby's conversational gestures are far more controlled. He'll turn toward the sound of your voice and wriggle with pleasure on seeing you. He understands that a smile is a happy greeting, his earliest "hello." Your baby will learn that being friendly is rewarding if you respond with interest, love, cuddles, comfort, and soothing noises. A child who is smiled at, smiles back and smiles in greeting. When you feed him, make this a time of physical intimacy. Hold him close, look into his eyes, and talk gently.

4 months By now your baby is such a social being that he'll cry soon after being left alone, even if he has many toys around him. He'll stop crying if you go to him, and he'll wriggle his body in anticipation. He'll be happy to respond to people who acknowledge him, but will have a special response for you and the rest of the family. Make eye contact as often as possible and exaggerate all facial expressions and gestures.

5 months At this age your baby has four main methods of communication: sounds, gestures, facial expressions, and crying, and unless he is asleep, he'll make the most of all four. Imitate all your baby's sounds with changes in pitch and loudness. Interest him in subtle sounds. Play soft music, crunch up tissue paper, and ring small bells. He can also tell the difference between an angry voice and a friendly one now, and will react to each differently. He now shows a certain shyness with strangers, but will smile at a familiar face.

6 months Your baby's social advances are far more physical now, even aggressive, but they may be offset by a growing fear of strangers, and a possessiveness over you. He'll explore much more with his hands, patting and touching your face and hands rather than just searching your face with his eyes. Help your baby by giving him lots of physical affection.

RESPONDING TO YOUR BABY

Any response you make to your baby's attempts at conversation will further his understanding of communication, so you must try to be positive all the time. If a baby's gurgling is met with silence, he'll soon grow tired of such an unrewarding game and may well give up on all but the most basic communication. Always encourage a "two-way" conversation, either by imitating your baby's gestures and noises in an overt way, or by chatting to him in order to elicit a response. Be animated with voice and gesture. The broader your gestures, the more he understands, the more fun he has, and the closer the bond becomes.

A young baby is sensitive to sudden noises, so bear in mind that, although a wide variety of noises are tranquilizing for him, harsh or very loud noises will frighten and upset him.

Encourage your baby to cope with new faces by introducing him to any visitors he hasn't met before. This will allow him to get used to strangers in the security of your home. The more your baby enjoys your company, the more likely he is to actively seek it as he grows older. Songs and rhythmic games will encourage him to equate joyful times with mixing with others.

DIFFICULT BABIES

A demanding baby, one who cries constantly and can't be comforted, can be difficult to cope with. It's vital that you share the responsibility with your partner and try very hard to control your temper. There are many causes of, and solutions for, a crying baby, and constant tears is a phase that is fortunately short-lived. If your baby is difficult, it's important to understand why he's crying, keeping you awake, or ignoring you. Whatever his particular problem, your calm, loving, and understanding approach will have a far more positive effect on him than being chastised or ignored. Your healthcare provider can offer advice and support.

If you have an antisocial baby—for example, one who is discontented when hungry, but never enjoys feeding or being held—you may feel rejected by him, or responsible for his unhappiness. Try to keep these negative thoughts at bay. No matter how much he rejects you, keep trying to engage his interest. It has to be said, though, that some babies are antisocial from birth and reject physical affection. Don't blame yourself once you've tried everything.

ONE OF THE FAMILY

Your baby is longing to be part of the family with all its routines, rules, and customs.

To become interested, he needs to learn how to fit in. For this reason, you should include him in family activities, outings, shopping, daily chores, and visiting friends from as early as possible. Talk to your child about all the members of the family and show him photos.

The family group will be the basis of your baby's learning about the workings of groups in general. His behavior with family members will teach him about his expected behavior with strangers, and will open him to the social customs of his society. Your baby learns chiefly through imitation, so by copying your behavior, he learns his own standards of social interaction.

Involve your baby
Try to include your baby in your activities, even if they don't directly involve her.

A WILL OF
HER OWN

From six months onward your baby will show assertiveness in her demands and preferences. Your older baby is:

• Very eager to show how grown-up she is becoming.

• Determined to be independent and to manage without help.

• Demonstrating likes and dislikes with certainty and assertion, if not consistency.

• Unable to consider consequences and gets very angry when she has to wait, often showing this with violent noises and actions.

• Aware that she is a separate being from you and, as such, is determined to have her own way.

• Often confused and unhappy at the conflict between her urge to be independent and her desire to love and please you.

• More willful than her intellectual maturity will allow.

• Extreme in her emotions, from great happiness to outbursts of temper tantrums.

• Seemingly infatuated with saying the word "no."

Social behavior

Your baby is becoming more socially adept by now, and takes a great deal of pleasure in meeting and being with other people. Her interactions with you are increasingly comprehensive as she learns to understand certain words and phrases, and uses the communication skills she has learned in order to mix with others in the world around her.

Touching, smiling, and all the contact of general company are vital to your baby's happiness at this stage, as she gradually learns to refine her conversational gestures and cries into recognizable signs of communication.

6–8 months Closeness to another baby will be a delight. She'll reach out and touch new friends and will enjoy social games like "Peek-a-Boo" and "Patty-Cake." She'll try to communicate with a series of shrieks, grunts, raspberries, and coughs, and will mimic facial expressions and conversational gestures. You should "answer" her in order to simulate these "conversations" and impress upon her that social interaction is a two–way activity.

8–12 months She will respond to her own name now, and will understand that a firm "no" means that she should stop whatever she is doing. She is affectionate and will demand closeness with you, particularly big hugs and intimate smiles. Certain social rituals are common to her now—like saying "bye-bye"—which she'll imitate with little prompting. She'll no longer calmly allow a toy to be taken away and she'll show anger if this happens.

12–15 months Her sociability is constantly expanding and she enjoys being in groups, especially when she can follow conversations and join in whenever there's a lull. Despite her outgoing attitude, she will still need to be close to you for reassurance and security, and will often look to you when meeting new people—just holding hands will give her the confidence she needs. She can say a few words, ask for things, and show thanks when things are done for her in an obvious way. She likes to be helpful, and enjoys sharing tasks with you.

15–18 months By now your baby is even more helpful with daily chores, and loves the independence of dressing and undressing herself. She is very affectionate, and shows love for her family, pets, and favorite toys. She imitates adult behavior and is fascinated by adult interaction and conversation. Despite being socially aware, she will tend to play alone and, although she will enjoy playing near another child, she will not tend to play with her.

HOW TO HELP

The concept of sharing is particularly difficult for your baby to grasp. It's unrealistic to expect your baby to give a toy to another baby if she is still playing with it. It is equally unfair to expect your baby to understand that she can't take another baby's toy simply because she wants it. This, then, gives rise to a situation whereby you can demonstrate the basics of give and take. Your child of 18 months is generally able to comprehend reciprocity, but you must demonstrate it in a way that is reasonable to her; if she takes another baby's toy, she must replace it with one of her own so that they can both play. Your baby is wholly capable of unselfishness and generosity, but any such act must be seen to be a pleasure for both parties. If your baby is willing to share her treats with other members of the family, encourage these small acts of generosity with others and try to build on them.

You should always include your baby in social gatherings and teach her the basic pleasantries from as early as possible. Introduce her to lots of new faces so that she doesn't become dependent on you and the family alone for social stimulation. It will help her to feel secure when she is away from you or her usual caregiver, although this shouldn't happen too frequently, or for long periods of time.

INTRODUCING DISCIPLINE

Discipline should be applied first with the tone of the voice, later with the word "no," then by distraction, and only finally with very mild punishment. Spanking, threats, and withdrawal of pleasures have no place with small children. If you are too severe or too lenient, your baby may become insecure. Before she is three, your child can't respond to reason, and she still can't grasp the connection between cause and effect. She'll understand that she's done wrong, or that you're angry, but it will take her some time to remember to connect a particular action with a particular outcome. For this reason, it's vital that you point out a mistake to your child immediately so that she links the action with the punishment. Bear in mind that your baby's memory is very short, so if you brood over your anger and act later, she won't understand and won't learn from your attempts at correction. During a baby's first year, there are very few reasons for saying "No." I kept the rules for my children to a minimum, and I had only one unbreakable rule in their first year: when they were doing something that was unsafe for themselves or others, I would say "No" firmly while removing an object or stopping my child from doing something dangerous. I didn't wait for my child to stop. As I was trying to teach what was unsafe, I always explained why I was stopping him.

Your baby will be very receptive to justice and fair play, and to their opposites. She immediately recognizes inconsistency, and so gently applied and consistent discipline will help your child to develop self-control and a conscience, which in turn will help her in her decision-making in later life. It will also give her a sense of responsibility toward others.

FEAR OF STRANGERS

It is not uncommon for a normally talkative and sociable child to become withdrawn, even tearful, when introduced to strangers or taken to a strange place. This is quite normal and should never be ridiculed or made into an issue.

Don't insist that she joins in immediately with the group. A gentle introduction from you works by far the best, and your baby will soon forget her nerves and find her place within the social gathering.

Even a very shy child, if gently encouraged, will join in with new friends after an hour or so, but rushing her may make her more insecure. A favorite toy will bolster her confidence, so don't take this security away. Once she feels relaxed, she'll play happily with her new playmates.

IDENTIFYING WITH OTHERS

By the time your child reaches the age of three, he'll begin the process of identification with himself and with other people around him.

You will start to see evidence of his self-awareness as he takes steps to command and control himself, showing that he can put himself in the position of others. You may overhear your child scolding himself when he thinks he has done something that you would disapprove of. He will begin to act out the part of the adults known to him, particularly you, often adopting phrases that you use regularly.

This will all become part of the process of his exploring and getting to know the way the world works and his own part in it. Now is the time to introduce him to the idea of a wider circle of people, teaching him to respect and be polite to them. Introduce him to visitors to the house—delivery people, mail carriers, and meter readers—as well as your own friends, and make meeting people part of his daily routine.

Social behavior

From his first moments, your baby looked to you as the center of his world—the main provider of affection and care. However, as he gets older and his self-awareness and life experiences develop, he'll begin to see you as a separate person and will extend his interest to other people. Although you can't make friends for him, you can help by introducing him to a few first companions. He will soon learn to adapt his skills and develop the social habits of older boys and girls.

18 months–2 years At this age, you should encourage your child to interact with other children. Invite children to the house and give him games and play material to facilitate socializing. Be patient; although his initial reaction may be self-centered, he will modify selfish behavior if it is played down. Avoid rivalry by praising your child's achievements—this will give him a good sense of self-worth. Praise all sharing.

2–2½ years As he is learning to share, encourage games that involve giving to others and respecting their wishes. He may demonstrate feelings of rivalry as a consequence and try to force his will on others. You'll need to use discipline fairly while still encouraging and supporting all his efforts and achievements, since approval is more important at this stage. Start teaching your child manners and respect for private property. Be consistent about unbreakable rules like those concerning safety.

2½–3 years As your child continues to socialize, he becomes more independent from you and more outgoing toward other children. He will start to be more generous and unselfish in play with others, and form stronger friendships with adults and children, showing signs of sympathy when others are in distress. It's never too early to introduce the need for truth and honesty. Always reward it even if it involves a confession to a misdemeanor. Reward the truth and deal with the misdemeanor next time. NEVER punish truth.

RIGHT AND WRONG

Your child will only learn the differences between right and wrong if they are clearly pointed out. In the first year, you can act out why hot or sharp things are dangerous using sounds and actions. If your child understands why you want him to do something, he is much more likely to do it willingly, so try to explain and then ask his opinion. There are situations that are nonnegotiable: where your child's safety is threatened, when the thoughts and feelings of others should be considered, and where your child is tempted to tamper with the truth.

You should be very firm on these points, and he will gradually learn a sense of responsibility for disciplining himself as he grows up. Cockiness can often be mistaken for impertinence, but unless your child is imposing on the feelings of others, he may be displaying nothing more than a healthy resistance to authority that can be useful, if sensibly directed.

A spoiled or overindulged child will behave in a self-centered way, and this may be the result of the overprotectiveness, favoritism, or unreasonably high expectations of his parents. The best cure is to let him go to preschool or daycare so that he can get used to mixing with other children.

SHARING
Young children are naturally selfish and usually begin to think of others only when they're taught to do so. Your child has to understand that other children feel as he does before he is able to grasp the importance of thinking of other people's feelings. Don't worry if your child seems to be slow in learning to share; it's very difficult, but with your patience he will successfully acquire this skill. Help by making sharing a game. Initiate games that involve giving things to others and he will learn to share with them.

Toys for sharing
Encourage your child to cooperate with others by getting him to complete a puzzle such as this one with a friend.

MEETING OTHER CHILDREN
Just like all the other lessons he has to learn through life, your child's ability to make friends could be slow to develop, so introduce it to him gradually. Invite friends over, one at a time at first, to your home where he is sure of himself. Stay nearby to give him help and support should he need it. He'll begin to build up a small circle of friends and gain confidence through his own place in it—an essential way to learn the ground rules for future friendships.

TANTRUMS

Toddlers between the ages of two and three often have temper tantrums as a means of venting frustration when they don't get what they want.

This is quite normal because your child won't have sufficient judgment to control his strength of will or the language to express himself clearly, but as his knowledge and experience of the world broaden, the occasions when his will is pitched directly against yours become rarer.

A tantrum may be brought on by such feelings as frustration, anger, jealousy, and dislike. Anger is brought on by not getting his own way; frustration by his not being strong enough or sufficiently well coordinated to do what he wants. It will usually involve your child throwing himself on the floor, kicking and screaming.

The best thing you can do is to stay calm, since any attention on your part will only prolong the attack. If he has one in public, take him outside or to a quiet corner, without fuss.

At home, an effective technique is simply to leave the room. Explain to your child that, while you still love him, you have to leave the room because you are getting angry. Never confine him in another room because this denies him the option of coming back and saying he's sorry.

GROWING UP LIKE MOM

By the age of three, your little girl is aware of the fact that she is female and that she'll grow up to be a woman.

This makes her very attentive to you—her mother. Her view of gender roles will be influenced by your attitudes. If you:

• Regard yourself as equal to your partner, your daughter will see this as normal.

• Treat other women as close friends and confidantes, your daughter will see relationships with adult women in this way.

• See working as integral to family life, your daughter will view a career as compatible with having a family.

A role model
When your little girl starts to realize that she will grow up like her mother, she will take a special interest in your activities.

Social behavior

Your preschooler faces many changes in how she sees herself as her independence grows and her personality matures. Sudden upheavals can cause your child to exhibit quite violent changes of mood as she tries to relate her changing identity to her family life and the guidelines she has learned for social behavior, both of which are relatively constant.

Be patient and allow her to mature in her own time. The difficult stages are easily outweighed by the thrilling ones, and your child must experience both in order to become a socially adept member of her community.

3 years If your child has been brought up to relate to new friends, she will separate from you easily from the age of three-and-a-half onward, and at about the same time she is learning to play interactive games, such as tag. She is generous and generally sympathetic when someone else is distressed. Unselfishness comes from being a team member so encourage your child to pull her own weight at home. Give appreciation whenever possible.

4 years During the fourth year, your child has an expanding sense of self, indicated by bragging, boasting, and out-of-bounds behavior. She begins to realize that other children are separate entities. Your four-year-old wants to be grown up. She becomes argumentative, and may be selfish, rough, or impatient, especially with younger children or brothers and sisters. She'll express affection at bedtimes but might be jealous of you and your partner together. Four-year-old boys, in particular, often have silly, boisterous humor.

5 years During the fifth year, your child may become rather serious, businesslike, and realistic. She gets very excited in anticipation of the future. At this age your little girl is sympathetic, affectionate, and loves to be helpful. She has a strong feeling for the family, and appearance is very important to her. She is not afraid to call people names. For a little boy, his Mom is the center of his universe. He takes others and himself for granted and is interested in immediate experiences.

SEXUALITY AND GENDER

3 years By the time she is three years old, your child already has an interest in her own gender and the differentiation of herself from boys. At about the age of three-and-a-half she'll express "I like" and then slightly later "I love," and she will affirm, if questioned, that she is a girl rather than a boy. She will begin to express interest in physiological differences between the genders and in boys' and girls' postures for urinating.

She makes no distinctions between gender at play and realizes that people touch out of friendship as well as out of love. She begins to become interested in babies and wants her family to have one. She will ask questions such as "What can the baby do when it comes?", or "Where does it come from?" and most three-year-olds don't understand when they get the answer that the baby grows inside its mother. It is still vital, however, that you answer your child's questions as frankly and honestly as possible so that her trust in you is not undermined.

4 years By the age of four, children are extremely conscious of their navel and under social stress they may grasp their genitals and may need to urinate. They may play a game of "show," indulge in verbal play or name-calling, and make jokes about passing urine or stools. They have an interest in other people's bathrooms and may demand privacy for themselves, but be extremely interested in the bathroom activities of others. They may begin to segregate themselves along gender lines. All your answers to your child's questions on sex should stress the aspects of loving, caring, and the responsibilities that an intimate relationship demands. Your child may also question how babies get out of their mothers' tummies and may spontaneously think babies are born through the navel. This is a time when gender-stereotyped behavior is learned more from peers than parents.

5 years At five your child will be familiar with, but not much interested in, physical differences between the genders. She'll be more modest and less self-exposing and will play less in the bathroom than earlier. She'll be aware of sex organs when she sees adults undressed and will wonder why her dad doesn't have breasts or her sister doesn't have a penis.

Most children of five take the opposite sex for granted and there's little distinction between the role of gender in play. There may be frequent boy–girl pairs. Girls' interest in babies continues: they may ask for a baby of their own and they may even dramatize this in games. Your five-year-old will constantly ask, "Where do babies come from?", and will accept "Mommy's tummy" as an answer, but some fix on the idea that you buy a baby at the hospital. She will make little connection between the size of a pregnant woman and the presence of a baby inside her.

GROWING UP LIKE DAD

Your little boy will have realized by the age of three that he will grow up to be a man, and he will become particularly interested in his father.

Your little boy will watch your partner and learn from him what it is to be a man. If your partner:

• Treats women, particularly you or his daughters, in a caring and considerate way, your little boy will believe that this is the correct way to treat women.

• Sees other men as friends, your son will also find older men approachable.

• Enjoys and participates in family life, your child will follow this example.

• Resolves disputes with rudeness and violence, he will too.

A sense of identity
Your little boy will gain his idea of what it is to grow up as a man by observing his father.

FAVORITISM

It is all too easy to favor one child above the other, or at least to treat him in a way that seems like favoritism.

If a child is born several years after a previous one and is much wanted, for example, he may be treated preferentially. Sometimes it happens that the mother's favorite is the boy, the father's favorite is the girl, and a third-born child is no one's favorite.

Favoritism reveals itself in many different ways, some of them apparently inconsequential, but very important in the mind of a child. A favored child may be:

• Reprimanded less

• Allowed to do a greater variety of activities

• Given more treats, such as rides on Dad's back, or candies

• Defended when he gets into trouble for being naughty

• Given more time and attention

Of course, all children have different needs, and it is impossible to treat them absolutely equally, but you should beware of favoring one child, or even appearing to; children are very quick to notice such behavior, and a child who feels left out will suffer a blow to his confidence.

RELATIONSHIPS

Children who grow up in a stable, secure environment and feel loved by their parents are likely to become well-adjusted adults. Ideally, you and your partner will have equal but complementary roles, and agree on strategy, so that your child can't play one of you against the other. The way a child interacts with his parents and siblings evolves gradually between the ages of three and five.

MOTHER AND CHILD
3 years At the age of three, children generally have good relationships with their mothers. Quite often the mother is the favorite parent with whom children like to discuss and relive past events. By three and a half, the mother–child relationship can sometimes become more difficult. Children can be simultaneously demanding and resistant. A child may refuse to eat, dress, or take a nap for his mother, but be quite compliant with someone else.

4 years By the age of four, your child will take pride in you, quote things that you say, and boast about you to friends, though at home he'll still resist your authority.

5 years The mother–child relationship is generally more smooth: your child likes to do things that you request, enjoys playing around you, and needs to be aware of your presence without having your full attention. Children quite often express affection, such as, "I like you, Mommy," and, although they accept punishment from you, it may not have a great impact on them. Boys may talk about marrying Mom.

FATHER AND CHILD
3 years At three years, the mother tends to be the favorite parent, but the father can take over in many situations. For instance, a child may cling less at bedtime and go to sleep more quickly in the presence of his father. At the age of three and a half, girls may express closeness to their fathers.

4 years Children boast about their fathers outside the home, and quote them as an authority. Some children may feel jealous of their father spending a lot of time with their mother and feel they are being deprived of maternal attention. If this is the case, a child may verbally express dislike for his father.

5 years By five years of age, children are likely to accept fathers taking a caring role if mother is busy, sick, or away. Relationships with father are generally smooth, pleasant, and undisturbed, and children often value special outings with their fathers. They usually accept

Sibling relationships
Your child will enjoy the companionship of a sibling to play with, but don't be surprised by quarrels, since these are quite natural.

punishment better from mothers than fathers. Fathers may have more authority and tend to be disobeyed less.

SIBLINGS

At the age of four, relationships with siblings can be turbulent. A child is old enough to be a nuisance to older siblings and can be selfish, rough, and impatient with younger siblings. Quarrels and physical fights over toys are common, and there will be complaints about fairness.

A five-year-old is usually good with younger siblings. Girls, especially, can be protective and kind toward younger members of the family, and are helpful rather than domineering. Having said this, a five-year-old is still too young to be responsible for younger siblings; and although he may be caring while an adult is present, he may resort to teasing when left alone with a sister or brother. Five-year-olds usually interact well with older siblings, sometimes adopting a baby role in domestic play.

THE ONLY CHILD

Although there are benefits to being an only child, such as lots of love and attention, there are also disadvantages. Without the presence of other children of a comparable age, the only child can sometimes feel lonely, and reticent about mixing in groups. As long as you're aware of this, you can do things to compensate. Introduce your child to other children at an early age. Encourage him to visit friends and invite them over to your house, and arrange outings with other young children.

There is also the tendency for some parents to be possessive and overprotective with their only child. This can be dangerous for both parent and child. If you don't allow your child a sense of adventure and the freedom to experiment and explore, he may become timid and wary of new people and experiences. You, meanwhile, will have a more acute sense of loss when your child does become independent.

An only child needs the same amount of discipline as other children. Try not to be overindulgent, and make your child realize that he can't always expect to have your undivided attention.

REJECTION

Although it is unusual, some parents emotionally reject their children, and this can express itself in criticisms and unfavorable comparisons to siblings.

The consequences of parental rejection can be acute. Signs of profound insecurity in a rejected child can be as follows:

- Excessive fear or shyness

- Crying a lot

- Aggressiveness and tantrums

- Jealousy and attention-seeking

- Excessive clinging to mother, thumb-sucking, or masturbation

- Bed-wetting or soiling

- Physical tics

- Head-banging

- Bullying, stealing, or lying

- Cruelty to animals

SHYNESS

Shyness is something that affects many children. Common types of shy behavior include disliking new experiences, reluctance to join in social gatherings, unwillingness to talk to unknown people, and difficulty in making new friends.

Don't think of shyness as something wrong with your child; many well-adjusted adults are quite shy. The best way of dealing with it is not by criticism or forcing change but by preparing your child for any situation she's likely to find difficult, perhaps with stories or role-playing. In most cases, time and patience are all that is needed. See opposite for suggestions on how to help a shy child at school.

Don't worry if your preschool child is not too popular at this stage. Friendships in this age group are casual and unstable, here today and gone tomorrow, and they are not likely to have important or lasting effects on the child's personality.

Playing together
Children will often play next to each other even if they are not involved in the same game.

MAKING FRIENDS

By the time your child reaches the age of four, she is likely to be able to play with other children in an interactive, imaginative, and sustained way. The members of your child's group may change rapidly and there may not be an allegiance to a special friend at this stage, though girls are more likely than boys to pair off with a particular friend. Although children may tease and chant at peers of the opposite sex, gender is not usually a criterion for selecting friends—neither is race.

By the age of five, children tend to select a single playmate, but their play is not necessarily interactive: children often play "in parallel," in that they sit at the same table doing different things. The most frequent grouping is of two children of the same gender, but even at this age, gender is still not a major selection criterion for making new friends.

Although group play demands some cooperation from children, this is quite superficial, since children can often play with their own ends in mind, and have little concern for the group as a whole.

SOCIAL GROUPS
Although children do not fit into rigid stereotypes, there are some common features in most groups of preschool children. The "star" is the child who is popular with everyone; the "rejectee" tends to be least popular; the "neglectee" doesn't evoke strong feelings in other children and, although she doesn't have any enemies, she probably has no friends; and the "clique" is a small group of children who repeatedly seek out each other's company.

The problems experienced by the rejectee are obvious and are usually quickly spotted by preschool staff. Neglectees, however, may suffer a form of social isolation that is more subtle but equally damaging. The typical neglectee is quiet, reserved, and may blend easily into the background.

THE LONER
Isolation in the early years of childhood can have several long term negative effects. Studies have shown that children who have problems interacting with their peers not only suffer in the preschool years but have more emotional disturbance in later life than "sociable" children, and this can incline them to suicide in adolescence and adulthood. The loner is also more likely to be truant and get involved in vandalism and petty crime. For this reason, making efforts to help an unpopular child is always worthwhile.

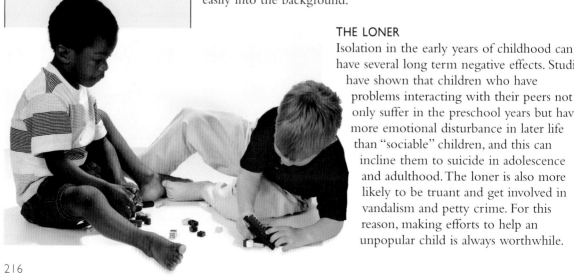

Encouragingly, preschoolers seem better able to develop new social skills than older children or adults.

The first signs that a child is a loner may appear when she starts nursery school. Whereas other children pair off or form groups, this child remains solitary. When children are asked to find a partner, the loner will be the last one left without a partner and, when asked to stand in a line, she will find herself at the back.

If you think that your child is being neglected, it's important to take steps to help her social development. Fortunately, preschool children can learn new social skills easily if helped by sympathetic staff and you.

HOW TO HELP

If your child has poor social skills, there are various ways that you or your child's nursery school teacher can help. These include attaching a child to something or someone that raises their standing, or giving a child a responsibility that will boost confidence.

Opposite pairing This involves pairing a neglected or unsociable child with a child who is outgoing and sociable. By being seen as the friend of a popular child, the neglected child will gain a significantly higher level of social acceptance in a short time.

Younger pairing Pairing a child with poor social skills with a younger child, can be another way of conferring status. A study carried out in the 1980s showed that when unpopular children between the ages of four and five played with children younger than themselves, their level of popularity increased by at least 50 percent. Younger playmates offer positive social experiences to neglectees and rejectees, which helps build their self-esteem and assertiveness.

Clique activities Although it might seem bad for children to form small, exclusive groups within a large group, allowing them to mix in their preferred clique motivates them to get along with their peers outside the clique. Clique-based activities give children a sense of security and confidence about all social relationships.

Small groups It's sometimes assumed that an unsociable child will become sociable when surrounded by a big group. In fact, small groupings are better at facilitating friendships because in a large group the unsociable child can remain in the background; in a small group she can't be ignored. A preschool teacher can help by placing the child in a small group, then gradually extending the size of the group.

Star responsibility Establishing definite roles, such as giving the most popular children responsible tasks to do, appears to have a settling effect on all children of nursery school age. Tasks could include giving out the straws for milk, or supervising cleanup time. Unsociable children appear to benefit from this strategy as much as other children.

YOUR CHILD'S NEW WORLD

Now that your child is socializing with children of her own age, whether at preschool or at play, she will have new concerns of which you will become aware.

• Clothes are one of the first ways of expressing individuality, and children may identify themselves with a particular peer group by the clothes they wear. By the time your child reaches preschool age, she will probably want to select her clothes each day. Encourage her sense of identity and independence by having a flexible attitude toward her clothes.

• Toys, sports equipment, any sort of collection, such as a stamp or sticker collection, books, and comics are all powerful indicators of status among children. Even earning money for doing odd jobs is a sign of prowess.

• Academic or athletic success, or popularity, also confer distinction. Some children also derive status from their parents—a high-profile or professional career, affluence, or being well-traveled are all things that carry prestige.

• If you feel that your child attaches too much value to a particular thing, or values something that is inappropriate, help her to reassess priorities and perhaps reward her for some achievement that you consider worthy.

EXPLAINING ABOUT LYING

If your child makes a habit of exaggerating the truth, it is important that you stress why telling lies is such a bad idea.

If he is old enough to understand, you could try telling him the story of "the boy who cried wolf." Afterward, talk about the story and make sure that he understands that if you can't tell the difference between what is true and what is not true, you might not know when something really important has happened to him.

LYING

In order for a child to tell a lie, he must have reached a stage in his psychological development where he can distinguish fantasy from reality. For example, if a 15-month-old baby is chastised by her mother for daubing poster paint on a wall, and he shakes his head vigorously in denial, he isn't lying—it may be that he has genuinely forgotten the action, wishes that he hadn't done it, or simply cannot recognize the difference between fantasy and reality. Only when a child reaches the age of three or four years will he be capable of lying, and most children will lie if they find a situation sufficiently threatening.

HOW SERIOUS IS LYING?

Children lie for many different reasons, and some types of lying are more serious than others. For instance, a make-believe lie is a natural part of a child's fantasy life, whereas a coverup lie is a conscious attempt to avoid punishment.

Exploratory lying This is done simply to see your response. For example, a four-year-old child will tell his mother that he didn't like his dinner even though he ate it all. This is designed to see how you will react. In most cases, your response to this kind of lying is enough to discourage him from doing it again. Some children, however, recognize that it wins attention and will employ it over and over again as they grow up. For this reason, it is serious and must be discouraged.

Bragging This type of lying usually takes the form of a greatly exaggerated story and is done to boost the child's self-confidence. A five-year-old will state boldly that he has received many expensive birthday presents or that he lives in a huge house in an attempt to impress his friends. Although bragging is generally harmless, you can discourage your child from this type of lying by reinforcing his genuine achievements.

For a small number of children, bragging can become a permanent habit. Children who brag frequently do so because they desperately want to impress their friends and parents and they want to be

Talking it through
If you discover that your child has been lying, explain what she has done wrong patiently but firmly, instead of getting angry.

loved. The danger is that people will come to view everything your child says with skepticism. Bragging lies can become a child's hallmark, and he may lose many friends as a result.

Make-believe lies These are lies that mix reality and fantasy, and they serve to add excitement to everyday experiences. For instance, a four-year-old may have a vivid imaginary world consisting of fairies, monsters, and invisible friends, all of which he can describe in colorful detail. Childhood fantasies don't really constitute lies, and they should be seen as a normal phase of child development.

Coverup lies Lies that aim to deliberately mislead are the type that parents worry about most. Children tell coverup lies to avoid being punished, and they learn this tactic at a relatively early age. In one survey, mothers were asked to identify the most common reason for their four-year-olds lying to them. Nearly half of them said that it was a lie to escape a reprimand. Coverup lies become more sophisticated and plausible as a child gets older.

Lies to avoid punishment can put parents in a difficult position. If you punish your child every time he does something wrong, he may learn to lie in response. On the other hand, if you don't reprimand your child, then he's likely to go on behaving in the same way. You need a balance between being too liberal and too punitive. I tried to encourage the truth with my children by saying that a child who told the truth would never be punished. They realized I was aware of the effort taken to be honest and promised not to lie; they rarely did.

DEALING WITH LYING

A study carried out several years ago investigated the impact of different parental responses on lying. It was found that children whose parents used moral principles to explain to their children why lying is wrong effectively reduced the frequency of lying. A parental response involving punishment increased the frequency of lying.

Children sometimes tell coverup lies not to escape punishment, but because they fear that their bad behavior will stop you from loving them. Therefore, any punishment for lying should be accompanied by reassurance. A child needs to be aware that punishment and parental love are not mutually exclusive. There is much research to show that parents who are honest with their children receive honesty in return. Make it easy for your child to confess to his misdeeds by speaking to him calmly rather than getting angry and making accusations.

Children often say things that are inaccurate or untrue, and one important reason is that they hear their parents doing it: adults frequently tell "white lies" to avoid hurting other people's feelings unnecessarily. Your child may hear you saying something that contradicts what you normally say. If the reason for such tactful conversation is not explained to him, he can't understand why it is wrong for him to do the same.

HELPING A CHILD WHO LIES

Because children lie for different reasons, every child must be treated individually. There are, however, a number of do's and don'ts that apply to all children.

- Act calmly—the child may genuinely be confusing reality and fantasy.

- Try to understand the motive for a lie. Your child is not lying because he wants to be malicious, but because he is afraid of the punishment he'll receive.

- Explain to your child why it is wrong to lie. Use examples that he can understand.

- Make punishments reasonable. If you over-punish your child, he will be more determined to lie in the future.

- Make your child aware that although you are angry with him, you still love him.

- Don't ridicule the child who persists with bragging lies. Bragging indicates low self-esteem, and you should work to increase your child's self-confidence with praise and affection.

- Don't use physical punishment on a child who lies. Research shows that constant spanking for lies only encourages children to lie more, because they are afraid of being spanked again.

STRESS

Children as well as adults can suffer from stress.

Clinginess and behavior problems can all be signs of stress. If your child is showing any of these symptoms, ask yourself if he is under strain, or if you are expecting too much of him.

WHEN THINGS GO WRONG

There are two broad categories of abnormal social development: habit disorders and behavioral disorders. The chart below sets out some of the most common and lists some of the factors that cause them. These are never sole causes, however, only characteristics of the environment created by parents. Many other factors may be involved. Of course, by no means will all children respond to these family traits with any kind of a disorder. The table is suggested only as a guide to help parents.

Factor	Habit disorder	Behavior disorder	Approach
Extreme strictness	Bed-wetting	Bullying, hitting other children, biting	Relax authoritarian attitudes to potty training. Don't scold. Give your child dedicated time. Show more affection and praise more.
	Fecal soiling (see also below)	Lying, blaming others, stealing, refusal to share	More relaxed attitude to bowel control. Never "potty-train."
		Destructiveness	Your child needs outlets for aggressive behavior. Allow boisterous play.
Overprotectiveness	Undereating (due to overfeeding)	Antisocial behavior, refusal to "join in"	Be more flexible and relaxed about food.
	Negativism, "sissy"	Becomes a loner	Encourage your child to be independent. Develop her self-respect and self-worth.
Lack of affection	Overeating to compensate	Stealing, lying, delinquency	Show your child affection and give praise.
Neglect or disorganized home	Pica (see p.222)	Lying, stealing	Give focused attention once a day.
	Fecal soiling (see also above)	Destructiveness, bullying	Give more dedicated attention every day.
Prudishness, repressiveness about nudity, extreme strictness	Possibly obsessive masturbation	Prurient interest in sex, very early sexual intercourse	Be open. Don't discourage questions about the facts of life. If you can, be relaxed about nudity.

Habit disorders involve problems with eating, passing stools, sleeping, or speaking, and behavior disorders involve problems with social conduct, such as stealing, truancy, or vandalism. Parents may sometimes feel that their child with a behavioral problem is being manipulative or vindictive. It should be realized, however, that preschoolers are generally too young to behave in a calculated way.

HABIT DISORDERS

Problems such as bed-wetting, fecal soiling, overeating, and fad-eating are found in most normal children and, as long as they only occur occasionally, they should not be perceived as disorders. However, when a child repeatedly wets her bed past the age when you would expect her to be dry, or overeats to the extent that she becomes obese, help should be sought. Habit disorders usually result from family factors, emotional trauma or conflict (such as a new baby in the family, a new home, or a change of schools), or delayed development. Occasionally, there is a physiological basis for bed-wetting and you should eliminate this possibility first.

Bed-wetting Enuresis is the most common habit disorder and is never the child's fault. It is usually nocturnal, and the most common reason is developmental delay. Most children are dry during the day and night by the age of five. Habitual bed-wetting in a seven-year-old could be considered abnormal, but is probably the result of stress on the child; it will improve when the stress is removed. Occasional bed-wetting is very common and is often caused by excitement, fear, illness, or a sense of threat, so it can be ignored.

In some families, there is a history of bed-wetting; a child should never be blamed for her slowness. Only about one in ten children suffering from enuresis has a physical or emotional disturbance, and these children usually suffer from enuresis during the day as well as the night. Physical causes include physiological or anatomical disturbance of bladder function, urinary infection, nocturnal epilepsy, and congenital abnormalities of the bladder.

Bed-wetting is sometimes an emotional response to excessive parental pressure to be clean and dry. Insufficient or inconsistent encouragement or unrealistically high expectations before the child is developmentally ready are common reasons. Bed-wetting is exacerbated by parental disapproval and teasing by siblings. Never scold or ridicule bed-wetting, and always praise success.

Measures such as restricting fluid before bedtime and waking and lifting during the night are occasionally helpful. The pad and buzzer or bedwetting alarm method of treating enuresis, in which a buzzer sounds when the bedclothes become wet, is successful in some cases, but it shouldn't be used on children under seven. The best approach to bed-wetting is to treat it as lateness rather than illness and not to draw attention to it. Very young children may stop bed-wetting if they are allowed to sleep in their parents' bedroom.

FECAL SOILING

Unlike bed-wetting, fecal soiling is unusual in potty-trained children and almost always indicates stress or emotional disturbance.

Nevertheless, a physical cause should be ruled out first, such as severe constipation with overflow of fecal material. There are three types of fecal soiling: soiling that has been present from babyhood; regressive soiling, in which a potty-trained child reverts to an earlier stage of development; and aggressive soiling, which is an emotional response to overly strict parenting, or severe or outdated potty training methods (see p.113).

Aggressive soiling usually occurs in children who have been potty-trained too early in life, because the parents place exaggerated emphasis on being clean. If a child feels stifled and isn't allowed to play and get dirty, she may express her frustration and anger through soiling.

The most effective way to deal with soiling is to reduce a child's anxiety. Very strict parents should become more relaxed, and stressful or traumatic events need to be dealt with sympathetically.

DEPRESSION

Children become depressed when they face stress they can't cope with: moving, changing schools and leaving friends behind, separation from parents, divorce, or being the subject of abuse are all examples.

It is now believed that any evaluation of learning disabilities in a child should include routine checking for depression, since the two often go hand in hand.

A depressed child may cry more than normal, lack interest in games and friends, and be irritable when efforts are being made to rouse him from his apathy. Depression rarely occurs on its own in children; it's usually combined with phobias, obsessions, and compulsive behavior. Sleep disturbance, anorexia, lack of concentration, which in turn causes difficulties at school, and tense, restless behavior are common features. Chronic depression affects the development of a child's personality—a depressed child who is hostile and rebellious may become antisocial and even delinquent as he grows up.

There are many ways to help a depressed child. If his environment is insecure, a period as a out-patient or in-patient in a children's hospital may be useful, provided it is combined with help from the whole family. Psychotherapy can help to relieve unconscious conflicts in the child, whether they are about growing up or overdependence on parents. Parents too, may need help and therapy—if they are overprotective, for instance. Every effort should be made to identify and reduce the stress on the child.

Eating disorders Refusing to eat, overeating, being excessively picky, and pica (eating things not usually considered edible) may all be classified as eating disorders if they occur frequently.

Persistent refusal to eat or picking at food is common in children of preschool age. Poor appetite may be the result of anxiety, or it may indicate a problem between parent and child. Parents may be overanxious, with exaggerated ideas about nutritional needs, or food may be used as a symbol of affection. Overfeeding results in undereating. Fortunately, food refusal in young children rarely leads to undernourishment—the best treatment is to adopt a more flexible approach to food and offer a wide range of foods.

Picky eating is common in otherwise healthy children and many children go through phases of "food fads" that eventually pass. Picky eating, unless it is excessive, is not really a problem. It is often a child's natural way of selecting a balanced diet.

Overeating is a more serious problem than food refusal or pickiness in that it can lead to obesity. Obesity is bad for a child's health, and means that he may be teased by his peers and suffer low self-esteem.

Children overeat for many different reasons; sometimes a child uses food to compensate for the fact that he feels unloved and insecure; sometimes a parent who feels inadequate will overfeed a child to make up for not giving them enough love and affection. To prevent overeating, it is essential to identify the underlying reason, whether it is insecurity on the part of the child, or conscious or unconscious overfeeding on the part of the parent. A doctor will be able to suggest a suitable reducing diet.

Pica is the consumption of substances without nutritional value, such as soil, gravel, chalk, paint, or even feces. It's most common among children who are neglected or live in dysfunctional or poor homes, but it may also be linked with iron deficiency and high lead levels. Children with pica may show other signs of disturbed behavior.

BEHAVIORAL DISORDERS

Antisocial behavior usually stems from a problem within the family or in the family's inability to adjust to society at large. A child may fail to identify himself as part of a family and to accept parental attitudes and standards of behavior. This is most likely to happen in homes where there are no consistent adult role models, or where a child is constantly being moved around, scolded, punished, or being mentally, physically, or socially abused. Common symptoms of behavioral disorders are bad language, temper tantrums, disobedience, aggression, stealing, and lying. As a child grows up, he may stay out late, be truant from school, and take drugs.

Psychologists, child psychiatrists, and social workers can provide a diagnosis of a behavioral disorder, and in some cases psychotherapy may be recommended. Since the problem often indicates an underlying problem in the family, the whole family, rather than just the individual child, may receive counseling and be assigned a social worker.

OTHER PROBLEM BEHAVIOR

Most children at some stage will indulge in behavior that you find worrisome, unacceptable, or just annoying. In the majority of cases, the reasons are quite innocent and the phase will soon pass.

Negativism Stubbornness, selfishness, and disobedience are all characteristics of negativism. To some extent, all preschoolers are negativistic. They may seem to delight in doing the opposite of what they are asked: when you want your child to go out, he decides to stay in, or when you want him to eat his food, he refuses it.

There are many reasons for resisting parental authority, and parents can misinterpret them. A child may be negativistic not because he wants to revolt against authority, but because he wants to continue what he's doing. He has no concept of time, and sees no reason why he should stop playing an enjoyable game. Reasons such as a mealtime or going to bed are irrelevant if he isn't hungry or tired.

Another explanation for negativism is that a young child can't distinguish between two opposites. He is inexperienced, his life is charged with alternatives, and often he finds it impossible to differentiate between yes and no, give and take, or push and pull. His interest in these double alternatives is so evenly balanced that he goes from one extreme to the other.

Flagrant negativism may be the result of insufficient parental encouragement. Even if your child is slow to perform a task or makes a mess, it's important that you encourage learning early on.

Stealing Between the ages of two and five or six, a child may be so attracted to an object—a toy, coins left on a table, or a candy bar—that he takes it when he hopes no one is looking. Sometimes he will do it in such a way that his theft will be discovered. Neither is a sign of a deep-rooted problem. Rather it is the normal result of overwhelming desire unchecked by social inhibitions. Don't punish the act, but don't ignore it. Tell your child clearly and calmly that it is unacceptable and insist that the object be returned. In all likelihood, one or a few such interchanges are all that's required to end the behavior.

Resistance to school A child who says he doesn't want to go to school or, more commonly, complains of a stomach- or headache on school mornings may be coming down with a mild illness; he may be unhappy about something in school; or he may not wish to leave you because of shyness or something he is worried about at home. It's best not to force your child to go to school at first, unless this is a recognized and often-repeated pattern. If an illness doesn't reveal itself in a day or two, or if your child perks up once the threat of school is removed, you should talk to his teacher to help uncover any problems. If all is well at school and reluctance to leave home is the possible cause, try a loving but firm goodbye and a warm, but restrained welcome home. If the behavior persists, consult your doctor.

SEXUAL MISBEHAVIOR

Adults tend to classify some aspects of normal development (such as games of "show") as prurient. They are quite normal stages of development, and it is only adult interference that leads to exaggerations of sexual play.

True sexual misbehavior may occur in isolation or together with other forms of antisocial behavior, such as truancy. Sexual curiosity and masturbation are common and normal features of childhood, and become abnormal only because of their frequency or the circumstances in which they occur. Unless you consider a child's sexual behavior completely unacceptable, it is important to retain a sensible attitude to this feature of childhood. Even if you do consider behavior questionable, consult your doctor before labeling your child's behavior abnormal.

CHOOSING A PRESCHOOL

When she's three or four years old, your child will be able to go to preschool, if you choose. Whether you feel this is the correct step will largely depend on her nature. For example, is she still shy and clinging, or naturally outgoing? Only you can know whether she is ready.

Before making a decision, visit several preschools in your area. Prepare a checklist of important points so you don't forget any of them. For example, are the teachers relaxed or formal? Is it a happy environment? What is the standard of facilities? How many children are there, and are they well supervised? What subjects are taught? Does the school feel safe? Are the children happy?

You should sit in on a few classes and spend a whole morning or afternoon there, and also speak to mothers whose children already attend. You will then have all the information you need to help you decide.

Early education

The decision to send your child to preschool will depend largely on the options available and whether they suit her individual needs. Find out what there is in your area and try to visit preschools and talk to teachers and other parents to get a good idea of what's provided.

CHOOSING PRESCHOOL EDUCATION

There is no single kind of preschool that is best for every child. Each child should be in a school that fits her particular needs. All evaluations of preschool education show mixed results. One long-term assessment showed that boys in Montessori programs sustained gains in reading and math throughout their school careers. Other research shows that intellectual gains are found in all but the poorest of programs. But it's difficult to know how long these benefits last. Evaluations of Head Start, for example, show that apparent IQ differences between children in Head Start and those who don't attend preschool diminish over time. Whatever the benefits of preschool education, there is no substitute for a loving and caring home environment.

Play groups often take children from as early as two-and-a-half years old. They provide the opportunity for interaction with other children of the same age and help develop early social skills, but in a less formal atmosphere than preschool.

Preschool has some benefits. Your child can develop a greater sense of confidence and therefore more self-control, as well as learning to share, to be concerned for the needs of others, and to take turns. Your child's skill in planning ahead and cooperating with others will improve through fantasy and group play.

WHAT PRESCHOOL CAN DO FOR YOUR CHILD

The opportunities for play in preschool enhance the various ways that your child thinks—that is, imaginatively, speculatively, and inventively. These are characteristics that are often found in intellectual and creative children. Some preschools are designed to help disadvantaged children by building up their confidence. Children who attend such preschools turn out to be less likely to repeat a grade in school than their peers who did not attend preschool. They are also less in need of special education, and less likely to show delinquent behavior later on when they reach adolescence.

I think there are very few risks to your child's attending preschool, certainly no more than when she ventures outside of the family; she'll just encounter them sooner. Risks may include minor health problems, or exposure to behavior you find objectionable, such as swearing and racy stories.

SETTLING IN

You can help your child adjust to preschool by taking her along for one or two visits well in advance of her start date. Encourage her to play with the other children, and to sit at one of the desks or play with some of the equipment. But try not to push her to socialize with other children if she doesn't seem eager at first. Some children are naturally more gregarious than others, and she will adjust in her own good time. The aim is to make her visits as enjoyable as possible. If you stress all the fun things she will do, her eager anticipation for school will be stronger than her worry about leaving you. If she is having trouble adjusting, most preschools will let you stay with her on the first day, and for steadily decreasing periods of time on the following days. Make sure you pick her up yourself for the first week, when she is most insecure. Once she is confident that she's not being abandoned, you'll be free to make other arrangements for picking her up.

Your child's personality, maturity, place in the family, and willingness to leave home will all influence the way she settles down at preschool. In general, boys are more likely than girls of the same age to cry when their mothers first leave them at preschool, and they tend to cry when frustrated or angry with a teacher or helper. On the other hand, your child may enjoy being with other children as much as she does anything else about preschool. It's not unusual for two little boys or girls to rush eagerly toward each other when they meet at school.

Although your child is now attending preschool, this doesn't mean that your part in her education is finished. Ask her what she did each day at preschool and who she played with. By getting her to talk over her school experiences, you will be consolidating the new words and skills she is learning. You can help her to improve her use of language by repeating what she says in the correct form, though not by directly correcting her. Your child will be constantly seeking new information, and you should always try to answer her questions truthfully. If you don't know the answer, it is best to suggest you both look it up in a book, or ask Daddy if he knows, rather than just try to fudge an answer or change the subject.

HOW CHILDREN BEHAVE AT PRESCHOOL

As a rule, boys are more task-oriented in preschool play, and little girls talk more about being friends, recognizing similarities in each other, admiring one another's clothes, discussing who's friends with who, and so on.

Dominant and aggressive behavior in little boys is very much in evidence in a preschool setting. Intelligence and ability to get along with others are as important to popularity in preschool as a boy's size or physical prowess. Popularity fluctuates from day to day. Hitting is a common form of aggressiveness. A few girls strike out at other girls, but their hitting is usually not effective. Boys take longer to learn not to hit others and make unprovoked, if rather mild, attacks on girls. They will, for example, push little girls or gesture menacingly at them.

APPROACHES TO PRESCHOOL

No single method of preschool has proved to be significantly better for every child. Many parents send their children to preschool to give them an opportunity to play and be sociable, others simply because it allows their children physical outlets that won't damage the furniture.

Structured classes are better suited to the needs of most small children. A chaotic environment may cause some boys to react in a way that some teachers describe as hyperactive. Structures vary within preschools. Some preschools follow a timetable for certain activities each day, along the lines advocated by Dr. Montessori, and organize the school around an orderly, child-sized environment with specific behavioral guidelines, such as putting things away when they are finished with.

A child who finds tasks easy and has lots of local friends may enjoy a traditional preschool. However, a child who has few local playmates and wants to socialize may enjoy a less structured preschool.

GIRLS AT SCHOOL

Girls, in general, have a greater aptitude for subjects involving language skills, such as reading. They're also more likely to prefer games that involve social interaction with other girls.

This innate tendency may be reinforced by parents and teachers who steer them toward certain activities that involve "playing quietly" and away from others more associated with boys. Whatever the reasons, girls at school generally follow certain patterns of behavior. They:

• Prefer to play with other girls in games involving a strong element of cooperation. They will often shy away from boys, especially those engaged in boisterous or aggressive play.

• Tend to choose activities involving books (words or pictures). On the other hand, they will be more anxious than boys about math and other number-based activities.

• Are generally well motivated and more willing to conform. However, this may mean that teachers assume they are coping well with lessons and so they may receive less attention than boys.

GOING TO SCHOOL

Starting school will be a great milestone for your child, and for you. You'll both have to make adjustments: your child will discover a new, exciting world, and you'll have to adjust to his growing independence.

IS YOUR CHILD READY?

Most children in the US start kindergarten at around six years of age—but many parents are eager to send their children earlier if places are available, to give them a "head start." It is biology and not the calendar that determines your child's readiness for school. Certain physical skills are therefore usually taken as signs that he has reached the level of mental development necessary for school success. These include being able to catch a large ball, hop on one foot, and run and stop on a signal. Your child must be capable of taking care of his bodily needs, such as going to the bathroom independently, fastening his shoes, and dressing himself. He should also know his full name and be able to ask clear and concise questions. Many five-year-olds are proud of learning numbers and their ability to count. They also demonstrate their maturity by making strong efforts to keep themselves under control. You can begin to introduce all these things to your child before he starts school.

If you are unsure whether your child is ready, ask a preschool teacher. A teacher with ten years' experience has probably taught over two hundred children and so should be very accurate at predicting whether your child will do well at school.

School readiness checklist

Your child need not have mastered every skill on the list. Use it only as a guide, and consult a teacher at your chosen school.

• Join in the shared activities of a group
• Listen to a story and retell events in sequence
• Join in and readily follow instructions for games or new activities
• Express ideas and needs clearly to others
• Hop, skip, and jump
• Help around the house doing simple tasks
• Recognize basic colors and shapes
• Recognize similarities and differences in sound
• Join in songs and know some simple ones by heart
• Cope with buttons, shoelaces, and zippers, and cut with scissors
• Copy simple figures, including a circle, square, and triangle
• Attend to personal hygiene needs

HELPING YOUR CHILD ENJOY SCHOOL

Your child is more likely to succeed at school if he has the right frame of mind to begin with. You can achieve this by preparing your child before he starts so that he is physically and mentally ready for the demands that school will make on him. Encourage him to carry out simple tasks so that he understands the concept of responsibility. Make sure his play involves imagination and creativity, as well as opportunities for learning and developing his memory. It is important, too, that the school provides the right environment for your child's education, with motivated teachers who have a good relationship with their pupils.

Your child will undoubtedly benefit if you take an interest in his schoolwork and can continue his education at home. However, there is a real danger that you will do more harm than good if your methods are very different from those being taught at school. Teaching methods change over the years, so the current system probably bears no relation to the way you were taught. To avoid this, talk to your child's teacher about the school's particular methods and find out at first hand about the subjects they are teaching and the textbooks that are in use. You may be able to borrow books and equipment overnight. Some schools actively encourage parents to sit in on classes as observers, or you may even be able to help out. But don't overdo the schoolwork. Home should also be a place of comfort and refuge, so you will need to strike a balance between helping your child progress with his education and overloading him with work.

YOUR CHANGING RELATIONSHIP

Your child's first days at school mark a change in his relationship with you. Until now, he has been dependent on you for everything, but now he'll have to begin to learn to become independent, responsible for all his own decisions and actions. This change doesn't happen overnight, but it is important to begin the process by encouraging your child to take on more and more responsibility. By now he should already bathe and dress himself and he might be expected to care for his schoolbag, books, and other equipment, and to lay his things out each night for the next day.

He'll feel very grown-up, and will not want to be fussed over, but you should always be ready to give a cuddle whenever he shows he needs one. It is hard for your child to accept that he isn't fully grown up, and the emotional drain of daily social interaction may occasionally be too much for him. As with most things, a hug from you is the best remedy and will set him up for the next day.

You may find that your child won't want such public displays of affection as he used to have, particularly not in front of his new friends. Don't feel snubbed. He is simply asserting himself as independent—grown up enough not to need a kiss from Mom. More than anything else, it's important not to push too hard, even in asking what happened during his day. Clever prompting will be all you need to hear about his time at school, but prying will only make him secretive.

BOYS AT SCHOOL

Boys, generally, have a greater aptitude for activities involving spatial skills, such as building games. They're likely to prefer games that involve competition and physical activity.

As with girls, this innate tendency may be strengthened by adults. Boys may be encouraged to take up "boyish" activities that "let off steam" or involve construction, and unconsciously discouraged from contemplative pursuits, such as reading. As a result, they tend to behave in certain ways at school. They:

• Prefer playing with other boys, especially in energetic games that involve physical activity, such as climbing or mock fighting.

• Concentrate on toys that aid mathematical and spatial skills. They will also persevere with a difficult math question until they solve it.

• Become more disruptive if they do not get attention or are having difficulty with a subject. This may mean that the teacher will spend a disproportionate amount of time with the boys compared with girls.

CHAPTER 4

Family life

If you've never had a child, you may imagine that you can incorporate a baby into your life with minimal disruption. This is rarely the case. A new baby is a 24-hour-a-day commitment, and you'll find that, at least for a few months, your normal lifestyle will change enormously. This will be all the more true if you have twins or even triplets.

Your relationship with your partner will also be different. There will be less time for intimacy and companionship, and you may find you need to stop and take stock of your joint responsibilities. Childcare is often thought of as a woman's job, but there is no biological reason why this should be so. Shared parenting will reap benefits for you and your partner, as well as your child.

You may want to involve other members of your family in helping to bring up your baby, especially if you are a single parent, or if you and your partner both go out to work. Alternatively, you may decide to employ a nanny, au pair, or babysitter, or send your child to daycare. Whichever choice you make, planning ahead and organizing your time is of paramount importance.

MOTHER
KNOWS BEST?

**The argument that women
are better equipped for
parenthood than men
is no longer valid.**

Sixty years ago it was not
uncommon for a women to have
ten children or more, and young
girls were more likely to be involved
in caring for them. Nowadays, most
mothers have never seen a newborn
until they give birth.

If a woman does have more
experience of caring for a baby than
her partner, it's important that she
doesn't mock his efforts, since
he may respond by withdrawing his
help altogether. When this happens,
the role of each parent becomes
polarized, increasing pressure on the
mother and isolating the father from
the family unit.

Becoming a family

No matter how many baby books you read, and no matter how
well prepared you are, you can still be knocked sideways by the
impact of a newborn baby on your life. As well as the physical
requirements of caring for a baby, your normal domestic chores,
such as doing laundry, will at least quadruple.

After the first few weeks, when relatives and neighbors stop dropping
by to offer congratulations, the novelty of being home alone with a
new baby can wear off rapidly. Mothers who have given up a job or a
career may find that what they miss is not their work, but their work
environment. They miss social interaction with their friends and
colleagues. In particular, they miss the difference between work and
home. With a young baby, you don't have the luxury of leaving your
work behind.

Many people also find that making the transition from being
a couple to being a family can prove more traumatic than they
imagine. The dynamics in a relationship need to adapt to a new
addition. Problems can arise when a couple finds it difficult to fit
another person into the complex equation of human emotions
that makes up a relationship.

NEW RESPONSIBILITIES

The arrival of a child means that choices become stark: beforehand,
for instance, if neither partner wanted to clean the bathroom floor,
it could be left until later. But a baby can never be left until later.
His needs take priority and somebody has to take immediate
responsibility for meeting them. Time that was previously spent
on other things must now be given to the baby.

Ideally, these lifestyle changes are shared
equally within a partnership, but in
practice women very often end up taking
on the main burden. Depending on
individual expectations, this can lead to
deep resentment within a relationship,
causing a couple to drift apart after the
birth of their baby.

Research in the US has shown that one
in every two marriages goes into decline
after the birth of the first child. All of the

Shared parenting
*Spend time with your partner
getting to know your child and
learning to be parents together.*

couples in the study, no matter how well-adjusted, experienced on average a 20 percent increase in conflict within their marriage during the first year of parenthood. Although conflict can sometimes be healthy, it is often not what new parents expect.

To reduce the stress placed on a partnership, it is vital that each partner has at least some idea of what to expect and is able to compromise. Having a baby means rearranging your life.

EQUAL PARENTING

Although the role of men in parenting has changed over the last few decades, the attitude that childcare is primarily a woman's responsibility still persists. Ideally, you and your partner should discuss your respective roles before your baby is born. Women should make their partners aware that being a good father doesn't just mean helping the mother: it means being a father to the child as well.

It's important for you and your partner to share the childcare as far as possible. If a father isn't involved in caring for his child, it can be limiting in two ways. First, a father's relationship with his partner may suffer if she feels resentment at a lack of help and support. Second, if a father doesn't play an active role in the early months and years of his baby's life, he may lose the chance to form a close childhood bond with his son or daughter. A detached father will have a negative effect on his child. Girls may have trouble interacting with men, and boys will be deprived of a male role model.

FATHERING

Many of us remember our fathers seeming more distant and unapproachable than our mothers, but there is no reason why a child can't enjoy an equally close relationship with both parents. A baby's relationships don't operate on an either/or basis and you should never worry that if a baby spends an equal amount of time with her father, she might love her mother less. All young children need as much love as they can get, and both parents should do their utmost to provide it.

Today it may be economic factors that determine who is left holding the baby. If a woman earns more than her partner, or if he is unemployed, many couples can't afford to let misplaced male pride reduce their monthly income. While the rise of the house-husband has undoubtedly benefited lots of families, it is important to bear in mind that the man left at home with a small child suffers from the same problems as a woman: isolation and boredom.

DADS—YOUR NEW ROLE

The way to conquer your new role is to assume it fully. There is nothing more unsatisfactory than having imagined yourself a headliner and being reduced to a walk-on part.

If you grasp fatherhood with both hands by actively caring for your child along with your partner, you will establish yourself as pivotal in your family and the rewards for you will be in the depth of the relationship with your child and in the strengthening of your relationship with your partner.

If you feel your life has been turned upside down by the arrival of your baby, you are one of the only two people who can put it right. Life won't ever be the same again, but that will only be a cause for regret if you stand on the sidelines of family life instead of fashioning it for yourself.

Parental bonding
Your child can't have too much love and attention, so both of you should give as much as possible.

231

A FATHER'S STORY

Anna and Henry Ewington experienced a bad few months after their son Alexander was born. Anna was exhausted, depressed, and overwhelmed, and Henry didn't feel very paternal.

Henry attributes this to the fact that he measured fatherhood in terms of doing things, and that Anna quickly took all responsibility for the baby.

Henry's frustration intensified Anna's difficulties. For the first three months she experienced periods of post-partum depression. Their sex life deteriorated, and Henry started to feel rejected by Anna, both physically and emotionally. In just a few months, they decided it was crunch time.

"We decided it had to be 'make' instead of 'break' when we found out Anna was pregnant with Leora only ten months after the birth of Alex. I realized then that I had to give Anna enormous credit for being able to cope with it all. I half expected her to cave in, but instead she became stronger, perhaps because of having to cope with Alex."

During the third month of Anna's pregnancy, she had a threatened miscarriage. She was advised to stay in bed, and Henry decided to take unpaid leave from work so that he could take care of her.

"For the first time since the birth, Anna felt as though I was doing my part, and I felt, for once, that I was the linchpin of our family unit. Despite the emotional strain, I'm glad we went through it. It has made me an equal parent with Anna, whereas before I felt like an observer."

GRANDPARENTS

With the arrival of a first child, grandparents can be supportive, or they can be the source of increased tension, especially if family relations are already strained. You will probably find that you see more of your in-laws once your baby is born, and hopefully this will contribute to a happier family life.

Sometimes, however, the intimacy and interdependency of family relations means there is a thin line between helpfulness and interference. Ideally, you and your partner will have discussed the role you want grandparents to play. Once both of you have decided how much help you do or don't want, you will find it easier to establish your authority by setting out the rules in advance.

Many grandparents, particularly grandmothers, want to show you how they coped with a crying baby or a disobedient toddler. This advice is usually well-meant and may be welcome. If it isn't, say so. Point out that he's your baby and caring for him is your responsibility. If you occasionally make mistakes, they will be your own. It's certainly worth persevering to overcome problems so that your child can benefit from a secure and loving relationship with his grandparents.

A SPECIAL RELATIONSHIP

A good relationship between a grandparent and grandchild is rewarding for the whole family. Grandparents can offer a more relaxed perspective about your children; parents can rest assured in the knowledge that when grandparents are in attendance, their baby will be well cared for; and a baby can learn to form an important emotional bond beyond his mother and father.

Grandparents can form special relationships with their grandchildren for several reasons. First, they see them less frequently than their parents, which alleviates the strain of day-to-day care. Second, ultimate responsibility for a child rests with his parents. This frees grandparents to enjoy the thrill of parenthood without the accompanying

Second time around
Your parents and your partner's parents are likely to have a relaxed attitude toward childcare.

worries and stresses. Third, a grandparent has already brought up at least one child, and problems are always easier to cope with the second time around. Grandparents are also likely to have more quality time to spend with their grandchildren.

As children become young adults with problems of their own, grandparents can offer a broader perspective on the difficulties facing them. A grandparent is likely to be the oldest person that your child will ever know as a friend, and can give your child an insight into how things were in the past.

Not all families, however, can enjoy the benefits of an extended family. This is particularly true today, as financial pressures force couples to move to where they can find work. Divorce can also limit grandparents' access to their grandchildren. This can be terribly upsetting for grandparents and grandchildren alike, and it helps if a child continues to see his grandparents regularly.

LOVE AND SECURITY

The most basic needs of any young child are physical care and emotional love and security. If a child feels well cared for, he will develop into a more outgoing and relaxed person. A child who is given enough love and security at an early age is likely to become less demanding as he grows older. Conversely, a child that is emotionally neglected may grow up insecure, clingy, and fearful.

It's important that parents don't shy away from giving their child adequate love and security for fear of "spoiling" him. Although it's true that a child shouldn't get into the habit of thinking he can have anything he wants, it's even more important that he doesn't get into the habit of thinking he isn't loved.

Remember, your child's way of seeing things is very different from yours. Small and apparently trivial displays of affection (a hug, a pat, a kiss) will do much more to shape the personality of your young child than anything else. It's no good loving your child and trying not to show it, in the mistaken assumption that this will make him a "stronger" person. In fact, the opposite is true.

Affection produces emotional and physical results. For instance, when young babies are held in their mother's arms, they breathe more slowly, have a steadier respiration, cry less, and sleep more. This isn't so surprising, since cuddling takes a child back to the comforting sensation of the uterus when he was warm and secure. Hugging is also the best way of communicating to a young child that you love and care for him. If your child sees his parents hugging each other, he'll know that, in spite of any arguments you might have, you still love each other.

Even if your child can feel that you love him through your physical affection, it's also important that he hears it. Toddlers especially need to hear that you love them. They have reached the stage where they can tell you that they love you, and they need this affection to be reciprocated. Never be shy about showing your love—it's the most important thing you will ever share.

GIVING AFFECTION

Loving touch is crucial to our well-being and, in the case of babies has even been shown to promote physical development.

If you're not sure how to increase the amount of physical affection you show your child, consider some of the following suggestions. These combine physical attention with love and companionship—exactly what every child needs.

• Try carrying a young baby in a baby sling; almost all newborn babies love the sensation of being strapped close to you.

• Every so often, give your baby a soothing rub with baby lotion or a massage (see pp.76–77).

• Share a bath together, but be sure to hold him close to you so that he feels warm and secure in the water.

• As he gets older, do some exercise together—this doesn't have to be anything more complicated than putting a record on and dancing around the room.

• Have a few rough-and-tumble games; many mothers leave this to the father or to other children, and particularly neglect to do so with girls.

• Curl up in bed with your child, and every now and then, sleep in together, so that your child starts the day knowing he is well loved.

The single parent

Case study

Name Nicole Killen
Age 34 years
Occupation Office manager
Obstetric history Normal pregnancy. Matthew born two days after due date

Name Matthew Killen
Age 15 months
Medical history Asthma diagnosed when 6 months old.

Nicole was convinced that one day she would meet a wonderful man who loved her completely, and hat they would have a caring relationship in a loving home. But it didn't happen. "Whether it was circumstance or coincidence I don't know, but

when I found out I was pregnant with Matthew, it seemed as though I was being given a chance to actively take control of my life, instead of waiting for someone else—who might never arrive—to do it for me."

When Nicole became pregnant with Matthew three years ago, she found herself in a difficult and unexpected situation. At the time, she was having a casual affair with a work colleague. "I found myself in a quandary because throughout my whole life, I never once envisioned myself as a single mother. I had grown up thinking a child should be the product of a loving relationship. But I knew that this wasn't a relationship I wanted to remain permanent."

FIRST REACTIONS

"The thought of becoming an unmarried single mother took a lot of getting used to. Initially, my own mother, who is quite conservative, reacted very badly, which made things even harder. She's come around to the idea now, but that's because Matthew is a lovable toddler whom she adores madly."

Nicole was entitled to three months' maternity leave by the Family Medical Leave Act, but since her employer was not obligated to pay her for this time she settled on taking two months, which was all she could afford. The first weeks went quite smoothly—Matthew was quite a placid baby, and by the eighth week he usually slept five hours each night. "In fact, although I was exhausted, Matthew gave me so much joy that I took an unexpected delight in having him all to myself."

UNEXPECTED PROBLEMS

After three months, Nicole was torn between staying at home and going back to work, but in the end, despite financial pressures, she decided to stay at home. "I felt Matthew was just too young to leave with an unknown babysitter. It was only toward the end of the fifth month that I started to experience problems.

"The worst part was never having anyone to vent to at the end of the day. You can't moan to a six-month-old. Little problems and nagging worries developed into overblown crises that kept me awake for hours at night. The week before my maternity leave was up, Matthew got a mild chest infection. Although it wasn't serious, I became so worried that I developed severe insomnia and was prescribed some tranquilizers."

Matthew's chest infection lasted for three weeks, and the doctor then diagnosed asthma. Nicole was immediately convinced that Matthew was a "sickly" baby who would be ill for the rest of his life. "If there had been someone else to share the worry with, I'm sure I wouldn't have reacted so badly," she recalls.

RETURNING TO WORK

"I felt I had to put off returning to work for another month. Then, when the day finally arrived, I was surprised by my own anxiety—not so much because I had to leave Matthew (I left him asleep with my mother) but because halfway to work I started to wonder if I could still do my job. The job I have is quite high-pressure—it's up to me to keep everything running smoothly from 9 a.m. to 6:30 p.m. I worked four days a week, and it wasn't easy worrying all day at work, and then worrying all night at home."

At this point, Nicole's mother moved in with her for five weeks so that she could have some time to adjust to being a single working mother. Having her there made Nicole realize that, although she couldn't afford it, she had to consider full-time help at least until the end of the first year. She contacted a local parents' group, who sent her advice on hiring a nanny.

EMPLOYING A NANNY

When Matthew was eight months old, Nicole hired her first full-time nanny. The cost, for someone on her salary, was crippling. She also realized that, although she got a bit more sleep, most of the time she found it impossible to stay in bed and leave it to the nanny when she heard Matthew crying. "It may have been that his asthma made me overprotective, or it may simply have been that I didn't like sharing my home with a relative stranger—whatever the reason, after two months I asked the nanny to leave, and decided to care for Matthew on my own."

This helped ease the financial situation, which by that point had become quite critical. It was still hard for Nicole to go out, because she couldn't afford to spend money on a babysitter and an evening's entertainment. She realized, nearly a year after the birth, that she hadn't been out socially since having the baby.

A LIFE OF HER OWN

"That was when I had the idea of having my first post-Matthew dinner party. About eight friends came around, each with a homemade dish, and we had a fabulous evening without waking Matthew once. Having the dinner party made an enormous difference to me. It was the first time I felt as though I was a social being again, rather than just a single mother. About a week later I managed to get off the tranquilizers permanently."

Two months after Matthew's first birthday, Nicole arranged daycare so that a nanny took care of him him three days a week, and he stayed with his grandmother one day a week. "This was the first time that things seemed to calm down enough for me to enjoy being a parent. I got used to the asthma attacks, and no longer panicked unnecessarily. My job was more under control and I even began to nurture an infrequent social life. I no longer feel any guilt about having Matthew on my own, because I know he is well cared for and that he receives a huge amount of love."

BE NICE TO YOURSELF

Learning to care for your new baby in the first weeks can be overwhelming, so remember to take care of yourself, too.

• Get your partner to help out with the baby so you can have some time to yourself.

• Don't expect to be a perfect mother right away. You have a lot to learn, and your baby is learning too.

• Let the housework go. Do only the essential tasks, and get someone else to do them if you can.

• Low potassium levels can contribute to a feeling of exhaustion. Eat plenty of potassium-rich foods, such as bananas, tomatoes, dried apricots, and plain yogurt.

• Don't be surprised if you get the "baby blues"—up to 80 percent of mothers do, and it will pass after about ten days. If depression persists, however, you should seek help very quickly.

Organizing your life

As any mother knows, the physical, emotional, and social demands on your life seem to multiply unendingly with the arrival of a new baby. Interrupted nights and hectic days, coupled with the psychological pressure of taking responsibility for a new person, combine to heap unexpected stresses onto a new mother.

Organization can be the key to survival. Pregnancy is the ideal time to sit down and take stock of the situation before you are swept away by the joys and traumas of parenthood. No matter what stage you are at, however, it is never too late to organize your time so that you get more out of it.

When you are planning your post-baby life, try dividing up things you have to think about into three or four areas: baby-related, work-related (house and/or office), partner-related, and you. This fourth category is usually undervalued, but happens to be one of the most important. If you aren't happy, your baby won't be happy. There are certain things that you will find helpful to think about in advance. For instance, if you are a working mother, have you spoken to your manager about if and when you want to return to work? Have you considered going back but working reduced hours? Is it possible for you to do a job-share?

If you will be working part-time, you should find out which benefits you're entitled to—they may not be the same as the ones you had previously. You don't want to discover that you might be facing a pay cut when you've already committed yourself to expensive childcare.

Establishing a routine A lot of the work you do in caring for your baby involves repetitive tasks, and these will be much easier to manage if you can work out some sort of timetable. Your routine should follow your baby's needs, not vice versa, so you won't be able to establish it right away; it will take your baby three to six weeks or longer to settle into a pattern of feeding and sleeping.

Be careful not to confuse organization with regimentation. You don't want your life to be inflexible, since the needs of a young child can change hourly. What is important is that the routine you create for yourself doesn't either bore you or ignore your needs.

TIME FOR YOURSELF

You are your child's universe, so it's best for her if you're not irritable, grumpy, and jaded. While you must make every effort to meet your baby's needs, you must also look out for your own needs.

Plan at least half an hour each day to devote entirely to yourself—you may want to take a bath, read a book, watch television, write a letter, meditate, exercise, listen to music, manicure your nails, or give yourself a facial. Before the baby arrives, finding half an hour for yourself seems simple, but once she is born it can seem like an impossible task.

If you are to make some space for yourself, the first thing you must do is learn to accept offers of help graciously. Too many mothers feel they are failures if they don't personally attend to their child's every need. This can be a dangerous route to go down. It is based on unrealistic expectations and eventually leads to nervous exhaustion or even breakdown.

GETTING AWAY

If you and your partner have already discussed how you are going to share the new workload (see Equal parenting, p.231), the next stage is discussing how you can make some time for each other once the baby has arrived. Try to arrange for a babysitter to come at least once a month or, better still, once a week, so that parenting doesn't take over every single waking second of your lives.

Look into the possibilities of nanny-sharing (see p.241) or, if you are not working full-time, see if you can arrange a "baby-swap" with another mother. Find out if your gym, or perhaps even a local college or university, offers babysitting. This is an ideal way to meet friends, take up an interest, or increase your qualifications while your child is cared for and socializes with other children of her own age.

Spending time apart from your child doesn't necessarily make you a worse parent—in fact, in most cases it makes you a better one. If you spend all your time with your child, she'll develop unrealistic expectations of relationships in general, and is likely to become overly demanding of friends and teachers alike.

Moreover, although your child needs a close and loving relationship with you, it is a mistake to think that she needs your company every second of the day. She will gain confidence and valuable social skills by learning to interact with adults and other children.

TIME AS A COUPLE

As well as making time for yourself, it's important to have some time as a couple, without your baby. It's hard to be spontaneous now, so planning to spend time together becomes very important.

It may seem odd to make a formal appointment to spend time with your partner, but it really can help you keep up a healthy relationship. It needn't be an elaborate arrangement—it could be something as simple as always having a cup of coffee and chat at the end of the day or planning to go swimming together every Sunday while a friend or relative looks after your baby. Don't feel guilty—keeping your relationship strong is as important for your baby as it is for you.

Handing over
Your baby doesn't need you every minute of the day, so let someone else take care of her now and then while you go out.

YOU AND YOUR PARTNER

TIPS FOR MOTHERS

Your partner will quickly start to feel he is neither wanted nor needed if you give all your attention to the baby.

• Always ask your partner for help; you can't expect him to know how much you need it unless you tell him.

• Involve him in the day-to-day care of the baby as soon and as much as possible.

• Don't refuse help when it's offered even if you feel you might do better on your own—it's his child, too.

• Do your best, no matter how unsociable you feel, to give your partner some of your attention and your affection.

• If he is turning out to be a reluctant father and you are at the end of your tether, leave him a phone number, hand him the baby, and go out for the evening—he'll soon realize how much hard work it can be!

Sharing feelings
Always make time to talk to your partner so you can avoid misunderstandings.

When your baby arrives, your relationship with your partner changes immediately. All the common interests and experiences that previously held you together (your social life, your sex life, hobbies, vacations, and so on) suddenly go out the window overnight. You are likely to be so exhausted that your partner's needs are the last thing on your mind.

The discipline that a new baby imposes on your life makes keeping excitement and sparkle in a relationship a great effort. That's why many couples feel it's just never the same—and they're right. Sometimes it's better than it ever was before, but problems arise when one partner, inevitably the father, feels excluded.

YOUR PARTNER'S FEELINGS

Although it is widely acknowledged that a mother undergoes huge upheavals during and after pregnancy, there is less appreciation of the effects that a new baby has on a father. Most fathers who accompany their partners through labor are in a state of shock after the birth. They are often traumatized by seeing their partners in considerable pain and distress. In fact, research has shown that nearly one in ten fathers suffers serious postpartum depression. One of the reasons suggested is that parental roles have changed so much in the last 20 or 30 years, making it more difficult than ever for fathers to adjust to parenthood.

Unless you make an effort with your partner, he may start to feel that "three's a crowd" and that he's being pushed out. It's unwise to let this type of situation develop, not just because you need your partner's help, but because he should spend as much time as possible with your baby at an early age. This will help him to build a close and loving relationship that lasts throughout your baby's childhood.

THE "REJECTED" FATHER

Be aware that barriers between you and your partner are likely to spring from the fact that, as one psychologist put it, "although men and women become parents at the same time, they don't become parents in the same way." There are many sociological, financial, and environmental reasons for this, but the result is often straightforward resentment or jealousy.

A man can quickly feel isolated within the family unit. He suddenly finds his partner's time monopolized by the new addition, and unless he is taking an active role in caring for the baby, he's no longer sure where he fits in. It is quite common to find a father becoming jealous of his own child. This situation may be exacerbated if there were differences of opinion about having the child in the first place (men often complain of being "pushed" into having a baby).

Your partner may find these feelings particularly difficult to deal with if he also feels rejected on a sexual level. Often men take a new mother's diminished sex drive as a personal rebuff. If possible, discuss the effects this may have on your relationship before the baby arrives.

POSTPARTUM SEX

If you haven't lost your desire for sex, that's wonderful and you should make the most of it. There's no reason to wait for your first six-week checkup to have sex if you feel physically fit enough, but check with your doctor first. For some women, however, especially those that have had episiotomies, sex isn't on the agenda.

After the baby arrives, your partner may share your lack of interest in sex, but if he doesn't, one sure way to make him understand is to let him feel your episiotomy scar—most men will be very sympathetic.

A reduced sex drive is natural in that nature is doing her best to furnish you with the most reliable contraceptive of all—abstinence. After all, the last thing any new mother wants is to find that she's pregnant again so soon after her first baby.

Try to impress upon your partner, however, that there may be emotional as well as physiological reasons for your not wishing to have sex, and he needs to respect these equally.

COMMUNICATION

During the initial months of parenthood, both of you should make real efforts to keep the lines of communication open between you. No matter how exhausted or disoriented you may be, it is essential that you find the time to explain your feelings to each other.

Having a child changes things forever. If you are the one to spend most time with your new baby, you'll be distracted from the fact that you have temporarily lost your lover. The same can't necessarily be said for your partner—if he isn't so involved in the day-to-day care of your baby, it's only natural that he feels the change in your relationship more acutely.

Let your partner help with the baby as much as possible (see Tips for mothers, left). Too often, women involve their partners by giving them tasks that are only indirectly linked to the baby. When a mother says, "I'll get Samantha ready while you run the bath," she is sharing some of the work, but not the child. Try reversing some of these options so that your partner spends sufficient time with the baby, and make sure that both of you consider the advice given in the columns on the left and right.

An active father
A father who helps care for his child will feel needed by both his partner and the baby.

TIPS FOR FATHERS

Once your baby is born, you need to be sensitive to the needs of your partner, and prepared for the physical and emotional difficulties that she may experience.

• Don't leave the entire care of your child to your partner, even if she doesn't seem to mind. There may be hidden resentment and you'll lose the chance to be a real father.

• Spend time alone with your baby; this will increase your confidence and give your partner a break.

• If you're working, talk to your employers about the new addition to your family. Consider taking at least two weeks off work when the baby is born, and see if you can change some of your working hours.

FEEDING

You must decide how you want your baby to be fed while you're out at work.

If you begin working before he is six months old—that is, before any mixed feeding—you will need to plan ahead. Introduce a routine so that feeding times are predictable and constant. If you feed your baby at breakfast and around 6 p.m., the person who takes care of him during the day need give only the expressed milk or milk formula for the other two daytime feedings.

If you don't want your baby to have any milk substitutes, freeze expressed breast milk; it will keep for up to three months in the freezer. It should take about two weeks to get into this routine. You will need to run down your daytime milk production before returning to work or you will be uncomfortable during the day.

RETURNING TO WORK

You will need to find out what the legal requirements are regarding when you need to return to work. When it's time for you to return to work, you may realize that you haven't given yourself enough time to readjust after pregnancy. It's always a good idea to consult your doctor, since there are health factors to consider about which she can advise you. Some mothers find that they can't bring themselves to leave their baby, while others—even though they adore the baby—are climbing the walls and ready to "escape."

If you have made the decision to return to work, be assured that as long as you arrange good childcare (see below), you will not be neglecting your child. There is no danger of your young baby forgetting who you are, or transferring his affection to his daytime caregiver. The really important thing is that when you get home, you spend quality time with your child.

I know from my own experience as a working mother that guilt pangs are inevitable. I felt certain, however, that my baby would instinctively know I was his mother. I was reassured when I later came across research showing that very young babies are quite able to single out their parents (whether biological or adoptive) due to the loving, interested attention that only parents can give. Similarly, it has been shown that premature babies can distinguish between the touch of their parents' hands through an incubator and the more matter-of-fact handling of nursing staff.

The important point is that it is the quality of the time you spend that counts more than the quantity. Love isn't measured in time: love is what you put into time, no matter how short.

CHILD AND CAREER

The job you face at home is twice as demanding as the one you face at work, and your terms of employment are worse. After all, you are expected to work seven days a week, 365 days a year. You will be frowned upon if you don't cook, clean, iron, entertain, and provide advice, nursing care, and sympathy continuously for at least 18 years, if not indefinitely. Your efforts will go largely unnoticed by society and, of course, you won't get paid a penny. In fact, you will have to pay for the privilege of being a parent—but as most parents will tell you, despite the job description, it's a privilege worth paying for!

Your child's first step, first smile, and first word are all priceless personal achievements. Helping to mold a tiny baby into a thoughtful, well-adjusted individual is a task requiring sacrifice, responsibility and, above all, love. It also yields huge emotional dividends. To my mind, this makes parenting one of the most important and rewarding jobs in the world. Given this, it is disturbing to see the low status attached to parenting, particularly for women, who shoulder much of the burden. Being a good parent involves helping your child's personality to develop in a positive sense, and being a good role model. If you want your children to grow up and work hard, then the fact that you work hard at your own job sets an excellent example.

Having to combine the role of principal parent with full-time career is not easy, but women are doing it with imagination and sheer hard work. The rise of the mythical "Supermom" has meant that we are often expected to do it all without any help. There are a lot of "Supermoms" around: they are the ones that manage everything day after day, at home and in the office, without failing to give love and energy to their children.

CHILDCARE
Start looking for reliable childcare six to eight weeks before you plan to return to work. For daycare, you may need to apply farther in advance, especially to popular sites that have waiting lists. Some companies provide onsite daycare, but unfortunately they're rare.

Friends and relatives Letting a relative help can be the perfect solution for many mothers, but consider the situation carefully before asking someone. You can start to feel uncomfortably indebted, or, conversely, they can feel taken for granted.

Because you don't have a "professional" relationship, it may be difficult to stipulate rules and guidelines that they don't take quite as seriously as you; discipline problems, for example, can soon become frustrating, particularly if your views on child-rearing diverge. On the other hand, if these problems are confronted early on, you can benefit immeasurably from the security, flexibility, and low cost of this type of arrangement. If you ask a friend, rather than a close relative, to help on a regular basis and you pay her, you will be required to pay social security taxes.

Babysitters
You will be able to tell from your child's reaction whether he feels loved and secure with his babysitter.

CHOOSING CHILDCARE

Your baby doesn't only need to be changed and fed: he needs the kind of loving attention that you would give him yourself if he is to learn to interact and become a sociable child.

Nanny or babysitters This kind of help can be expensive, but you might consider sharing a nanny with another family. You can find one through an agency, or by advertising in local newspapers and magazines. Joining a "Mommy and me" group in your neighborhood is a good way to meet other mothers who might be interested in sharing a nanny or a babysitter for just a few hours or most of the day.

Daycare/family daycare The benefits of a good daycare center are many, including well-trained staff and lots of opportunities for your child to learn important social skills. Some daycare centers also encourage early learning skills and offer a story hour, along with arts and crafts, music, and other organized activities. Although some employers offer onsite daycare, it is still a rarity in most cities. Family daycare provides another good alternative for the care of your child. Family daycare is offered in a caregiver's own home, often with her own children. This kind of care is very often the most economical for large families.

241

EFFECT ON YOUR CHILDREN

Research suggests that children can be better off with two unhappy parents than with divorced parents.

However, the research gives no indication of the different divorce situations, which are critical in determining the effect on the child.

An amicable divorce may be barely damaging and its effect entirely different from that of a bitter, acrimonious divorce. The main reason for this is that in an acrimonious situation, each parent usually does his or her best to turn the children against the other parent. This has a very negative and damaging effect on children, and should be avoided at all costs.

Separation and divorce

At some stage in every relationship, problems arise. In rare cases, couples live happily ever after, but the vast majority don't. This doesn't necessarily reflect a lowering of moral values; it is more an indication of the complexities and pressures of modern life. Support systems are weaker and expectations higher.

Statistics show that today, two in three divorces are initiated by women, many of whom feel they are asked to do too much without adequate support from their partners. The average marriage lasts about eight years—a depressing fact of life for growing numbers of children brought up without two parents.

PERIODS OF CHANGE

The problem for nearly all couples is that in the long term, people change. Although this can be difficult, it can also be invigorating and constructive. If you learn to develop together, you will prevent boredom and stagnation from building up in your relationship.

At the end of periods of change, which are often fraught with emotional insecurity, you will either grow together or grow apart. Whatever happens, it is vital that your children feel secure about their future at all times. For young children, change within a family unit (or fear of that change) is very damaging. Children don't have the defense mechanisms to protect themselves from the severe emotional insecurity that a breakup can cause.

EXPLAINING TO YOUR CHILDREN

A young child is like a sponge that soaks up emotional signals, whether or not they're directed at her. If you are happy, the chances are your child will be happy; if you are sad, she'll be sad. Although it's worth making an effort "for the sake of the children," don't fall into the trap of thinking they won't know what's going on. They usually sense when something is wrong, whether or not you have a smile on your face.

Because of this, it's always best to explain, at least partially, what is going on. If you don't, children will invent their own explanations, mistakenly blaming themselves for problems in the family. This is because children under five only conceive the world in relation to themselves. If you don't give a plausible explanation of why you and your partner are arguing or splitting up, they may come up with explanations that are inconceivable to an adult, but make perfect sense to a child, such as: "Daddy left because I don't clean my room," or "Mommy is upset because I wet the bed/I'm clumsy/I lost my allowance money." Feelings of guilt are very damaging, especially for a child already struggling to come to terms with the emotional turmoil and insecurity that marital breakups can trigger. Doubt is one of the worst fears in a child's mind, so never leave your child in any doubt that you love her and that you'll continue to take care of her.

DIVORCE

If you reach the point where the only option left is divorce or separation, don't assume automatically that your children will be devastated. Some will be, but the effect on your child will depend greatly on age, personality, the circumstances of the divorce, and the prevailing social attitudes in the school and community.

I know of one elementary school class, for instance, where out of 35 children, only five had parents who were still together. They were regularly teased by the others from "broken homes" who saw these five children as materially disadvantaged: the children whose parents were still together only got one set of presents on their birthday or at Christmas, and they only had one house. Although having divorced parents is nothing to boast about, many of these children did. This may be deeply shocking to a lot of people, but it is just one more indication of the different times that our children are growing up in.

MOVING OUT

If the time comes when you have to leave, it's vital to let your child know that you are not taking your love with you, and that you'll continue to be an active parent. Let your child know specifically when you plan to see her and, no matter how difficult it is, try never to break these arrangements.

If you are the parent left with full-time responsibility for your child when your partner has moved out, try not to be upset if she misses her father or mother. Don't try to make her forget that the other parent exists, and don't speak abusively about the other parent, since this will only confuse your child further.

Even if your child appears to be unaffected by a marital split, keep a close eye on her and ask her teachers if they notice any difference in her at school. Some children have fewer questions than others and keep their feelings of insecurity to themselves, but they may still need extra attention and love. Increased bed-wetting, thumb-sucking, and general "clinginess" are all signs that your child is in need of extra reassurance.

Grandparents can be a great boon at the time of the divorce. If possible, do encourage your child to see both sets. Don't let bad feelings act as a cutoff. Think of your child first—she needs continuity, security, and reassurance, and grandparents are second to none at providing these, as long as they don't bad-mouth either parent.

Ask your children about their worries and anxieties and give them space to voice them. Listen and take them seriously. Act on them. They will almost certainly be things you haven't thought of, or would dismiss as trivial if you did.

ACCESS

Whatever your feelings are about your partner, it's best for your child if you're easygoing and generous about access.

Don't be stingy, and don't be confrontational—it causes your child such anguish. Try to meet somewhere civilized, like one of your homes, not somewhere like a park or shopping mall, or your child will feel like a commodity.

Plan well ahead, don't break promises at the last minute, and if your partner is late, be relaxed about it, otherwise your child will worry about both of you. Don't make it an opportunity to denigrate her father or mother; be casual, and keep your child calm: "Oh, there must be a traffic jam," or "Should we play a game until he gets here?"

If your partner is consistently late or unreasonable, arrange a separate meeting to discuss this, out of earshot of your child. The only time to consider preventing your ex-partner from having any access to your child is if you think she's at risk of being kidnapped or otherwise harmed. In such cases, it is best to seek professional advice, through either counseling services or a lawyer.

Multiple births

New parents are often surprised at the amount of work involved in caring for a newborn, and this is even more true for mothers who have multiple births.

• Many mothers of twins don't realize how much help they will need, though mothers who have already had one baby tend to be more realistic about this. Don't underestimate the task of caring for twins, and don't for one minute imagine that asking for help reflects badly on your adequacy as a parent.

• Helpers can create extra work. This is particularly true of a friend or relative who moves in to "help" you and then expects you to cook for her every evening, so consider this carefully before accepting long-term help.

• You may find that everyone wants to help with the babies and no one wants to do the housework. They're your twins, and you must learn to mother them yourself, so don't be afraid to be firm about what help you need.

Twins are by far the most common multiple births. Identical (monozygotic or uniovular) twins are formed by the splitting of a single fertilized egg: the two babies develop from one egg and one sperm, and share a placenta. Twins that develop from the fertilization of two eggs by two sperm and have a placenta each are called nonidentical, fraternal, dizygotic, or binovular. Multiples can occur in any combination of identical and fraternal.

PREGNANCY AND BIRTH

Early rapid weight gain is a common sign of twin pregnancy. The minor complaints of pregnancy can become more uncomfortable, and there are a few clinical conditions that are relatively more common in multiple pregnancies, such as anemia or fluid retention. Make sure you eat well and get plenty of rest.

For a mother carrying two babies, pregnancy is naturally more tiring than for a mother carrying only one. But it's usually shorter—37 weeks rather than 40 weeks. Delivery is reassuringly straightforward and, while it's been known for the birth of the second baby to be delayed by days, this is rare and the gap between babies is usually less than half an hour. Twins are more likely to be premature.

FEEDING

There are some special considerations if you are trying to feed twin babies and, while I would always advocate breastfeeding, you may want to consider the pros and cons set out in the chart below. When you come to establishing daily routines, there are several ways in which you can try to get your twins to feed and sleep at similar times, though

Breast	Bottle
• Breastfeeding is slightly more difficult to establish than the bottle, and it's not easy when you're on an outing.	• An advantage is the freedom for your twins to be fed by their father (or anyone else) if you're tired, and in public.
• There are all the usual advantages of breastfeeding, especially protection against infection—very important to twins because prematurity is more common than with single babies.	• Neither you nor your babies will find your return to work a difficult transition to make, since bottle-feeding is already established.
• You can hold both your babies and feed them at the same time, giving them equal attention and nourishment.	• It's virtually impossible to bottle-feed your two babies at the same time, at least not holding them close to you in the crook of your arm, while making eye contact.

initially one may wake early and want feeding and the other may simply sleep on. You could feed the baby who wakes first while waiting for the second, then reverse them; or feed both at once and spend time talking or playing afterward.

SHOULD THEY SLEEP TOGETHER?

Almost serendipitously, it was found that premature twins, if placed in the same incubator, were happier, more contented, and gained more weight than when they were nursed alone. A moment's reflection is enough to understand why this must be so. After all, twins share a very confined space for nine months and solitude will be quite difficult to bear. Once at home, you can extend this theory into the nursery by placing both your babies in the same crib. This will suit tranquil sleepers, but restless babies may disturb each other. The next step might be to try adjacent cribs. Another equally good approach is to treat twins simply as siblings, and have them sleep in the same room, but not in particular close proximity. The crying of one twin doesn't seem to bother the other unduly.

DIAPER-CHANGING

Try to share the diaper-changing between you, otherwise life becomes one long diaper change for one of you. Most parents of twins opt for disposable diapers, though even the newborn size may swamp your twins if they were premature. But you can make them snug by wrapping your babies in plastic pants with ties placed on top of the disposable diaper and tying securely. You'll probably find that it will be several weeks before your twins are big enough for the next size of disposable diapers. Unless two of you are working together, it's best to change your twins one at a time.

IMPORTANCE OF PLAY

Because of the demands they make on your time, twins are likely to receive less adult stimulation through play and physical contact than single babies, but they get far more peer stimulation and company. Loving interaction with you is essential to their physical, mental, and social development. Set aside time for play every day, or arrange the babies' sleeping times so that they are awake in the evening when both parents can play with them.

THE FATHER'S ROLE

Most fathers want to be closely concerned with the care of their babies and will enjoy watching either or both of them to give you a break.

A father fulfills a pivotal role in a family with twin babies, and a couple should discuss in some detail the sort of activities he will help with or have sole responsibility for when the babies come home. Some are obvious, others are not, like going to the supermarket, and doing household chores, cooking, and laundry. Night duty is particularly important to give respite to a mother who is overtaxed during the day and exhausted at night.

Helping out
With the amount of work involved in caring for twins, your partner's help will be indispensable.

DRESSING TWINS

Many parents wish to dress twins alike, especially if they are identical, and this can look very appealing.

From the outset it's only fair to twins to think of them and treat them as individuals. It's difficult enough for a single child to achieve a sense of self and self-worth without having to battle with a doppelganger who looks alike and is dressed identically. Not only that, twins find they have to distinguish between themselves to friends, relatives, and strangers; dressing them individually goes a long way to avoiding such embarrassment.

As your twins get older, I think it's much better to let them decide for themselves what they wear; if you've always dressed them differently, they will probably continue to do so themselves.

BEING A TWIN

Twins have a close and intuitive understanding of each other and enjoy the companionship of a child of the same age. Having the support and approval of another person can be very reassuring as they grow and encounter new experiences.

PHYSICAL DEVELOPMENT

Don't make the mistake of expecting your twins to do too much too soon, and don't compare them to other babies of the same age. Like any other babies born preterm, if your babies were premature, their progress will be slower than that of babies who went the full 40 weeks.

The development of a preterm baby can be slow and erratic; for some, every day can be an uphill struggle. It's very encouraging to know, however, that twins born after 32 weeks will develop quite normally, though they may achieve their milestones somewhat later than full-term babies, so for each milestone, add on anything up to three months for the dates given for full-term babies.

If progress seems slow, be consoled by the knowledge that, in one study, twins were shown to have caught up in height by the age of four and weight by eight. Don't make the mistake of expecting your twins to develop identically even though they look alike. Nonidentical twins rarely do, and of course a boy and a girl would develop in different ways at different rates, with growth spurts occurring at different stages and skill acquisitions at different times.

TWINS AS INDIVIDUALS

Much of family life militates against twins being treated as individuals. It's just easier and simpler for them to be placed alongside each other in their high chairs and fed from the same dish, even with the same spoon! When small, they may have played together with the same toys at the same time. It's irresistible for parents, family, and friends to treat twins as a single identity, where individuality is submerged. But there are some safeguards that can be put in place. Choosing names that sound very different is one; different clothes is another. Different-colored bed linen and towels help, too. Also, try to be alert to differences in personality and help them to flower.

Individuality
Encourage each twin's sense of identity and individuality by dressing them in different clothes or colors.

THE SPECIAL BOND

The extra-strong bond that exists between twins is legendary. Even after separation, twins can seem to be governed by a unifying force, marrying on the same day, buying the same type of house, even choosing identical cars. Very often, each relates to the other more intimately than to any other person, including parents and, later on, even wives. It's as though there are unspoken ties that defy explanation and love that outweighs all others. And, of course, twins do understand each other in a way no one else can because they spend so much time together, attending to one another, covering each other's weaknesses, and fortifying their strengths. Also, they often face situations together, which makes them feel strong and confident as a team, but also gives each one an unique insight as to what makes the other tick.

TALKING TO TWINS

Parents may find it quite difficult to talk to their twins because nearly half of all twins develop a secret language so weird it excludes the adult world and holds it to ransom. But you may find that your twins are slow to talk, and there may be several reasons for this. An Australian study suggests that twins generally have more difficulties to deal with from the outset, and so milestones can be late, not just with speech, but with motor skills, too. But it must be remembered that twins share the parental attention that a single child would enjoy undiluted, and so there are fewer opportunities to learn and, in particular, busy or tired parents feel less like talking to their babies. Research bears this out. The mothers of twins talk less and use grammatically simple sentences and apply reasoning and reassurance less often. It's important, therefore, not to concentrate on the more gregarious twin but talk as freely to the quiet twin.

BECOMING SOCIABLE

Make sure your twins feel at home with any social group, be it family or friends, or other toddlers, from a very early age. There's a danger of not mixing with other children because twins have each other for company. For the same reason, you may find that your twins are quite happy to be left with strangers from an early age as long as the other twin is present. Indeed, they may seem rather bossy and self-centered to other children.

On the other hand, they may opt to play exclusively with each other as a twosome and will have to be persuaded to join in. Gradual separation can often work if activities are split between parents and friends. Dad might get one twin to help in the yard while Mom takes the other shopping. You might try inviting a friend of each twin over to play on different days. Later on, you could encourage teachers to place your twins in different activity groups so that they mix with other children and have a chance to make friends—or even consider sending them to different preschools.

SIBLINGS

The advent of twins in the family can put everyone under strain, not least other brothers and sisters. For a three-year-old, the "dethronement" that follows the arrival of a new baby seems like a double whammy when twins arrive.

It's very difficult to give older children the attention they're used to and deserve when twins absorb every ounce of time and energy you possess. But for their sake, plans should be laid and a real attempt made to soften the blow, otherwise children will feel neglected, unloved, and insecure; revert to bed-wetting; become antisocial; and misbehave.

Twins should be heralded throughout the household with charts, pictures, and story books so that siblings can grow accustomed to the idea and role-play with dolls. Involvement with equipping the babies' room helps make the absent twins seem real, and their return from the hospital can seem acceptable if Mom's arms are free to gather up the children waiting excitedly for the new arrivals, while someone else carries the twins. Each child should receive a small gift from each twin (named), and it's a good idea to set aside the first half-hour for playing with them before seeing to the twins.

Make sure that each child has half an hour a day of your undivided attention. Then he will feel valued. It's a good idea for you and your partner to take the children out on their own so that they have you entirely to themselves, and feel secure in your love despite the two new interlopers.

CHAPTER 5

Special needs

There are many reasons why a child may need more care and attention than her peers. Your child may have a chronic condition, such as asthma; a learning disorder, such as dyslexia; a developmental disorder, such as autism; or she may simply be very advanced for her years. Whatever the case, she'll need extra support and consideration in order to maximize her potential. This may take the form of special medical treatment, home care, or special education. The same goes for a very bright child who might outstrip older brothers and sisters and even parents. This can put a unique strain on your family, so get expert help so that your child is given the chance to fulfill her potential.

Early identification of special needs is very important. A severe condition such as cerebral palsy will be apparent soon after birth, but others, such as dyslexia, can go unnoticed for years. Never be afraid to act on your suspicions; seek professional advice if you are at all worried, and make sure you seek out any help or advice that is available. You are still your child's main caregivers, whatever her needs, and the better informed you are, the more you can do for her.

The special child

Although all children develop at different rates and the range of what doctors and psychologists consider "normal" is wide, a small number fall at either end of the developmental spectrum. At one end are children who are unusually advanced for their age in both motor and intellectual skills; at the other end are children who haven't acquired basic skills such as language, and children who learn very slowly. In between are children with developmental or learning disorders such as autism and dyslexia.

Perhaps surprisingly, very advanced children have needs similar to those of children with a learning disorder: lots of stimulation, attention, and love. You might say that all children need these things—and you'd be right—but without them, children with special needs will suffer more. If such children don't receive the correct stimulation, they may not turn out to be "just average"; they could develop serious behavioral problems.

The monitoring of a child's growth, development, and behavior may involve a number of people, including your healthcare provider and the school psychologist and school nurse.

RECOGNIZING THE SIGNS

If your child does have special needs, an early diagnosis is very important so that he can get help. Some learning disorders are difficult to spot,

especially those characterized by behavior that may be considered positive, such as quietness, infrequent crying, or excessive sleeping. Autistic children, for example, are often described by their parents as well-behaved before other signs of their illness emerge. A gifted child, on the other hand, may be disruptive and not do well in school, making it hard for teachers to recognize his potential.

The following are some signs that might indicate that your child has special needs. However, bear in mind that children vary enormously, so what you regard as delayed speech in your child, for example, could be just a normal variation in development. If you're worried, check with your doctor.

DEVELOPMENTALLY DELAYED CHILD

• Not speaking by the age of two-and-a-half years

• Failure to interact with other people—to join in appropriately in conversation, for instance

• Repetitive routines or habits beyond the normal age, such as asking the same question over and over

• Problems reading and writing, inability to tell left from right, and poor coordination

• Overactivity and short concentration span

GIFTED CHILD

• Very early and fluent language skills

• Very independent behavior, or a preference for the company of adults

• Tendency to be bored by repetitive tasks

• Precocious development accompanied by bad behavior such as temper tantrums

• Unusually long concentration span

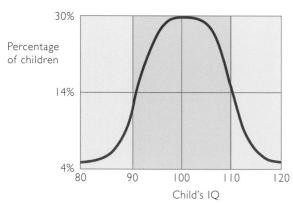

IQ chart
The few very gifted children appear at the extreme right of the curve. At the left is the small group of children with impaired mental abilities. Most children fall between these extremes.

GIFTEDNESS

A gifted child is one who has advanced cognitive (understanding) skills and motor skills for his age. He can walk, talk, and reason earlier than average. He will be a high achiever in most areas, and he may have an IQ over 150. Having a gifted child is rare. Although many children may be advanced for their age in a particular skill at a particular time, only about 2 percent of the population are truly gifted. If your child is gifted, however, it is likely that you as a parent will be the first to notice.

DIAGNOSIS

Diagnosing a gifted child becomes easier as the child gets older, but one of the first signs is early language acquisition, particularly speaking fluently before the age of two. Early reading may be another sign of giftedness: many able children learn to read at the age of three or four, and 6 percent learn to read before the age of two. Other possible qualities of gifted children are as follows:

- Good powers of reasoning
- A good memory for places and names
- A strong creative and imaginative drive
- Sharp powers of observation
- Being curious and always asking questions
- More at home with adults than with children
- An ability to grasp abstract ideas
- Independence
- Ability to solve problems or puzzles
- Having an extensive vocabulary
- Assimilating facts very quickly
- Long concentration span
- Ability to describe events, people, and situations accurately and vividly
- Eagerness to spend time studying or learning
- A specific talent, such as artistic ability
- A high IQ

SPECIAL NEEDS

Although you may perceive giftedness as an asset rather than a problem, your gifted child may not always be provided for adequately at school, and he will have specific emotional needs that are different from those of the average child.

The gifted child may find it hard to relate to his peers. He may be impatient with other children for being slow, and this may make him unpopular. Although your child may be condescending toward other children, he will probably still want to be part of their group, and this may lead to frustration and isolation. Alternatively, your child may try to conceal his talents in order not to seem different, so that he will be accepted by other children.

Interacting with adults can also be a problem. Teachers may treat gifted children as arrogant, precocious, or cocky. Gifted children are likely always to know the answers to questions and to be able to point out inconsistencies, and question the reasons for doing something. The gifted child does not mean to be attention-seeking or trouble-making, and the negative response he gets from adults can make him withdrawn and antisocial.

A gifted child who is denied the chance to exploit his potential may show a confusing mixture of intellectual prowess and immaturity. He may sulk and have temper tantrums; he may be bored by basic school subjects; and, if he's restless and inattentive, his teachers, far from recognizing his talents, may believe that he is of low ability. You may have to intervene and discuss with your child's teacher the kind of specialized or accelerated learning your child requires and make sure that he gets it.

Can giftedness be cultivated?

Intelligence is wholly innate and overrides all cultures and backgrounds; cleverness is partly innate and partly environmental.

Evidence suggests that some gifted children come from relatively affluent homes with educated parents who spend time stimulating and encouraging their children; the extra boost can turn a very bright child into a gifted one. Being overly pushy as a parent will not help to cultivate giftedness in your child, however. You can help him fulfill his potential, but you can't change that potential.

HOW YOU CAN HELP

It is important to know that your child is gifted, since it may help to explain a lot of her behavior, especially behavior that is construed as deviant: social withdrawal, aggressiveness, tantrums, moodiness, and so on. It is also important in that it means you can start to cater to your child's specific needs. If you have a gifted child, don't adopt the attitude that she can simply wait until others reach her level. Gifted children need lots of intellectual stimulation, and they will be deprived if they don't get it.

If your child is of school age, you should enlist the help of her teacher. If a teacher doesn't understand that your child is gifted, then he or she may perceive her as a threat or a problem. A sensitive teacher, however, will help your child to integrate with other children and will prevent her from becoming isolated. Some schools have provisions for gifted children and in some areas there are enrichment programs that will supplement your child's learning. You can contact the National Association For Gifted Children (see **Useful addresses**, p.344) for more information.

As a parent, it is important that you treat your child sympathetically. Although she may be very advanced in some ways, she will still be emotionally immature, so avoid treating her as a "little adult." You can provide plenty of intellectual stimulation for your child in the following ways:

• Provide toys that promote interactive learning. Limit television viewing, as it is a passive way of learning.

• Give your child freedom to play and try not to intervene too much, unless she asks for your help.

• Encourage any specific talents such as painting.

• If you have a particular talent of your own, share it with your child and try to communicate your enthusiasm to her.

• Send your child to summer school, and introduce her to other gifted children.

• Encourage her to ask questions and, if you don't know the answer to a question, help her to look up the information in a book.

• Read her stories that will enrich her imagination.

• Involve her in your everyday tasks.

UNDERACHIEVERS

Whereas gifted children acquire skills very early, underachievers or developmentally delayed children acquire skills at an unusually slow rate. Some of the first indications that your baby is "behind" are docility, quietness, and sleeping for very long periods.

Your baby will not make much noise, will not interact with her environment in the same way as the average child, and will be late in smiling, responding to sounds, and learning to chew. When you try to engage your child in activities, she will have a short attention span, and she will spend brief periods doing lots of different things rather than devoting all her energy to one task or game. As she grows older, she may demonstrate a tendency to be overactive, and she may have a below-average IQ.

DIAGNOSIS

A developmentally delayed child will be later than usual in achieving some of the important developmental milestones (see below). It is important, however, to eliminate the possibility that your child has a physiological problem such as partial deafness or blindness. You should also find out whether your child has a severe developmental disorder, such as autism (see p.258), or whether she is simply developing at a rate that is below average. Ask your doctor to refer your child to a psychologist for assessment. Your child may need remedial help.

BEHAVIORAL MILESTONES

There are various clues or signs that your baby or child is developmentally delayed or underachieving. Although children vary in the speed at which they develop, behavioral milestones do exist—if your child has not reached the following stages, then she may have a learning or developmental disorder.

Hand regard Your baby becomes aware of her hands at about the age of eight weeks, shortly after she begins to play with her feet. Between the age of 12 and 16 weeks your baby will stare at her hands and wiggle her fingers—she's discovering that she can control her hand movements. Hand regard may go on for as long as 20 weeks, however, in developmentally delayed children.

The grasp reflex If you put your finger (or any object) into a baby's palm, she will close her fingers around it in a tight grip. This reflex usually lasts about six weeks after birth, but will persist longer if your child is developmentally delayed.

Mouthing At about six months, your baby will put everything that she can into her mouth. This behavior will last until around a year in a normal child and longer in a developmentally delayed child.

Casting Children up to the age of 16 months will throw objects out of their crib or playpen—a behavior called casting. Developmentally delayed children may continue to do this for much longer.

Drooling Slobbering and drooling should stop at around one year. Developmentally delayed children may still be drooling at the age of 18 months.

HOW YOU CAN HELP

Intellectual development is determined by both nature (inherited qualities) and nurture (things such as physical and social environment, and diet). Your child's IQ is decided before birth, but it can flower through the stimuli that your child is exposed to after birth. If your child is not encouraged to interact with other people from an early age, and she is not encouraged to engage her senses in the world around her, chances are she will not reach her full potential, even if that potential is limited.

If you suspect that your child is lagging behind, spend lots of time reading aloud and talking to her, playing with her, taking her out, showing her new things and new people, and encouraging her to play imaginative games with her toys. Give her toys that are educational and plenty of colorful books and pictures to look at.

Behavior modification techniques may be helpful. Put simply, this means rewarding your child's responses with praise and affection and being patient with her efforts, however slow they are. If you punish her for slowness, she may become discouraged and lose her desire to learn.

DYSLEXIA

This is a learning disorder that affects reading, spelling, and written language. Although dyslexia particularly affects your child's mastery of written symbols—letters, numbers, and musical notation—she may have difficulties with spoken language too. Dyslexia is a specific neurological disorder and is not the result of poor hearing or vision, or low intelligence. One in 20 children is dyslexic.

DIAGNOSIS

Many bright children are dyslexic, and the condition is often diagnosed earlier in these children since parents become aware of the gap between their child's obvious intelligence and her level of achievement in specific areas. The main symptoms of dyslexia are difficulty in reading and writing. Your child may have problems perceiving letters in the correct order, or she may confuse similarly shaped letters such as "b" and "d," and "p" and "q." Labeling a child dyslexic if she is not is just as harmful as failing to recognize it if she is. A correct diagnosis can only be made by an expert. The following may help you to recognize dyslexia in your child:

- Poor spelling and poor coordination

- Difficulty in remembering lists of words, numbers, or letters, such as the alphabet or tables

- Difficulty in remembering the order of everyday things, such as days of the week

- Problems telling left from right

- Jumbled phrases, such as "tebby dare" instead of "teddy bear" and difficulty learning nursery rhymes

DYSCALCULIA AND DYSPRAXIA

Dyscalculia and dyspraxia are related conditions. Dyscalculia is rarer than dyslexia but shares many of the same features. The child's core problem is in handling numbers and mathematical concepts. Common signs of dyspraxia are clumsiness, poor posture, awkward gait, and confusion about which hand to use to perform a task. The child may also have difficulty catching a ball, poor body awareness, and find it difficult to hop, skip, or ride a bike. Both conditions are treated in the same way as dyslexia.

EFFECTS OF DYSLEXIA

The problems listed on p.243 may occur in children who don't have dyslexia. The difference is that dyslexic children will suffer more severe symptoms and won't grow out of them.

Recent research suggests that as well as having problems with literacy, dyslexic children also have problems with distinguishing different sounds, and with memory and balance. For example, dyslexic children will find it much more difficult to balance on one leg than nondyslexic children.

A dyslexic child's strengths are likely to be sensitivity, intuition, and impulsiveness. Skills associated with the left side of the brain, such as dealing with written symbols, responding to instructions, and putting things in order, are weak in the dyslexic child. Some dyslexic children may be very creative and have an aptitude for drawing and painting.

SPECIAL NEEDS

One of the main problems that dyslexic children face is incorrect diagnosis. It is common for children to attempt to learn to read and write, fail to do so, and then be labeled "slow" or even disabled. This is very demoralizing for the child and is bound to affect his school performance overall. Parents and teachers often confuse dyslexia with a low IQ, but in fact most dyslexic children have an average or above-average IQ.

If dyslexia is recognized early, remedial education is very effective. If a child is diagnosed as dyslexic at the age of four or five, when he goes to school, he will probably only need about half-an-hour of extra tuition each day for a period of six months to bring his reading and writing up to normal standards. If dyslexia is not diagnosed until he's seven or eight, he will have a lot of catching up to do.

HOW YOU CAN HELP

You can do three things to help your dyslexic child at home. First—and this is sometimes overlooked—acknowledge that your child actually has a problem. If you are told that your child will catch up or will learn to read eventually, don't listen—dyslexia is a specific learning disorder that will respond only to the appropriate remedial treatment. Second, be supportive and positive, especially if your child is having problems at school. Third, play lots of learning games with your child.

Emotional support If your child is at school and is lagging behind other children, his self-confidence may be low, and it is very important that you make him feel successful at home. Don't show any impatience. Encourage him to do the things that he is good at, and help him do things for himself.

Give him self-help aids, such as "left" and "right" stickers on his tricycle, and, if he finds a particular task difficult, tell him to take it slowly. The International Dyslexia Association (see **Useful addresses**, p.344) gives advice on coping strategies and remedial education for children with dyslexia. They can also provide helpful leaflets and books.

Home learning games Playing games with letters, words, and sounds can be very useful. The following are all ways in which you can have fun and enhance your child's learning:

• Say nursery rhymes out loud together, or try making up your own rhyming poems or limericks. This will familiarize your child with the concept of rhyming words.

• Teach your child rhymes or songs that involve sequences of things such as days of the week.

• Play "Simon Says." This will help your child to follow instructions.

• Play "Hunt the Thimble." This will encourage your child to ask questions involving relationships such as under, on, and inside.

• Introduce the concept of left and right.

• Ask your child to set the table at mealtimes.

• Play clapping games. Give one clap for each syllable of a word and get your child to repeat it. Clap a rhythm to his name.

• Give your child groups of words and ask him to pick the odd word out.

• Get your child to think of as many words beginning with a particular letter as he can.

• Play "I Spy." If your child has difficulty with letter names, make the sound of the letter instead.

• Encourage your child to trace words and letters, or to make letters out of modeling clay.

ADHD

This stands for Attention Deficit Hyperactivity Disorder and is one of the most common childhood disorders seen by psychologists. Children with ADHD may be hyperactive. Although they are not noted to be "overactive" from birth as such, they are likely to have been colicky, demanding babies. They are impulsive, inattentive, and easily distracted.

WHAT CAUSES ADHD?

The current theory about ADHD is that it is a disorder of perception and understanding. Four times as many boys as girls have ADHD, and it is caused by both genetic and environmental factors. In the past, problems such as ADHD and hyper-activity were thought to have a dietary origin. Diets high in chemical additives and lacking in essential vitamins and minerals were thought to cause aberrant behavior in some children, though this has proven not to be so.

Some hyperactive children have benefited from cranial osteopathy—a very gentle yet effective technique. Cranial restrictions can arise at the time of birth as a result of obstructed labor, forceps, or vacuum extraction. If a hyperactive child had a difficult birth, then it is possible that releasing any cranial restrictions will help to calm the child.

EFFECTS OF ADHD

A child with ADHD may be unpredictable and disruptive. Even before he goes to school, he may have problematic relationships with adults and have acquired a reputation for rebelliousness. This has a negative effect on his self-esteem, so that when he does go to school, he starts off on an unequal basis with other children. His performance may be variable: one day he might be quite compliant; the next he won't be able to sit still for more than a few minutes and will fidget incessantly. He may become a low achiever at school, with a reputation for poor concentration, and he may be thought to have a low IQ, though he doesn't. Certain early physical symptoms are associated with ADHD. In babies, these include colic (your child may be difficult to feed either by breast or bottle) and excessive drooling and thirst. In children, they include poor appetite and sleeping problems. Boys with ADHD seem to suffer more than girls with ADHD, in that girls are likely to be better adjusted socially and more achievement-oriented. Boys in particular may be criticized for overactivity, and this can make the problem worse.

SPECIAL NEEDS

If your child is having problems at school—if he is irresponsible, careless, disorganized, and suffers from poor concentration and motivation—then you need to eliminate the possible causes. Consider the possibility that he is dyslexic (see p.253) or gifted (see p.251). If his behavior has started recently, has he experienced a traumatic event? Does he have other behavioral problems such as lying (see p.218) or resistance to school (see p.227)?

Your child may need to be referred to an educational or child psychologist or a pediatric neurologist who will be able to diagnose ADHD and decide on appropriate action to meet your child's individual needs.

HOW YOU CAN HELP

It is important for a child with ADHD to have an orderly home life and a structured, well-disciplined routine. If your child knows that he has to do certain things at set times of the day, he is less likely to be unruly. You should also remember that, if your child has problems with self-control, he probably has low self-esteem, because he meets with adult disapproval all the time. Always praise and reward good behavior. and he will learn that certain types of behavior win your approval, while others don't. When you want your child to do something, make requests clear and simple and give them one at a time. Praise effort as well as achievement.

Drug treatment is reserved for severe ADHD in children over six and the main drug used is methylphenidate hydrochloride (Ritalin), among others. The drugs have significant side effects, so their use is closely monitored. Parenting a child with ADHD can be demoralizing, since your child may have a reputation for being a troublemaker. Many parents feel isolated because their child is rejected by preschools, and even unwelcome in friends' homes. Don't blame yourself for your child's behavior—take time away from your child when it all gets to be too much. Organizations such as Children and Adults with Attention Deficit Hyperactivity Disorder (see **Useful addresses**, p.344) can offer help and advice.

STUTTERING

When your child is learning to talk, it is normal for her to stumble over words, repeat words, and hesitate. It is only when hesitations dominate your child's speech and cause her considerable distress that she is said to have a stutter. Whereas normal hesitation is the relaxed repetition of a word at the beginning or the end of a phrase, a child with a stutter will get stuck on a word, and repeat one of its syllables over and over again. Occasional stuttering is a natural part of language acquisition that will disappear and should never be made an issue of or treated as a problem. Making a fuss about it may cause your child to become anxious and so lead to a true stutter.

IS IT SERIOUS?

When children are learning language, they are not always able to convey their thoughts in words as quickly as they would like to. Your child lives very much in the present, and she will want to convey the intensity of her feelings immediately—when her vocabulary isn't wide enough or her language skills aren't advanced enough, she may stutter in her rush to get the words out.

Most children stutter at some stage. Your child may stutter on some days and not others; she may stutter when she is tired, excited, or in a particular situation or environment. It doesn't matter, though, unless she stutters in a lot of situations and gets very upset because of it.

WHAT CAUSES STUTTERING?

If your child is to become a fluent speaker, then she needs to have plenty of support and encouragement to boost her confidence. A combination of the

---

HOW YOU CAN HELP

You can influence your child's speech by the way you talk to her. If you speak very quickly and you appear distracted, your child may feel that she has to keep up and that you are not interested in what she has to say. Always try to speak slowly and appear attentive and interested. Look at your child and, if possible, talk to her on the same physical level. Use language that is simple, and talk about very immediate things that can be seen. Avoid asking too many questions—instead, describe your own feelings or experiences; this will encourage your child to contribute. Above all, never react negatively to your child's stutter or she will become more self-conscious and the stutter will get worse. When your child is struggling with a sentence, try not to complete it for her or supply a word.

If your child is very anxious about stuttering, talk to her about it. If she knows that you understand, this will lessen her sense of suffering alone. If you don't talk about her stuttering, your child may feel that it is something to be ashamed of. If your child is very young and is having problems with speech, return to games and activities that involve looking or listening rather than speaking. If your child is at school, try discussing the following strategies with her teacher:

• Your child may need extra help with reading. If she is worried about particular words, this can cause her to stutter. Reading aloud in unison with another child may reduce stuttering.

• Children tend to be more fluent when they are talking about something personal or a subject that they know a lot about. This should be encouraged whenever possible.

• If a teacher is observant about what encourages fluency and what increases stuttering, she can prevent your child from feeling embarrassed. When she needs information from your child, it may help if she asks questions that require a "yes" or a "no" answer, particularly if your child is distressed.

• Some methods of speech promote fluency and should be encouraged. These include saying words that have a rhyme or a rhythm, saying words that have actions to go with them, reciting lists, or counting, acting, or singing.

• It may be a good idea for your child's teacher to broach the subject of stuttering with her in a matter-of-fact way, since your child will then feel that it has been noticed by a sympathetic adult and that she doesn't have to hide it.

following three conditions can cause a stutter to develop:

• Parental demands that overestimate the child's ability, such as asking lots of questions; insisting on clear speech; and expecting fast replies and grown-up behavior.

• Your child wanting to perform well to impress people before her vocabulary is large enough.

• Stressful situations in which your child is tired, anxious, or frightened, or where people are talking very fast, or there are lots of interruptions.

Stuttering is not inherited. A stuttering child believes that speaking hesitantly is in some way wrong or bad. Your child becomes acutely self-conscious and focuses on the way she speaks, and this leads to worse stuttering. She may avoid situations that involve speaking, especially to new people, and if your child is of school age she may pretend that she doesn't know answers to questions to avoid having to speak in front of other children.

SPECIAL NEEDS

If your child has a severe stutter, she may need the help of a speech or language therapist. A therapist may visit your child at school or advise parents and teachers. The National Stuttering Association (see **Useful addresses**, p.344) provides contacts, advice, and a helpline.

DELAYED SPEECH

At the age of about 11 months, your baby will probably be able to say simple words, such as "mama," "dada," "dog," and "cat," and by two years she will probably be able to form simple sentences, such as "Daddy in garden." Speech will become progressively more sophisticated during the third and fourth year. As with all aspects of development, the age at which milestones are achieved varies widely, but if your child is very far behind other children of the same age, then there may be something wrong.

There are many causes of delayed speech, the most important being deafness—have your child's hearing tested at once if you suspect she may be deaf. Middle ear effusion (see p.285) can result in problems with hearing. Your child may be late in speaking because she hasn't received the correct stimulation—this can happen to children who have been institutionalized or children whose parents simply don't talk to them enough. Boys are more prone to delayed speech than girls, and twins may speak later than average (see p.247).

Very occasionally, delayed speech is due to a physiological defect or a disease of the speech muscles, larynx, or mouth. There are also disorders that affect the part of the brain that controls speech.

Children vary in the age at which they begin to speak, but if your child is not talking at all by the age of two-and-a-half, you should seek medical help. Deafness can lead to late development of speech and this is why testing for hearing (see pp.178–179) is very important. A baby will not learn to speak if she is deaf. If your child is deaf, she may need a hearing aid; if she has a severe speech defect, she may need help from a speech therapist.

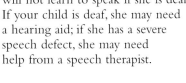

Tambourines or maracas can be used to beat out a rhythm

Improving fluency
Singing, or any kind of rhythmic speech, can reduce stuttering, so tapping out a rhythm to rhymes and songs can help your child feel more confident.

AUTISTIC SPECTRUM DISORDER

Also known as autism, this is a condition in which a child has problems relating to people and situations and may show an obsessive resistance to any change in routine. A complex disorder that varies from mild to severe, it typically appears within the first three years of life and can be linked to other problems such as dyslexia and physical disorders such as epilepsy. It is four times more common in boys than in girls. It used to be thought that autism was caused by emotional deprivation or some negative aspect of the child's background or upbringing. We now know that it has a physiological origin and results from an abnormality in the brain. There may be a genetic basis to the disorder.

DIAGNOSIS

Because autism is a developmental disorder it may take a while for you to become aware that your child is different from others. You may notice that your baby is uncommunicative in the first year of his life, but you may not attach any significance to this until later, when other signs become apparent. Most parents know that their child is autistic or that "something is wrong" by the time he is about three.

EFFECTS OF AUTISM

Children with autism vary considerably in their abilities, but there are three main traits that all autistic children share: problems with social interaction, communication problems, and impaired imagination. Many autistic children display repetitive behavior, and some have very sophisticated memories.

Social interaction If autism is severe, your child will be indifferent to other people. In babies, this manifests itself as crying that can't be appeased by holding and cuddling, quietness, poor eye contact, and failing to return or respond to gestures such as smiling, waving, or facial expressions.

Autistic children show a lack of interest in interacting with other people, particularly children.

They don't make friends and, when they do approach people socially, they may behave inappropriately: they may repeat snatches of conversation that have just been spoken, they may be aggressive, or they may use confusing language. In less severe forms of autism, your child may accept social contact, but will not be very responsive or respond in a stilted, repetitive way.

Communication From an early age, most children show a desire to communicate with other people. Even before they can form words, they will communicate nonverbally using facial expressions and body language. Autistic children seem to lack this desire. Even if your child does speak, he will tend to talk at people, rather than with them, or his speech may be restricted to conveying his immediate needs. Your child may exhibit echolalia (repetition of words that he has just heard), and he may use specific words or phrases in a repetitive or inappropriate way. It is common for autistic children to be confused about when to use "I," "you," or "he."

Imagination An autistic child doesn't use his imagination when he is playing with toys and, rather than perceiving things in their entirety, he may become overly interested in a small detail of a toy, person, or object. When playing with a toy train, for example, he might concentrate on one small part, such as a wheel or the cow-catcher, rather than using it as a make-believe train.

Some autistic children do pursue activities that engage the imagination, such as reading, but these tend to be repetitive and stereotyped. For instance, your child may read one book again and again.

Repetitive behavior Repeated tapping, rocking, head-banging, teeth- grinding, grunting, screaming, finger-flicking, spinning objects, and standing up and jumping from the back foot to the front foot are some of the behaviors that can occur in autism. The type of repetitive activity that your child indulges in is dependent on his level of ability. More sophisticated types of behavior include arranging objects in complex, repeating patterns, and collecting large numbers of a particular object. Your child may be interested in a particular topic and will ask the same questions about it and demand the same answers over and over again. You may also notice that your child likes repetitive routines, even inappropriate ones, to be observed without fail. For example, he may want exactly the same sequence of activities carried out when he goes to bed each night.

Memory Some autistic children are able to store a memory and retrieve it exactly as it was first perceived, and the results can be very impressive. An autistic child may, for example, draw perfectly from memory a building he has seen, or repeat whole conversations or lists of information.

SPECIAL NEEDS

The severity of your child's condition depends on several factors: whether he has any other learning disorders (such as dyslexia, see p.253); whether he has any accompanying physical disorders (such as epilepsy, see p.270), the type of education he has access to; and his personality or disposition, which will affect how he reacts to his disabilities. It is important to diagnose autism and associated disorders as early as possible so your child's needs are met.

The Autism Society of America helps parents with autistic children, offers various publications on care and education, and also hold conferences and workshops (see **Useful addresses**, p.344). Depending on the severity of your child's autism, he may be able to go to a regular school, where he

may receive extra help, and a few autistic children manage to do this; otherwise he will need to go to a special school for children with learning or developmental disorders.

HOW YOU CAN HELP

You will probably find that your child's behavior is most problematic between the ages of two and five, and there may be an improvement between the ages of six and 12. As he grows up, your child will probably become more responsive and sociable. Although no cure exists for autism, there are many different therapies designed to improve the behavior and adjustment of your child:

Behavior modification This therapy concentrates on replacing dysfunctional behavior (tantrums, head-banging, aggressiveness, and so on) with desirable behavior, using a system of rewards.

Relaxation and massage The child is taught how to relax using massage, music, touching, and verbal cues. Later, the verbal cues can be used on their own when the child shows signs of tension; because he associates them with feeling relaxed, they should dissipate the tension. Massage helps autistic children bond to people through touch.

Holding therapy This involves giving the autistic child plenty of hugs and cuddles, regardless of his indifference. The theory is that if you insist on holding your child, he will be comforted and reassured without the problem of having to initiate the interaction in the first place.

Speech therapy Some cases of autism are diagnosed by speech therapists, because poor language development is often the first sign. Speech therapy can also improve your child's communication skills. If your child doesn't speak or his speech is very limited, it may help to teach him a sign language such as Makaton, which complements rather than replaces speech.

Psychotherapy This involves working with the whole family so that parents understand the behavior of the autistic child and its consequences. In some cases, the child himself might receive individual psychotherapy.

Using sign language
If your child finds talking difficult, you can use a sign language or picture symbols to communicate—it can help to clarify your language to her.

Signs can be used to complement speech but not replace it

Living with chronic conditions

The word "chronic" is used to describe an illness, such as cerebral palsy or asthma, that is long-lasting, where the symptoms are present on a daily basis, or where they flare up occasionally. In contrast, an acute illness, such as tonsillitis, comes on suddenly, and the duration of symptoms is quite short. Chronic conditions may be lifelong and you, your family, and your child will need to make some changes in your lifestyle in order to cope with the condition on a day-to-day basis.

DEALING WITH ILLNESS

The most common emotional reaction to the news that your child has a chronic condition is anxiety, combined with fear, bitterness, and possibly guilt that you yourself have done something to cause the condition. After the initial shock, many parents become very involved in learning about their child's condition and how to manage it. The first thing you need to know is what the treatment program entails—this may be daily injections, occasional blood transfusions, or just making sure that your child always carries an inhaler. You will also need to familiarize yourself with the symptoms of an attack or the possible dangers to your child, and learn what to do in an emergency.

When your child first shows signs of a chronic condition, apart from the physical unpleasantness of being ill, she will most likely find the experience of visiting doctors and hospitals quite stressful. Stay calm in front of your child, and don't fuss or panic. She'll see your anxiety and interpret it in her own way and become more anxious herself; she may even become terrified that she is going to die. Talk to your child rationally about her condition and explain what is happening to her. If she doesn't understand what's wrong with her, this can be more frightening than the illness itself.

Because you are worried about your child's health, it is quite natural for you to pay special attention to her. You should be careful, however, that you don't exclude other members of your family, especially if you have other children.

Research is being conducted into chronic conditions and management programs are becoming progressively more advanced—many children can live a near-normal life. (For self-help groups on the conditions described here, see **Useful addresses**, p.344.)

ASTHMA

Asthma is a common chronic illness affecting one in ten children at some time in childhood. The symptoms of asthma—coughing, wheezing, and shortness of breath—are caused by narrowing of the airways, and episodes can be brought on by various triggers. The severity of episodes varies greatly. There may be a family history of asthma or the allergic conditions eczema and hay fever—this is called atopy. Asthma is more common in boys than girls and may improve as a child gets older.

Risk factors The reasons for the increase in rates of asthma are not entirely known, although parental smoking, pollution, viruses, low birth weight, and bottle-feeding instead of breastfeeding are possible factors. Smoking is the only proven factor, particularly if you smoke during pregnancy, and you or your partner smoke during your child's early years. Boys are twice as likely as girls to have asthma.

There is good research to suggest that children who are not exposed to a wide variety of viruses and bacteria in early childhood, and who therefore never have their immune system challenged, are more vulnerable to developing asthma. Children who are raised on farms are less likely to have asthma than city-dwellers.

DIAGNOSIS

Many young children have wheezing episodes during winter with a cold, cough, rapid breathing, and difficulty feeding, but this doesn't make them asthmatic. It's the pattern of symptoms that develops over time that shows whether a child has asthma or not.

It can be quite difficult to spot asthma in very young children for three reasons. First, a third of all children will have at least one attack of wheezing during their first five years. Most of these children will never have breathing problems again, even though wheezing may be severe enough to warrant hospital admission. Second, doctors use a variety of words to describe asthma, such as wheezing, reactive airway disease, or hyperactive airways. Third, a "peak-flow meter," the device normally used to measure how well the lungs work, can only be used with children who are over five years of age.

Before reaching a diagnosis, your doctor should wait and see how the pattern of your child's symptoms develops. It is this pattern, not individual symptoms, which dictates the diagnosis of asthma. Typical symptom patterns are as follows:

• Repeated attacks of wheezing and coughing, usually with colds.

• A persistent cough may be the only symptom in small children.

• Many restless nights caused by attacks of wheezing or coughing.

• Wheezing or coughing between colds, especially after exercise or excitement, or when your child is exposed to cigarette smoke and allergens such as pollen or dust-mite droppings.

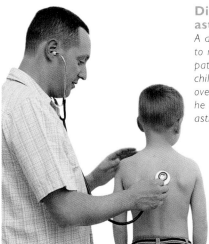

Diagnosing asthma
A doctor will need to monitor the pattern of your child's symptoms over time before he can diagnose asthma.

Many people believe that wheezing is the only symptom of asthma, but for young children, a dry and irritating cough may be the only symptom. Healthy children don't cough persistently.

Children under the age of one year are most likely to suffer from wheezing, which is set off by virus infections such as a cold or a runny nose. In fact viruses, are an almost universal trigger for young children. Breastfeeding may help improve a child's resistance to viruses.

TRIGGERS
If your child does suffer from asthma, you will find that certain substances or activities can trigger an attack. Once you have identified triggers, help your child to avoid them.

Smoking Help your child avoid cigarette smoke, because it's especially harmful to growing lungs, and can trigger asthma attacks. Never smoke around children, and don't allow visitors to your home to smoke in the house.

Cold air You may notice that your child coughs or wheezes initially on going outdoors. Keeping your child indoors, however, is not the answer. A dose of reliever medicine (see p.262) just before going out may be all that's needed.

Activity If laughter, excitement, or exercise trigger asthma in your child, it may be a sign that the asthma is not properly controlled. Consult your doctor, since it is very important for children to join in the fun and enjoy themselves. The symptoms of activity-induced asthma may be prevented if your child takes a dose of reliever medicine beforehand. Your child should warm up before playing games— several 30-second sprints over five to ten minutes will allow her to exercise for up to an hour or so. Swimming provides an excellent form of exercise for children who are suffering from asthma, and it seldom provokes an attack unless the water is very cold or heavily chlorinated.

Allergies Minimize your child's exposure to potential allergens, such as mites, pollen, and fur. Complete avoidance of house dust is impossible, but the following measures will help: avoid feather pillows, comforters, and carpeting; cover your child's mattress with a plastic sheet; clean and vacuum your child's room regularly.

TREATMENT

Your doctor can prescribe medicine that will control your child's symptoms, though they can't cure asthma. Most medications come in the form of an inhaler. There are two types: preventers and relievers. Children should always use their inhalers with a device called a spacer, which delivers the drug directly to the airways.

Relievers When an asthma attack occurs, a reliever, or bronchodilator, makes breathing easier by relaxing the tiny muscles in the narrowed airways and letting them open up. They may also be taken several times a day to stop symptoms from developing. A child who suffers occasional asthma attacks must have a reliever medicine on hand at all times.

Preventers Your child will probably have to take a preventer if he usually needs to use a reliever more than twice a week. These stop asthma from starting by reducing inflammation in the airways and making them less sensitive to irritants. Preventers must be taken regularly, even if your child is well. They take about 7–14 days to become effective from the time they are first taken. Once the symptoms are well

Spacer
Spacer devices make inhalers easier for young children to use and more effective.

under control, your doctor may reduce the treatment. If your child uses a preventer as well as a reliever, label the pump clearly.

Treatment devices The drugs can be given in different ways, depending on the age of the child and his ability to coordinate his breathing with the use of the inhaler. The following is a general guide, but children vary as to which they can master:

up to 2	Nebulizer or spacer with face mask
2–4	Aerosol inhaler with spacer
5–8	Powder inhalers
8 up	Powder inhalers or aerosol inhalers

— *Drug is forced into mouth by pump mechanism*

Dry-powder inhalers
These are good for giving preventer medicines, but they can't be inhaled very well when the child is wheezing or is tight-chested because a good breath in is needed to trigger the device. An aerosol may still be needed for relieving these symptoms.

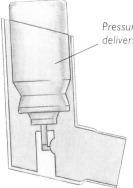

Pressurized container delivers a metered dose

Aerosol inhaler
A metered dose is inhaled directly into the lungs. This requires good coordination, thorough instruction, and a careful assessment of the technique with each type.

Some very young children need a nebulizer, which produces a fine mist of medicine. For most children, however, spacers are the best solution. The drug is delivered into the spacer and the child inhales it over several breaths. For an older child, make the spacer a toy by putting stickers on it, or play games in which you count out loud as your child takes five breaths from the spacer. Nebulizers or steroid tablets or liquid may be needed for severe attacks.

A recent study has shown that it is possible to control asthma by using a combination of drug treatments so that patients suffer few or no symptoms. These medicines are a combination of an inhaled steroid to reduce inflammation and a long-acting bronchodilator to help airways stay open for a long time. They help treat the underlying cause of asthma—inflammation—and are taken on a daily basis to help prevent asthma symptoms and attacks.

HOW YOU CAN HELP

Although there is no known cure for asthma, modern asthma management can effectively reduce a child's symptoms and allow him to lead a full and active life. Regular contact with your doctor and close monitoring of your child are important. Some healthcare providers hold asthma clinics with highly trained nurses.

Your doctor will develop an asthma management plan with you, and explain when to use the preventer and reliever, and what to do if your child's symptoms get worse. This should be written down for you to keep. A vital part of any plan is a review meeting with a doctor or nurse every few months. Monitor your child's symptoms closely and consult your doctor if you notice any of the following:

- Wheezing and coughing in the early morning.

- Increased symptoms after exercise or exertion.

- Waking at night with a cough or a wheeze.

- Increased use of reliever therapy.

An emergency plan Any asthma attack can be life-threatening, so have an emergency plan of action agreed with your doctor for very severe attacks.

- At the start of the attack, give your child his usual reliever. Wait about ten minutes, and if there is no improvement, call 911.

- Repeat the treatment until the breathing symptoms improve or until help arrives.

- Give your child steroid tablets or liquid if they've been prescribed by your doctor.

- Keep your child in an upright position.

- Call your doctor or 911, or take your child to the nearest hospital emergency room.

CYSTIC FIBROSIS

An inherited condition that affects mainly the lungs and the pancreas, cystic fibrosis (CF) produces thick and sticky mucus in the lungs and the pancreas. CF is the most common inherited disease of its kind and affects approximately one in every 2,500 children, though in differing degrees. The gene responsible for CF has been discovered, and there is now a chance that there will be a cure by the time your child reaches adulthood.

WHAT CAUSES CF?

The disease occurs when both parents carry the gene for the disorder. One person in every 25 is a carrier of CF, but an affected gene will be masked by a normal gene from the other parent, and even where two carriers of CF have a baby, there is only a one-in-four chance that the baby will have CF. These chances apply anew for each pregnancy. They don't change the more pregnancies you have. CF affects girls and boys in equal numbers.

DIAGNOSIS

All babies born in the United States have a sample of blood taken when they are in the newborn nursery, usually from a prick in the heel. These spots of blood are tested for the signs of several diseases, one of which may be CF. The diseases tested for vary from state to state.

Another test measures the amount of salt in the sweat; children with CF have more salt in their sweat than normal children. (Some parents comment that their child tastes salty when they kiss him or her, even though children with CF don't sweat more than other children.) This sweat test is carried out on any baby who has recurrent bouts of pneumonia or fails to thrive, and on the brothers and sisters of a child with CF.

Your feelings Once the diagnosis is made, you may have trouble accepting it, especially if your child seems well. You may feel angry, or guilty, but eventually you will realize that no one is to blame. Recriminations are not only pointless, they will do great harm to relationships within the family and to your CF child.

You may seek a second opinion or even consider alternative therapies. You should discuss this with your doctor. Write down the questions you want to ask as you think of them, in case you forget later. Doctors will be happy to provide a second opinion, particularly if you have not yet had the chance to visit a special clinic for CF.

Some people find complementary therapies helpful, but they must be taken in addition to conventional therapy and should be discussed with the child's doctor. It is essential for the future health of your child that conventional medicines are given in the prescribed way.

It's important to try not to overprotect your child. Remember, she is a normal child who happens to have CF. She will be naughty and have all the same emotions as other children, and there's no reason to treat her differently in relation to discipline, education, or physical activities. If you do, you will not only be doing her a disservice, but will also be creating problems for yourselves in the long run. If you're the parent of a newly diagnosed child, you may find it helpful to talk to other parents with CF children. Support groups can put you in touch.

Learning about CF Much of the treatment for CF is carried out at home, and to be as effective as possible, you should try to understand as much as you can about the disorder. CF is a complicated condition, however, and each child will be differently affected, so other people's experiences may differ from yours. Bear in mind that you can't learn everything immediately, and no one will expect you to. Moreover, you will be given a huge amount of information and advice from various sources, some of which will be conflicting.

DIGESTIVE PROBLEMS

The pancreas is a gland in the abdomen. It produces insulin, which passes directly into the blood, and digestive juices containing enzymes, which pass into the intestines where they help with the digestion of food. In CF, the small channels down which these juices flow to reach the intestine become blocked with sticky mucus, and the enzymes can't reach the intestines to digest food. The children often have large appetites, but fail to thrive and pass large, pale, greasy stools since food can't be absorbed properly.

Treatment Most of the missing digestive enzymes can be replaced with pancreatin, which is given in a

powder or a capsule form. For a young baby, the powder can be mixed with a little cooled boiled water or milk, and given before each feeding from a spoon or feeding bottle. It should not be mixed with a whole bottle of milk, because it will curdle the milk. Once your baby is on solids, she should eat whatever the rest of your family is having. Vitamins are not well absorbed in CF, so your child will need a dose of vitamin drops each day.

RESPIRATORY PROBLEMS

Inside the lungs there are lots of tiny tubes, the bronchioles, down which air passes to reach special air sacs, the alveoli; here, oxygen enters the bloodstream and carbon dioxide leaves the blood to be breathed out. CF children have normal lungs at birth, but the mucus produced in them is abnormally thick, so it blocks some of the smaller airways and leads to infection, and later to lung damage.

Treatment The aim of treatment is to keep the lungs as normal as possible in two main ways:

• Clearing the sticky mucus with physical therapy, breathing exercises, and physical exercise.

• Prevention and prompt treatment of chest infections, usually with antibiotics.

HOW YOU CAN HELP

Even with pancreatic supplements, a child with CF may not absorb all the nourishment she needs in order to grow normally. Your child will therefore need more calories, so high-energy snacks between meals, such as milkshakes, are helpful. It's important to be sure that your child is growing well, since this shows she's absorbing nourishment; you can plot her measurements on the charts on pp.318–25.

You can only learn how to clear the thick mucus from your child's chest from a physical therapist and with lots of practice, so don't be afraid to ask for help. You should start the physical therapy from the time of the diagnosis, and it's important to get into a routine right away. You will need to do it twice a day when your child is well, and more often when she has a chest infection.

You should communicate very closely with your doctor about the prevention and treatment of chest infections. Should an infection occur, your child will need extra physical therapy and antibiotics.

WHEN TO SEE THE DOCTOR

Your CF child is very vulnerable to chest infections, so it's important to seek medical help promptly if you think something is wrong. The following symptoms may indicate that a trip to the doctor's office is needed:

- Decreased or poor appetite
- Weight loss
- Stomachaches
- Frequent or loose stools
- Increased or frequent coughing
- Vomiting
- Increased sputum
- Change in the color of sputum
- Breathlessness
- Unwillingness to exercise
- Fever
- Cold symptoms

Immunizations and CF

Babies with CF are particularly at risk from the common childhood infectious diseases, especially those that may affect the lungs.

A child with CF must stick rigidly to the normal immunization schedule (see p.283), and injections should only be postponed in very exceptional circumstances and after consultation with your doctor. Having a cold or a cough is not sufficient reason to delay immunization. CF children should also be immunized against the flu every winter.

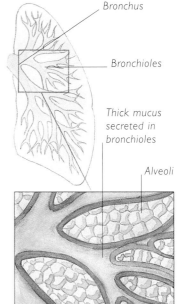

Bronchus

Bronchioles

Thick mucus secreted in bronchioles

Alveoli

Blocked airways
Thick mucus blocks the airways, starving them of oxygen and ultimately causing parts of the lung to collapse.

Physical therapy
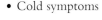
To clear the thick mucus from your child's chest, use physical therapy twice a day, and more often during chest infections.

Make sure your child is comfortable during physical therapy

DIABETES MELLITUS

A chronic disease, diabetes mellitus in children is due to a lack of insulin from the pancreas. This results in an increase in blood glucose concentration (hyperglycemia), causing excessive urination and constant thirst and hunger. An accumulation in the body of chemicals called ketones occurs when there is a severe lack of insulin. A high sugar level is not in itself dangerous, but high ketone levels are. Most diabetic children need insulin injections and a strictly controlled diet.

IS THERE A CURE?

Diabetes occurs because cells of the immune system attack the insulin-producing islet tissue in your child's pancreas. Any cure must therefore replace the damaged tissue in some way. For this reason, transplantation offers the only viable therapeutic approach, but rejection of the transplanted tissue poses a serious problem.

There is promising research going on that suggests we might be able to graft tissue into the body that will not be recognized as foreign. Already this approach has worked experimentally and has been used to reverse diabetes in a number of animal models, without the need for antirejection therapy. It is quite possible that diabetes will be cured with transplants in your child's lifetime. Progress has also been made with genetic research, and the recent discovery of two new genes has opened up the possibility that the condition could be prevented.

Subcutaneous injection
Pinch the skin gently and insert the needle at 90°. A needle will deliver the insulin to the layer of fat just below the skin.

ADJUSTING TO DIABETES

It can be quite frightening when you're told that your child has insulin-dependent diabetes (Type I diabetes), but the disease will not prevent your child from leading a full and active life.

How you and the family handle your child's diabetes helps to determine the way in which your child accepts or denies the disease and becomes a balanced, mature person. You will soon know a lot about diabetes itself, the need for insulin, the technique for injection, and about the importance of proper food intake and exercise. You will also need to know how to recognize the signs of a low/high blood sugar level.

CONTROLLING DIABETES

The aim of diabetes treatment is to keep blood sugar levels as near to normal as possible. Too high a level (hyperglycemia) can lead to fatigue, excessive urination, constant thirst, weight loss, and an increased level of ketones in the body. Too little blood sugar (hypoglycemia) can lead to weakness, dizziness, confusion, and even seizures. Proper levels are achieved by a combination of dietary control and regular meals, with particular attention paid to the intake of sugar and carbohydrates, insulin injections, and regular physical exercise.

After a diagnosis is made, treatment is started by a pediatrician who specializes in diabetes, usually supported by nurses certified as diabetes educators and dieticians. Other members of the diabetes medical team include an ophthalmologist and a pharmacist. There are many different insulin preparations available, but essentially they are of two types—short-acting and longer-acting. Short-acting insulins are used before the main meals of the day, whereas longer-acting preparations are used twice a day. It is likely that your child will need to use a combination of the two. These are now available in cartridge form and they can be given conveniently via a cartridge pen. The hospital team will also talk to you about the value of blood

Injection sites
To avoid scarring, vary the injection sites. Suitable sites include the upper arms, thighs, buttocks, and stomach.

glucose self-monitoring, which both you and your child can do at home to help control the diabetes. The hospital diabetes team will want to see your child regularly. In particular, they will be aiming to keep blood glucose under control, and they will also monitor growth and development. This is likely to involve regular blood tests.

Perfect control is too much to hope for. Even if your child is completely trustworthy about insulin and food, he will still occasionally have raised blood sugar. If your child eats candies and other sweets occasionally, it won't be life-threatening, so don't make too much fuss.

One bite of chocolate will not make any child sick, not even a child with diabetes. Even if your child has followed your advice, you will have to accept that blood sugar can sometimes be a little high or a little low. Be realistic.

IMMUNIZATIONS AND DIABETES

Diabetic children are more vulnerable to infection so annual flu shots are recommended. Additionally, your child will be offered the pneumococcal vaccine after the age of two. This may need to be repeated after three years, depending on the antibody response. Your child must also have the usual childhood vaccinations.

HOW YOU CAN HELP

You will need to exercise skill to help your child accept his condition with the minimum of fuss. Supervise invisibly while giving your child some responsibility so that he learns self-care and control.

Children with diabetes tend to worry more than children without the disease, and this is only to be expected; they have to assume important responsibilities, and they know, or will come to know, that diabetes can do some very unpleasant things. Diabetes makes children feel tired and confused, and can make them lose consciousness. A child who is diabetic has to plan ahead when leaving home, and remember always to take along some candy or sugar and insulin and syringes. Your child is threatened both physically and psychologically by diabetes, so you need to be sympathetic without becoming overprotective. As your child grows older, however, he will gain mastery over the situation, learn self-care, and understand what needs to be done.

Blood glucose self-monitoring

A system is available that enables you to measure your child's blood sugar level accurately at any time. Precise monitoring and testing of blood sugar may reduce and even reverse some of the complications of diabetes.

You begin by obtaining a drop of blood from a tiny finger-prick. The blood is dropped onto a chemically sensitive strip. The strip is inserted into a machine that measures the blood glucose and shows it on a digital display. Another method relies on comparing the strip visually with a color-coded chart. Each method gives accurate results.

Blood glucose self-monitoring allows you to measure your child's blood sugar levels frequently and accurately without visiting the doctor and waiting for lab results; with it, you can respond promptly to a low blood-sugar count by giving high-carbohydrate foods, or to a high blood-sugar count by giving an insulin injection. Your doctor can recommend the proper insulin dosages or other medications according to blood glucose levels.

While it involves a small element of pain, blood testing is more accurate than urine tests, since there is a delay between the rise of blood sugar and the time it shows up in the urine. Another problem is that urine tests only show high glucose readings when the levels are well above acceptable limits.

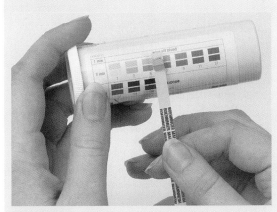

Test strip
The strip will change color to indicate your child's glucose level. Read the blood glucose level by comparing the strip with the color chart on the side of the strip container.

CEREBRAL PALSY

In the US each year about seven in 1,000 babies are born with or develop cerebral palsy. It is a disorder that affects both boys and girls from all races and social backgrounds.

WHAT CAUSES CEREBRAL PALSY?

Cerebral palsy is caused by an injury to the brain, usually before, around, or soon after the time of birth. Causes of such injury include a difficult or preterm birth, perhaps because the baby fails to breathe properly; cerebral bleeding, which may occur in preterm babies; or bleeding into cavities of the brain (intraventricular hemorrhage), which may also occur in preterm babies; or an infection in the mother during the first weeks of pregnancy—rubella or cytomegalovirus, for example. Occasionally, a baby's brain is formed abnormally for no obvious reason, or the disorder is inherited even if both parents are healthy.

TYPES OF CEREBRAL PALSY

If a child has cerebral palsy, part of her brain does not function normally. The affected area is usually one of the parts of the brain that controls certain muscles and body movements; the disease interferes with the messages that normally pass from the brain to the body. In some children, cerebral palsy is hardly noticeable at all; others are more severely affected. No two children will be affected in quite the same way. There are three main types of cerebral palsy:

Spastic cerebral palsy Here, the cortex, which is the outer layer of the brain and controls thought, movement, and sensation, is affected. Tight and sometimes jerky muscle movements result.

Athetoid cerebral palsy This type involves the basal ganglia, which are groups of cells lying deep within the brain. The basal ganglia promote organized, graceful, and economical movement, so an abnormality can cause movements that are bending and wavelike.

HOW YOU CAN HELP

It's difficult to predict the effects of cerebral palsy, particularly on a young child. It doesn't become more severe as your child gets older, though some difficulties may become more noticeable, and your priorities will change: when your baby is young, for example, you might concentrate on helping her to sit up, but later you will be more concerned with communication skills and talking.

There is no cure for cerebral palsy, but if children are lifted, held, and positioned well from an early age, and encouraged to play in a way that helps them to improve their posture and muscle control, they can learn a lot and lead fulfilling lives.

There's no question that you're going to have to work very hard with your child, and there will be difficult moments when you feel that it's all too much. These feelings are natural, and most parents feel that they gradually get less severe. Indeed, many parents say they find bringing up a child with cerebral palsy a challenging and fulfilling task.

Children with cerebral palsy often tend to lie or sit in certain ways, because their muscles are sometimes in spasm, and they can have problems with their joints. Having physical therapy as soon as cerebral

palsy is suspected can help reduce the risk that these complications will develop.

• Your child may get stiffer and have more muscle spasms when she's lying on her back, so lay her on her side or stomach instead, supporting her with a cushion if necessary. It's also a good idea to change her position every 20 minutes or so.

• Help your child to learn to use her hands right from the start by letting her feel things with different textures, and encouraging her to hold toys and other objects. Toys securely strung over her chair can be useful.

• Enable your child to learn shapes by showing her different simply shaped objects, and encouraging her to handle them and play with them.

• A child of three or four years with cerebral palsy may want to help with everyday tasks around the house like any child her age. Explain to your child what you're doing, let her watch you, and if possible, let her join in.

Ataxic cerebral palsy This indicates that the cerebellum, which is located at the base of the brain, is affected. Because the cerebellum is responsible for coordinating fine movement, posture, and balance, an abnormality can result in an uneven gait and difficulty in walking.

EFFECTS OF CEREBRAL PALSY

Some children with cerebral palsy will have difficulty talking, walking, or using their hands, and most will need help with everyday tasks. Very often, a child's other abilities—vision or hearing—may be affected. The child with cerebral palsy may suffer slightly or severely from slow, awkward, or jerky movements, stiffness, weakness, floppiness, or muscle spasms. Some children are prone to involuntary movements. There are a number of disorders associated with cerebral palsy, due either to poor muscle control or to other abnormalities in the brain.

Eyesight The most common eye problem is a squint, which may need correction with glasses or, in severe cases, an operation.

Hearing Children with cerebral palsy are more likely to have severe hearing difficulties than other children. It is important that hearing difficulties be diagnosed early (see p.178). An affected child may be able to wear a hearing aid.

Speech The ability to control the tiny muscles in the mouth, tongue, palate, and voice box is necessary for speech. Difficulty in speaking and problems with chewing and swallowing often occur together in children with cerebral palsy. Speech therapists can help with both kinds of difficulties and ease communication problems.

Spatial perception Some children with cerebral palsy can't perceive space and relate it to their own bodies; for instance, they're not able to judge distances or think in three dimensions. This is due to an abnormality in a part of the brain that is not related to intelligence.

Epilepsy About one-third of children with cerebral palsy are affected by epilepsy (see p.270), but it is impossible to predict whether, or when, your child may develop seizures. In some children, they start in infancy; in others, not until adulthood. If your child does develop epilepsy, it can be controlled with medication.

Learning difficulties People who are unable to control their movements very well, or to talk, are often assumed to have a mental disability. Some people with cerebral palsy do have learning difficulties, but this is by no means always the case; many people with cerebral palsy have average intelligence.

Help for your child
It's important to help children with cerebral palsy to lead as normal a life as possible. This little girl is having fun with a toy while sitting in a special seat and table designed to support her and correct her postural problems.

CHOOSING AND USING TOYS

Despite their difficulties with movement, children with cerebral palsy need stimulating play as much as any child, but choosing toys can be problematic. Most toy companies make goods suitable for children with cerebral palsy. If you are planning to buy an expensive toy, ask your physical therapist or occupational therapist for advice, or join a toy library and experiment to find out which toys your child will find most rewarding. Wedges, for support, and standing frames can greatly help children with cerebral palsy to enjoy their toys. Once again, your occupational therapist will be able to help.

• When your child is playing, let him choose from two or three toys, then put away the ones he doesn't want. If he's surrounded by lots of toys, he will easily be distracted.

• Always show your child how a new toy works, not once but many times.

• Help him to use his imagination by telling him stories about his cuddly toys while you play with him, for example, or encourage him to have a tea party with them.

• If your child doesn't seem to want to play, start showing him how much fun it is by starting to play with his toys yourself, and ask him to join in.

Conductive education

This learning system is designed to help adults and children with certain kinds of motor disabilities, including children with cerebral palsy, to become much more independent.

It was developed at the Pëto Institute in Hungary and has helped some children to gain skills that their parents never believed possible. The aim is to help people to function as normally as possible—physically, intellectually, and socially. It is based on a consideration of the child as a whole person, intensive group work with parents and children, and the encouragement of every small movement toward gaining independence.

The Inter-American Conductive Education Association (see **Useful addresses**, p.344) is establishing a network of schools where parents and their preschool children can learn the basics of conductive education together.

EPILEPSY

More than 2.7 million Americans of all ages are living with epilepsy. This brain disease tends to run in families. The normal electrical impulses in the brain are disturbed, causing periodic seizures.

EPILEPTIC SEIZURES

There are several forms of epileptic seizure. One, called "grand mal," involves recurring attacks of seizures and difficulty breathing with loss of consciousness followed by stiffening of the body lasting a minute or less, and then a series of rhythmic jerks of the limbs, clenching of the teeth (when your child might bite his tongue), and frothing at the mouth.

In another form, called "petit mal," there are no abnormal movements, only a second or two of unconsciousness, very much like daydreaming. Your child's eyes will glaze over and he appears not to see or hear anything. This is not easily recognized, and may go undiagnosed. Although not as dramatic as grand mal, petit mal seizures can interfere with a child's life, particularly with paying attention and performance at school, and with some physical activities where loss of control could pose a danger.

Epilepsy is not to be confused with febrile seizures (see p.281), which are fairly harmless and are caused by a high temperature preceding or during an infectious illness.

HOW SERIOUS IS IT?

Epilepsy is by no means life-threatening. Most children grow out of the petit mal form by late adolescence, but those who suffer from the grand mal form can also improve with age and some grow out of it. However, some children with grand mal epilepsy need special attention throughout life, even though the condition can usually be controlled by drugs. It can take time to establish the level of medication required, and a young child may go through times when the epilepsy is not absolutely controlled by drugs. Consult your doctor, who can raise the dose for better control. Dosage of the anti-epileptic treatment will need to be increased as your child grows and puts on weight, since treatment is based on weight. If your child has a seizure of any kind, consult your doctor immediately.

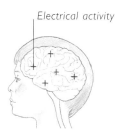

Electrical activity

Excessive electrical
activity causes
seizure

**Normal brain
activity**
*The level of electrical
activity in the brain
is relatively low.*

**Brain activity
in a seizure**
*When an excess of electrical
energy builds up, signals are
sent to the body, causing a
seizure.*

WHAT TO DO DURING A SEIZURE

• Loosen the clothing around your child's neck
or chest.

• As soon as your child stops moving violently,
put him in the recovery position (see p.329).

• During a petit mal seizure, guide your child
to safety and stay with him until it has passed.

• Make a note of what happens during your child's
seizure so you can tell your doctor.

• Don't try to restrain the limbs.

• Don't try to hold your child's teeth apart if they
are clenched, or put anything into his mouth.

TREATMENT

If your child has a seizure, your doctor will ask
you about it and examine him to decide what
form of seizure he's had. If the doctor suspects the
seizure may be the onset of epilepsy, the child
will be referred to a pediatric neurologist for an
examination that may include blood tests, an EEG
(electroencephalogram), and a brain scan.

Epilepsy can be controlled, but not cured. Anti-
convulsive drugs taken on a daily basis will reduce
the frequency of grand mal seizures and eradicate
them in most children. Selective drugs are now
available that target a precise area of the brain
and don't cause the side effects associated with
older drugs.

Your child's condition will be reviewed
periodically by your doctor, and if there are no
seizures for a year or two, he may try phasing
out the drugs.

Surgery may be used if drugs are not effective and
if damage to a single area of the brain is thought
to be the cause. Your doctor will advise you as to
whether this might be appropriate.

HOW YOU CAN HELP

It could be a shock to realize that your child has
epilepsy, but you must try to remain calm. You and
your child will both need to get your confidence
back. You can do this with the help of your
doctor, who can advise you on how to cope
with the seizures.

It is important to observe your child's condition
so that you can report back to your doctor. Make a
note of the frequency of your child's seizures. If he's
on medication, watch him carefully and report any
mental or personality differences that may be caused
by the drugs. You should never stop your child's
medication without seeking medical advice first.
To do so could result in a severe, prolonged seizure
after a few days.

Treat your child as normally as possible all
the time. Tell his friends and teachers about the
condition so that they're not scared or shocked if
your child has a seizure when they're there. Your
child should always wear a medical alert bracelet or
tag engraved with information about his epilepsy.

When your child is old enough, teach him to
recognize the signs of an oncoming attack. Many
sufferers of epilepsy experience sensations such as an
unpleasant smell, distorted vision, or an odd feeling
in the stomach just before a seizure. If your child
can identify these sensations as warning signs, he
may be able to avoid having an accident.

THE OUTLOOK FOR YOUR CHILD

The aim of caring for a child with epilepsy is to
control the seizures with a minimum of side effects
and enhance his quality of life as he grows up.
Seizure control should never be established at
the cost of drug side effects, since they may result
in cramping of important brain functions that allow
your child to develop normally.

Monitoring your child's condition is very
important. Don't rely on your doctor to do this;
establish a plan of action that involves regular visits,
and if your child has more than one or two seizures,
visit the doctor immediately for reassessment;
the medication may need to be adjusted.

SICKLE CELL DISEASE

This inherited disease is most common in people of African or West Indian descent, but may also occur in people from South Asia, the Middle East, and the eastern Mediterranean. A sufferer will have bouts of pain and may be at risk from other disorders, but will feel well most of the time.

TYPES OF SCD

Sickle cell disease is caused by an abnormality of hemoglobin, the oxygen-carrying substance in red blood cells. There are three main types: sickle cell anemia, which is the most common and severe form, hemoglobin SC disease, and sickle beta-thalassemia.

Sickle cell anemia When oxygen levels are low, the abnormal hemoglobin (known as type S) becomes crystallized, making the red cell fragile and ridged. These sickle cells—so called because of their characteristic sickle or crescent shape—can then become trapped in the blood vessels, causing a blockage that prevents blood flow. This accounts for the excruciating pain that is characteristic of an SCD attack.

Sickle cells last only about 20 days in the body, as opposed to the usual 120 days for normal red cells, and the early death of red cells leads to anemia. Sometimes aplastic crises occur, where the blood-forming activity in the bone marrow is reduced temporarily, decreasing the level of red-cell production and shortening the life of the red cells. As a result, the bone marrow may become inactive, which can be life-threatening.

Hemoglobin SC disease In this form of SCD there are two abnormal hemoglobins—type S and type C. The disease appears later, and in a milder form, than sickle cell anemia.

Sickle beta–thalassemia This is similar to sickle cell anemia in that there is an abnormality in the hemoglobin that results in abnormally shaped cells. Sufferers inherit a sickle cell gene from one parent and a thalassemia gene from the other.

SICKLE CELL TRAIT

Sickle cell trait is found in areas where malaria was or is endemic, and offers some protection against malaria. It's not surprising, therefore, that around 10 percent of Afro-Caribbeans, 25 percent of Nigerians, and a smaller but significant number of Middle Eastern and Mediterranean people have the trait.

A child can only inherit sickle cell disease if both parents pass on the abnormal trait, and even then the chances are only one in four. If only one parent passes on the trait, then the sickle cell gene will be masked by a healthy gene from the other parent. A carrier is unaffected, but the trait shows up in blood tests.

EFFECTS OF SCD

Apart from causing anemia and acute attacks of pain called "crises," sickle cell disease can cause other problems, including infections and jaundice. There is also a small risk of a stroke occurring during a crisis.

Infections Children with SCD are particularly vulnerable to infections—for example, in the lungs or bones. An overwhelming infection can cause a dramatic loss of blood cells in the spleen or liver, resulting in a massive drop in hemoglobin levels, which is potentially fatal if treatment is not given immediately.

Pain crises When sickle cells block a blood vessel, there may be oxygen starvation of tissue supplied by that blood vessel; this can occur nearly anywhere in the body, although the feet and hands are particularly vulnerable.

These crises are one of the most distressing aspects of SCD; the pain is violent and unpredictable, and as a parent it is very difficult to watch your child in pain and be unable to help her. The crisis can be treated with painkilling drugs, however. Sometimes crises are brought on by infections, strenuous exercise, low temperatures, or dehydration caused by vomiting or diarrhea

Jaundice The rapid breakdown of red cells can result in increased levels of a pigment called bilirubin (see **Jaundice**, p.25). This causes a yellowish appearance in the whites of the eyes, which often increases with the severity of the crises. Skin may also have a yellowish tinge.

Development Children with SCD may experience a slowdown of their growth (in both height and weight), and puberty may also be delayed. They may exist in a permanent state of chronic anemia leading to a rapid decline in their condition when ill.

SCREENING

Genetic and supportive counseling are essential for couples at risk or with SCD in their families. In some areas, all babies are screened for hemoglobin abnormalities regardless of ethnic origin. Early detection means the condition can be managed properly right from the start, and in particular that long-term treatment with penicillin can begin promptly, to minimize the risk of lung infections and sickle cell crises.

Prenatal screening is available to find out if a baby's hemoglobin is normal and can be carried out at the time of amniocentesis (usually about 16 weeks into the pregnancy). Screening is advisable for pregnant women who are aware that they have the sickle cell trait. Couples at risk will be offered counseling to clarify the risks of having children.

TREATMENT

If your child has SCD, she'll need frequent doses of penicillin to nip bacterial infections in the bud. This should be given from the time of diagnosis

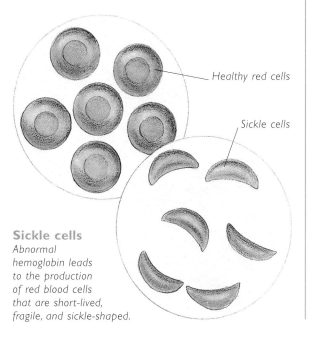

Healthy red cells

Sickle cells

Sickle cells
Abnormal hemoglobin leads to the production of red blood cells that are short-lived, fragile, and sickle-shaped.

throughout life. All affected children need folic acid supplements. They should drink plenty of fluids to prevent dehydration and should always keep warm, to encourage normal circulation. Although over-exertion can cause problems, your child should exercise regularly and find her own energy tolerance level—exercise will improve the health of her heart and circulation. Pain and symptoms of infection should be treated promptly.

Where millions of red blood cells have been destroyed, exchange transfusion in hospital may be necessary. Sometimes many exchange transfusions will have to be given. Although this is a lengthy procedure, it will allow your child a near-normal life. Painkillers, fluids, and possibly inhaled oxygen and antibiotics may be given, too. With experience, parents can learn to manage mild crises at home.

HOW YOU CAN HELP

Although knowledge about the disease is incomplete, it is important that you are as well informed as possible, so that you can help your child avoid pain crises. Counseling will give you a safe, confidential way of exploring your feelings, and provide a source of encouragement and support (see **Useful addresses**, p.344).

When your child starts school, you should inform her teachers and the school principal of her condition, making them aware of the problems it can impose on education. Your child may miss classes, for example, because of hospital admissions or a crisis. Reassure your child and encourage her to express her feelings and anxieties.

Your child's feelings must be given great consideration. Many children with SCD can experience difficulties with their classmates at preschool and school. Your child's teachers should educate the other children about SCD so that your child does not suffer from feelings of alienation or isolation—as she might if, for example, they thought they could catch the disease from her.

Once they can speak, many SCD children express a fear of dying or being deformed. Others feel different and alienated, thinking they're the only ones who are suffering from this condition and that nobody understands them. Still others are afraid of expressing when they are in pain in case nobody believes them. You can help enormously by making sure that your child knows she has your sympathy, understanding, and care whenever she needs it.

CHAPTER 6

Medicine and healthcare

Most childhood illnesses are minor, and others
are easily preventable; immunizations are effective
against most infectious diseases. In a baby, however,
seemingly minor illnesses can cause complications:
a cold that develops into a throat infection,
for instance, may cause breathing difficulties.

You will be understandably anxious if your child
is sick or has had an accident. Sometimes, deciding
whether to seek medical help can be equally
stressful. You should never worry that you are
being too cautious—if you find yourself wondering
whether it is worth consulting a doctor, then you
probably should.

The main cause of death in young children is
accidents, but fortunately, many injuries are
preventable. Reduce the likelihood of accidents
by making your home safe and taking precautions
when your child is away from home. Learn first
aid. Don't just read this book; attend a first-aid
training course (see p.327) and learn the
emergency procedures on pp.326–33 by heart.

Dealing with illness

It's fairly easy to recognize when your child is ill: he'll be pale and listless, and lose his appetite. You can treat him at home for most things. If you're ever worried or in two minds about the seriousness of the illness, however, call your doctor. Some symptoms always require immediate medical attention: see p.277. Even when you are sure your child is ill, you might not know what's wrong with him. To help your doctor as much as possible, observe everything you can about your child's symptoms; the more information the doctor has, the better his chances of making an accurate diagnosis.

WARNING SYMPTOMS

If you think your child is falling ill, monitor his temperature, appetite, and breathing rate.

Temperature The normal body temperature for a child is 98.6°F (37°C). If a baby has a temperature, seek medical advice. For an older child with a raised temperature, always consider his overall condition to decide how sick he is. Take into account how alert and communicative he is, whether he is eating and drinking, and any other symptoms, such as an earache. Your child's temperature does vary according to how active he has been and the time of day. His temperature is lower in the morning than during the day, and higher in the evening. It will also be higher if he has been running around.

Diarrhea Loose, watery bowel movements mean the intestines are inflamed and irritable, and there is not enough time for water to be reabsorbed from the stool. Gastroenteritis is the most common cause, but diarrhea can be caused by gastric flu or an infection elsewhere in the body. Diarrhea is always serious in babies and young children because it can lead to dehydration. If your baby is under one year old and has had diarrhea for six hours, consult your doctor immediately.

Vomiting Check with your doctor if your child has been vomiting for six hours or more, especially if he has diarrhea or fever. Vomiting is usually caused by gastroenteritis or food that disagrees with your child, but there may be a more serious cause.

Taking your child's pulse

A rapid or undetectable pulse may indicate that your child is ill. The pulse rate varies according to health, age, and physical exertion.

The average pulse rate for a baby is 100–160 beats per minute; this slows to 100–120 for a one-year-old, and 80–90 for a seven-year-old.

When taking your child's pulse, use the first two fingers, not your thumb. Count the number of beats over a 15-second period and multiply this figure by four to get the rate per minute. Do not use your thumb, since it has a pulse of its own.

Checking heartbeat
For a child under a year, the best way to take a pulse is to put your palm on her chest at the level of the nipple and count the number of heartbeats (you'll also find a pulse on the inner side of the arm above the elbow.)

Radial pulse
In a child over one year, it should be relatively easy to find the pulse on her wrist. Place your middle and index fingers on the spot on the wrist immediately below the thumb, and count the beats.

Use your index and middle fingers, not your thumb

Pain You should see your doctor if your child complains of headaches, particularly after he's bumped his head or if the headache comes on a few hours after the head injury, or if there is blurred vision, nausea, dizziness, or stomach pain, particularly on the lower right side of the abdomen.

Breathing Difficulty in breathing is a medical emergency and requires immediate help. Breathing may be labored and you may notice that your child's ribs are drawn in sharply each time she takes a breath. If her lips turn blue, you should treat this as an emergency and call 911.

Appetite Sudden changes in appetite may indicate underlying illness, especially if your child has a fever, even a mild one. Your doctor should be alerted if your child refuses food for a day and seems lethargic, or, if he is under six months old, has a poor appetite and doesn't seem to be thriving.

CALLING THE DOCTOR
It is only natural for a new parent to be anxious, and you may worry because you are not sure whether your baby is genuinely ill. Along with many doctors, I quickly learned that the one person whose opinion can't be dismissed is the mother's. So your guideline should be, whenever in doubt, call a doctor. Don't feel shy about asking your doctor questions if something is worrying you, however trivial it may seem.

What to tell your doctor In order to make a diagnosis, a doctor will need the following information: a description of your child's symptoms; when they started; in what order they occurred; how severe they are; and whether anything precipitated them (eating something poisonous, for instance). In addition to this, your doctor will need to know your child's age and medical history.

Be prepared to give details of any injury or accident. Did your child lose consciousness? Has he had anything to eat or drink (in case he needs an anesthetic)? Was he bitten by an insect or animal? What was it and what were his symptoms? If he has swallowed a toxic substance or plant, keep some of it to show to the doctor.

The specific questions your doctor may ask about an illness are: Has your child vomited or had diarrhea? Does he have any pain? Where is it? How long has it lasted? Have you given him anything for

it? Is his temperature high? How quickly did the fever come on and what was his highest temperature? Has he lost consciousness at any time? Have you noticed swollen glands or a rash? Has he had any dizziness or blurred vision? The doctor will also ask general questions about your child's appetite and sleeping patterns.

What to ask your doctor If your child is prescribed medications, make sure you know when they should be taken (some medications need to be taken on a full stomach), how long they should be taken for, and whether there are any side effects. Find out how your child should be nursed and how soon his symptoms can be expected to go away. Ask your doctor about preventive measures for a child who has a recurring condition like cold sores.

With an infectious disease, you'll need to know whether it's safe to have visitors, how long your child will have to be out of school, and whether the illness has any long-term effects.

EMERGENCIES
Some situations demand immediate medical attention. Call 911 or take your child to the nearest hospital emergency room by car should any of the following serious situations happen:

- A bone fracture or suspected fracture (see p.339)
- A severe reaction to a sting or bite from an insect or animal (see p.341), or after eating nuts
- Head injury
- Symptoms of meningitis (see p.304)
- Pale blue or gray coloration around the lips
- A burn or scald (see p.336) that is larger than the area of your child's hand
- Poisoning or suspected poisoning (see p.334)
- Unconsciousness (see pp.327–29)
- Severe bleeding from a wound (see p.335)
- Contact with a corrosive chemical, especially involving the eyes (see pp.334 and 338)
- Difficulty breathing, or choking (see p.333)
- Any injuries to the ears or eyes (see pp.284, 287, and 338)
- An electric shock (see p.334)
- Inhalation of toxic fumes such as smoke or gas

TEMPERATURE

Take your child's temperature whenever you suspect she is ill. Normal body temperature for a child is between 96.8°F (36°C) and 98.6°F (37°C). Anything over 100.4°F (38°C) is classed as a fever. Never take your child's temperature just after she has been running around or eaten something hot or cold.

Take care

Don't use a mercury thermometer in your child's mouth; she may bite it and swallow mercury, which is a poison. Digital thermometers are harder to break and are safe and easy to use with children of all ages. They are battery-operated, so be sure to have some spare batteries available.

Thermometers

A hot forehead may be the first sign that your child has a fever, but to be sure, take your child's temperature with a thermometer. Take it again after 20 minutes.

The most accurate way to take your child's temperature is with a digital thermometer. Ear thermometers are also very accurate and give a reading in seconds. Strip thermometers are less accurate than others, but simple and safe to use. Always wash a thermometer after use in soap and cold water and store in its own case.

Digital thermometer
Window shows the temperature reading

Ear thermometer
Window shows the temperature reading

Strip thermometer
A glowing panel indicates your child's temperature

TAKING YOUR CHILD'S TEMPERATURE

Using a digital thermometer
A digital thermometer can be used in the mouth or under the arm. To take the mouth temperature, ask your child to open her mouth and raise her tongue. Place the thermometer under her tongue. Ask your child to place the tip of her tongue firmly behind her lower front teeth—this will hold the thermometer in place. Then ask her to close her lips—but not her teeth—over it. Leave until the thermometer beeps, remove, and read the number in the window. With a young child, you may find it easier to take her temperature under her arm. Put the thermometer into her armpit and lower her arm over it. Hold her arm down until the thermometer beeps, then remove and read it.

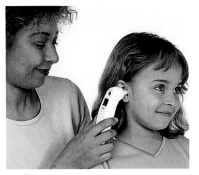

Using an ear thermometer
Digital ear thermometers are a quick, safe method of taking a child's temperature. Gently insert the tip into your child's ear and read the temperature from the display. The ear thermometer has a hygienic disposable tip.

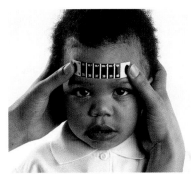

Using a strip thermometer
The strip thermometer is easy to use. Carefully position the heat-sensitive side on your child's forehead and hold it there for a minute or so, keeping your fingers clear of the panels. The temperature should light up on the outside of the strip.

MEDICINES

Most medicines for children come in syrup form with a spoon or dropper to administer them. If your baby refuses medicine, get your partner to help you, or wrap her up in a blanket so that you can hold her steady. Using droppers or letting your baby suck the medicine from your finger are the best ways to give medicine if your child can't yet swallow from a spoon. Older children may be cajoled into taking medicine by the promise of a favorite food to take the taste away.

GIVING MEDICINE

Dropper
Hold your baby in the crook of your arm, put the dropper into the medicine, and draw up the right amount by squeezing the bulb at the top. Place the dropper in the corner of your baby's mouth and gently release the medicine by squeezing the bulb.

Spoon
The spoon should be sterilized with boiling water or sterilizing solution. Hold your baby in a semi-reclining position, pull his chin down with your finger, and place the spoon on his lower lip. Raise the angle of the spoon so that the medicine trickles into his mouth.

Finger
Measure out the correct dose of medicine into a small container. Dip your finger in it and allow your baby to suck it off your finger. Continue until he has taken the whole dose.

APPLYING DROPS

Eye drops
Lay your baby on his back and tilt his head in the direction of the affected eye. Put the dropper into the medicine, and draw up the right amount. Gently pull his lower eyelid down with your finger and raise his upper lid. Let the drops fall into the corner of his eye. Get someone to help if necessary.

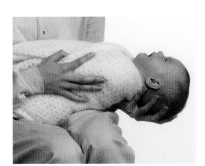

Position for nose drops
Lay your baby on his back with his head tilted backward. Put the dropper into the medicine, and draw up the right amount. Hold the dropper above your baby's nostrils and let the required number of drops fall into each nostril.

Position for ear drops
Lay your baby on his side. Put the dropper into the medicine, and draw up the right amount. Hold the dropper over your baby's ear opening and let the required number of eardrops fall into the center of his ear. Keep him still for a few moments while the drops spread into the ear canal.

NURSING YOUR CHILD

You don't need special skills or medical knowledge to care for your sick child. Relax the rules and try to hide your anxiety. Don't insist that he eats while he's ill, but do encourage him to drink a lot of fluids.

GENERAL NURSING

As well as whatever treatment the doctor recommends, the following routines will help your child to feel more comfortable while he is sick:

• Air your child's room and bed at least once a day.

• Leave a bowl by your child's bed if he is vomiting or has whooping cough.

• Leave a box of tissues by your child's bed.

• Give small meals frequently; your child may find large portions unappetizing.

• Sponge your child down with tepid water if he has a fever.

• Give liquid acetaminophen or ibuprofen for pain relief or fever.

SHOULD YOUR CHILD BE IN BED?

At the beginning of an illness, when your child is feeling quite sick, he will probably want to stay in bed, and he may sleep a lot. As he starts to feel better he will still need bed rest, but he will want to be around you and may want to play. The best way to accommodate this is to make up a bed on the sofa in a room near where you are working so that he can lie down when he wants to. Don't insist that your child goes to bed just because he is ill—children with a fever, for instance, don't recover faster if they stay in bed. When your child is tired, however, it is time for bed. But don't just leave him alone. Make sure that you visit him regularly (every half-hour), and stay to play a game, read a book, or do a puzzle. When he's on the road to recovery, make sure that enough happens in his day to make the distinction between night and day.

GIVING DRINKS

It is essential that your child drinks a lot when he's ill—when he has a fever, diarrhea, or is vomiting—because he will need to replace lost fluids to avoid becoming dehydrated. The recommended fluid intake for a child with a fever is 1½–2½ fluid ounces per pound (100–150 milliliters per kilogram) of body weight per day, which is the equivalent of 1 quart (1 liter) per day for a child who weighs 20 pounds (9 kilograms).

Encourage your child to drink by leaving a drink at his bedside (preferably water or fruit juice), by putting drinks in glasses that are especially appealing, and by giving him flexible straws to drink with.

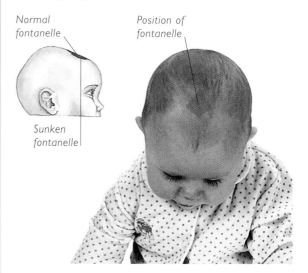

Normal fontanelle

Position of fontanelle

Sunken fontanelle

Dehydration

If your baby is under 18 months and has been vomiting or has had diarrhea, she may be dehydrated. One sign of dehydration is sunken fontanelles, which indicate that your baby needs immediate medical attention.

OCCUPYING YOUR CHILD

Illness is an occasion when you can completely indulge your child. When he is not resting, spend time playing games and talking to him. Relax all the rules and let him play whatever games he wants to, even if you've previously not allowed them in bed. If your child wants to do something messy, like painting, just spread an old sheet or plastic shower curtain over the bed. If you can, move a television into his room temporarily—this will keep him entertained and make him feel special, as well.

Let him do some painting; read aloud to him; get out some of his old toys and play with them together; buy him small presents and let him unwrap them; sing songs or make up a story together; ask him to draw a picture of what he is going to do when he feels better; and, unless he has an infectious illness, let some friends visit him for a brief period during the day. As your child gets better, let him play outside, but if he has a fever, discourage him from running around too much.

VOMITING

Your child will probably find vomiting a distressing experience, and you should try and make him as comfortable as possible. Get him to sit up in bed and make sure there is a bowl or a pail within easy reach, so that he doesn't have to run to the bathroom. Hold back long hair, and when he's being sick, hold his head and comfort him. Afterward, help your child to brush his teeth, or give him a mint to suck to take the taste away.

When your child hasn't vomited for a few hours and he's feeling hungry, offer him bland foods, such as pasta or mashed potatoes, but don't encourage him to eat if he doesn't want to. More important than eating is having plenty of fluids. Avoid milk and give him water or diluted fruit juice.

TREATING A HIGH TEMPERATURE

The first sign of a raised temperature is often a hot forehead, but to check if your child is feverish, take his temperature (see p.278). Call your doctor if the fever lasts more than 24 hours or if there are any accompanying symptoms. Temperatures over 100.4°F (38°C) should be taken very seriously in children under six months, but doctors do believe a high temperature is a protective mechanism for killing off viruses and bacteria. To reduce fever, lower the temperature in your child's room and give iced drinks

Try to cool your child down by tepid sponging if his temperature is over 104°F (40°C)—children risk febrile seizures if their temperature is too high. Wet a washcloth in tepid water and wring gently, so that it is still dripping. Starting from the head, and using gentle strokes, sponge your child's whole body. Re-wet the cloth in the tepid water when it starts to feel warm. Check your child's temperature every five minutes and stop sponging when it drops to 100.4°F (38°C). Never use cold water, since this will cause his blood vessels to constrict, preventing heat loss and increasing temperature.

When sponging with tepid water fails to lower your child's temperature, try giving him liquid acetaminophen or ibuprofen (aspirin is unsuitable for children under 12). It's still important for him to drink lots of fluid, since he will be perspiring a lot.

Febrile seizures

The most common cause of seizures in babies and children between six months and three years is a raised temperature that accompanies a viral infection. It's known as a febrile seizure.

During a seizure, the muscles of the body twitch involuntarily due to a temporary abnormality in brain function. The child loses consciousness. Other symptoms include the stiffening of the body, rhythmic jerking of limbs, and clenching of teeth, with sleepiness and confusion on coming around. The child may also be incontinent. You should clear a space around him so that he doesn't hurt himself. Wait until his body has stopped jerking and then place him in the recovery position (see p.329).

You will need to sponge your child with tepid (never cold) water to reduce his temperature. Don't leave him alone, don't try to restrain him, and don't put anything in his mouth. Call a doctor as soon as your child has come around. Should the seizure last more than 15 minutes, call an ambulance.

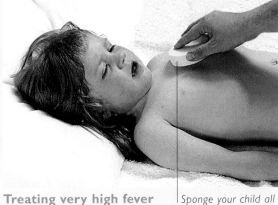

Treating very high fever
If your child's temperature is over 104°F (40°C), undress her and cool her down by sponging her with tepid water.

Sponge your child all over to cool her down

HOSPITALS

At some point in your child's life she may have to go into the hospital. This could be because she has an accident, a childhood illness, or a chronic condition, such as sickle cell disease (see p.272), which requires regular blood transfusions, or she needs to have an operation.

TEACHING YOUR CHILD

Given a little forethought on your part, a stay in the hospital does not have to be upsetting or frightening for your child. If you don't like hospitals and you convey this attitude to your child, you may inadvertently make her stay more difficult than it has to be. Try to teach her that a hospital is a friendly place where people go to get better. Whenever the chance arises—if you have a friend or a relative in the hospital, for instance—take your child along when you go to visit, and be matter-of-fact, not gloomy, about their illness. If a child's first experience of a hospital is when she becomes sick, it will seem more alien than it would otherwise.

If you know that your child is going to the hospital, read her a story about a child who goes into a hospital, and role-play doctors and nurses with toy stethoscopes. Be as honest as you can about why she's going to the hospital, and emphasize that it's to make her better. Reassure her that you will be with her as much as you can, and if she is old enough to understand, tell her when she'll be well enough to come home.

If your child requires an operation, she'll probably be curious about what's going to happen to her. Answer her questions as honestly as you can—if she asks you whether the operation will hurt, don't pretend that it won't, but tell her that doctors have medicines to make the pain go away quickly.

WHAT TO TAKE

You can help your child prepare for a stay in the hospital by packing a bag with her. One of the most unsettling things for her will be the unfamiliar surroundings and the change of routine, so let her have some of her own things with her: a personal stereo and CDs or a radio, travel games, cuddly toys, and a photograph for her bedside. On a practical level, for a short stay, pack the following items:

• A toiletry bag containing a hairbrush, comb, soap, washcloth, toothbrush, and toothpaste

• Three pairs of pajamas or three nightgowns, although some hospitals will want the child to wear a hospital gown to allow easy access

• A bathrobe and a pair of slippers

• Three pairs of socks

• Three pairs of pants

IN THE HOSPITAL

Most hospitals expect parents to stay with their children 24 hours a day. Whether yours does or not, try to spend as much time as possible with your child, especially at first, when her surroundings are unfamiliar. Let her know when you will come, and always keep your promises about visiting. Ask the nurses if you can bathe, change, and feed your child. If she is well enough, you can read and play games with her. If you can't stay all the time, encourage your partner, friends, and relatives to visit at different times rather than all at once so that your child has someone she knows well almost all the time.

COMING HOME

Depending on how long your child has been in the hospital, you may notice some changes in her habits. She probably woke up and went to sleep much earlier in the hospital than she does at home, and these sleeping and waking patterns may carry on for a while. She may resent the discipline at home after having been spoiled and indulged a little, and she may be reluctant to go back to school. The best approach to these things is to be tolerant; your child will soon adapt to life at home again.

IMMUNIZATION

The incidence of potentially fatal childhood diseases such as diphtheria has declined dramatically since the introduction of vaccination programs, which provide immunity. Some vaccines are long-lasting (rubella), others need to be "boosted" at regular intervals (tetanus).

There are two types of immunization: passive and active. The former works by introducing already-formed antibodies into the body. The latter involves injecting a weakened form of the infection that encourages the immune system to produce its own antibodies—this is why immunization can sometimes produce mild symptoms of the disease it is intended to protect against.

In the first five years of your child's life, she will need immunizations for polio as well as measles, mumps and rubella, and Hib, diphtheria, tetanus, pertussis (whooping cough), pneumococcus, and varicella (chicken pox). Vaccines don't provide instant protection against disease; in some cases they take up to four weeks to be effective. Give acetaminophen to ease any discomfort.

IMPORTANCE OF IMMUNIZATION

Because immunization programs have been so successful, it is easy to forget how prevalent diseases like pertussis (whooping cough) or polio once were. Many first-time mothers nowadays have never seen a child in leg-braces—a common sight in their parents' generation, when the possibility of paralysis or even death from polio was a very real one.

Immunization protects both individuals and whole communities from infectious diseases. Every child should therefore be properly immunized. Some mothers are alarmed by stories about the side-effects of vaccinations, but these are actually quite rare. Your child shouldn't be vaccinated, however, if she has an acute illness with a fever, or if she's had a severe reaction to a previous dose of vaccine. Your healthcare provider will advise you.

TETANUS INJECTIONS

There is a danger of tetanus with any penetrating wound. Tetanus bacteria only thrive where there is hardly any oxygen, so superficial wounds carry little risk. Tetanus bacteria and spores live in soil and manure, so it's dirty wounds that are dangerous. The bacteria produce a poison, which attacks the nerves and brain, causing muscle spasm, particularly of the face—hence the common name "lockjaw." Patients always require hospital treatment. Tetanus can be completely prevented by immunization. The first three tetanus injections should be given before 12 months and boosters should be given before starting school and every ten years thereafter. If your child has a dog bite or a deep, dirty cut and has not been immunized, she must have preventative injections right away in a hospital emergency room.

What is given	When
• Diphtheria, tetanus, acellular pertussis (DTaP)	• Generally given at 2, 4, and 6 months
• Polio	• Generally given at 2, 4, and 6 months
• Hib	• Generally given at 2, 4, and 6 months
• Pneumococcus (also called pneumococcal conjugate vaccine, brand name Prevnar)	• Generally given at 2, 4, and 6 months
• Hepatitis B	• Generally given at 2, 4, and 6 months
• MMR (measles, mumps, rubella)	• Given at approximately 1 year old
• Varicella (chickenpox)	• Given at approximately 1 year old
• Influenza vaccine	• Generally given yearly from age 6 months to 24 months
• DTaP	• Given at age 4–6 years
• Polio	• Given at age 4–6 years
• MMR (measles, mumps, rubella)	• Given at age 4–6 years

Since there are now many combination vaccines, most children will not get more than three shots per visit.

Common complaints

Any illness in a child is different from, and more serious than, the same illness in an adult because the immune system is not fully developed and because complications can occur. A throat infection in a child, for example, can easily spread to the chest because the airways are so short.

In this section I've described the most common childhood complaints, and given advice on when you need a doctor, and what you can do at home. Try to become familiar with the material in these pages; it'll help you to take prompt and appropriate action whenever your child complains of feeling ill.

EARS

Ear infections are common in children because their eustachian tubes are narrow and horizontal, so drainage is poor and they are easily blocked, leading to middle ear infections.

WAXY EAR

Ear wax is produced by glands in the outer ear canal and protects the ear from dust, foreign objects, and infection. Children tend to produce more ear wax when they have a cold or sore throat, and if this dries and hardens, it can result in hearing loss. Although it's not usually serious, you should consult your doctor.

Symptoms Ear wax can become hard and compacted and cause impaired hearing, a ringing sound in the head, or a sensation of fullness in the outer ear. It may be possible to see the wax buildup.

Treatment Ear drops may be effective. Drops are more likely to be used if the wax has formed a hard plug—they will soften it, allowing it to come out. You should never try to insert anything into your child's ear to try to clear wax, not even a fingernail or cotton swab. They will only push the wax farther into the canal or damage the lining of the ear.

OUTER EAR INFECTION

The passage leading to the eardrum from the ear flap can sometimes become infected as a result of excessive cleaning or scratching, or the presence of a foreign object in the ear. This can be painful, but is not usually serious.

Symptoms Your child will complain of an earache, and his ear flap and outer ear passage may be red and tender. You may notice a puslike discharge from the ear, and a dry scaly look. If your child is in great pain, he may have a boil in the ear canal.

Treatment Home treatment includes keeping the ear flap clean, and giving liquid acetaminophen to relieve pain and keep the temperature down. Your doctor may prescribe antibiotics or ear drops. Any foreign object or boil in the ear must be dealt with by your healthcare provider.

MIDDLE EAR INFECTION

Otitis media or infection of the middle ear is quite common in children. Infections are caused by bacteria entering the middle ear from the nose and the throat via the eustachian tube. If middle ear infections are left untreated, they can result in permanent hearing loss. Recurrent middle ear infections are often linked with middle ear effusion.

Symptoms The most prominent symptoms are a severe earache and loss of appetite. Your child may also have a fever or a discharge from the ear, and there may be some hearing loss. A baby with a middle ear infection may be distressed and pull and rub her ear, which will be very red; she may also have general symptoms such as loss of appetite, vomiting, and diarrhea.

Treatment The usual treatment is pain-relieving medication. At home, you should keep your child comfortable and cool and give lots of drinks as well as his medicines. Your child should avoid getting water in the ear until the infection has cleared. Antibiotics may be prescribed in severe cases, especially if the child is feverish and vomiting.

MIDDLE EAR EFFUSION

If your child has repeated infections of the middle ear, it can gradually fill with jellylike fluid. Since the fluid can't drain away through the eustachian tube, it becomes gluelike and may impair hearing because the sounds are not being transmitted across the middle ear to the inner ear, where they are actually heard. Most cases clear up without any treatment, but if the condition persists, your child may need treatment to prevent hearing loss, leading to poor learning and speech development

Symptoms Middle ear effusion generally causes no pain, but partial hearing loss and a feeling of fullness deep in the ear may occur. A child with this condition may sleep with his mouth open, snore, and speak with a nasal twang. If middle ear effusion is not treated, it can cause prolonged deafness, resulting in speech and learning problems.

Treatment The fluid may drain away if left for a few weeks. Your doctor may prescribe decongestants to help drainage. If the fluid doesn't clear, surgery may be recommended; it involves making a tiny hole in the eardrum and sucking the fluid out. Then a typanostomy tube may be inserted—this is a tiny plastic tube that allows air to circulate in the middle ear. Any fluid that forms can drain away through the typanostomy tube and down the eustachian tube.

The tube usually falls out after a few months, and the eardrum heals. Occasionally, the tube has to be inserted again if the fluid reaccumulates. Children can go swimming, but shouldn't dive. When washing hair, use ear plugs to stop water from getting into your child's ears.

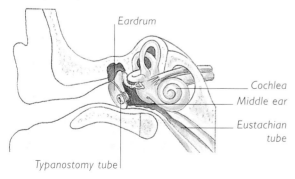

Eardrum

Cochlea

Middle ear

Eustachian tube

Typanostomy tube

Typanostomy tube
This is a tiny plastic tube that's fitted to allow air to circulate in the middle ear. Any fluid that forms can drain away through the tube.

NOSE

A stuffed-up nose, due to a cold, flu, or more rarely from an allergy, is quite common in childhood. Minor nosebleeds are also quite common. Neither is usually serious.

STUFFED-UP OR RUNNY NOSE

Excess mucus in the nose, which results in sniffing or a runny nose, is usually caused by a cold virus (see p.294). The mucous membranes lining the nasal passages become inflamed, swollen, and congested and hence block the nose. Other causes include allergic rhinitis (see p.293) or a foreign body, like a bead, lodged in the nose (see p.343).

Symptoms The secretions produced by a cold virus usually start off being clear and runny, but may become thick and yellow by the time the body's defenses attack the infection.

Treatment Encourage your child to blow his nose often. Demonstrate how to clear one nostril first, and then the other. Inhaled menthol in the form of a chest rub or drops on your child's pillow or clothes may help. Call your doctor if a runny nose lasts more than three days and your child is unwell.

NOSEBLEED

Most nosebleeds can be stopped quite easily. If a nosebleed is severe, lasts more than 30 minutes, or follows a blow to the head, you should take your child to the doctor. Nosebleeds in children are often caused by nose-picking.

Symptoms The bleeding usually comes from tiny blood vessels on the inner side of the nostril. A clot may form in the nose; it shouldn't be removed.

Treatment Sit your child down with his head forward over a bowl or a sink while you gently squeeze the soft part of his nose. Keep applying pressure for about ten minutes, after which the bleeding should have stopped. Don't let your child blow his nose for at least three hours afterward. Never put your child's head back, or he may swallow blood and vomit. If a nosebleed is severe and does not stop after squeezing the nose for another ten minutes, take your child to the emergency room.

THROAT

Throat infections such as tonsillitis are rare in babies under one year. They are more common in children who have just started school and are being exposed to a new range of bacteria.

SORE THROAT

An uncomfortable or painful throat is usually due to infection by a bacterium such as streptococcus, or a virus such as the cold or flu viruses.

Symptoms Your child may tell you that she has a sore throat, or you may notice that she finds it hard to swallow. Depress her tongue with a spoon handle and tell her to say "aaahhh" so you can look down her throat for inflammation or enlarged red tonsils.

Treatment Give lots of drinks, and purée your child's food if she finds it difficult to swallow. Your doctor may prescribe an antibiotic if there is a bacterial infection or tonsillitis. Use acetaminophen to ease pain and fever.

TONSILLITIS AND ADENOIDS

The tonsils, situated on both sides of the back of the throat, prevent bacteria that invade the throat from entering the body by trapping and killing them. This can sometimes result in the tonsils becoming swollen and infected. The adenoids, which are at the back of the nose, are usually affected too.

Symptoms Your child will have a sore throat and may find swallowing difficult. The tonsils are red and enlarged, possibly with whitish spots. She may have a raised temperature, the glands in her neck may be swollen, and her breath may smell bad. If the adenoids are swollen, her speech may sound nasal.

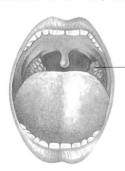

Whitish spots
on tonsils

Tonsillitis
Swollen, infected tonsils cause a sore throat and difficulty in swallowing. Yellow or white spots may also appear on the tonsils.

Treatment Consult your doctor, who may take a throat swab and examine your child's ears and glands. As for a sore throat, give lots of drinks and purée your child's foods. Use acetaminophen to ease discomfort and fever. Antibiotics may be prescribed for bacterial tonsillitis. Removal of the tonsils is considered after many severe recurrent attacks or if the ears are badly affected, too.

LARYNGITIS

An infection of the larynx or voice box may accompany any cold or sore throat. As long as it doesn't develop into croup (see p.296), laryngitis is rarely a serious condition.

Symptoms The most common symptoms are hoarseness or loss of voice. Your child may find it uncomfortable or painful to swallow, and may have a dry cough and a mild fever. Sometimes laryngitis develops into croup (see p.296).

Treatment Most cases of laryngitis are short-lived. Your child should rest, preferably in a humid environment in which the air can circulate. Give her lots of fluids and encourage her to rest her voice. If her temperature remains high, she may need antibiotics. Make sure she doesn't overheat (see p.281) and should croup develop (see p.296), seek medical help as soon as possible.

Lymph nodes

With a local infection, extra white blood cells are produced at the lymph nodes closest to the site of the infection, to mop up and kill the bacteria. The production of white cells causes lymph glands to become inflamed and sore.

Swollen glands
Lymph nodes in front of the ear and below the angle of the jaw swell due to throat infections. To feel them, run your finger down your child's neck from a point just below his ears; they feel like a string of beads.

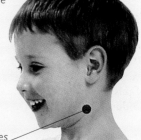

Lymph nodes

EYES

The most common childhood eye problems are infections or inflammations that can be cured with good hygiene, and sometimes antibiotic eye drops.

BLEPHARITIS

This is inflammation of the eyelid margins, found in conjunction with eczema and cradle cap, and is usually recurring. It is not serious and can usually be alleviated with simple self-help measures. Consult your doctor if your child's eyes become sticky or if the condition does not clear up within a week.

Symptoms The eyelid margins appear red, scaly, and inflamed, and you may notice tiny crusts of dried pus on your child's eyelashes.

Treatment Take a cotton ball dipped in a solution of warm boiled water and half a teaspoon of salt, tell your child to close her eyes, and wipe each eye from the nose outward. Use a fresh cotton ball for each wipe. Do this every morning and night until the skin has healed. Your doctor may prescribe eye drops or ointment if there is an infection.

CONJUNCTIVITIS

In this common eye complaint, the membrane covering the eyeball and lining the eyelids (the conjunctiva) becomes inflamed and red. There are three main causes of conjunctivitis: infection by a virus or bacteria, damage due to the presence of a foreign body, and an allergic reaction. Infective conjunctivitis is very contagious, and if one eye is infected, the other one is likely to become infected if you don't take precautions.

Symptoms Inflammation causes pain on blinking, and your child may find it uncomfortable to look at bright lights—a symptom called photophobia. When conjunctivitis is caused by an infection, the eye will be sticky and there may be a collection of pus in the lower eyelid. Allergic conjunctivitis produces clear, watery tears and swollen eyelids.

Treatment Conjunctivitis can be treated by wiping the eye with saline solution or water. Even if the

infection is only in one eye, both need to be treated because the infection is easily transferred from one to the other. When a foreign body is visible, remove it with the corner of a clean tissue. Always seek medical advice for a child who has a "red eye." For an infection, your doctor will prescribe an antibiotic ointment or eye drops. Anti-inflammatory eye drops and antihistamines are used for allergic conjunctivitis.

STY

When the follicle of an eyelash becomes infected, a sty, or small abscess, develops on the margin of the eyelid. Rubbing the eyes may encourage them. A sty may require medical treatment if it's very sore.

Symptoms At first, the eyelid appears red and a bit swollen, then the swelling fills with pus and the sty may protrude noticeably from the eyelid.

Treatment Although sties are not as contagious as other eye infections, you should still keep your child's washcloth and towel separate from the rest of the family's. Your doctor may prescribe antibiotic ointment. If the eye is very sore, warm compresses may be helpful.

STRABISMUS/MISALIGNMENT

Your baby's eyes may appear to be pointing in different directions, sometimes convergent (toward each other) and sometimes divergent (away from each other). Until the age of about eight weeks, this is perfectly normal, but if the baby's eyes have not aligned by two months you should seek advice. The usual causes of strabismus are an imbalance in the muscles of the eyes, or one eye being far-sighted and the other being near-sighted.

Symptoms If you suspect that your baby has a misalignment, confirm by observing how light is reflected in her eyes. It should be reflected from exactly the same place in each eye; if not, then she almost certainly has strabismus. Consult your doctor.

Treatment The usual treatment is to cover the strong eye with a patch, since this forces the muscles in the weak eye to become stronger. The eyes should become aligned within about five months, though it can take longer. If your child's squint is related to far- or near-sightedness, she should get glasses from an optometrist.

MOUTH

Childhood mouth problems are generally minor; thrush is the only condition that needs immediate medical attention, since it does not respond to the usual self-help measures. Your child may refuse food when his mouth is sore. Give him puréed bland foods that he can suck through a straw.

TEETHING PAIN

A child's teeth usually begin to come through at about six months and are complete by his third birthday (see p.175). During the period when the teeth are erupting, the gums are red and swollen.

Symptoms If you touch the swollen, red gums you may feel a hard lump beneath. Your baby will salivate and drool more than usual and will chew objects. He may have trouble sleeping and be more irritable and clingy. Eating may be painful.

Treatment Acetaminophen may be used for pain relief, but medical treatment is not usually necessary. Other symptoms, such as loss of appetite or vomiting, are not caused by teething. Call your doctor.

The ring can be cooled in the refrigerator

Pain relief
Chewing on a cool teething ring— never frozen—or firm-textured foods such as carrot fingers or pieces of apple can ease the pain.

MOUTH ULCERS

Open sores in the mouth occur inside the lower lip, although they are common on the tongue, gums, and inside the cheeks. Aphthous ulcers are the most common kind and appear as round or oval yellow spots with an inflamed outline. They should go away by themselves in 10–14 days, but if they're recurrent, or prevent eating, seek medical help.

Symptoms All mouth ulcers are painful. Your child may have difficulty eating, especially food that is acidic or salty, and may refuse food.

Treatment If your child has an aphthous ulcer, try applying a topical anesthetic to the affected area, or giving oral painkillers such as acetaminophen or ibuprofen. Your doctor may prescribe an anti-inflammatory cream if the ulcer is severe. Avoid anything containing a local anesthetic, since allergies may occur.

Try to eliminate the underlying cause: ask your dentist to file down any rough teeth; discourage your child from biting his cheeks; or, if you are bottle-feeding your baby, try using a softer nipple. Whatever the type of ulcer, you should purée your child's foods, give him a straw to drink through, and avoid salty or acidic foods.

THRUSH

The mucous membranes can sometimes become infected by a fungus called *Candida albicans*. The growth of candida is usually kept in check by the presence of other bacteria, but when these bacteria are eradicated by taking antibiotics, candida begins to multiply unrestrictedly. Alternatively, thrush can be passed on from a mother at the time of birth when the baby passes through the vagina. Although thrush is not serious, it can cause a young baby discomfort while he is sucking or feeding.

In children, thrush may only be seen in the mouth, but it can infect the whole gastrointestinal tract and the anal area, where it is sometimes confused with diaper rash (see p.111).

Symptoms Thrush produces white, curdlike patches on the gums, cheeks, tongue, and roof of the mouth. If you attempt to wipe them off, they become raw and may bleed. Around the anus, thrush appears as red spots or a rash. If your child has diaper rash as well, there may be white flaky patches.

Treatment Thrush can be treated quickly and simply with antifungal medications, in liquid form or gel for oral thrush, and cream form for anal thrush. These are available over the counter.

Puréed, bland, cold, or lukewarm foods are best if your child has oral thrush, particularly natural yogurt (not for very young babies).

Fungi flourish in warm, moist conditions, so if your baby has anal thrush, you should keep him as dry as possible. Leave his bottom exposed to the air as much as you can, and avoid using plastic pants. Be meticulous about hygiene, and always keep your child's hands clean.

SKIN

Childhood skin complaints may be caused by an infection, an allergy, or a response to very high or low temperatures. Most of them are minor and can easily be treated. Rashes occur with a variety of complaints, some of which are serious; if you are at all worried about a rash, consult your doctor.

CHAPPED SKIN

Chaps are little cracks in the skin, sometimes raw and deep. Exposure to the cold makes skin dry and prone to chapping, particularly the extremities, where circulation is poor—hands, fingers, and ears. Damp skin around the lips chaps, too. Failing to dry properly after washing, and washing so frequently that the skin's natural oils are removed, can both contribute to chapping.

Symptoms Chapped skin has a dry, cracked appearance. If the cracks are deep there may be some bleeding and severe pain, and if they become infected you may notice pus and inflammation.

Treatment Unless chapped skin becomes infected or is very slow to heal, you can probably solve the problem with self-help measures. Apply rich emollient creams to your child's skin, use lip salve on his lips, avoid using soap (use baby lotion instead), and dress him warmly in cold weather. Avoid icy winds and sudden changes in temperature. Infected chapped skin should be treated by your doctor.

CHILBLAINS

Children who are sensitive to cold may get chilblains. Constriction of blood vessels in the skin is a normal reaction to cold, but in a cold-sensitive child, the fine network of blood vessels beneath the skin may overconstrict, and then overdilate when your child returns to a warm environment. Where overdilatation occurs, a bump will form in the skin.

Symptoms A chilblain is a red or purple lump of any size. The main symptom is intense itchiness when the body starts to warm up after exposure to cold. Chilblains usually occur on the feet, the backs of the lower legs, the hands, the tip of the nose, and the edges of the ears.

Treatment Chilblains, although irritating, are not serious and usually heal themselves if kept warm. A simple application of talcum powder or calamine lotion can often alleviate itchiness and discourage your child from scratching.

If your child is susceptible to chilblains, make sure that he is dressed warmly when he goes out in cold weather, paying particular attention to vulnerable areas of the body. As damp conditions increase the likelihood of getting chilblains, make sure that he has waterproof clothing to wear in wet weather.

COLD SORES

The virus responsible for cold sores is called herpes simplex and is a relative of chicken pox and shingles. All sufferers from cold sores carry the virus in their skin, where it lies dormant in the nerve endings. The virus is transmitted from parent to child during kissing. A rise in skin temperature due to intense sunlight, flu, a cold, stress, or overexertion can reactivate the virus and result in a cold sore. Cold sores are not usually harmful except near the eye where, rarely, they can cause ulceration of the conjunctiva (the transparent covering of the white of the eye).

Symptoms There is usually warning of an attack in the form of a hot, itchy, tingling sensation for 24 hours before the cold sore appears. The skin becomes red and then tiny blisters appear, usually around the lips or the nostrils. The blisters enlarge, join together, and then burst, revealing the classic cold sore. Fluid from the blisters then forms a crust, which gradually shrinks and falls off as the skin underneath heals. This takes 10–14 days. While a cold sore is at the blister-and-weeping stage, it will be very painful, and your child may complain of pain over the whole side of the face, an earache, and pain when he chews because the facial nerves are inflamed by the virus.

Cold sores are very contagious, and your child can spread them to other parts of his face by touching them with his fingers.

Treatment Your pharmacist can recommend, or your doctor will prescribe, an antiviral cream to be applied every two or three hours as soon as the skin begins to tingle. This will prevent future cold sores from developing into their full-blown form. He may prescribe an antibiotic cream if the cold sore becomes infected.

Discourage your child from touching her face, from kissing other children, and from sharing her washcloth and towel for the duration of an attack. Applying petroleum jelly may stop a cold sore from cracking and bleeding. Rubbing alcohol may help to dry the sore out, but it stings and I don't approve of using it on children.

It's helpful to identify the triggers that bring on your child's cold-sore attacks. For instance, if it is strong sunlight, your child should wear a high-SPF sunblock around her lips in summer.

BOILS

When a hair follicle becomes infected, a red, pus-filled swelling can result. Boils are rarely serious if they are treated appropriately, but they can cause pain, particularly if they are in an uncomfortable place such as the armpit or buttock. Boils rarely heal by themselves, and left untreated can form a carbuncle (a cluster of several boils).

Symptoms Initially the skin is red and swollen. As the yellow pus collects beneath the skin, the swelling increases. Boils usually appear singly, but, because hair follicles are so close together, it's possible for infection to spread and for a crop of boils to appear.

Treatment Seek medical help if your child has several boils, if there are signs that the infection is spreading, if the boil is causing severe pain, or if it has not burst after a couple of days. Your doctor may decide to lance the boil to drain the pus away, which provides immediate pain relief. Crops of boils require antibiotics and investigation of the cause.

Don't try to burst or squeeze a boil at home; this will be excruciatingly painful and will spread infection. Instead, dab the affected area with rubbing alcohol or antiseptic and cover with a gauze dressing. Warm compresses can also help.

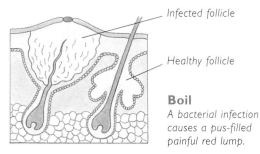

Infected follicle

Healthy follicle

Boil
A bacterial infection causes a pus-filled painful red lump.

IMPETIGO

The bacteria staphylococcus, which is present in the nose and on the skin, can sometimes cause a skin infection around the nose, mouth, and ears and elsewhere. Impetigo is characterized by a bright yellow, crusted rash or small pus-filled blisters; it is highly contagious, and you should keep your child home from school until it has cleared.

Symptoms The first sign of impetigo is reddened skin. This is followed by the appearance of blisters full of pus, which burst, leaving patches of oozing skin. The fluid dries into a yellow crust. Impetigo spreads rapidly if left untreated.

Treatment Take your child to see the doctor, who will prescribe an antibiotic cream and dressings to keep the skin covered, and possibly antibiotic pills. Be meticulous about hygiene—wash away crusted areas with warm water and pat dry with a paper towel. Use disposable cloths and towels to protect the rest of the family from infection.

INFANTILE ECZEMA

This inflammatory skin condition is caused by an inherited tendency plus a trigger factor such as an allergy or an infection. Occasionally, it is simply a response to stress. The type of eczema that usually affects children is atopic eczema. The reason for including this here is that it appears in the first weeks or months of life and is worrisome for parents, who are at a loss as to how to manage it.

Symptoms Skin affected by atopic eczema is raw, dry, scaly, red, and itchy, and there may be small white blisters, like grains of rice, that burst and weep if scratched. Seborrheic eczema looks similar to atopic eczema, but is less itchy and occurs in quite different places (see right). Itchiness is the most irritating symptom of eczema.

Treatment If you suspect your child has eczema, see your doctor, who may prescribe an anti-inflammatory cream and antihistamines to curb itching and combat any allergy. If the skin is infected, antibiotics may be necessary. Your doctor will also try to identify the cause: a pet, laundry detergent, or food, for example. Keep contact with water to a minimum, and if you have to bathe your child, put unguent emulsificants or unscented bath oil in the water. Stop using soap, and make sure that clothes

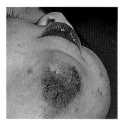

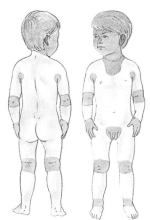

Affected area
Atopic eczema (above) typically occurs on the face, hands, neck, ankles, and knee and elbow creases. The gray areas indicate the usual sites of seborrheic eczema.

are thoroughly rinsed and contain no trace of laundry detergent or fabric conditioner. Minimize her contact with potential allergens, use emollient cream on her skin, and keep her fingernails short so that she can't scratch. Use cotton fabrics, never wool. At each diaper change, use a generous amount of aqueous cream to keep the skin moisturized.

DERMATITIS

This is an inflammation of the skin that occurs in response to stress, to an allergy such as nickel sensitivity (contact dermatitis), or occasionally to light (photodermatitis). Seborrheic dermatitis (or seborrheic eczema, see p.290) affects the face, especially the nostrils, eyebrows, eyelids, and scalp.

Symptoms Dermatitis, no matter what type, is a red, itchy, and scaly rash, sometimes with blisters. In contact dermatitis, the rash usually appears where the skin has been in contact with the allergen. Photodermatitis appears as clusters of spots or blisters on skin that has been exposed to the sun.

Treatment If dermatitis is very severe, your doctor may prescribe a weak steroid cream. Make sure that your child keeps the affected areas clean, doesn't scratch them, and doesn't expose them to oil-stripping agents such as soaps and detergent.

HEAT RASH

A hot, poorly ventilated environment in which the skin can't cool encourages heat rash; the body responds by sweating excessively and the sweat glands become enlarged and red. Heat rash is quite common in babies because their sweat glands are not working properly yet.

Symptoms A faint red rash appears on parts of the body that get hot easily and where sweat glands are most numerous. Typical areas include the neck, the face, and skin folds such as the groin, elbows, armpits, and behind the knees.

Treatment Don't overdress or swaddle your baby. Bathe her in tepid water and pat her dry, leaving her skin slightly damp. Make sure the temperature of her room is not too high, and keep air circulating by opening a window slightly. Consult your doctor only if the rash has not cleared up after 12 hours to exclude other possible causes.

SUNBURN

Spending too much time in the sun or being exposed to sunlight that is too intense can cause sunburn. All children should wear a high-SPF sunscreen and cover up with a hat and clothes. If your child is fair-skinned or unused to being in the sun, you should be especially cautious about letting her play outdoors. Children should be well protected from hot sun (see p.147). Sunburn can be painful, and in extreme heat, it may be associated with heatstroke (see p.340). In the long term, sunburn can lead to skin cancer, particularly in fair-skinned people.

Rashes

Infectious diseases like chicken pox, rubella, or measles, as well as allergies and blood disorders, may all cause rashes.

A rash may be discrete or blotchy, flat or bumpy; it may disappear on pressure or not; and it may contain blisters. If your child has a rash, check to see if she has a fever (this may indicate an infectious disease), and consider whether she has been exposed to any potential allergens (see p.292). An itchy rash between her fingers may indicate scabies.

A rash that doesn't disappear on pressure, such as purpura, is nearly always serious and can result from a fault in the blood clotting mechanism or from bacterial toxins, as in meningitis. You can spot purpura by pressing a drinking glass to your child's skin to see if the rash remains visible through it. If it does, see your doctor immediately.

Symptoms The affected skin is hot, inflamed, red, and tender. Sometimes the skin looks "bubbly" and blistered. After a few days, the dead skin will flake and peel, at which point your child may complain of itchiness. If sunburn is severe, particularly on the back of the neck, look out for symptoms of heatstroke—fever, vomiting, and dizziness—and if they are present, seek medical help immediately.

Treatment Immediate relief can come from applying calamine lotion and cold sheets or towels to the affected areas. Liquid acetaminophen may also be helpful for keeping your child's temperature normal. Treat sunburned skin very gently; let your child go without clothes indoors, and cover the skin with loose-fitting clothes and bare skin with total sunblock if he is going outdoors. A hat should cover the nape of the neck. Your doctor may prescribe an anti-inflammatory cream for sunburn.

WARTS

Warts may occur singly or in great numbers. Most disappear without treatment after two years. There are more than 30 different types of wart viruses. Children usually get common warts on the hands or areas subject to injury, such as the knees, and plantar warts on the soles of the feet. Although contagious, warts are not at all serious.

Symptoms Common warts, such as those found on the hands, appear as firm, flesh-colored or brown growths. They are composed of dead skin cells. Although they may look unsightly, common warts should not be painful unless cracked and bleeding. Unlike other warts, plantar warts may be very painful because they are pressed into the sole of the foot as the child walks.

Treatment Unless warts are painful, unsightly, or could be passed on to other children, don't worry, since they may disappear spontaneously. If you do decide to treat a wart at home, there are several products available in pharmacies. Never use these on the face or the genitals; they are too harsh and can scar delicate skin. If you consult your doctor, he will discuss treatment options with you and may recommend that your child have the warts removed. If you suspect that your child has genital warts, see your doctor right away. Plantar warts should be kept covered at all times to prevent them from being passed on to others.

ALLERGIES

An allergy is an abnormal response of the immune system to a specific chemical or substance. The most common form of allergy is hay fever, which is an allergy to pollen, but children may be allergic to a range of things, from foods and plants to light and drugs.

ERYTHEMA TOXICUM (RASH)

An allergic skin rash that takes the form of itchy, raised red blotches with white centers, erythema toxicum is most commonly caused by contact with a stinging nettle plant (nettle rash), but can be the result of an allergy. Histamine (a chemical found in cells throughout the body) is released in response to contact with an allergen or nettles, and it causes fluid to leak into the skin from the blood vessels, leading to the typical weal. Newborn babies sometimes have an erythema rash (see p.14).

Symptoms The skin is extremely itchy and there are raised white lumps (weals) surrounded by a flare of inflammation. The weals are small and circular or large irregular patches. The rash usually appears on the limbs and the trunk, although it can appear anywhere on the body. Erythema toxicum lasts for a few minutes, disappears, and then reappears at a different site. It can be accompanied by facial swelling (angioedema), which is a reason to consult your doctor without delay. Occasionally, erythema toxicum can affect the mouth, tongue, and throat, and cause difficulties with breathing (anaphylaxis). This should always be treated as an emergency.

Erythema toxicum
Raised white lumps form, surrounded by inflammation. Sometimes these join together, forming large patches on the surface of the skin.

Treatment Apply calamine lotion to your child's skin or give him a fairly cool bath. Your doctor may prescribe antihistamine tablets. If your child has had a previous severe allergic reaction, consider carrying an epinephrine auto-injector.

HAY FEVER (ACUTE ALLERGIC RHINITIS)
When the mucous membranes are exposed to an allergen (usually pollen), they become inflamed and the child suffers the symptoms of allergic rhinitis (see below). The condition usually occurs in the spring and summer months when the pollen count is high. Hay fever is relatively unusual under the age of five. It tends to run in families, and it may disappear spontaneously.

Symptoms Hay fever symptoms include sneezing, a runny nose, and red, itchy, watery eyes. Hay fever is distinguishable from a common cold in that it is seasonal and there is no fever.

Treatment While it is impossible to prevent your child from being exposed to pollen, you can note the pollen count in the weather forecast and discourage him from playing outside if it is high. Antihistamines often help relieve symptoms. Your doctor may also arrange for skin tests to identify the particular pollen causing the symptoms and may prescribe a course of desensitizing injections. Eye drops and steroid nasal sprays are additional treatments.

CHRONIC ALLERGIC RHINITIS
Chronic or perennial allergic rhinitis is just like hay fever, but happens year-round. It starts in the same way as hay fever (see above) but the culprit is usually house dust mites rather than pollen. Other causes are feathers and cat and dog fur.
.

Symptoms The symptoms of chronic or perennial allergic rhinitis are the same as those of hay fever—runny nose, watering of the eyes, itchy nose and eyes. Diagnosis is confirmed by skin tests.

Treatment The most effective treatment is avoidance of the allergen or allergens, which show up in skin tests. You may have to get rid of a favorite pet, or change bedding or vacuum the room frequently.

Antihistamines and other drugs help prevent symptoms occurring. Intra-nasal steroids, given in very small, safe doses, often bring rapid relief.

PHOTOSENSITIVITY
This condition is an allergy to light, or rather to certain wavelengths of light. A very rare form is inherited, but more commonly photosensitivity is caused by swallowing a photosensitizing substance or applying it to the skin. Examples of such substances are some drugs, dyes, chemicals, and plants.

Symptoms Photosensitivity usually shows as a rash, easily distinguishable because the skin that is covered by clothes is free of inflammation and there is a clear line demarcating the skin that has been exposed to sunshine.

Treatment The photosensitizer and/or sunlight should be avoided until the rash clears. A susceptible child should cover up and wear total sunblock.

FLEA BITES
Children quite often get one flea bite, develop an allergy to it, and then break out in a rash of spots. These spots may be mistaken for more bites, but are in fact an allergic rash, which is very itchy. It will subside in 10–14 days.

Treatment The family cat or dog will have to be sprayed for fleas. You will also have to spray any carpets or soft furnishings that may harbor flea eggs. Your doctor may prescribe an antihistamine medicine to contain the itching and scratching.

DRUGS
The most common drug allergy is to penicillin or its derivatives. Once diagnosed, your child should wear a bracelet or tag stating that he is allergic to penicillin so that he won't be given it again, since further reactions can be severe. Any drug at any time, however, can cause an allergy, particularly if there's a family history of allergies, eczema, and asthma. The worst form of drug allergy is anaphylaxis, in which blood pressure drops and the tongue and throat may swell up; it needs emergency treatment.

Symptoms A rash appears up to ten days after exposure to the drug, possibly with swelling of the face and tongue. Problems with breathing, vomiting, and diarrhea need urgent medical attention.

Treatment For mild allergies, antihistamines are usually sufficient. Once a drug is identified as an allergen, it must be avoided for life.

COLDS AND INFLUENZA

Infections with cold or flu viruses are common in childhood because children haven't yet developed immunity to specific viruses. There are roughly 200 cold viruses, which all produce similar symptoms—your child will never get the same cold twice.

Clearing the sinuses
Get your child to inhale dissolved menthol crystals in warm water. Cover his head with a towel to keep the vapors in.

COMMON COLD

Colds are not serious unless your baby is very young, or a complication such as bronchitis (see p.295) sets in. Colds are more frequent when your child starts preschool, because she's suddenly exposed to lots of new viruses.

Symptoms Most cold viruses start with "catarrhal" symptoms (stuffy or runny nose, cough, sore throat), fever, and listlessness. The nasal discharge is first clear and then thick and yellow as the body's defenses take over. The rise in temperature can cause cold sores (see p.289), hence their name.

Treatment Only symptoms can be treated, not the virus itself; there's no cure for the common cold. If a secondary infection such as sinusitis or bronchitis arises, then your doctor will prescribe antibiotics; otherwise, home remedies suffice. Give your child plenty of fluids, encourage her to blow her nose frequently, showing her how to clear one nostril at a time, and apply petroleum jelly to her nostrils and upper lip if they become sore or chapped. When congestion is severe, make sure that she sleeps with her head propped up with pillows, and try applying a menthol rub to her chest. Your doctor will prescribe nose drops if a blocked nose interferes with sleeping or eating. Liquid acetaminophen reduces fever and eases aches and pains.

SINUSITIS

The sinuses are cavities in the bones around the nose and cheeks and above the eyes, and are lined with mucous membranes. Mucus usually drains from them into the nose. Sinusitis occurs when drainage is impaired, usually with a cold or flu or if an infection spreads to the sinuses from the throat.

Symptoms Nasal secretions are clear and runny at first with a cold. A change to a thick, yellow discharge is normal, but if it is persistent, sinusitis has probably developed. Other symptoms include a feeling of fullness and discomfort around the top of the nose, a headache, a diminished sense of smell, a stuffed-up nose, and sometimes fever.

Treatment Sinusitis can be treated with antibiotics, decongestants, and nose drops. At home, keep the atmosphere humid, prepare menthol inhalations for your child, and give her liquid acetaminophen if she complains of pain in her face and forehead.

INFLUENZA

This is a viral infection similar to the common cold, but it produces more severe symptoms. Influenza, or the flu, can be very debilitating, and is potentially serious because it can weaken the body and make the ears, sinuses, and chest vulnerable to secondary infections by bacteria.

Symptoms Flu symptoms resemble cold symptoms, but in addition to the usual sore throat, runny nose, and cough, your child will have quite a high temperature, a headache, and a backache, and she may complain of feeling hot, cold, and shivery. She will be lethargic and weak, and may feel nauseous.

Treatment The only remedies available for flu are symptomatic ones. Let your child rest in a warm, ventilated room, and give her liquid acetaminophen and plenty of fluids. Take your child's temperature regularly—if it fails to come down, or if other symptoms develop, such as persistent nasal discharge, an earache, or a chesty cough, seek medical advice.

CHEST INFECTIONS

In very young children, the air passages, sinuses, and the ears, nose, and throat are really all one system because the tubes are so short. A chest infection can therefore develop from an infection elsewhere in the upper respiratory tract. Chest infections are always serious. The airways may become so narrow that breathing is difficult and impaired and pneumonia may develop. If your child's breathing is ever labored, you should always seek medical help immediately.

COUGHS

The cough is a reflex action that clears the throat of any irritant such as mucus, food, dust, or smoke. A cough may be due to the irritation of a cold, sore throat, tonsillitis, or a chest infection. The cause should be treated, not just the cough alone, which is merely a symptom of an underlying condition.

Symptoms There are two types of cough: a productive cough, in which phlegm is produced, and a nonproductive cough, in which there is no phlegm. The first has a "wet" sound, while the second is dry and hacking. Both will prevent sleep. In a small baby, mucus running down the back of the throat can cause vomiting. A cough may also be a nervous symptom. If a cough is hacking or croaking, your child may have croup (see p.296). Violent coughing can cause vomiting.

Treatment If you suspect that your child has croup (see p.296) or asthma (see p.260), you should seek medical help right away. An underlying acute infection such as tonsillitis should be treated separately. As long as they don't stop your child from sleeping or eating, most other coughs can be treated at home. Discourage your child from running around, since breathlessness may bring on a coughing fit, and get her to lie on her stomach or side at night; this prevents mucus from running down the throat. Give your child plenty of warm drinks. If she is coughing up lots of phlegm, use a liquid expectorant, and lay her over your lap and pat her on the back. Suppress a dry cough, but never suppress a productive cough.

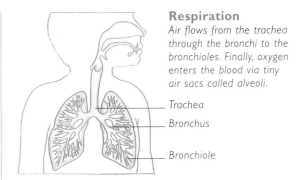

Respiration
Air flows from the trachea through the bronchi to the bronchioles. Finally, oxygen enters the blood via tiny air sacs called alveoli.

— Trachea

— Bronchus

— Bronchiole

BRONCHITIS AND BRONCHIOLITIS

The larger airways in the lungs are called the bronchi and the smaller are called the bronchioles. Bronchitis or bronchiolitis occur when a viral infection causes the linings of these airways to swell and mucus to build up. Bronchiolitis tends to be more serious because it can cause severe breathing difficulties. Bronchiolitis is most common in babies and very young children. Bronchitis is not usually serious in children over a year old.

Symptoms The symptoms of bronchiolitis are a cough and breathlessness, which may lead to difficulty in feeding. Your child may have a raised temperature and may wheeze. She may be pale and appear quite sick. There may be drawing in of the chest (in the struggle to get air into the lungs) and the lips and tongue may appear blue. The symptoms of bronchitis are a dry cough that develops into a cough producing green or yellow phlegm, raised temperature, and possibly a loss of appetite. If the phlegm, is swallowed your child may vomit it up. If your child becomes more unwell, possibly with difficulty breathing, this may indicate severe infection or even pneumonia.

Treatment You should consult your doctor if you suspect that your child has a lung infection. She will prescribe antibiotics as necessary. Labored breathing and a gray or blue complexion should always be treated in the hospital, where your child will be put in an oxygen tent to help her breathe.

Keep your child warm and rested, give plenty of fluids, and encourage her to cough up the phlegm. If she has a fever of more than 104°F (40°C), sponge her down with tepid water (see p.281) and give her liquid acetaminophen to keep her temperature down. Don't give your child a cough suppressant—it is important to bring up the phlegm.

PNEUMONIA

This is a severe and serious inflammation of the lungs, caused by a virus or bacterium. Your child will be ill for two reasons: first, because of the bacterial or viral toxins, and second because the affected lung is out of action. The initial cause of pneumonia is often a cold or flu. Conditions like asthma, cystic fibrosis, whooping cough, and measles increase the risk of pneumonia. Pneumonia is always serious, and small children are often treated in the hospital because oxygen is needed.

Symptoms Usually starts with a fever and cough, and your child may be breathless. He may look pale and unwell and seem lethargic. His breathing may be rapid and shallow.

Treatment Labored breathing is always a reason for you to seek medical advice urgently. You should consult your doctor right away if you suspect your child has pneumonia. Your doctor will prescribe antibiotics and may decide that immediate hospitalization is necessary if your child is in need of oxygen therapy.

CROUP

When a small child's air passages become inflamed and congested as a result of an infection, breathing can become difficult and croup can result. The croup sound is due to air being drawn in through a swollen and narrowed larynx, usually as a result of a viral infection. Croup usually occurs in children between the ages of one and four years. It can come on suddenly: your apparently well child will wake in the night with croup.

Symptoms The main symptom is a barking cough, accompanied by hoarseness and noisy breathing. In severe cases your child may be fighting for breath and his face may turn gray or blue. Attacks occur at night and are often short-lived.

Treatment Stay calm. If your child is upset, his breathing will become even more labored. Make sure the air around your child is damp—get him to lean out of a window if it's wet outside, or take him to the bathroom and run the hot faucet.
    If your child's face turns blue, you must get medical help immediately. Croup may need hospital treatment or treatment with a nebulized steroid. Even if croup is mild, report it to your doctor.

PARASITES

Parasites are very contagious, so if your child has lice or worms, the whole family should be treated. Always inform your child's daycare, preschool, or school of the infestation. Infestations can be uncomfortable, but they're not serious and can be eradicated.

HEAD LICE

Head lice are common in children of school age. The louse is a small insect that lives on blood from the scalp, lays eggs, and cements them to the base of the hairs; the eggs, called nits, become visible as the hair grows. Contrary to the belief that lice are a sign of uncleanliness, head lice prefer clean hair.

Symptoms Your child will complain of an itchy scalp, which feels worse in hot weather. You may see white eggs firmly attached to the hair near the scalp.

Treatment Tell your child's school that he has head lice. To treat, wash the hair and saturate it with conditioner while damp. Comb the hair thoroughly for 20 minutes with a nit comb, cleaning the comb after each stroke. Rinse and dry the hair. Repeat this treatment every two or three days until the hair is clear of nits—this will take at least two weeks. Alternatively, wash your child's hair in insecticidal shampoo. The whole family should be treated.

Louse and nit
The adult louse lays its eggs (nits) at the root of the hair (left). The eggs become firmly attached and hatch after about two weeks unless they are removed by combing or the hair is treated with insecticidal shampoo.

— *Adult louse*

SCABIES

This is an infestation by a microscopic mite that burrows into the skin and lays eggs. Although it is not serious, it can be very itchy, especially at night, and it is highly contagious. A child can get scabies by physical contact with someone suffering from scabies or from infested bedding.

Symptoms The backs of the hands, finger clefts, feet, ankles, and toes are affected by an intensely itchy rash. Burrows are usually visible as gray, scaly trails across the skin with a black pinhead spot (the mite) at the end.

Treatment Your doctor will probably prescribe a lotion to treat scabies. This should stay on overnight, rinsed off in the morning, and the treatment repeated in a week. The whole family should be treated.

Mites can live independently of human skin for up to six days, so you should wash all your clothes and bed linen to prevent reinfection.

Scabies mite
The mite burrows into the skin and the opening of the burrow is visible as a gray, scaly swelling. The classic site of the rash is between the clefts of the fingers. The mite may be visible as a dark spot at the head of the burrow.

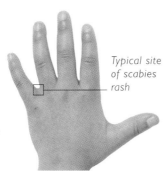

Typical site of scabies rash

PINWORM
Pinworms are extremely common in children, but are not serious and are easily eradicated. If a child eats food containing worm eggs, they will hatch in the intestines. As the larvae mature, the females move down the intestine and lay eggs around the anus. This causes itchiness, and a child can easily pick up the eggs on his fingers and transfer them to his mouth, thus beginning the whole cycle of infestation again.

Cycle of infestation
Pinworms enter the body through the mouth and lay eggs around the anus. A child can become reinfested by scratching the anus, then transferring the eggs to his mouth.

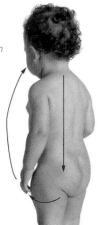

Eggs are swallowed and hatch into larvae inside the intestine

Female worms lay eggs around the anus at night, causing itching

Eggs are passed from the anus to the mouth via the fingers

Symptoms The most distressing symptom is the intense itchiness around the anal area, which feels worse at night when your child is hot and can prevent him from sleeping. There may also be tiny white worms present in the stools.

Treatment If you notice worms in your child's stools or find he's suffering from anal itchiness, tell your doctor, who will prescribe a medication for the whole family. Pay special attention to hygiene: encourage hand-washing often after using the toilet, keep your child's fingernails short, and get him to wear pants in bed to discourage scratching.

ROUNDWORM
This type of worm is very rare in the West and is usually only brought in by people living in tropical climates, especially in areas where hygiene is poor. The parasite is a cylindrical worm approximately 6–16 inches (15–40 centimeters) long, and enters the body in egg form via contaminated food. Once in the body, the eggs hatch and the worms mature and lay new eggs, which may be passed in the stools.

Symptoms Roundworms inhabit the intestine and produce few or no symptoms. Sometimes the worms may be visible in your child's stools. Where roundworm is endemic, it leads to poor growth and a failure to thrive.

Treatment Roundworm is treated with tablets that kill the worm. Laxatives may also be given so that the worms pass quickly and easily in the stools. Scrupulous hygiene is absolutely essential if treatment is to be successful.

After traveling overseas

If you have recently been in the tropics and your child is suffering from persistent diarrhea, he may have contracted amebiasis (amebic dysentery).

This is caused by an amoeba—a tiny single-celled organism that lives in the large intestine—which is picked up only in tropical countries. It is a serious illness with fever, diarrhea, and stomach pain. If you suspect amebiasis, take your child and a stool sample to the doctor. He'll need drugs to get rid of the parasite and rehydration therapy if diarrhea has been severe.

STOMACH AND ABDOMEN

Babies are affected by few of the conditions that cause abdominal pain in adults, like gallstones and peptic ulcers. Several causes of abdominal pain in infants and children are, however, potentially very serious, so you must call your doctor immediately if a child with abdominal pain is distressed or if the pain is accompanied by a fever, diarrhea, or vomiting.

Any tension in the house, between parents, between siblings, or at school, can cause a child to feel nauseous, vomit, and suffer abdominal pain. When all other causes have been eliminated, stress should be considered as a cause of pain. Ask your healthcare provider for advice.

COLIC

This type of crying usually occurs in the first four months of life, then clears spontaneously without treatment. It's thought to be due to spasms of the intestines, though there is no proof of this and the cause remains unknown. The condition is harmless, though distressing for parents.

Symptoms Your baby, who is otherwise well, will have bouts of crying when she screams and draws her legs up toward her abdomen.

Treatment No drugs are needed. Your baby may be soothed by any rhythmic activity such as rocking, swaying, being taken in the car for a ride, or being laid on her tummy on your lap while you rhythmically pat her back. Often, nothing will calm a colicky baby, but try to remain calm yourself. Since colic often occurs at the same time each day, typically in the evening, you should try to plan your day accordingly so as to reduce the stress on you.

GASTROENTERITIS

Inflammation of the stomach and intestines, usually due to bacteria or viruses in contaminated food, causes diarrhea and vomiting; pain is a lesser symptom. There are various noninfectious forms of gastroenteritis caused by food intolerance, spicy foods, and antibiotics. The complaint is extremely common and fairly mild. It rarely lasts for longer than three days, and the child tends to recover without any specific treatment other than replacement of fluid and minerals. A small baby, however, can't tolerate dehydration, and if she vomits or has diarrhea for longer than three hours, you should contact your doctor without delay.

Symptoms The first symptom is loss of appetite, followed by vomiting and possibly diarrhea. Your baby may become dehydrated, in which case the fontanelles of her skull will be sunken (see p.280) and her mouth dry.

Treatment Mild cases can be treated at home by your doctor, but if vomiting or diarrhea continue, your baby must be treated in the hospital, where fluids will be given intravenously.

INTUSSUSCEPTION

In this rare and unexplained condition of babies, the intestine telescopes on itself, forming a tube within a tube, usually causing a blockage of the intestine, which is very serious. It's most common at the junction of the small and large intestines.

Symptoms Your baby may scream intermittently and draw up her legs. There may be vomiting and diarrhea, and she may pass blood and mucus. Her abdomen may be swollen and she may become dehydrated. The condition may be complicated by a ruptured bowel and peritonitis (inflammation of the lining of the abdomen) if left untreated.

Treatment Passing air into the bowel can cause the intussusception to unfold. If it doesn't, then in practically all cases surgery is successful. In severe cases, a segment of bowel may have to be cut out.

Folded intestine
A section of the small intestine telescopes on itself, like a finger in a glove being turned inside out. Intussusception is rare, and very serious.

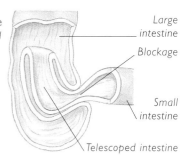

Large intestine

Blockage

Small intestine

Telescoped intestine

APPENDICITIS

Inflammation of the appendix, a small, fingerlike sac at the junction of the cecum and the ileum in the small bowel, is a common cause of abdominal pain. The cause is not known, but it may be obstructed by a small piece of feces or very occasionally by pinworms. The appendix becomes inflamed, swollen, and infected. Appendicitis is not a serious condition as long as it is diagnosed early. However, if the symptoms are mistaken for something else, such as constipation, and there is any delay in treatment, the appendix can burst, and an appendix abscess or even peritonitis (inflammation of the abdominal lining) can result.

Symptoms The first symptom is pain around the navel which, after a few hours, shifts to the right lower side of the abdomen, where it becomes intense. Your child may have a slight temperature and refuse food. The tongue may become coated and there may be vomiting, diarrhea, or constipation.

Treatment Consult your doctor immediately. The appendix must be removed before it ruptures. If this is not done soon enough, it will perforate and cause an internal abscess. The abscess must then be drained and the appendix removed after treatment with large doses of antibiotics.

Site of pain
The first symptom of appendicitis is a slight ache in the navel area. This develops into a sharper, more localized pain, which is usually most intense in the lower right-hand side of the abdomen.

Sharper pain in lower right side | Initial pain around navel

Type of pain	Other symptoms	Cause
Sudden pain causing your baby to scream and draw her legs up	Common in babies under four months	Colic (see opposite)
Crippling abdominal pain that causes your baby to scream	Blood and mucus in the stools and vomiting	Intussusception (see opposite)
General mild abdominal pain	Vomiting and diarrhea	Gastroenteritis (see opposite)
Severe pain near the navel that moves toward the lower right of the abdomen	Slight temperature, refusal of food, coated tongue, vomiting	Appendicitis (see above)
Generalized stomachache	Anxiety, clinginess, tearfulness, aggression, and nausea	Stress (see introduction opposite)
Sudden crippling pain in the lower abdomen	Swelling and pain in the scrotum	Torsion of the testis (see p.301)
Generalized stomachache	Sore throat, nasal congestion, and slight fever	Throat infection (see p.286), common cold (see p.294), or middle ear infection (see p.284)
Dull abdominal ache spreading around into the back or down into the groin	Pain on urinating, bed-wetting when previously dry, and rarely blood in the urine	Urinary tract infection (see p.300)

UROGENITAL COMPLAINTS

Symptoms such as painful urination or blood in the urine may result from an infection of the bladder, a kidney disorder, or, rarely, an injury. Correct diagnosis is important in all such complaints so they don't become chronic. The most common genital emergency is torsion of the testis (see opposite).

URINARY TRACT INFECTION

The urinary tract consists of the kidneys, where urine is produced from water and waste products; the ureters, which carry urine from the kidneys to the bladder; the bladder, which stores urine; and the urethra, which carries urine away from the bladder. The female urethra is much shorter than the male urethra, so bacteria entering the female urethra have a much shorter distance to travel to the bladder, increasing the likelihood of infection.

   The most common cause of urinary tract infections is poor hygiene; the main type is cystitis, though only in girls. A tendency to have repeated infections can be due to an anatomical abnormality of the urinary tract, although this is quite rare.

Preventing infection
Urinary tract infections are usually spread from the rectum via the urethra to the bladder or kidneys. Girls should always wipe from front to back after passing a stool.

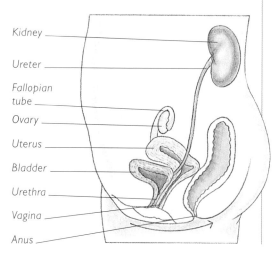

Kidney

Ureter

Fallopian tube

Ovary

Uterus

Bladder

Urethra

Vagina

Anus

Symptoms Urgent, frequent urination is the most prominent symptom of a urinary tract infection. Your child may complain of a burning or stinging sensation at the beginning and end of urine flow. This is due to the bladder muscle contracting down on the inflamed lining. Your child may also pass urine involuntarily, and start to wet the bed again at night. Pain in the lower abdomen and back is common. Severe back pain, fever and chills, refusal to eat, and a headache mean your child has a kidney infection and will be very ill. Blood in the urine indicates a severe infection or kidney damage.

Treatment All urinary tract infections require medical treatment. Your doctor will take a sample of urine to confirm the presence of a bacterial infection and find the most suitable antibiotic to treat it. A bladder infection can spread upward toward the kidneys, but if you seek treatment early, this should not happen.

   All children under age three who have a urinary tract infection are referred for further testing. The pediatrician will look for anatomical abnormality and check for kidney damage.

   Give your child plenty of fluids to keep the bladder flushed out. Encourage your child to urinate as often as possible. Liquid acetaminophen and a wrapped hot-water bottle on the lower abdomen can help to relieve pain.

   Show your daughter how to wipe herself from front to back after passing a stool. For the duration of an attack, washing should be very gentle, since the urethra is sensitive.

BALANITIS
This is an inflammation of the foreskin and head of the penis as a result of bacterial infection. The foreskin is nearly always tight. Products such as laundry detergent can cause irritation and swelling.

Symptoms The glans (tip of the penis) and foreskin are red, swollen, and tender to the touch, and you may notice pus coming from inside the opening. Your child won't let you retract his foreskin and will have pain on passing urine.

Treatment Medical treatment is always necessary or your son could develop a stricture of the foreskin, causing it to become too tight to retract. Your doctor will give you an antibiotic cream and, if your son is not already circumcised, may suggest circumcision if the foreskin is tight—either now or, if it doesn't stretch. by the time he's six.

Things you can do yourself include changing diapers frequently, keeping the penis clean, applying antiseptic cream to any soreness, and applying a barrier cream to the entire genital area. Always make sure your child's clothes are thoroughly rinsed to remove any traces of detergent.

UNDESCENDED TESTES

Before a baby boy is born, his testes develop inside his abdomen, and descend into the scrotum (the pouch that hangs below the penis) shortly before birth. Occasionally, one of the testes fails to descend. The testes need to hang outside the body, where the temperature is lower, for efficient sperm production to take place; a testis at body temperature can't produce sperm. Even if only one of the testes is undescended, treatment is carried out to achieve the best possible fertility later in life, because there is an increased risk of malignancy in an undescended testis, and for cosmetic purposes.

Retractile testes withdraw into the abdomen in response to cold or touch. This is normal in young children, and can persist into adulthood. It doesn't affect fertility.

Symptoms One or both testes are absent from the scrotum. This condition is otherwise symptomless and will not cause your child any discomfort.

Development of the testicles

In a fetus, the testicles grow inside the abdomen, near the kidneys. Not long before a boy is born, they move downward into their normal position in the bag of skin called the scrotum.

Testis developing with the kidney

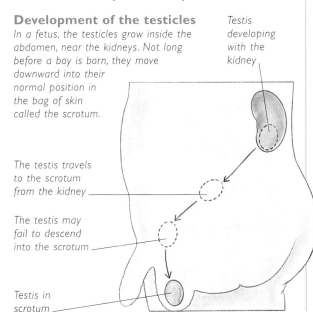

The testis travels to the scrotum from the kidney

The testis may fail to descend into the scrotum

Testis in scrotum

Treatment Often, the testes descend during the first year of life. If they don't, corrective surgery may be carried out when your child is older, usually between one and two years.

TORSION OF THE TESTIS

If one of the testes becomes twisted on its stalk, the blood supply will be interrupted and it will become red, swollen, and very painful. If left untreated, the testis will be irreversibly damaged, so you should seek medical treatment right away.

Symptoms The first symptom is severe pain. Later, the testis becomes swollen and tender. Your son could feel sick and may vomit. The scrotum turns red, purple, and then blue.

Treatment The testis must be surgically untwisted as soon as possible in order to restore blood flow. Occasionally, the testis will untwist spontaneously, but you must not wait for this to happen.

BLOOD IN THE URINE

The medical name for blood in the urine is hematuria. It may be only a streak or sufficient to color the urine deep red. The cause may be in any part of the urinary tract from the kidneys to the urethra. Cystitis (inflammation of the bladder) and urethritis (inflammation of the urethra) are two common causes. Nephritis (inflammation of the kidneys) is less common but more serious.

If you notice any blood in your child's urine, you should seek medical advice immediately. Although infections such as cystitis are not serious, they cause great discomfort, and it's important to stop bacteria from spreading from the bladder up to the kidneys.

Symptoms Slight bleeding may be invisible, and found only when urine is examined under a microscope, or when a special diagnostic dipstick is put into the urine. The symptoms of a urinary tract infection (see opposite) may be present or your child may have a kidney infection or glomerulonephritis.

Treatment Since blood in the urine is only a symptom of an underlying disorder, your doctor will perform special tests to determine the cause and treat it. The urine must be cultured to check for infection and urinary tract X-rays performed to find any anatomical abnormalities.

INFECTIOUS DISEASES

An infectious disease is one that is caused by a microorganism—that is, a bacterium or a virus. The infection is most commonly spread via the air or by direct contact, though it may also be spread via food, water, or insects, particularly in poor conditions. In countries where standards of sanitation are high, appropriate drugs are readily available, and health and nutrition are generally good, infectious diseases pose far less of a threat than they once did. In addition, many serious infectious diseases have been virtually eliminated in the West by immunization (see p.283). The characteristics of many childhood infectious diseases are similar: a rash on the body, a fever, general malaise, and cold symptoms. If you notice a rash and your child's temperature is raised, consult your doctor. The dangers with most illnesses are that your child may become dehydrated from vomiting or refusing food and drink, have difficulty breathing due to constricted airways, or suffer febrile seizures (see p.281), and some diseases can lead to complications if left untreated.

Mumps
The salivary glands will swell up, changing the shape of your child's face; the swelling may appear on either or both sides of the face, just below the ears or the chin.

Applying lotion
The rash that accompanies chicken pox is very itchy. Rub calamine lotion on to soothe the itch; the spots may leave scars if they are scratched vigorously.

Disease

Chicken pox A common and usually mild viral disease.

Incubation 17 to 21 days

Rubella A viral infection, which is usually mild in children.

Incubation 14 to 21 days

Mumps A viral illness, which is seldom serious in children.

Incubation 14 to 21 days

Measles A highly infectious and potentially serious viral illness.

Incubation 8 to 14 days

Whooping cough A bacterial infection that causes inflammation of the airways.

Possible symptoms	Treatment	Complications
Red, itchy spots that become fluid-filled blisters and then scabs. Headache and slight fever.	Apply calamine to the rash, keep your child at home, and discourage scratching. Your doctor may prescribe an anti-infective cream.	In rare cases, chicken pox may lead to encephalitis (inflammation of the brain) and, if aspirin is mistakenly given, Reye's syndrome, a serious illness with symptoms of vomiting and fever.
Small red spots, first on the face and then all over the body, slight fever, and enlarged lymph nodes at the back of the neck and behind the ears.	There is no specific medical treatment. You can give your child liquid acetaminophen if he has a fever, and you should try to keep him in isolation.	The biggest risk is to pregnant women who are not immunized and come into contact with a child with rubella, since it causes birth defects. There is a slight risk of encephalitis.
Tender, swollen glands below the ears and beneath the chin. Fever, headache, and difficulty chewing and swallowing. May also complain of earache. Less common symptoms are painful testicles in boys—very rare pre-puberty.	There is no specific medical treatment. You should keep your child home from school, give him liquid acetaminophen and plenty of fluids, and purée his food.	Occasionally, meningitis, encephalitis, and pancreatitis. Sometimes one of the testes is affected, and decreases in size. If both testes are affected, this can lead to infertility, but this occurs very rarely.
Brownish-red spots appear behind the ears and then spread to the rest of the body. White spots in the mouth (Koplik spots) are the diagnostic sign. The child is feverish, has a runny nose, a cough, and a headache. He may have sore eyes and find it hard to tolerate bright lights.	Keep your child in bed for the duration of the fever and keep him home from school for 7 days after the appearance of the rash. Give him liquid acetaminophen and plenty of fluids. Your doctor may prescribe eye drops for sore eyes and antibiotics for secondary infections.	Ear and chest infections that require treatment with antibiotics may occur. There is also a slight risk of pneumonia, encephalitis, and seizures.
A cough with a distinctive "whoop" sound as the child tries to breathe, common cold symptoms (see p.294), and vomiting. Coughing may stop your child from sleeping.	Your doctor may prescribe antibiotics, and in severe cases your child may need to go to the hospital for oxygen therapy and treatment for dehydration. Encourage your child to bring up phlegm by laying him over your lap and patting his back as he coughs; don't let him exert himself, and keep him away from cigarette smoke.	The main danger is dehydration due to persistent vomiting. Sometimes a severe attack of whooping cough can damage the lungs and make your child prone to chest infections. Small babies are most at risk. They may stop breathing for short periods and are also at risk from seizures, pneumonia, brain damage—and very rarely, death.

Meningitis

Putting myself in the position of the parent of a child, I'd want to know how to be alert to the possibility of meningitis. The warning signs are:

• Headache and sensitivity to bright lights.

• Stiff neck—your child won't like pulling her head forward when lying on her back.

• A rash that doesn't disappear when you press a glass on it.

If you spot any of these signs, call your doctor immediately.

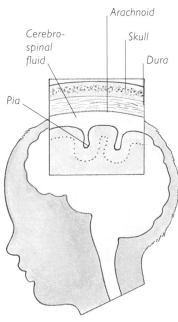

Cerebro-spinal fluid

Pia

Arachnoid

Skull

Dura

Meningitis
The three membranes that cover the brain and spinal cord—dura, arachnoid, and pia—are called the meninges. Inflammation of the meninges results in meningitis.

Disease	Possible symptoms
Hepatitis An inflammation of the liver caused by a viral infection. There are many viral causes, but Type A is the most common in children.	Loss of appetite, nausea, and jaundice. In some cases, your child may pass dark brown urine and pale stools.
Meningitis An inflammation of the membranes that cover the brain and spinal cord. Hib vaccination immunizes against one cause—Haemophilis influenza B. Pneumoccal conjugate vaccine gives protection against another of the causes.	The symptoms of meningitis are fever, stiff neck, lethargy, headache, drowsiness, and intolerance of bright light; there may also be a purple-red rash (purpura, see **Rashes**, p.291) covering most of the body. In babies under 18 months old, one noticeable symptom is that the fontanelles will bulge slightly.
Scarlet fever A bacterial infection that causes tonsillitis accompanied by a rash. It is rarely serious.	Fever, enlarged tonsils and a sore throat. A rash of small spots that starts on the chest then spreads, but doesn't affect the area around the mouth, and a furry tongue with red spots.
Roseola A viral infection whose symptoms resemble those of scarlet fever.	A high fever for about three days. Red or pink spots on the trunk, limbs, and neck appear as the fever wanes. The rash fades after about 48 hours.
Diphtheria A serious and highly contagious bacterial infection. It is now very rare because of widespread immunization.	The tonsils are enlarged and may be covered by a gray membrane. Your child may have a mild fever, a cough, and a sore throat. Breathing difficulties may develop.
Tuberculosis A highly infectious bacterial infection that most commonly affects the lungs, but can also affect other parts of the body, such as the kidneys, meninges, and bones.	Persistent coughing (possibly with blood and pus in the sputum if the lungs are affected), chest pain, shortness of breath, fever (especially at night), poor appetite, weight loss, and tiredness.

Treatment	Complications
Your child should be isolated and rest in bed for at least two weeks. Be meticulous about hygiene—hepatitis is highly contagious—and give her plenty of fluids. If she won't eat, add a spoonful of glucose to her drinks.	Some children suffer post-hepatitis symptoms for up to six months. These may include moodiness and lethargy.
Intravenous antibiotics are used to treat bacterial meningitis, and painkilling drugs relieve the symptoms of viral meningitis. If a purple rash appears on the skin, your child should be taken straight to the hospital.	Viral meningitis is not usually serious and clears up within a week. Bacterial meningitis is potentially fatal and so should always be treated as a medical emergency.
Your doctor may prescribe antibiotics. Home treatment includes giving your child plenty of fluids and puréeing food to make it easier to eat. Give liquid acetaminophen to lower temperature.	If your child is sensitive to the streptococcus bacterium, it may cause complications, including nephritis (inflammation of the kidneys) and rheumatic fever (inflammation of the joints and heart). These are rare.
Keep your child rested and sponge her down with tepid water to reduce her fever if it is above 104°F (40°C). Give liquid acetaminophen to lower her temperature.	If your child's temperature is very high, she may have febrile seizures (see p.281).
Diphtheria is very serious because of the possibility of breathing difficulties, and your child should be hospitalized immediately. She will be given strong antibiotics and she may need a tracheotomy to help her to breathe—that is, a small tube will be inserted into the windpipe to bypass the blockage in the throat.	Without treatment, diphtheria can cause other serious and potentially fatal complications. Bacteria can release a toxin that damages the heart and nervous system. This can cause heart failure and paralyze the muscles needed for breathing.
Tuberculosis is a serious disease if left untreated. The disease can usually be treated at home. Your doctor will prescribe antibiotics.	The possible complications of tuberculosis of the lungs include pleural effusion (collection of fluid between the lung and chest wall) and collapse of areas of lung tissue (air between the lung and chest wall).

Checking the throat
Use a spoon or spatula to hold your child's tongue down while you check his throat. Enlarged tonsils and a sore throat may be symptoms of scarlet fever.

SAFETY

Many everyday household items are dangerous to children. Every year a large number of children are admitted to the hospital because they have fallen from windows, burned themselves on stoves or been scalded by hot drinks, choked on small objects, or swallowed household chemicals. Your child is naturally adventurous and inquisitive, and it is all too easy to underestimate the dangers he faces as he explores his environment, especially in the light of his developing mobility and manipulative abilities.

FALLS

The causes of accidents from falling vary according to the age of the child. Babies under the age of one are most likely to fall from a carriage or a stroller, or from a raised surface, such as a tabletop, whereas children aged between one and four are more likely to tumble down stairs, fall out of windows, or topple off play equipment.

You can minimize the risk of your child's falling by careful supervision—make sure you never leave your baby unattended on a raised surface—and by making a few changes in your home, such as installing window locks and safety gates on the stairs. Make sure that the railings on balconies and banisters are no more than 4 inches (10 centimeters) apart or your child may fall through or get his head stuck between the rails.

If you don't have a harness for your baby's high chair, carriage, or stroller, you should buy one. The built-in harness that is supplied may not always be adequate. Full harnesses are available from department stores and baby stores—look for one that is easy to fasten and adjust. Make sure you buy one and use it.

WINDOWS AND DOORS

The types of accidents associated with windows and doors include falling out of an open window, being cut by broken glass, and getting limbs and fingers trapped in closing doors. Various door-slam protectors are available to prevent fingers from being caught in closing doors.

The glass that is usually used for doors and windows is particularly dangerous because it breaks into long, sharp shards. Safety glass, on the other hand, is less likely to break, and when it does break, it doesn't form sharp pieces. Laminated glass stays in one piece when it is broken, and toughened glass shatters into small rounded pieces. A cheaper option is to use safety film, but this can only be used on unpatterned glass that is completely flat, and, once applied, can't be removed.

Never place furniture under windows—children will climb up on it, creating a greater risk of falls. To prevent your child from falling out of a window, you can install window locks that only allow the window to open by 4 inches (10 centimeters). Bear in mind, though, that windows can be an essential escape route if there should be a fire in your home, and figure out how you would escape from the window in an emergency. Consider taping the key to part of the window frame so it's always there if you need it.

Safety equipment	
Smoke detectors	Your home should be protected with smoke detectors on each floor. These detectors are inexpensive and easy to install. They must be attached to the ceiling to be effective; follow the manufacturer's instructions.
Fire extinguisher and blanket	The kitchen is the most likely place for a fire to start, so you should keep firefighting equipment there. Extinguishers need to be checked regularly for pressure, and may need to be replaced annually.
Safety locks	Make sure that windows remain firmly closed, or can be opened only a little way, especially on upper stories.
Stair gates	These can be installed at the top or bottom of the stairs. The bars should be vertical so that your child can't climb up them, and the gate should have a childproof lock.

FIRE SAFETY

House fires can be fatal if you or your child inhale smoke and toxic fumes. Fortunately, there are lots of ways that you can minimize the likelihood of a fire and lessen the damage that it can do.

• Don't smoke indoors.

• Don't leave pans containing hot fat unattended.

• Keep flammable liquids locked up.

• Use fireplace guards on any open fireplace.

• Store matches out of your child's reach.

• Buy flame-retardant furniture.

• Replace fire extinguishers every year.

• Keep a dry powder extinguisher and a fire blanket in the kitchen.

• Install smoke detectors, and check the batteries regularly.

• Smother a frying-pan or fat-fryer fire with a fire blanket, damp cloth, or pan lid.

• If you light candles in your home, keep them well out of the reach of children and pets. Never leave a lit candle unattended.

• Make sure everyone in your home knows what do if there's a fire.

BURNS AND SCALDS

Scalds occur when a child is exposed to hot liquids—they usually affect the face, neck, chest, and arms. As a child gets older and his hand–eye coordination improves, he will be able to pull saucepans, mugs, and kettles containing hot liquids off work surfaces. Another cause of scalding is putting a baby in water that is too hot, or leaving him unsupervised in a bathroom where there is a tub or sink full of hot water. A child can be scalded by less water, at a lower temperature, than an adult.

A good way to avoid scalds is to turn your hot water thermostat down to 129°F (54°C). At this temperature, scalding will only start to occur after 30 seconds of exposure. When running a bath for your child, put the cold water in first and then add the hot water afterward; don't leave a young child unsupervised in the bathroom.

In the kitchen, you can stop your child from pulling things off work surfaces by making sure that there are no trailing cords. Try to buy coiled cords for your iron or coffee-maker, or shorten the existing cords and use hooks to keep them out of reach. After you are finished with a mug, teakettle, or pan full of hot fluid, empty it immediately. Fit a guard to your stove, and, when cooking on the range, use the back burners in preference to the front ones and always keep pan handles turned in.

ELECTRICAL SAFETY

Make sure your child is aware of the dangers of electricity, and cover unused outlets with heavy furniture or with outlet covers. These are plugs made of plastic that prevent your child from sticking his fingers or objects into the outlet. Avoid brightly colored socket covers, since these will only serve to attract your child's attention.

POISONOUS SUBSTANCES

Children between one and three years old are most prone to accidental poisoning because they learn how to climb and open cupboards. Before the age of 18 months, children can't tell by taste whether something is likely to be bad for them. Common household poisons include bleach, kerosene, disinfectants, detergents, medications such as antidepressants and tranquilizers, and painkillers such as aspirin and acetaminophen. Fortunately, only one in 500 incidents of accidental poisoning has very serious consequences.

Poisoning is largely preventable. Keep all drugs and household chemicals in a high place out of reach of your child, or preferably in a locked cupboard. When using them, watch your child the whole time—this is when most accidents happen. Both prescription and over-the-counter medications should be kept in bottles with child-resistant caps— avoid taking them out of their original containers— and throw away any outdated or unused drugs.

Household chemicals, such as bleach, should also be stored in an inaccessible place, and you should never put chemicals into bottles that are familiar or attractive to children, such as soda bottles. Keep pet food bowls away from children, since they can harbor bacteria, and don't keep toxic plants or flowers, such as daffodils and irises, in the house.

SAFETY AT HOME

There are some general rules that apply to all rooms of the house. These include avoiding trailing cords, loose carpets, rugs, and flammable items of furniture, and choosing furniture that is child-friendly—for example, avoid tables with sharp corners. Keep all electric outlets covered, and install window locks. Teach your child from an early age that hot things such as fireplaces and ovens are dangerous and that she should never go near them, but maintain safety precautions until your child is at least three years old.

When your child visits other people's homes, scan the room for potential dangers. If you are in a house where there are no children, carry out a quick check for breakable items, heavy ornaments that can be pulled off surfaces, open, low-level windows, and sharp objects.

KITCHEN

• Install a stove guard and always point pan handles toward the back of the range.

• Keep matches out of your child's reach and install a smoke detector.

• Set the hot water thermostat to a maximum of 129°F (54°C)—at this temperature, it will take half a minute for serious scalding to occur.

• Keep plastic bags out of reach.

• Store sharp knives and cutlery in a drawer with a child lock.

• Don't use tablecloths. Your toddler can pull them, and everything on the table, onto her head.

• Don't leave hot pans or mugs containing hot drinks sitting around.

• If you spill grease or liquid on the floor, clean it up right away.

• Always keep harmful cleaning products in a secure place.

• Keep hot items, such as trays that have just come out of the oven, away from the edge of counters so that children are not able to reach them.

• If you are not using the iron, put both the iron and the ironing board away. Never leave your child unattended if the iron is on.

• Keep bowls of pet food out of reach to avoid bacterial infection.

• Never leave your child unattended while he is eating—he could choke.

• Stay in the kitchen while cooking. If you must leave the kitchen briefly, turn down the heat on appliances and return to the kitchen quickly.

LIVING ROOM

• When you replace the glass in patio doors, choose laminated glass or toughened glass.

• Use a fireplace guard in front of the fireplace.

• Use outlet covers to stop your child from poking objects into outlets.

• Avoid trailing cords on lights and TV, stereo, and video equipment.

• Avoid poisonous houseplants (see p.311).

• Don't leave alcohol, cigarettes, matches, or lighters lying around.

• Keep fragile, breakable items out of reach.

• Don't place hot or heavy objects on low tables.

• All shelving should be securely fixed to the wall.

HALL AND STAIRS

• Install a safety gate at the top and the bottom of the stairs.

• Make sure halls and stairways are well lit.

• Don't leave objects lying on the stairs.

• The stairway should be protected on both sides by walls or banisters.

• The gaps between the banisters should not be more than 4 inches (10 centimeters) wide so your child can't get an arm or a leg caught in them.

• Stair carpets should fit the stairs exactly so that your child can't trip on them.

• Repair any loose or frayed carpet on the stairs without delay.

• Make sure that it is impossible for your child to get out the front door and run into the street.

BATHROOM

• Store medicines in a locked cabinet or on a high shelf and throw away unused or old medicines.

• Keep disinfectants and bleach locked up, in their original containers, preferably with child-resistant tops, and make sure they are always out of reach while you are using them.

• Never leave a child alone with a filled bathtub.

• When preparing your child's bath, always add hot water to cold, never the other way around.

• Use nonslip mats in the bath.

• Keep the toilet lid closed.

• Place heated towel rails out of your child's reach.

BEDROOM

• Crib toys should not have strings that are longer than 1 foot (30 centimeters).

• Never leave your baby with the crib side down.

• Never leave your baby alone on the changing table, even for a second.

• Put window locks on windows.

• Avoid lights with trailing cords.

• rib bars should not be too widely spaced (over 2½ inches or 6 centimeters apart), since your child could get part of her body stuck between them.

• Don't use a pillow in your baby's crib until she's one year old.

• Choose furniture with rounded corners.

• Don't leave fires burning or space heaters running when your child is alone in a room.

PLAY AREAS

• Keep older children's toys away from younger children's toys. Toys with small parts, modeling kits, and chemistry sets can also be dangerous to babies and toddlers.

• Store toys safely in a box and don't leave them lying around on the floor.

• Throw broken toys away so they don't injure your child.

• A playpen is a good way of keeping a young child out of potential danger. Make sure that it is at least 2 feet (60 centimeters) deep.

• Store toys and games within your child's reach so he doesn't have to stretch or climb to get them.

SAFETY AT PLAY

The most common accidents that result from playing are cuts and bruises from falling over or off toys, or injuries from swallowing part of a toy or inserting it into a nostril. Sometimes an accident occurs because the child is not properly supervised, or because a toy is broken, of a poor standard, or simply too sophisticated for the child. Construction kits, toy cars and trains, and rocking and wheeled toys cause the most injuries. Even soft toys can choke or suffocate a child.

TOY SAFETY CHECKLIST

• Check packaging and labels to be sure the toy is appropriate for your child's age. In general, toys with small components are not suitable for children under the age of 36 months.

• Check warning labels for flammability or for any toxic ingredients.

• Don't stick pictures on the inside of your baby's crib—he may put them in his mouth.

• Crib toys should not be suspended on strings of more than 1 foot (30 centimeters) long.

• If your baby can stand up in his crib, remove toys from the side, since he can use them as a stepping stone to climb out.

• For a child under three, avoid toys with small detachable components, since these can be swallowed by very young children.

• If you have children of different ages, store each child's toys separately.

• Show your child how to use a toy.

• One- and two-year-olds can easily fall off rocking toys and wheeled toys, so keep an eye on your child, especially if he is playing on hard ground.

• Regularly check the batteries in battery-operated toys. Replace them if there's any leakage.

• Make sure toys have no sharp or abrasive edges.

• Throw broken toys away rather than giving them to charity or selling them at a rummage sale.

• Store toys safely away in a box with a lid that doesn't slam shut.

• If a toy comes wrapped in a plastic bag, unwrap it for your child, and dispose of the plastic bag.

Choke hazard tester

Once your baby acquires the pincer grasp, he is in danger of picking up and swallowing small objects.

A choke hazard tester checks if an object is small enough to lodge in a child's windpipe. If the object slips into the tester, it's potentially dangerous for your child.

Toys

It's tempting to buy toys on impulse, but check for potential hazards first.

The edges should be curved or flexible, not sharp or rigid

The paint should be nontoxic

Eyes should be firmly attached

Ears should be firmly stitched on

The wheels should be nondetachable

The fabric should be flame-retardant

Check for splits or tears; loose stuffing might be eaten or inhaled

OUTDOOR SAFETY

Your child will enjoy playing outdoors—he will be able to run around freely, get dirty, and explore a different environment. The main danger associated with playing outside is that he may run out of the yard or playground and into the street. Drowning is also possible if there a pool or pond in the yard. You can prevent this by making sure that your child always plays in an enclosed environment and that gates are locked with child-resistant locks. Drain or fence ponds, put fences around swimming pools, and empty wading pools after use. The other main dangers include ingesting poisonous plants, animal feces, and chemicals used in gardening.

YARD SAFETY CHECKLIST

• Make sure that any poisonous plants (see right) are removed, and pull up all types of fungi as soon as they appear.

• Store garden tools and chemicals, such as weedkiller, in a locked garage or shed.

• Make sure that lawn furniture is always set up properly—injuries can be caused by unstable deck chairs and loungers.

• Check the safety of play equipment regularly.

• Put climbing toys on grass, not on paved areas.

• Make sure your child can't run out of the yard into the street by locking the gate if you have a fence.

• If you have a pond or a swimming pool and your child is under the age of two, you should drain it, cover it, or fence it off.

• Fix broken glass in greenhouses right away.

• Don't use power saws or mow the lawn if your child is running around. Always put power tools away after use.

• Cover sandboxes to prevent fouling by animals.

• Don't allow animals to defecate in the garden.

• Cover old wells or rain barrels.

POISONOUS PLANTS

Although eating garden plants is rarely fatal, they can cause unpleasant symptoms, ranging from irritation of the skin, mouth, throat, and stomach, to nausea and vomiting. Tell your child never to eat any plants or berries without asking you first, and remove plants that you know are poisonous. Daffodils, hyacinths, irises, buttercups, snowdrops, sweet peas, and privet cause irritation of the gastrointestinal tract, and rhubarb, many fungi, tomato leaves, willow, laurel, rhododendron, mistletoe, and lily of the valley cause general poisoning.

Playgrounds

Young children need challenging equipment to test their skills and use up energy, but make sure they're safe.

• The play area should be surrounded by a fence so animals can't get in

• Young children should sit in box swings, not open ones

• Swings should be enclosed by a fence

• Climbing equipment should be situated on grass or sand so children don't injure themselves

• Your child should not put his feet under a merry-go-round or jump off one when it's moving

• Slides constructed on an earth mound will break a fall

• The surface of a slide should have no seams in it

• Equipment at ground level, like tubes and tires, is safest for toddlers

Sandbox safety
Make sure sandboxes are shallow so a child can't get buried.

CAR AND ROAD SAFETY

The most basic rule of car safety is to make sure that your child is always strapped in. Rear-facing seats are best for infants and can be used in the front or back of the car. Use child locks on the rear doors of your car, and don't let your child lean out of the window, or stick her hands and arms out. Never take your eyes off the road to turn around and talk to your child when you are driving. If she needs your attention, stop the car first. Accidents can happen when a car is stationary as well as when it is moving. A child can get her fingers stuck in car doors or windows as they are being closed, or can be hit when getting out of a car on the traffic side.

BABY SEATS

The safest way for your baby to travel by car is in a baby seat. A seat belt alone is not sufficient for a child under the age of ten months because her pelvic bones are not strong enough to protect the pelvic organs from the pressure of the belt in the event of a crash. Baby seats are designed for babies from birth to 12 months and up to 20 pounds (9 kilograms), and should be used only in the back seat, even if the airbag is disabled. The best design is

Take care

Children under the age of 12 should never sit in the front seat of a car. In the event of a crash, the airbag comes out of the dashboard at speeds of up to 200 miles per hour (320km/h), inflating with such force that the impact can seriously injure or kill a child.

a rear-facing seat buckled into a seat belt. This means that in a crash the impact is against the baby's back, and not the delicate pelvic organs. Some models will convert to a forward-facing child seat.

BABY CARRIER

Certain baby seats can also be used as infant carriers. However, you will have to reinstall them every time you return to your car, increasing the likelihood that, at some point, you will do so incorrectly. Baby carriers that can be used as car seats have a harness that goes over the baby's shoulders.

CHILD SEATS

By the age of one year, your baby will need a child seat. Some of these are installed with a four-point anchorage kit, although these are not practical for all types of cars; other types are secured with the adult seat belt. All have built-in five-point harnesses. Make sure you install your child seat according to the manufacturer's instructions, since a badly installed seat will not offer any protection in a crash. When your child has outgrown a car seat—some types will last until she is six—she can use a booster seat with an adult seat belt.

Child safety
Babies over the age of twelve months need a child seat. This is a forward-facing seat. As with baby seats, the child is protected by a five-point harness.

Baby safety
The best seats for babies from birth to twelve months are rear-facing.

ROAD SAFETY

Road accidents are usually more serious and require longer hospitalization than any other childhood accidents, so this is an area where safety is of paramount importance. The responsibility for your child's safety when out in traffic lies with you, of course, not just when she is in her stroller but when she reaches school age. Children don't develop the ability to judge the speed of traffic until they are about ten or 11 years old, and they are not good pedestrians until the age of 12. You can, however, instill the basics of road safety from an early age, by teaching her and, more importantly, by setting her a good example.

TEACHING YOUR CHILD

The first thing that your child must learn is that roads are dangerous places. It doesn't matter what the circumstances are—whether she has lost her ball or pet, or wants to greet someone —she must never run out into a road. Unless your road or street has no traffic, don't let your child play on the sidewalk— encourage her to play in parks, playgrounds, or in the back yard instead, and make sure that these areas are secured with a fence or a locked gate. Tell your child that she must never play on a bike or scooter near the road, that she shouldn't stand in between parked cars, and that if she loses a ball in the street, she should ask an adult to retrieve it.

SETTING AN EXAMPLE

The best way to teach your child road safety is to show her how you behave as a pedestrian. Most of us develop bad habits as adults, such as weaving through traffic, or crossing a road without allowing ourselves sufficient time. When you are with your child you should follow all the rules of street safety, even if it takes you longer to reach your destination. This way, your child will learn by example.

When you cross the road with your child, hold her hand and explain what you are doing and why. Go to the curb and tell your child that it is the safety line that must not be crossed without an adult. Look left and right and wait for a clear break in the traffic before you cross. If you are pushing a stroller, keep it on the sidewalk until you are ready to cross. Demonstrate to your child how to press the button at a pedestrian crossing, if necessary, and how to wait for the traffic to stop before you enter a crosswalk. Never run across the road in front of traffic when you are with your child.

Your child's awareness of road safety is in part determined by the area she grows up in. A child who grows up in the country and only has to cross quiet country roads may need extra supervision when she goes to a city because she hasn't made a strong association between roads, traffic, and danger. If this is the case with your child, you can still teach her about road safety when you are driving in the car. When you stop at a crosswalk, point out what it is for and how pedestrians use it. Show your child sensible places to cross, such as straight stretches of road, and point out the dangers of crossing at places such as sharp bends or between parked cars, where you can't see traffic coming. Point out pedestrians who are crossing well or badly, and explain why.

ENVIRONMENT

Make a careful assessment of the traffic and road conditions on your street. Although traffic speed is an important factor, recent research has shown that busy main roads pose six times as great a risk to pedestrians as residential streets. In other words, if you live on a busy route, you should never allow your child to go out of the house on her own.

If you live in a residential area, you could try to increase the safety of roads by asking your city to install speed bumps or to narrow the road at specific points. If possible, get together with other parents from your area and discuss a campaign for safe neighborhood play. Your local government can play an important role in helping you achieve this.

The road safety code

This simple road safety routine is really intended for children of eight years and upward, but you should start to teach it as soon as your child is old enough to follow your example.

Repeat these steps to your child every time you cross the road together.

• Find a safe place to cross the road, such as a crosswalk or other marked pedestrian crossing.

• Stop, look, and listen for traffic.

• If there is any traffic, let it pass.

• Look in both directions (even on a one-way road) and when the road is clear, walk across. Keep looking and listening as you cross the road.

NOTES

PERSONAL RECORDS

Your baby's early milestones—his first smile, his first word—will seem unforgettable to you, but as time passes, you'll find that your memory becomes hazy, not just about small details like when he first held his head up, but about crucial ones like vaccination dates.

Birth record: first baby

Name _____

Date and time _____

Place _____

Estimated date of delivery _____

Length _____

Weight _____

Blood group _____

Duration of labor _____

Type of delivery _____

Doctor _____

People present _____

Development record: first baby

First smile _____

Achieves head control _____

First tooth _____

Sits unsupported _____

Starts solids _____

Feeds self _____

Responds to
own name _____

Uses mature
"pincer" grip _____

Learns to "ungrasp" _____

First word _____

Understands "no" _____

Crawls _____

Fully weaned _____

Jargons _____

Stands _____

Bowel control _____

Bladder control _____

Walks _____

Makes simple
statements _____

Dresses self _____

Obeys simple requests _____

Climbs stairs
unsupported _____

Runs _____

Jumps _____

Counts to ten _____

Draws a circle _____

Starts preschool _____

Starts school _____

These pages will help you keep track of these important events. The medical records on pp.316–17 are particularly important. Use them to refresh your memory each time you take your child to the doctor; they may remind you of some forgotten detail that seems relevant. Fill in your own medical history, too, and that of your partner; these can often provide important clues to your child's state of health.

Birth record: second baby

Name _____

Date and time _____

Place _____

Estimated date of delivery _____

Length _____

Weight _____

Blood group _____

Duration of labor _____

Type of delivery _____

Doctor _____

People present _____

Development record: second baby

First smile _____

Achieves head control _____

First tooth _____

Sits unsupported _____

Starts solids _____

Feeds self _____

Responds to own name _____

Uses mature "pincer" grip _____

Learns to "ungrasp" _____

First word _____

Understands "no" _____

Crawls _____

Fully weaned _____

Jargons _____

Stands _____

Bowel control _____

Bladder control _____

Walks _____

Makes simple statements _____

Dresses self _____

Obeys simple requests _____

Climbs stairs unsupported _____

Runs _____

Jumps _____

Counts to ten _____

Draws a circle _____

Starts preschool _____

Starts school _____

MOTHER'S MEDICAL HISTORY

Illnesses

Allergies

Chronic conditions

Medical records: first baby

Name

Illness	Date	Comments

Injuries

Allergies

Immunizations: first baby (see p.283)

Type	Date	Reaction
Diphtheria, tetanus, acellular pertussis (DTaP) **Polio** **Hib** **Pneumococcus** **Hepatitis B** Generally given at 2, 4, and 6 months		
MMR (measles, mumps, rubella) **Varicella (chickenpox)** Given at approximately 1 year old		
Influenza vaccine Generally given yearly from 6–24 months		
DTaP, Polio **MMR** Given at 4–6 years		

FATHER'S MEDICAL HISTORY

Illnesses

Medical records: second baby

Name

Illness	Date	Comments

Injuries

Allergies

Allergies

Immunizations: second baby (see p.283)

Type	Date	Reaction
Diphtheria, tetanus, acellular pertussis (DTaP) **Polio** **Hib** **Pneumococcus** **Hepatitis B** Generally given at 2, 4, and 6 months		
MMR (measles, mumps, rubella) **Varicella (chickenpox)** Given at approximately 1 year old		
Influenza vaccine Generally given yearly from 6–24 months		
DTaP, Polio **MMR** Given at 4–6 years		

Chronic conditions

LENGTH, HEIGHT, AND WEIGHT

The most important criteria in assessing your baby's progress are happiness and general well-being. If these are apparent, there's no need for you to worry about his measurements; your healthcare provider can do that for you.

You may find it interesting to plot your baby's increasing height and weight on the following charts, but you should only become anxious about it if his growth pattern veers away from the centile line (see below). Don't compare your child to others of his age.

The range of "normal" heights or weights at a given age is very wide. A newborn boy may weigh anywhere from 5½ to 10 pounds (2.5 to 4.5 kilograms) without giving cause for concern; a five-year-old boy from 28 to 56 pounds (13.5 to 26.5 kilograms).

Each chart shows the range of heights or weights into which the vast majority of children will fall. The black line in the middle of each colored band represents the 50th centile; that is, 50 percent of children will fall below the line and 50 percent above it. The outer lines represent extremes beyond which very few children (fewer than 0.5 percent) will fall. If your child does, you should consult your doctor.

A child's measurements, plotted regularly, should form a line roughly parallel to the central line. If not, the measurements may not have been correctly plotted or the correct chart may not have been used. If in doubt, consult your healthcare provider.

GIRL'S LENGTH 0–6 MONTHS

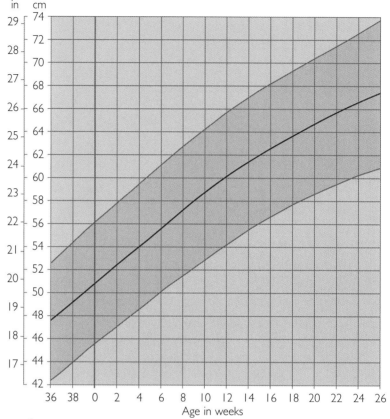

Age in weeks

GIRL'S WEIGHT 0–6 MONTHS

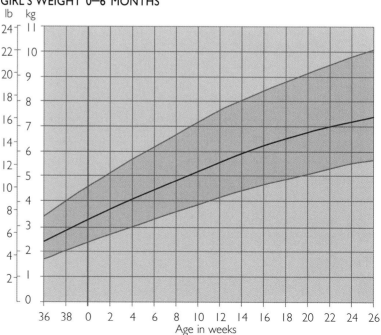

Age in weeks

BOY'S LENGTH 0–6 MONTHS

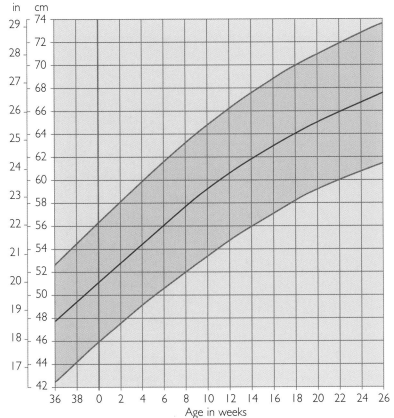

Age in weeks

USING THE CHARTS

I believe that no baby needs weighing and measuring if he's thriving, but we've included charts for parents who are eager to follow their child's progress.

• You will probably need to ask your healthcare provider for your baby's birth weight and birth length.

• For a baby, you could fill in the charts using the measurements taken by your healthcare provider.

• For a preterm baby, you will have to adjust his age accordingly, at least until he is a year old. If, for example, your baby was born at 36 weeks, start recording his measurements at the appropriate point to the left of zero on the chart, and continue to subtract four weeks from his age each time you fill in the chart.

• To measure your child's height once he's three or four, get him to stand against a wall with his feet together and his heels and shoulder blades touching the wall. Make sure he holds his head up straight by gently tilting his chin upward. If you like, measure him again at six-month intervals so he can see how he's growing.

• To enter your child's measurements on the chart, find his age along the bottom axis and draw a straight line up from it. Now find his weight or height along the vertical axis, and draw a line across. Mark a solid dot where the two lines meet. The row of dots is your child's growth curve.

BOY'S WEIGHT 0–6 MONTHS

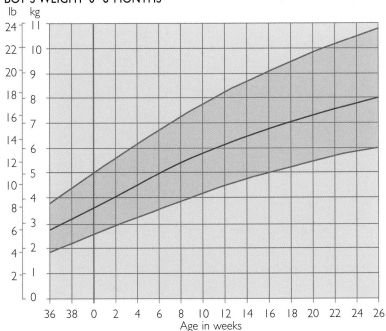

Age in weeks

NOTES

GIRL'S LENGTH 6–18 MONTHS

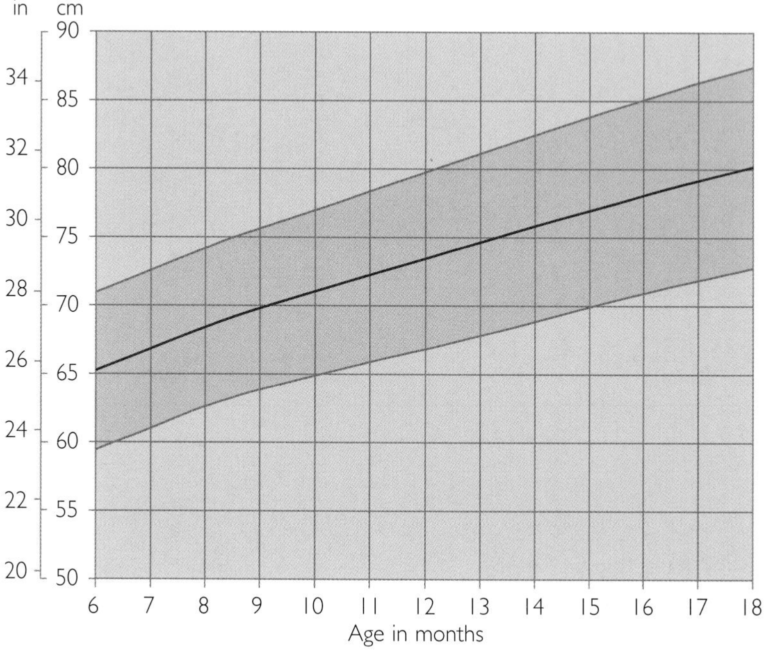

Age in months

GIRL'S WEIGHT 6–18 MONTHS

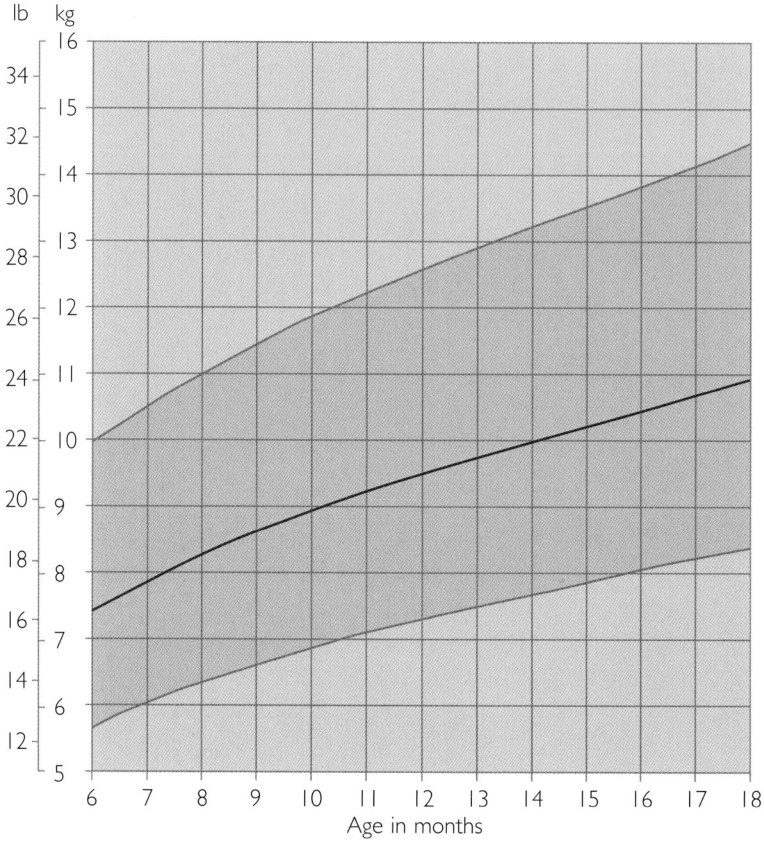

Age in months

BOY'S LENGTH 6–18 MONTHS

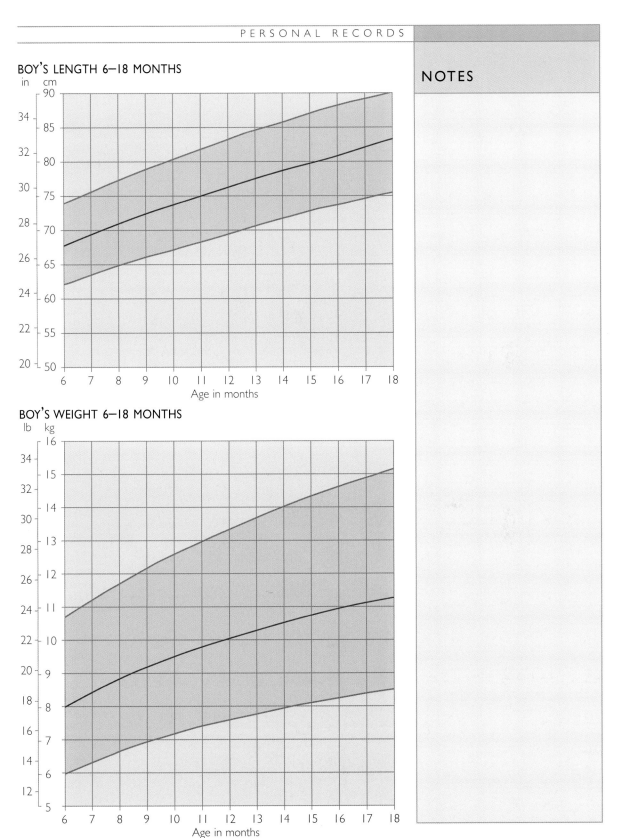

Age in months

BOY'S WEIGHT 6–18 MONTHS

Age in months

NOTES

GIRL'S HEIGHT 18–36 MONTHS

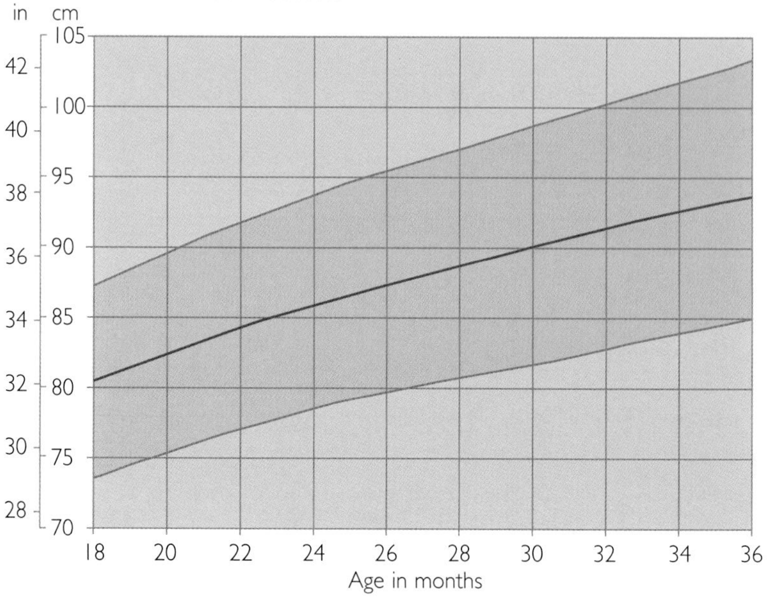

Age in months

GIRL'S WEIGHT 18–36 MONTHS

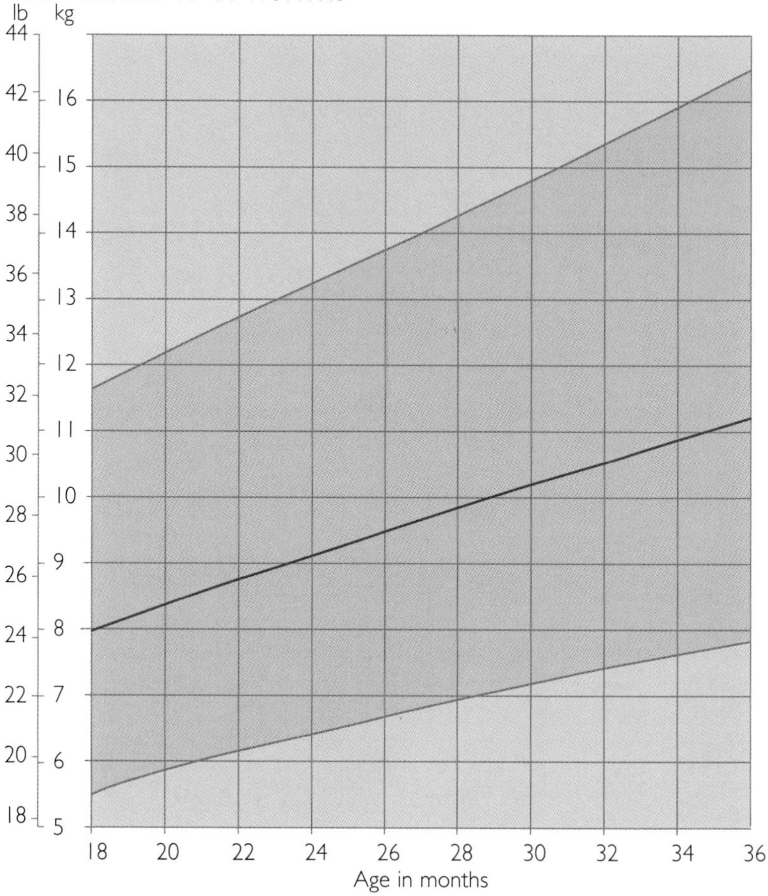

Age in months

BOY'S HEIGHT 18–36 MONTHS

NOTES

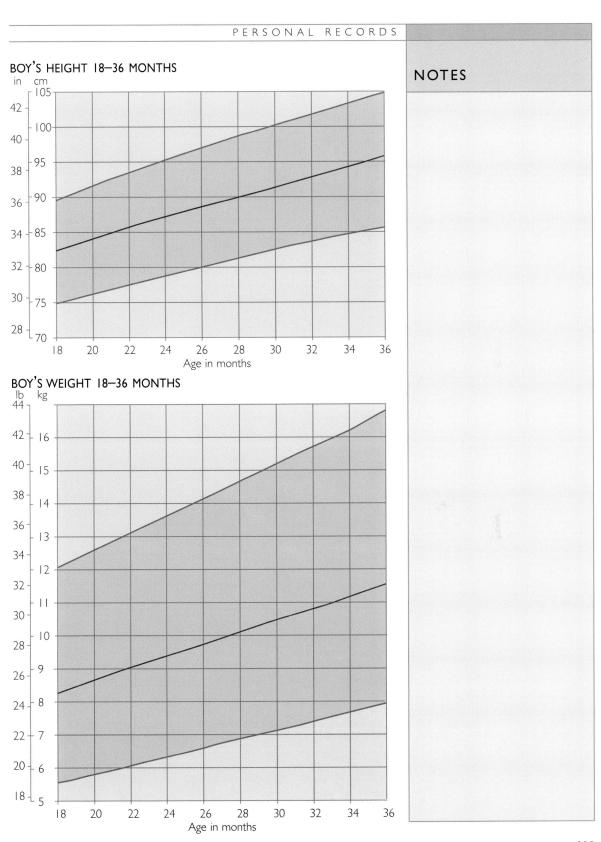

BOY'S WEIGHT 18–36 MONTHS

NOTES

GIRL'S HEIGHT 3–5 YEARS

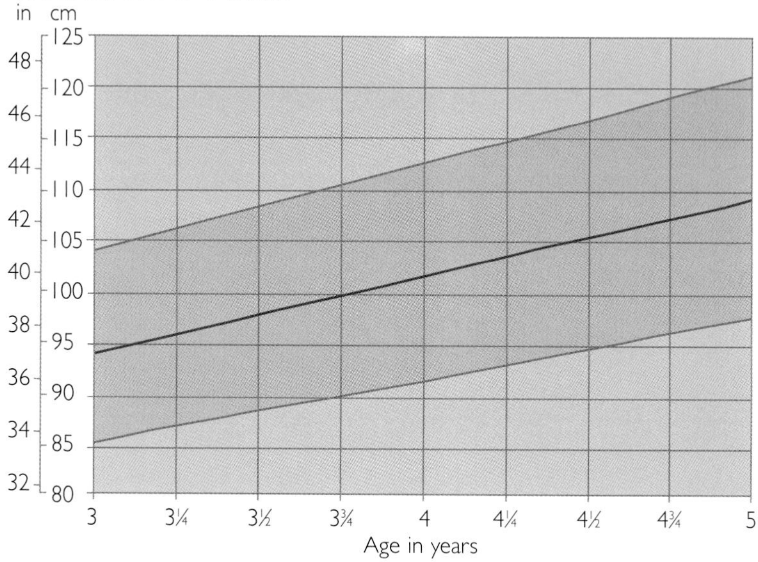

Age in years

GIRL'S WEIGHT 3–5 YEARS

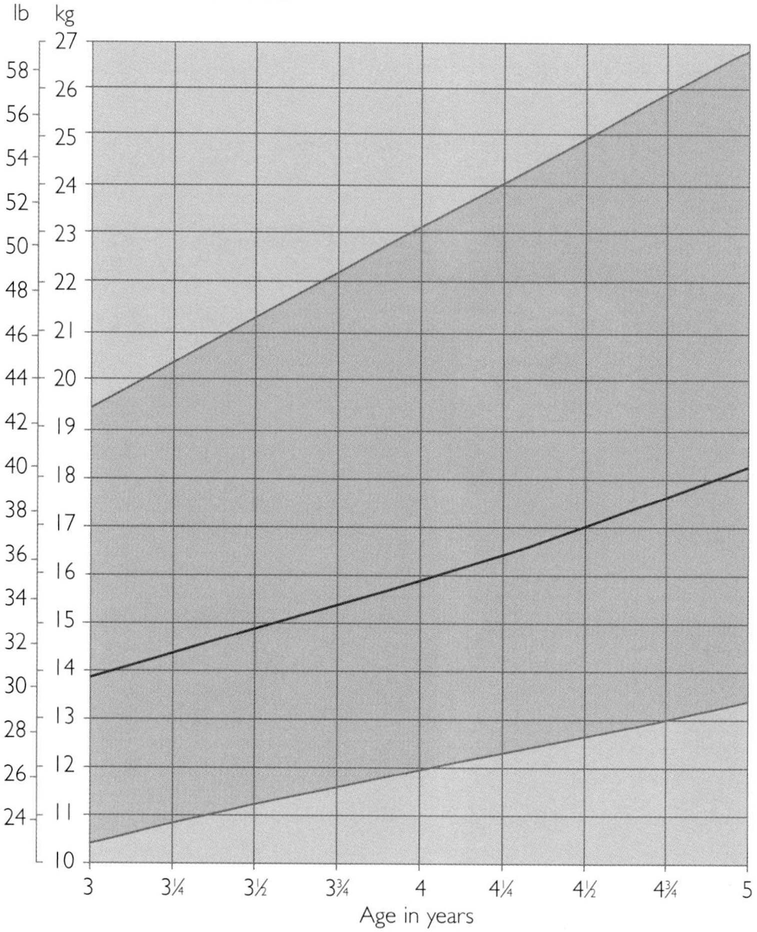

Age in years

BOY'S HEIGHT 3–5 YEARS

NOTES

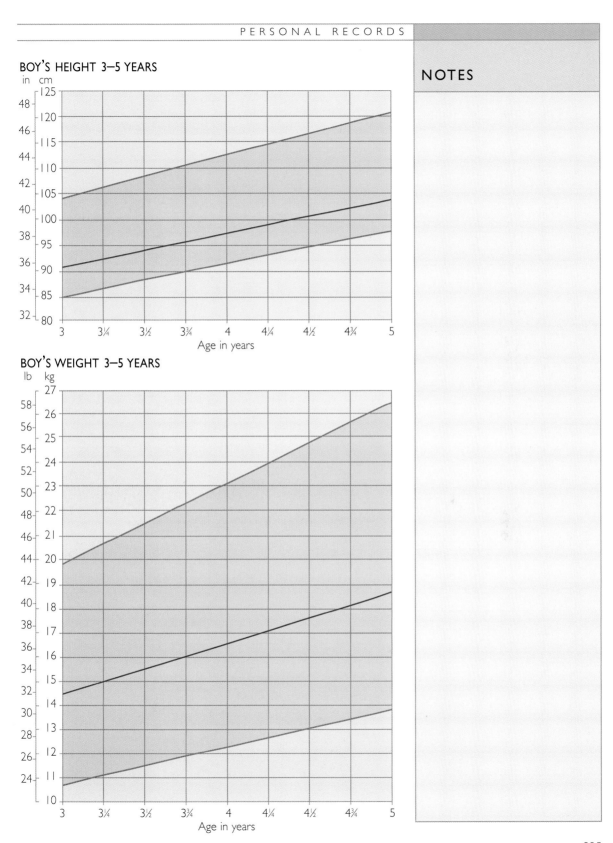

BOY'S WEIGHT 3–5 YEARS

FIRST AID

You will inevitably have to cope with minor accidents and cuts and bruises as your child grows up, but you should also be equipped to cope with major accidents or emergencies if necessary. All parents should know the basic first-aid techniques to deal with accidents quickly, effectively, and calmly. To give first aid effectively, you need to understand and practice the techniques detailed on the following pages, and you should keep a first-aid kit accessible in an emergency, but out of your child's reach.

EMERGENCY FIRST AID

A severe accident with the loss of much blood or other body fluids may precipitate shock (see p.332), which is always serious. Other emergencies include choking (see p.333), a very severe respiratory tract infection that blocks the airways, drowning, and unconsciousness. Prompt action on your part can be life-saving.

PRIORITIES

When your child has an accident, you must get your priorities right. Tell any adult present to call 911 while you go through the checklist (below). Detailed instructions for the procedures involved are shown on pp.328–333. If there isn't anyone around to help, you should go through the checklist before calling 911.

Is your child in danger? If appropriate, remove your child from the danger or the danger from your child. Don't put yourself at risk, and don't move your child unless you are in danger.

Is she conscious? Keep calling her name clearly and loudly.

Is her airway blocked? Open your child's airway by tilting her head back, clearing any obvious obstruction, and lifting her chin (see p.328–29).

Is she breathing? Lean close to your child's mouth to listen for breathing and feel it against your cheek. Look at her chest to see if it is rising and falling. If there are no signs of breathing after ten seconds, give two effective rescue breaths (see p.330).

Triangular bandage

Open-weave bandages

Gauze dressings

Adhesive bandages

Thermometer

Scissors

Home first-aid kit
Keep these items in a clearly marked box with an airtight lid. Make sure you know how to use each one properly. You may also like to keep some infant acetaminophen for treating pain or fever in young children.

Crepe bandages

Antiseptic wipes

Calamine lotion

Cotton batting

Wound dressings

Surgical tape

Dumbbell bandage

Tweezers

Safety pins

First-aid training

You must learn the procedures on these pages by heart in order to make use of them. If you have to waste time referring to this book to refresh your memory, your delay could be the difference between life and death.

To be thoroughly prepared for a medical emergency, you should complete a certified course of instruction in infant and child first aid and CPR. You can locate a course in your area by contacting the local chapter of the Red Cross (see **Useful addresses**, p.344).

Does she have signs of circulation? Look for breathing, coughing, or movement for no longer than ten seconds. If signs are absent, give alternate chest compressions and rescue breaths (see pp.330–31) for one minute, call 911, taking your child with you if you can, then continue resuscitation.

Call 911 If your child is having breathing difficulties or is unconscious, then call 911, or get another adult to do so. Try not to leave your child unattended and be prepared to carry out resuscitation on her.

RESUSCITATION

In order for vital organs such as the brain to function, they need a continuous supply of oxygen. If any part of the process by which oxygen is carried to body cells and tissues goes wrong, unconsciousness may result. Air must be inhaled to supply oxygen to the blood, and the oxygenated blood must be pumped around the body by the heart. If the brain is deprived of oxygen for more than three minutes, it will begin to fail. If the heart fails, death will occur unless emergency action is taken.

Resuscitation is necessary if, for whatever reason, your baby or child has stopped breathing or if her circulation has stopped (see p.328–29).

HOW RESUSCITATION WORKS

Oxygen supply

Three factors are involved in getting oxygen to the brain. The air passage, or airway, must be open so that oxygen can enter the body; breathing must occur so that oxygen can enter the bloodstream in the lungs; and the heart must be pumping so that the blood travels around the body (circulation) taking the oxygen to all the tissues, including those of the brain.

Air must be inhaled to provide oxygen

Oxygen enters the bloodstream via the lungs

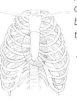

The heart pumps the oxygenated blood around the body

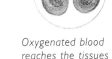

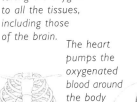

Oxygenated blood reaches the tissues

The ABC of resuscitation

In an emergency, when your child stops breathing or loses consciousness, you must remember to carry out the following checks in the order given:

A is for Airway To open the airway, tilt the head back, clear any obvious obstruction from the mouth, and lift the chin (see p.326). Never sweep the back of the throat if your child is choking (see p.333).

B is for Breathing If your child shows no signs of breathing, you will have to breathe for her with rescue breaths (see p.330).

C is for Circulation Check that your child has signs of circulation—breathing, coughing, or movement. If there are none, you will have to give chest compressions combined with rescue breaths (see p.331).

RESUSCITATION

If your child has lost consciousness and isn't
breathing, he's at risk of brain damage and heart
failure. You need to make a fast assessment of his
condition in order to know what first-aid treatment
to give. If he is unconscious but still breathing and
has circulation, then you should call 911 and place
him in the recovery position (see p.329). If he's
unconscious and not breathing but has signs
of circulation, you will need to give rescue breaths
(see p.330). If he's not breathing and has no signs
of circulation, you must give chest compressions
combined with rescue breaths immediately (see
p.331). All of these procedures differ slightly for
babies and children.

ASSESSING A BABY

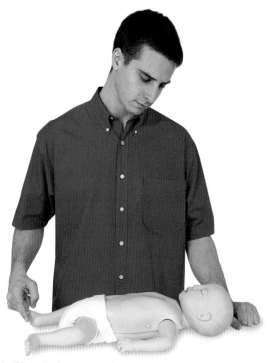

I Check for consciousness
See if your baby is conscious by calling his name and
tapping or scratching the sole of his foot. If he doesn't
respond after about ten seconds, shout for help.

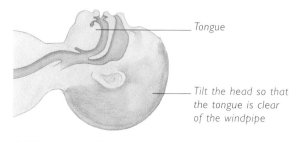

Tongue

Tilt the head so that
the tongue is clear
of the windpipe

2 Clear the airway
Look in your baby's mouth. If you can see an obvious
obstruction, remove it with your fingers, but be careful not
to poke it farther in. Open the airway by lifting the chin
with one finger and tilting the head back very slightly.

3 Check for breathing
Look, listen, and feel for signs of breathing. Look along your
baby's chest and abdomen to see if they are moving up
and down. Listen closely for sounds of breathing and feel
for his breath on your cheek. If there are no signs of
breathing after ten seconds, you should give two rescue
breaths (see p.330), and then look for signs of circulation.

4 Check for signs of circulation
Look for breathing, coughing, or movement for no more than
ten seconds. If there are no signs, give chest compressions
and rescue breaths (see p.331) for one minute, then call
911 and continue.

ASSESSING A CHILD

1 Check for consciousness
See if your child is conscious by tapping her shoulder. Keep calling her name. If she doesn't respond, call for help.

3 Check breathing
Look, listen, and feel for signs of breathing. Look along your child's chest and abdomen for movements; listen for sounds of breathing; and feel for her breath on your cheek. If she is not breathing, give two rescue breaths (see p.330), then check for signs of circulation.

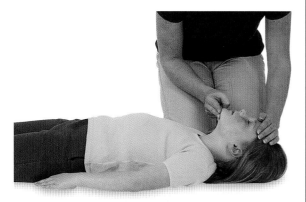

2 Clear the airway
Look in the mouth to see if it is obstructed. If it is, clear it with your fingers, but be careful not to push any obstruction farther in. Open the airway by tilting her head back by placing one hand on her forehead. Put two fingers under your child's chin and lift her jaw.

4 Check for signs of circulation
See if your child's heart is still beating by checking for signs of circulation. Look for breathing, coughing, or movement for no more than ten seconds. If there is no circulation, you must give one minute of chest compressions combined with rescue breaths (see p.331), call 911, then continue CPR.

The recovery position

An unconscious child who is breathing should be placed in this position to keep the airway open and to allow liquids to drain from the mouth.

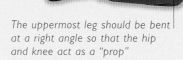

The uppermost leg should be bent at a right angle so that the hip and knee act as a "prop"

Place the arm at right angles to the body with the elbow bent

For a baby
Cradle him in your arms facing slightly toward you, with his head lower than his body in order to keep the airway open.

1 Position nearest arm
If your child is lying on his back or side, kneel beside him. Straighten his legs and place the arm nearest to you at right angles to his body with the elbow bent.

2 Position other arm
Bring the other arm across the chest and place the back of the hand against the cheek.

3 Bend leg
Still pressing your child's hand to his cheek, grasp the thigh that is farthest away from you and pull the knee up, keeping the foot flat on the ground and placing it next to the closer knee.

4 Resting position
Roll your child over into a resting position with his knee bent and his head resting on his hand.

RESCUE BREATHING

RESCUE BREATHING FOR BABIES

1 Open the airway
If your baby has stopped breathing, lay her down on a firm surface and gently tilt her head back. Check her mouth. If you can see an obvious obstruction, remove it with your fingers, but do not poke a finger down your baby's throat. Lift the chin with one finger.

2 Give rescue breaths
Inhale, put your lips over your baby's nostrils and mouth, making a complete seal, and breathe out gently into her mouth and nose so that her chest rises. Remove your lips and let the chest fall. Give two rescue breaths at a rate of one every three seconds.

3 Check for signs of circulation
After two rescue breaths check for signs of circulation—breathing, coughing, or movement (see p.328). If there are no signs, give chest compressions (see opposite) combined with rescue breaths. After one minute of this, call 911, taking the baby to the phone. If there are signs of circulation, continue to give rescue breaths, checking for signs of circulation every minute.

RESCUE BREATHING FOR CHILDREN

1 Open the airway
If your child has stopped breathing, lay her down on a firm surface and tilt her head back. Check for anything obviously

obstructing the mouth—if you see something, remove it, but don't stick your finger down your child's throat. Place two fingers under her chin and lift the chin.

2 Give rescue breaths
Using your finger and thumb, pinch your child's nostrils closed. Inhale, put your mouth over her mouth, making a complete seal, and breathe out until her chest rises. Remove your mouth and watch the chest fall. Give two rescue breaths—one every three seconds.

3 Check for signs of circulation
After two rescue breaths, check for signs of circulation—breathing, coughing, or movement—for no more than ten seconds (see p.329). If there are no signs of circulation, give chest compressions (see opposite) combined with rescue breaths for one minute, then call 911. If there are signs, continue rescue breaths, checking the circulation every minute.

CHEST COMPRESSION FOR BABIES

1 Position the fingers
Chest compressions combined with rescue breaths, known as cardiopulmonary resuscitation (CPR), are necessary when your baby has no signs of circulation, and is not breathing. Lay her down on a firm surface and position two fingers only in the middle of the chest just below an imaginary line between the nipples.

2 Give chest compressions
Press down sharply on the chest with the tips of your two fingers. You should give five compressions during a three-second period, and you should push down to a depth one-third of the depth of the chest. Be careful not to thrust too vigorously or too deeply, or you could harm your baby.

3 Give rescue breaths
After five compressions, give one breath (see opposite). Alternate chest compressions with rescue breaths: for every five compressions over a three-second period, give one breath. After one minute of this, call 911, taking the baby to the phone with you. Continue resuscitation until help arrives.

CHEST COMPRESSION FOR CHILDREN

1 Positioning the hand
Place your child on her back on a firm surface. Put the middle finger of one hand on the tip of the breastbone (the bone where the ribs meet in the middle) and the index finger above it. Position the heel of your other hand so that it rests just above the index finger.

2 Give chest compressions
Take your fingers away from the breastbone and, using the heel of the other hand, press down sharply to a depth one-third of the depth of the chest. Give five compressions in three seconds.

3 Give rescue breaths
After five compressions, give one breath (see opposite). Don't stop to look for signs of circulation unless she shows signs of reviving. Alternate five compressions every three seconds with one breath. After one minute, call 911, then continue.

SHOCK

Shock is commonly thought of as an emotional response to a distressing event, but in a medical context, "shock" refers to a perilous drop in blood pressure resulting in insufficient blood reaching the body tissues. If it is not dealt with quickly, the vital organs can stop functioning and the child can die.

Symptoms Initially, the body responds with a flow of adrenalin. This gives rise to a rapid pulse, pale, grayish-looking skin, especially around the lips, sweating, and clamminess. As shock progresses, your child may be thirsty, he may feel sick, and he may vomit. He is likely to be weak and dizzy, his breathing will be shallow and fast, and his pulse (see p.276) will be fast and irregular.

As shock progresses, the body withdraws the blood supply from the surface of the body to its core, and the oxygen supply to the brain weakens. In very severe cases, when the oxygen supply to the brain is insufficient, your child may become restless and anxious, and he may be yawning and gasping for air ("air hunger"). Eventually he will lose consciousness and the heart will cease functioning.

WHAT TO DO
If you suspect that your child is suffering from shock, you should call 911 as soon as possible. If he's lost a lot of blood, try to stop the bleeding (see p.335), and deal with any burns (see p.336), or any other obvious cause of shock. Move him as little as possible, but get him to lie down with his legs raised

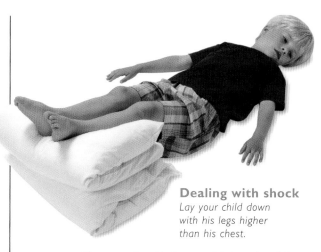

Dealing with shock
Lay your child down with his legs higher than his chest.

on some pillows so that his legs are higher than his chest; this makes it easier for blood to flow back to the heart. Undo any fastenings around the neck, chest, and waist and observe him in case he starts to vomit.

Your child will be very anxious, so it is important to stay with him and keep reassuring and talking to him. Fear and pain both tend to worsen shock, so keep your child as calm and as comfortable as you can under the circumstances. Make sure that he is warm, but not too hot. A blanket on top of him and around his head will keep him insulated. (In a very young child, the blanket should be wrapped around the body.) If your child is suffering from shock as a result of an injury, he may need surgery when he gets to the hospital, so don't give him anything to eat or drink. If he is thirsty, wet his lips with some water. Keep checking his breathing, and be prepared to give resuscitation (see pp.330–31) if necessary.

Causes of shock

There are two main causes of shock: a sudden drop in blood pressure due to paralysis of the nerves, as in electric shock, or a loss of blood or body fluid, as in severe burns.

An accident may lead to profuse bleeding, either internally or externally (see p.335), resulting in a reduced volume of blood circulating around the body. Severe untreated dehydration can lead to shock, especially if your child has a fever, vomiting, or diarrhea and the lost fluids are not replaced.

Your child's blood pressure will drop rapidly if he has a severe allergic reaction to, say, a wasp or bee sting, a food, or a drug. The allergens cause the blood vessels to dilate, tissues to swell, and the air passages to constrict. Insufficient oxygen reaches the tissues and he will be in danger of suffocation. This is known as anaphylactic shock.

Other causes of shock include peritonitis (inflammation of the abdominal lining), spinal injury, and some types of poisoning.

CHOKING

If your child's airway becomes completely blocked or he is unable to get sufficient oxygen into his lungs, he may lose consciousness. Normal breathing may return when he loses consciousness and the muscles relax. If he doesn't breathe, start resuscitation (see pp.328–31). Remove the blockage. Encourage a baby to cough out the foreign object by patting his back. If this doesn't work, follow the steps below. (For a baby or small child, follow the sequence for a baby; abdominal thrusts can injure small children.) If the procedure doesn't work, repeat it until help arrives or the obstruction clears.

FOR A BABY

1 Back slaps

Lay your baby face down along your forearm, keeping his head low and supporting his head and shoulders on your hand. Slap him sharply five times between the shoulder blades.

2 Check the mouth

Turn your baby face up and look in his mouth. If you can see the obstruction, use a finger to hook it out, but don't put your finger down his throat.

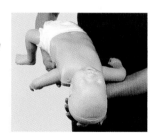

3 Chest thrusts

If slaps haven't worked, place two fingers on the lower half of his breastbone (in the center of his chest just below the nipples), and give five sharp downward thrusts. Check the mouth again. If the blockage hasn't cleared, repeat steps 1–3 three times and then call 911, taking your baby with you to the phone. Continue steps 1–3 until help arrives.

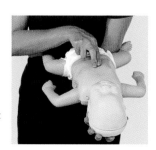

FOR A CHILD

1 Clearing the obstruction

If your child is breathing, encourage him to cough; this may clear the obstruction. If he cannot speak or cough, proceed to steps 2 and 3. If the obstruction does not clear the first time, repeat steps 2 and 3 up to three times. If the obstruction still has not cleared, dial 911 or call EMS.

2 Correct hand position for clearing an obstruction

Wrap your arms around your child's abdomen just above the hips (make sure your child is bending forward). Make a fist with one hand and place the thumb side of your fist against the middle of his abdomen, just above his navel. Get him to cough up the obstruction if he can.

Fist should be just above child's navel

3 Abdominal thrusts

Try abdominal thrusts. Put your arms around your child's upper abdomen. Make sure he is bending well forward. Place your fist between the navel and the bottom of the breastbone, and grasp it with your other hand. Pull sharply inward and upward up to five times. Stop if the obstruction clears. Check his mouth.

Press into abdomen with quick upward thrusts

ELECTRIC SHOCK

Your child may get an electric shock from frayed cords or wires, light switches, defective electrical appliances, or from touching an appliance with wet hands. It is important to warn your child about the hazards of electricity from an early age and stress that water and electricity are a dangerous combination. Replace frayed wires and put covers on any electrical outlets not in use.

Symptoms In severe cases, your child may lose consciousness and her heartbeat may stop. In mild cases, she may have slight burns.

WHAT TO DO
Before you go to help your child, you must break the contact between her and the source of electricity. If it is safe to do so, pull the plug out. If you have to break the contact manually, make sure

you do it safely: push your child away using an object made of a nonconducting material, such as wood or plastic, and stand on an insulating material while you do it. If there is no alternative, drag your child away by her clothes. This can be very dangerous, however—if you touch her skin or if her clothes are damp, you will get a shock, too.

Once the contact has been broken, you should examine your child for burns. If burns are severe or your child is unconscious, you should call 911. In the meantime, treat the burns by pouring on cold water and then placing a sterile dressing on them (see p.336). Monitor your child's condition closely; if she starts to suffer from shock (see p.332) you may have to resuscitate her. If she is unconscious but breathing, place her in the recovery position (see p.329).

POISONING

Common poisons include bleach, weedkiller, fungi, and plants such as berries, irises, and daffodils. Leave medicines and chemicals in their original containers, which should be tamper-proof where possible, and lock them up. Call your doctor or contact your local Poison Control Center if you suspect poisoning.

Symptoms A corrosive chemical often burns around the mouth, and it's common for the child to feel nauseous and vomit or have diarrhea. With very poisonous chemicals, your child may lose consciousness or have seizures. There may be a poisonous substance, such as berries, pills, or a bottle containing household chemicals lying around—keep this to show to your doctor to help her decide how to treat your child.

Use a wooden object to break contact with the source

A telephone directory makes a good insulator

Breaking contact
Stand on a dry insulating material while you push your child's limbs away from the source with a nonconductive object of wood or plastic. Do not touch your child's skin with your hands.

WHAT TO DO

If your child collapses or loses consciousness, check her breathing and, if necessary, resuscitate her (see pp.330–31). When she is breathing, put her in the recovery position (see p.329) and call 911. If she is conscious and breathing, call the Poison Control Center at (800) 222-1222 for emergency advice.

Try to identify the poison, and keep a sample in case medical staff need it later. If possible, tell the 911 operator or Poison Control Center how much your child swallowed and when.

Never try to induce vomiting unless told to do so by the Poison Control Center. If certain chemicals are regurgitated, they will cause as much damage on the way back up as they did when first swallowed. Instead, Poison Control staff may direct you to give your child sips of milk or water. Traces of poison on hands or face should be washed away with water.

DROWNING

A child can drown in just 2 inches (5 centimeters) of water, so it's very important not to leave your child alone near a wading pool, a bathtub, or even a pail of water. If a drowning child is not rescued quickly she will be asphyxiated.

RESCUE

Drowning in a large body of water is a hazard to you as well as your child, so first try to rescue her without entering the water. Try to reach her with your hand or a pole, or throw her a life preserver. Get into the water only if there is no alternative. In shallow water, carry your child to land by wading through the water; tow her only if she is already unconscious. While you are carrying her, make sure that her head is lower than her chest—if she vomits, there will be less risk of her inhaling vomit.

WHAT TO DO

Take your child to the nearest warm, dry place and, without undressing her, lay her down on blankets or a coat. Check her airway and breathing (see pp. 328–29), and give resuscitation if necessary (see pp. 330–31). If she is unconscious but still breathing, put her in the recovery position (see p.329) and monitor her breathing all the time. Change her wet clothing

and insulate her from the cold. Your child should receive medical attention as soon as possible; either call 911 or take her to the hospital yourself, because even if she appears to recover, there is a chance that she may suffer from "secondary drowning," where the air passages swell up. Your child may also need treatment for hypothermia.

BLEEDING

Cuts and grazes (see p.342) are rarely serious and, unless infected, can be dealt with at home. Severe external bleeding or internal bleeding, however, can lead to shock and eventually loss of consciousness. These should be treated as emergencies, and you need to act quickly.

WHAT TO DO

Profuse bleeding is both serious and distressing. It should be dealt with quickly before your child goes into a severe state of shock.

SEVERE EXTERNAL BLEEDING

Expose the wound if it is covered (cut away clothing if necessary) and apply pressure to the wound with a clean dressing or cloth. If there is glass sticking out of the wound, don't remove it. Instead, apply pressure on either side; this will compress the ends of the damaged blood vessels. Lay your child down, keeping the injured part of the body in a position above the heart to slow the flow of blood to the wound.

Do not use a tourniquet to stem bleeding, but do apply a dressing to the wound and secure it with bandages after applying pressure to the wound. If blood appears through the bandage, put another one on top. If there is glass sticking out of the wound, build up the bandages on either side until you can bandage over the top without pushing the glass deeper into the wound. Call 911 or take your child to the hospital.

INTERNAL BLEEDING

If your child is showing signs of shock (see p.332), if there is pattern bruising (bruising that follows the pattern of the object that crushed against the body), or if there is bleeding from the ears, nose, mouth, or vagina, you should suspect internal bleeding. Treat your child for shock (see p.332) and call 911.

BURNS AND SCALDS

Burns are usually described in terms of the amount of damage to the skin. First-degree burns are the least serious and can result from a minor spillage or touching a very hot surface. Second-degree burns are more serious, and fluid-filled blisters form on the skin. Third-degree burns are very serious, since all layers of the skin are damaged, fluid loss is high due to weeping of the skin, and the nerves and underlying muscles may be damaged. Unless a burn is very minor, you should always seek medical help.

WHAT TO DO

If the burn is minor, run cold water over the affected part of the body for about ten minutes. Cover it with a sterile dressing to protect it from bacteria. A clean plastic bag will make a good temporary dressing if you have nothing else suitable.

If the burn is major, call 911, then lay your child down and pour water over the affected area for ten minutes or until help arrives. Check to be sure your child is breathing. You may need to treat him for shock (see p.332). If he loses consciousness, be prepared to resuscitate him (see pp.330–31). Unless your child's clothes are sticking to the burned area, you should gently take or cut them off him.

DO NOT

• Touch the affected area or attempt to burst any blisters that form.

• Apply lotion or fat to the area.

• Stick a bandage or adhesive dressing to the burn.

• Cover the burn with a "fluffy" dressing or any cloth that sheds lint.

• Remove anything that is sticking to the burn: you may cause further damage to the skin or tissue and introduce infection.

• Overcool your child if he has severe burns; this could lead to hypothermia (see p.340).

CLOTHING ON FIRE

If your child's clothing should catch fire, the first priority is to stop him from moving. Any rapid movement will make the flames worse.

WHAT TO DO

• Stop him from running around in panic, because this will fan the flames. Lie him on the floor with the burning side uppermost.

• Wrap him in a heavy woolen coat or blanket to stifle the flames. Never use nylon—it will start on fire.

• Roll him on the ground to put out the flames. Douse him with water if you have some, or with another nonflammable liquid.

• Don't try to remove any clothing. It may be sticking to the skin, and moving it will cause further damage.

Take care

Severe burns are dangerous: a child can rapidly go into shock (see p.332) because of the loss of body fluids. Untreated shock leads quickly to unconsciousness. The larger the area of the burn, the greater the likelihood of severe shock. If more than one-tenth of your child's body is burned, he will need immediate treatment for shock; you should call 911 immediately.

HEAD INJURIES

If your child bumps his head, he will normally recover within minutes. If he hits his head quite hard, he may have some temporary swelling. Head injuries that should cause concern are those that cause severe bleeding or concussion, even hours later. Look for drowsiness, headaches, and nausea.

Symptoms   Mild symptoms resulting from a slight bump include a headache and a lump or swelling where the impact occurred. If the injury is more severe, your child may lose consciousness and the symptoms of concussion may follow (see below right). He may be drowsy, stunned, or dazed, and he may suffer nausea and vomiting. Disturbances in vision and headaches are common. If the skin of the scalp is cut, bleeding may be profuse.

Straw-colored fluid or watery blood leaking from the ears or the nose may indicate a skull fracture. Other symptoms include a depression of the scalp and unconsciousness. A suspected skull fracture should be treated as an emergency.

WHAT TO DO

If your child is unconscious, call 911 and place him in the recovery position (see p.329). Keep checking his breathing and his level of response (see pp.328–29) and be prepared to give resuscitation if necessary (see pp.330–31). If he comes around after a short time, keep checking his level of consciousness by getting him to respond to his name. Don't leave him alone.

If there is bleeding from the scalp, nose, or ears, press a clean pad firmly on the area to stop the flow. If there is a wound, don't touch it with your fingers. If the bleeding stops, clean and dress the wound, though not if this causes the bleeding to start again. If the wound is long or jagged, take your child to the hospital to have it stitched. If bleeding results from a small cut, clean it with soap and water and place a dressing on it.

Any discharge from the ear should be allowed to drain away. If your child is conscious and you think that he may be concussed, take him to see your doctor.

If you don't have a sterile dressing, any clean fabric pad will do

Scalp wounds
Apply firm, steady pressure to the wound with a sterile dressing or clean pad for ten minutes or until the bleeding stops. The pad should be larger than the wound.

Concussion

A child who has suffered a blow to the head may show symptoms of concussion, which is a temporary disturbance of the brain.

Your child will lose consciousness for a short time and then recover completely. He may feel dizzy or nauseous and have a slight headache, and may even be unable to remember what led up to his injury. Concussion can occur several hours after a blow to the head, so you should monitor your child closely for 24 hours for these symptoms. If the symptoms persist for more than a few days or if they recur, consult your doctor.

Cause of concussion
Because the brain is not fixed rigidly inside the skull, it is free to move around a little. This means that if there is a blow to the head, the brain is shaken or knocked against the skull, giving rise to the symptoms of concussion.

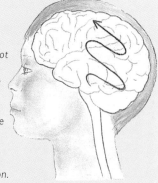

SEIZURES

The most common causes of seizures are fever (see p.281), epilepsy (see p.270), head injuries, diseases that damage the brain, and poisoning. Seizures may also occur for no apparent reason. During a seizure, there is a disturbance in the normal electrical impulses in the brain, causing muscles to jerk involuntarily. It is important that the child is not restrained in any way. Seizures usually occur on isolated occasions, but children with epilepsy suffer repeated attacks.

Symptoms Children with epilepsy may suffer from minor seizures (known as "petit mal"), which appear as a lapse of concentration or daydreaming, or from major seizures ("grand mal"). In a mild seizure, your child may experience a tingling or twitching in some part of her body, such as her arm or leg. In a grand mal seizure, your child may cry out and then lose consciousness and fall to the floor. Her body will become stiff and she will hold her breath. This "stiff" phase is followed by rhythmic jerking movements of the arms and legs and arching of the back. Your child has no control over her bodily functions and she may become incontinent. She may clench her teeth and bite her tongue, or froth at the mouth.

After the seizure, your child's muscles will relax and she will begin to breathe normally again. When she regains consciousness, she is likely to be dazed or confused, and she will want to sleep. When she wakes up, she won't remember the seizure.

WHAT TO DO
It's very important that you don't try to intervene while your child is having a seizure. Don't try to hold your child down. Even if you think she is at risk of biting her tongue, you should not try to open her mouth or put anything in it. Clear a space around your child so that she can't hurt herself, call a doctor, and stay with your child all the time. If your child remains unconscious, put her in the recovery position (see p.329).

You should make a note of the duration and the symptoms of your child's seizure to tell the doctor since it will help her diagnose the cause.

EYE INJURIES

Any injury to the eye should be taken seriously. Common injuries include a foreign object or chemical in the eye, a blow to the eye causing bruising or a black eye, and a cut in or near the eye.

Symptoms These vary according to the type of injury, but may include bruising around the eye socket, pain, inability to open the eye fully, or spasms of the eyelid. There might be impaired vision, a bloodshot appearance, and, if the eyeball has been punctured, blood or fluid leaking from the eyeball.

WHAT TO DO
This depends on the injury, but you must act quickly and may need to take your child to the ER.

• If your child has a foreign object in her eye, try to remove it using the corner of a handkerchief, or by flushing out her eye (see below). If it is embedded in the eye or is on the iris, tape a pad over her eye and take her to the hospital.

Flushing out the eye
Sit your child down with her head tilted in the direction of the affected eye. Pour clean water into the corner of the eye so the water washes over it and flushes out the object.

• For a blow to the eye, place a pad soaked in cold water over the eye to minimize bruising.

• If your child has a chemical in her eye, take her to the hospital, but first try to flush out the eye with water from a pitcher (see above) or under a faucet.

• If your child cuts her eye, hold a sterile pad against the wound and take her to the hospital.

FRACTURES AND DISLOCATIONS

The most common type of childhood fracture is a greenstick fracture, in which the bone bends and splits. Other types of fractures include closed fractures (a clean break) and open fractures (the bone breaks through the skin). A dislocation is a bone that is displaced from its joint, usually after a wrenching force.

Symptoms Typically, there is difficulty moving and a limb may look oddly shaped. There will be pain, swelling, bruising, and possibly a wound at the site of the injury. With a dislocation, your child may experience a "sickening" pain.

WHAT TO DO

All fractures and dislocations should be treated promptly in the hospital. You should keep your child as still as possible until an ambulance arrives, and don't let her have anything to eat or drink. You can prevent the worsening of an injury by immobilizing the joints above and below a fracture.

TYING A SLING

Support the injured arm

1 Positioning the bandage
Bend the injured arm across the chest. Place the bandage (use a triangular bandage or a square of cloth folded diagonally) between the arm and the chest. Pull one corner around the neck to reach the shoulder of the injured arm.

Secure with a reef knot

2 Tying the bandage
Bring the bottom of the bandage up over the child's forearm and tie the bottom corner of the triangle with a reef knot to the corner resting at the injured shoulder. Tuck in the ends of the knot.

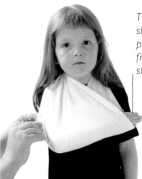

The fingers should protrude from the sling

3 Fastening the corner
Using a safety pin, secure the loose point of the bandage at the front of the elbow. If you don't have a safety pin, tuck the point into the sling. The hand should be left exposed.

LEG INJURY

Keep your child as still as possible while an ambulance is called. Don't take her to hospital yourself—she will need a stretcher. Your child could go into shock (see p.332), especially if her thigh bone is broken.

Support the joints
Sit or lay your child down, and encourage her to stay still. Hold the joints above and below the injured area to prevent any movement. Support her leg with pillows or blankets and call 911.

Take care

If you suspect that your child has fractured her spine or her neck, there may also be damage to the delicate spinal cord carried by the vertebrae. It is essential that you don't move your child until an ambulance arrives, and don't let her move her head. If there is spinal cord injury, your child may experience burning, tingling, or even a loss of sensation in her limbs.

HEATSTROKE

When the body overheats as a result of exposure to extreme heat, the temperature control mechanism in the brain fails and the sweat glands stop working. Your child can't lower his temperature in the adult way. This is a relatively common occurrence among children who go out in strong sun before they acclimatize to it. Your child's temperature may rise above 104°F (40°C) and in extreme cases he may lose consciousness and stop breathing. Most cases, however, are mild.

Symptoms Although the skin looks and feels hot, it remains dry. Your child will seem drowsy and lethargic, and he may have a rapid pulse rate. In severe cases, your child may become confused, start to lose consciousness, and stop breathing.

WHAT TO DO
Take your child's clothes off and lay him down in a cool place. Call a doctor if your child's temperature is 104°F (40°C) or higher and, while you are waiting, sponge him with tepid water or wrap him in a cool wet sheet. Place a covered ice pack on his forehead, give him lots of cool drinks, and direct a

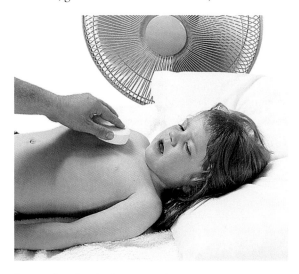

Lowering body temperature
Take your child out of the sun, and sponge her with tepid water or direct a fan on to her skin.

fan on to his body. Monitor his pulse rate and temperature closely. Check his temperature every minute until it lowers to 99°F (37.2°C), then stop cooling, but continue to monitor his temperature.

If he begins to lose consciousness, you should check his breathing and then place him in the recovery position (see p.329). If he has stopped breathing, give rescue breaths (see p.330) and then call 911.

HYPOTHERMIA

If your child gets cold as a result of being exposed to cold, wet, and windy weather, a near-drowning, or simply being in a room that is too cold, she may suffer from hypothermia. Clinically, hypothermia is defined as a body temperature of below 95°F (35°C). Deep hypothermia occurs when the body temperature drops to below 79°F (26°C). You need to know what to do if this happens—it can be fatal, since the heart, liver, lungs, and intestines may slow down and cease functioning.

Symptoms Your child may be shivering and his skin will feel cold and dry. He may look pale and blue (although babies may look pink) and his breathing may be slow and shallow. He will be lethargic and there might be behavioral signs, such as apathy, confusion, and quietness. In severe cases of hypothermia your child may start to lose consciousness.

WHAT TO DO
Take off any wet clothing, wrap your child in warm, dry clothes and blankets, and hold him close to your body. Call 911.

Older children can be warmed up with a warm bath and warm (not hot), sweetened beverages. Monitor your child's temperature constantly with a thermometer or by feeling his skin. If your attempts to warm him up are not working, or if he loses consciousness, call 911. If he seems to be warming up, put him in a warm bed and stay with him until the ambulance arrives or you are sure his temperature is back to normal. Never place a direct source of heat, such as a hot-water bottle, on your child's skin.

EVERYDAY FIRST AID

As your child grows up, he will inevitably experience some commonplace accidents, such as cuts, bruises, blisters, bites, and stings. Most of the time, these accidents are not serious and can be treated at home with comfort and some simple first aid techniques.

ANIMAL BITES

Animal bites can happen if your child is teasing or playing boisterously with a domestic pet, usually a dog or a cat. Although being bitten can be traumatic for your child, bites are not usually serious. The main danger is that if the animal bites deep into the flesh, bacteria will be lodged in the wound, making your child vulnerable to infection. If your child is bitten by any animal other than your own pet, seek medical treatment at once, since anti-rabies injections may be needed.

The first thing you should do is reassure your child, since he will probably be quite frightened. If he was bitten because he was teasing the animal, you should explain this to him and emphasize that it is an isolated incident.

WHAT TO DO

Wash the wound thoroughly with warm water and cover the bite with a dressing. If the bite is severe, try to control the bleeding with direct pressure and by raising the wounded part of the body and wrapping it tightly with a bandage. Cover the wound with a dressing and take your child to the hospital emergency room. He may need a tetanus injection if he hasn't been immunized.

SNAKE BITES

If your child is bitten by a snake, you should make a note of the snake's appearance so that the appropriate antidote can be given if the snake turns out to be a venomous one. Depending on the species of snake, the symptoms of a bite can include cuts or puncture wounds in the skin, intense pain, redness and swelling around the bite, and, in severe cases, labored breathing, sweating, vomiting, and impaired vision.

WHAT TO DO

It is important to keep your child calm, since if he panics, this can speed the spread of venom around the body. Wash the area of the bite with water, immobilize the affected part of the body with bandages, and call 911.

INSECT BITES AND STINGS

These are not usually serious unless there is an allergic reaction. Stings in the mouth or throat, however, are serious, since the swelling they cause can obstruct the airway. Stinging insects include bees, wasps, and hornets; biting insects include fleas, mosquitoes, and ticks. A sting is felt as a sudden, sharp pain and appears as a raised, white area on an inflamed patch of skin. A bite is less painful and normally causes mild discomfort and inflammation.

WHAT TO DO

Apply a cold compress and, later, calamine lotion to the bite or sting to relieve discomfort. If you can see the stinger sticking out of your child's flesh, scrape it off gently with a credit card or your fingernail.

If your child is bitten by fleas, have your family pet treated and your house disinfected. Mosquito bites can be avoided with insect repellent. When traveling in areas where malaria is a problem, always use malaria prophylaxis medicine. Tick bites are painless, but can cause infection and disease, so you should seek medical treatment.

If your child is stung in the mouth, give him an ice cube to suck (unless he is under one year old) and seek medical help at once, since swelling can restrict breathing. If your child has an allergic reaction to a sting, you should treat it as an emergency. Symptoms of an allergic reaction include swelling of the face and neck, puffy eyes, impaired breathing, red blotchy skin, wheezing, and gasping.

Removing a sting
If the sting is still in the skin, remove it by scraping it off with your fingernail or a credit card.

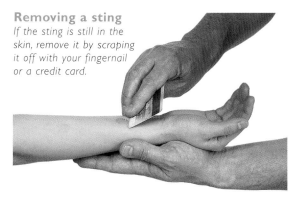

JELLYFISH STINGS

If your child steps on a jellyfish, she may experience a severe local reaction—jellyfish have stinging cells that discharge venom when touched. The severity depends on the type of jellyfish. Some jellyfish are not very toxic and are unlikely to produce severe symptoms—just a rash that may itch or be slightly painful. Others are more poisonous, and in extreme cases, their stings can cause vomiting, shock, breathing difficulties and unconsciousness, and can even lead to death.

WHAT TO DO

The stinging cells that stick to your child's skin release their poison gradually as they burst. You can help by inactivating the cells or preventing them from bursting. Alcohol or vinegar will do this, and any fine powder, like talcum powder, will make the cells stick together. If your child experiences a severe reaction to any sting or wound caused by a marine creature, take her to the hospital.

BLISTERS

When the skin is burned or subjected to pressure or friction, a blister may form as a protective cushion. Blisters are bubbles of skin with tissue fluid underneath. They are common on the heels of the feet if your child's shoes don't fit correctly or if she wears shoes without socks. Blisters are not usually serious unless they are the result of bad sunburn, they burst and become infected, or they are very large and painful; then you should consult your doctor.

WHAT TO DO

Do not burst a blister. In a day or two, new skin will form underneath the blister, the tissue fluid will be reabsorbed, and the blistered skin will dry and peel off. To aid this healing process, you should cover the blister with a clean dressing (not an adhesive bandage, since this can burst the blister when you peel it off) and keep it dry. If your child's blister is very large, your doctor may decide to lance it.

CUTS AND GRAZES

As long as a cut is superficial and is not infected (this is a risk with cuts by fingernails, plants, or animals), it should not require treatment. A graze is simply an abrasion of the skin that leaves the surface raw and tender. A cut that bleeds profusely can lead to shock (see p.332), so treat it as an emergency.

A very jagged cut may require stitches, and with a deep or dirty cut there is a risk of tetanus (see p.283).

WHAT TO DO

Run cold water over the wounded area. Using a gauze pad or a very soft brush, gently wash the graze with soap and water. Wipe away from the wound and use a clean piece of gauze for each wipe. Dry by patting with a clean tissue and cover with a sterile dressing or a plaster. If your child has an incision wound where the cut has two straight edges, you can hold them together using skin closure tape. If the wound is dirty or deep, there is a risk of infection and you should take your child to the hospital to see if she needs a tetanus injection.

If a cut is very deep or bleeds profusely, you should take your child to the hospital right away, since she may need stitches. Before she gets to the hospital, apply pressure to the wound using a clean handkerchief or pad (or your hand if you have nothing suitable) and make sure that the wounded part of the body is raised to slow the flow of blood.

SPLINTERS

Small shards of wood, glass, metal, or a thorn or spine from a plant can easily become embedded in your child's skin, particularly if she is playing outside. Unless splinters are embedded in the flesh or they prove too painful to remove, they can be dealt with very easily at home.

WHAT TO DO

First try to find out from your child what kind of splinter it is. If it is glass, you should not try to remove it yourself or you could cut your child. Seek help from your doctor. Look for the end of the splinter. Take a pair of sterilized tweezers (you can

Pull the splinter out in the same direction it went in

Removing a splinter
If the end of the splinter is visible, use sterilized tweezers to pull it out gently. Don't try to remove a glass splinter yourself; you could cut your child.

sterilize them by holding them over a flame; then let them cool) and gently pull the protruding end of the splinter out. Squeeze the area to make it bleed a little, since this will help clean it. When you have removed the splinter, clean the skin with soap and water. If the splinter is completely embedded in your child's skin, it may need to be removed by your doctor under local anesthetic—don't poke or probe the area with a needle. If you think that there may be dirt in the wound, your child may need a tetanus injection (see p.283).

BRUISES

Active children often get bruises from falls and bumps, and they are rarely serious; they usually take 10–14 days to disappear completely.

WHAT TO DO

Minor bruises need no treatment, just a hug if your child is upset. If the bruise is large, apply a cold compress for half an hour or so to contain the bruising. Consult your doctor immediately if pain on the site of a bruise gets worse after 24 hours (this could indicate a fracture) or if your child repeatedly has bruises with no apparent cause (this could indicate a serious condition).

CRUSHED FINGERS

This is a fairly common accident in very young children who don't understand how doors, windows, and drawers operate. A crush injury can be serious, so it is vital to release the trapped hand as quickly as possible and to comfort your child.

WHAT TO DO

If the skin is not broken, then once the finger or fingers have been released, hold your child's hand under a cold running faucet or hold a bag of crushed ice or frozen food against it. When the pain has subsided a little, wrap the hand in a bandage. If the crush is very severe and there is internal bleeding or swelling, call 911.

FOREIGN OBJECT IN THE EAR

The most common objects for children to push into their ears are small beads, pieces of crayon, and small components from construction toys. Occasionally an insect can fly into the ear, or cotton fibers can be left behind after cleaning. A foreign object in the ear may cause temporary deafness, lead to an ear infection, and/or damage the eardrum.

WHAT TO DO

If your child has an insect in her ear canal, lay her on her side with the affected ear uppermost and pour tepid water from a pitcher into the ear. The insect should float out. Any other type of foreign object needs to be treated by a doctor. If you attempt to remove it yourself, you may cause more damage. Your doctor can remove it and treat any resulting infection or damage to the skin. You can reduce the risk of foreign objects in the ear by making sure your child isn't given toys with small parts, particularly if she is under three years old.

FOREIGN OBJECT IN THE NOSE

If your child has pushed something into her nose, you may not notice, though she will probably complain of pain. Occasionally it takes several days for symptoms to become apparent. Your child might develop a blood-stained discharge from the nose, she may find it difficult to breathe, and there may be swelling, inflammation, and bruising around the bridge of the nose. A foreign object in the nose is rarely serious, but there is a risk that your child will inhale the object, so it requires hospital treatment.

WHAT TO DO

Don't try to remove the object—you could cause your child an injury, or push the object in farther. Keep her calm, get her to breathe through her mouth, and take her to the hospital.

At the hospital, a doctor will remove the foreign object using a pair of forceps; if your child is very young, she may need a general anesthetic beforehand.

PENIS CAUGHT IN ZIPPER

This can happen if your child is careless when closing his zipper. The tip of the penis gets caught between the teeth of the zip, and, although there should be no long-term damage, it is very painful.

WHAT TO DO

You should not attempt to open the zipper. Instead, take your child to the hospital and relieve the pain in the meantime by placing wrapped ice cubes over the zipper and penis. A doctor will open the zipper after giving your child a local anesthetic. Aftercare includes giving liquid acetaminophen to relieve pain. Your child should pour warm water over his penis as he urinates, to dilute the urine and prevent stinging.

Useful addresses

POSTNATAL SUPPORT

La Leche League
1400 North Meacham Road
Schaumburg, IL 60173-4808
(847) 519-7730
www.lalecheleague.org

Family Planning Council
260 South Broad Street
Suite 1000
Philadelphia, PA 19102
(215) 985-2600
www.familyplanning.org

National Healthy Mothers, Healthy Babies Coalition
121 North Washington Street,
Suite 300
Alexandria, VA 22314
(703) 836-6110
www.hmhb.org

The New Parent's Network
P.O. Box 64237
Tucson, AZ 85728-4237
(520) 327-1451
www.npn.org
Support for new and expectant parents.

Maternity Center Association
281 Park Avenue South, 5th Floor
New York, NY 10010
(212) 777-5000
www.maternitywise. org

PARENTS' GROUPS

Preemie Parent Support
www.prematurity.org

The Research Foundation for Children with Challenges
P.O. Box 1405
Santa Clarita, CA 91386-1405
www.specialchild.com
Help for parents with special care babies.

Foundation for the Study of Infant Death
509 Augusta Drive
Marietta, GA 30067
(800) 232-SIDS
www.sids.org

Child Development Institute
3528 East Ridgeway Road
Orange, CA 92867
(714) 998-8617
www.childdevelopmentinfo.com

Parents Without Partners
650 South Dixie Highway
Suite 510
Boca Raton, FL 33432
(561) 391-8833
www.parentswithoutpartners.org

The National Parenting Center
www.tnpc.com

Center for the Study of Multiple Births
333 East Superior Street
Suite 464
Chicago, IL 60611
(312) 695-1677
www.multiplebirth.com

Program for Early Parent Support
4649 Sunnyside Avenue North, #324
Seattle, WA 98103
(206) 547-8570 Ext. 10
www.pepsgroup.org

CARE AND EDUCATION

National Association for Education of Young Children
1509 16th Street, NW
Washington, DC 20036
(866) NAEYC-4U
www.naeyc.org

Nation's Network of Child Care Resource and Referral
1319 F Street
Suite 500
Washington, DC 20004
(800) 424-2246
www.naccra.org
www.childcareaware.org

National Institute for Early Education Research
Rutgers State University of New Jersey
120 Albany Street
Suite 500
New Brunswick, New Jersey 08901
(732) 932-4350
www.nieer.org

FIRST AID AND SAFETY

American Red Cross
2025 E Street, NW
Washington, DC 20006
(202) 303-4498
www.redcross.org

American Academy of Pediatrics
141 Northwest Point Boulevard
Elk Grove Village, IL 60007
(866) THE-AAPI
www.aap.org

National Association of Poison Control Centers
3201 New Mexico Avenue
Suite 330
Washington, DC 20016
(800) 222-1222

The American Medical Association
515 North State Street
Chicago, IL 60610
(800) 621-8335
www.ama-assn.org

Center for Disease Control and Prevention
1600 Clifton Road
Atlanta, GA 30333
(888) 232-3228
www.cdc.gov

SPECIAL NEEDS

Arthritis Foundation and American Juvenile Arthritis Organization
PO Box 7669
Atlanta, GA 30357-0669
(404) 872-7100
(800) 568-4045
www.arthritis.org

Asthma and Allergy Foundation of America
1233 Twentieth Street, NW
Suite 402
Washington, DC 20036
(202) 466-7643
www.aafa.org

Children and Adults with Attention Deficit Hyperactivity Disorder
8181 Professional Place, Suite 150
Landover, MD 20785
(800) 233-4050
www.chadd.org
For information and support

Autism Society of America
7910 Woodmont Avenue
Bethesda, MD 20814-3067
(800) 3-AUTISM
(301) 657-0881
www.autism-society.org

American Foundation for the Blind
11 Penn Plaza, Suite 300
New York, NY 10001
(212) 502-7600
(800) AFB-LINE
www.afb.org

Pediatric Brain Tumor Foundation
302 Ridgefield Court
Asheville, NC 28806
(828) 665-6891
(800) 253-6530
www.pbtfus.org

Celiac Disease Foundation
13251 Ventura Boulevard, #1
Studio City, CA 91604
(818) 990-2354
www.celiac.org

Inter-American Conductive Education Association
P.O. Box 3169
Toms River, N.J. 08756-3169
(800) 824-2232 or (732) 797-2566
www.iacea.org

Crohn's and Colitis Foundation of America
386 Park Avenue South, 17th Floor
New York, NY 10016-8804
(800) 932-2423
www.ccfa.org

Cystic Fibrosis Foundation
6931 Arlington Road
Bethesda, MD 20814
(800) 344-4823
(301) 951-4422
www.cff.org

Alexander Graham Bell Association for the Deaf and Hard of Hearing
3417 Volta Place, NW
Washington, DC 20007
(202) 337-5220
(202) 337-5221 (TTY)
www.agbell.org

American Diabetes Association
1701 North Beauregard Street
Alexandria, VA 22311
(800) DIABETES
www.diabetes.org.

Juvenile Diabetes Research Foundation International
120 Wall Street
New York, NY 10005-4001
(800) 533-CURE
www.jdrf.org

Association for Children with Down Syndrome
4 Fern Place, Plainview, NY 11803
(516) 933-4700
www.ACDS.org

International Dyslexia Association
Chester Building, Suite 382
8600 LaSalle Road
Baltimore, Maryland 21286-2044
(800) ABCD123
(410) 296-0232
www.interdys.org

National Eczema Association for Science and Education
4460 Redwood Highway, Suite 16-D
San Rafael, CA 94903-1953
(415) 499-3474
(800) 818-7546
www.nationaleczema.org

Epilepsy Foundation
4351 Garden City Drive
Landover, MD 20785-7223
(800) 332-1000
(800) 332-2070 (TTY)
www.epilepsyfoundation.org

National Association for Gifted Children (NAGC)
1707 L Street, NW, Suite 550
Washington, DC 20036
(202) 785-4268
www.nagc.org

National Center for Learning Disabilities
381 Park Avenue South, Suite 401
New York, NY 10016
(888) 575-7373
(212) 545-7510
www.ncld.org

The Leukemia and Lymphoma Society
1311 Mamaroneck Avenue
White Plains, NY 10605
(914) 949-5213
(800) 955-4572
www.leukemia.org

National Multiple Sclerosis Society
733 Third Avenue
New York, NY 10017
(800) FIGHT-MS
www.mssociety.org.uk

Muscular Dystrophy Association
3300 E. Sunrise Drive
Tucson, AZ 85718
(800) 572-1717
www.mdausa.org

Sickle Cell Disease Association of America
200 Corporate Pointe
Culver City, CA 90230
(800) 421-8453
www.sicklecelldisease.org

Federation for Children with Special Needs
1135 Tremont Street, Suite 420
Boston, MA 02120
(617) 236-7210
www.fcsn.org

Spina Bifida Association
4590 MacArthur Boulevard, NW,
Suite 250
Washington, DC 20007-4226
(800) 621-3141, (202) 944-3285
www.sbaa.org

National Stuttering Association
119 West 40th Street, 14th Floor
New York, NY 10018
(800) We Stutter 937-8888
www.nsastutter.org

Index

Acknowledgments

MEDICAL CONSULTANTS
Dr. Margaret Lawson; Dr. Frances Williams;
Dr. Penny Preston; Kate Mactier

MEDICAL CONSULTANTS FOR REVISED EDITION
Dr. Vivien Armstrong; Dr. John Mitchell; Lizzie Ette;
Dr. Aviva Schein

ADVICE AND ASSISTANCE
Talia Krikler for assistance with props and
photography; Association for Spina Bifida and
Hydrocephalus; Child Accident Prevention Trust; Child
Growth Foundation (height and weight charts); Cleft
Lip and Palate Association; National Childbirth Trust;
The Vegetarian Society.
The first aid information on pp.326–343 has been
validated by Joe Mulligan, Training Officer, British Red
Cross, and Dr. John Mitchell.

ART DIRECTION FOR PHOTOGRAPHY
Sally Smallwood

MODELS
Julia Alcock; Milo Baraclough; Cassie-Ella Bernard;
Gertrud Blomberg; Lena Larsson Blomberg and
Fredrik; Zoë Bothamley; Georgina and Elliot Bourke;
Alison Briegel, Alice, and Charlie; Jayde Caines; Niyazi
Caykara; Oliver Clarke; Ricardo Cohen; George
Cooper; Hannah and Charlotte Coster; Ella Crawley;
Cora Eugene and Kairone; Emily Fogarty; Keitel and
Stone Frankle; Joseph Gavshon; Julia Gibbon; Candy
Gummer; Hannah Heyes; Katie Hogben; Natalie
Joseph; Elliott Kenton; Sami Khan; William King;
Beverley Lagna; Malcolm Langton; Lee Lawer; Angela
Loveday and Jack; Georgina McCooke; Ursula
Macfarlane and Josiah Ackerman; Kelly MacNabb; Joan
Marcello and Marco; Antonio Marcello; Joseph Milner
Sweeney; Cordelia Nelson; Reiss Ng; Stephanie Parker
and Daniel; Jordan Raymond; Temuera Reefman;
Millie Satow; Caroline Sims and Michael; Alice Smith;
Jayde, Mairéad, and Michael Snell; Aisling Walsh; Tess
Watson; Mark Weegmann; Beresford
Williams; Jessica Williams; Albert Wood

Revised edition: Ivor with Art Baddiel; Brigid
O'Connell with Lee and Rosie Godwin; Marta Bird
with Max Brusniak; Sarah McCabe with James
Hartley; David with Merei Kong; Doug with Gil
Krikler; Net Workneh, Abs Beyene with Azaria and
Menna Beyene; Keren with Roy Boulter; Holly
Warnes, Mrs. Warnes with Jesse Begon; Caroline Cox
with Zita Hinshelwood; Deborah Tammer with Ruby
Katz; Deborah Golend and David Pratt with Anya
Golend-Pratt; Seemah Burgess with Findlay
Nahome-Burgess; Megan with Millie Aslan; Alex
and Emma with Dylan and George Krikler; Anna
with Talia; Susu Lawrence with Anna Lawrence-
Wasserberg; Shirley and Sharnah with Rohan
Karper; Annabel with Amelia Lermer; Nicole with
Glisha Izsak; Terumi Ehara with Mirei Kong; Tsega
with Elud and Lamek Neftalem; Julie with Charli
Pactor; Anna Josse with Elijah Lifton; Keith with
Shana Horwood.

PHOTO CREDITS
Getty Images: Vincent Oliver 26, Mel Yates 246,
Christopher Bissell 311; **Image Source Express**
(Royalty Free) 103; **Mother & Baby Picture
Library/EMAP** 33, 302; **Science Photo Library**:
Taeke Henstra/Petit Format 12, Ron Sutherland 15,
Horacio Sormani 48, Saturn Stills 266, Antonia
Reeve 269, Dr H.C. Robinson 291, John Radcliffe
Hospital 292; **Janine Wiedel Photo Library** 25.

All other images © Dorling Kindersley. For further
information see: www.dkimages.com

PICTURE LIBRARY
Romaine Werblow

ILLUSTRATION
Aziz Khan: 50, 104, 105, 109, 175, 262, 265, 271,
273, 285, 291, 295, 298, 300, 301, 327, 337;
Coral Mula: 29, 290, 304; Ian Thompson: 286

INDEX
Anne McCarthy